FROM ENRON TO EVO

Dedicated to my father, Roderick Hindery:

For your enduring love and encouragement, and for inspiring me through your pioneering publications on comparative ethics, critical thought, and indoctrination

From Enron to Evo

Pipeline Politics, Global Environmentalism, and Indigenous Rights in Bolivia

DERRICK HINDERY

FIRST PEOPLES
New Directions in Indigenous Studies

THE UNIVERSITY OF
ARIZONA PRESS

TUCSON

The University of Arizona Press
www.uapress.arizona.edu

Printed in the United States of America
19 18 17 16 15 14   6 5 4 3 2

Cover design by Leigh McDonald
Cover photo by Derrick Hindery

Publication of this book is made possible in part by the proceeds of a permanent endowment created with the assistance of a Challenge Grant from the National Endowment for the Humanities, a federal agency.

Library of Congress Cataloging-in-Publication Data
Hindery, Derrick, 1972–
From Enron to Evo: pipeline politics, global environmentalism, and indigenous rights in Bolivia / Derrick Hindery ; foreword by Susanna B. Hecht.
    pages. cm. — (First peoples : new directions in indigenous studies)
    Includes bibliographical references and index.
    ISBN 978-0-8165-3140-0 (pbk. : alk. paper)
    1. Indians of South America—Land tenure—Bolivia—Territorio Indígena Parque Nacional Isiboro-Sécure. 2. Indians of South America—Civil rights—Bolivia—Territorio Indígena Parque Nacional Isiboro-Sécure. 3. Indians of South America—Bolivia—Territorio Indígena Parque Nacional Isiboro-Sécure—Politics and government. 4. Indigenous peoples—Ecology—Bolivia—Territorio Indígena Parque Nacional Isiboro-Sécure. 5. Petroleum industry—Bolivia—Territorio Indígena Parque Nacional Isiboro-Sécure. 6. Natural gas pipelines—Bolivia—Territorio Indígena Parque Nacional Isiboro-Sécure. 7. Environmental protection—Bolivia—Territorio Indígena Parque Nacional Isiboro-Sécure. 8. Environmental justice—Bolivia—Territorio Indígena Parque Nacional Isiboro-Sécure. 9. Fossil fuel power plants—Brazil—Cuiabá (Mato Grosso). 10. Territorio Indígena Parque Nacional Isiboro-Sécure (Bolivia)—Social conditions. 11. Territorio Indígena Parque Nacional Isiboro-Sécure (Bolivia)—Environmental conditions. I. Title.
    F3319.1.T47H56 2013
    306.0984—dc23

2012044179

♾ This paper meets the requirements of ANSI/NISO Z39.48-1992 (Permanence of Paper).

Contents

Illustrations

Foreword

Che Guevara passed his last days in Vallegrande in the Andean foothills just above the Bolivian Amazon, and as he waited for his inevitable end, he might well have gazed toward the east, over a landscape that was just turning from its latifundist past and beginning its slow gyre toward its modern agroindustrial and hydrocarbon booms and its emergent native resistance. These were still wisps on the horizon, futures slowly being gridded out over the flatness of the Bolivian Amazon, the "Oriente." Che chose this part of South America because he believed that revolution fomented here would radiate throughout the continent from this tropical heartland. In many ways it has, but not as he imagined. What Leninist Che saw as atavistic remnants—its Indigenous populations—could scarcely be imagined as the socioenvironmental vanguard and the architects of successful resistance to energy juggernauts like Enron and Chevron, the quintessential incarnations of extractive-industrial monopolies.

Hardly known in the mid-1960s, the Amazonian-Andean interface stretches in an arc through Bolivia, Peru, Ecuador, Colombia, and Venezuela and contains some of the most extensive oil and gas reserves that lie under some of the richest tropical forests in some of the most remote parts of the planet. In the Amazon the hydrocarbon economy has pitted what seemed like the most powerless "backward" populations against some of the richest actors in global capitalism: transnational oil corporations. There is a simple David-and-Goliath story that could be told, but the virtue of Derrick Hindery's book is that he does not relax into this easy and well-known narrative, because we do not know how this story ends—and the account in any case is more complex, engaging both global and local actors on all sides. The conflict is profound and territorial and now exemplifies a twenty-first-century politics of energy in Amazonia where native populations and their allies, using arguments based in human rights, the "rights of nature," and questions about the planetary future and extractive capitalism itself, have been surprisingly successful in their redress against big energy, whether these take the forms of Chevron's defeat in Ecuador, the Camisea project in Peru, the relentless politics of Brazil's Belo Monte, the enormous dam on the Xingu River, or the expansion of biofuel monocultures. Hindery gives us the deep background, and a nervous cautionary tale, but a remarkable one about how this new tropical economy is being constructed in the neo-extractivist states, how it works ideologically in policy and practice, and how native Amazonians have risen in an unmatched form of insurgent citizenship to resist it.

Bolivia has had a complex history with extractivism, since it was home to that mountain of silver, Potosí, which swirled into global commodity circuits in 1557, defining the new-world contours of international trade for the next few centuries, lofting (and financing) Spain into its new Empire. Silver revenues lubricated global mercantilism and the states and institutions that supported it and structured the labor regimes that generated it. Rubber played that role in the late nineteenth and early twentieth century, as empires commanded by the industries needing this remarkable commodity went to the most remote reaches of the earth to acquire it. Extractivism defined Amazonia in this era. The realm of the rubber baron Nicolas Suarez stretched from the native lands of the Chiquitania that border Brazil to the headwaters of the Madeira and Beni rivers, even bumping into those foothills near Vallegrande, only to wither when plantation rubber from Asia even managed to outcompete latex produced by indentured Indigenous peoples in Amazonia. Later, tin clawed from Andean mines defined its political economic culture until the middle of the twentieth century. Bolivia's state institutions and its political and economic elites remained tethered to extractivism even as the booms and busts mirrored the caprices of global markets and widespread corruption. In earlier extractive economies, environment was of no concern, and Indigenous peoples were of interest only as a form of semi-slave labor. While Bolivia has a deep history of labor insurgency and, indeed, had one of the earliest postwar revolutions in Latin America, from 1952 to 1964, the authoritarian period of Cold War dictators was especially brutal in the country and persisted from 1964 to 1982, producing hyperinflation and a moribund economy.

In the mid-1980s, Bolivia became a kind of living laboratory for Harvard economist Jeffrey Sachs to test the ideas of structural adjustment and neoliberal trade rules. These reached fruition in the mid-1990s, as privatization of state sectors, large-scale enclosures, massive reductions of state employment, deregulation, decentralization, and free trade policies were implemented through a sharp recession, increasing inequality, and contraction of state services—the usual story. While Sachs seems to have repented this period, it inaugurated a time of deep instability, one in which economic power shifted from the cold arid highlands to the tropical realms of the Bolivian lowlands. Amazonia, which had resided in a tropical torpor since the rubber era, burst onto the scene with the powerful global economies of coca, soybeans, and oil and gas. A gutted and acquiescent state presided over the rise of agroindustrial deforestation and made deep compromises with international energy companies, the World Bank and other international financial institutions acting as midwives to the new, neo-extractivist economic regime. The part of the economy with its own autonomous sources of wealth was clandestine: the world of the coca producers, the Aymara and Quechua Indigenous populations that gave rise to and elected Evo Morales who vowed protection of Indigenous rights, territories, and autonomy and nationalization of some of the energy resources. This more Left version of the neo-extractivist state relied, as had regimes before it, on the now enormous returns from energy sector royalties as the means of expanding investment. In the case of Morales, social policy was better than the earlier regimes, but the central problem was that the macropolicies did not particularly shift. Long on rhetoric about environment, autonomy, and Indigeneity, the actual energy strategy increasingly focused on some of the most hyper-biodiverse native territories and national parks—the Chiquitano forest, Madidi National Park, and the Isiboro-Sécure Indigenous Territory and National Park—for hydrocarbon development, roads, and pipelines. Amazonian Indians found themselves arrayed against the coca communities and even conservation groups, which negotiated a $20 million conservation program with Enron and Shell that essentially green-stamped the destructive Cuiabá pipeline. The environmental program excluded Indigenous participation in determining the forms that conservation might take in their native territories. This book elaborates how these politics unfolded, and how the forms of collusion among energy corporations, states, and environmental organizations glossed over the effects of their actions with a baseless conservation discourse.

These actions stimulated active resistance and politics rooted in place and identity but mobilizing global legal norms, allies, and the languages of historical and human rights. Derrick Hindery's lively prose and careful documentation bring to light the dynamics that produced the neoliberal context and how the deals were cut and helps us understand why and how

Indigenous resistance has been successful. The book does what no other does: it gives us a template for understanding the "energy wars at the ends of the world" in the twenty-first century. It changes how one reads both energy and environmental headlines and clarifies the operations of neo-extractivist states. It gives us a history of places that are assumed not to have any, and thus open to a succession of predatory cycles and exclusionary politics, and shows us how the deep dialectic of tropical politics unfolds. Global climate, new development approaches, new ideologies, and a recasting of what it means to be a citizen increasingly are shaped by actions in the Global South, especially, I would argue, in Amazonia. Hindery's book shows in detail what is the essential truth of Amazonia: like the river itself, its history is always turbulent, always insurgent.

Susanna Hecht
Professor
Luskin School of Public Affairs
Institute of the Environment and Sustainability
University of California at Los Angeles

Acknowledgments

This book was made possible by generous support from various individuals, institutions, and communities. I would first like to express my deepest gratitude to the Chiquitano and Ayoreo people of Bolivia, who took their precious time to collaborate and shared their important experiences with me. I am sincerely grateful to leaders of various local, regional, and national Indigenous organizations, including the Federation of Indigenous Peoples of Bolivia (Confederación de Pueblos Indígenas de Bolivia), the Coordinator of Ethnic Peoples of Santa Cruz, the Chiquitano Indigenous Organization (Organización Indígena Chiquitana), the Indigenous Center for the Reclamation of Rights of Ángel Sandoval Province (Central Indígena Reivindicativa de la Provincia Ángel Sandoval), the Center for Indigenous Communities of Chiquitos-Turubó (Central de Comunidades Indígenas de Chiquitos-Turubó), the Indigenous Center for Native Communities of Lomerío (Central Indígena de Comunidades Originarias de Lomerío), and the Ayoreo Native Center of Eastern Bolivia (Central Ayorea Nativa del Oriente Boliviano). I owe special thanks as well to the Confederation of Peasant Workers of Bolivia (Confederación Sindical Única de Trabajadores Campesinos de Bolivia), the Bolivian Syndicalist Confederation of Colonizers (Confederación Sindical de Colonizadores de Bolivia), and various local committees from across the Chiquitano region that monitored social and environmental impacts of the Cuiabá and Bolivia-Brazil pipelines.

Many nongovernmental organizations in Bolivia and the United States were immensely helpful in collaborating, providing information, and sharing contacts. In Bolivia, I am most indebted to staff at the Collective for

Applied Studies and Social Development (Colectivo de Estudios Aplicados y Desarrollo Social), who helped me tremendously in the field and were unique in their dedication to supporting autonomy, self-sufficiency, and protagonism throughout the Indigenous communities where they worked. I give special thanks also to the Bolivian Forum on Environment and Development (Foro Boliviano sobre Medio Ambiente y Desarrollo), the Center for Juridical Studies and Social Investigation (Centro de Estudios Jurídicos e Investigación Social), Biosphere Productivity and Environment (Productividad Biosfera y Medio Ambiente), and the Bolivian Documentation and Information Center (Centro de Documentación e Información Bolivia).

In the United States, I am especially grateful to Atossa Soltani, executive director of Amazon Watch, for allowing me to volunteer and later work for the organization as part of its Bolivia program. This was essential in establishing contacts and eventually led me to shift my dissertation topic from linking neoliberal reforms with deforestation to connecting them with natural gas development. Many thanks to Janet Lloyd, Kevin Koenig, Leila Salazar, Greg Bernstein, Thomas Cavanagh, and Natalie van Zelm for their close comradery, intellectual inspiration, and support. I also wish to express my gratitude to Jon Sohn (formerly at Friends of the Earth), Nadia Martinez (formerly at the Institute for Policy Studies), and Kari Hamerschlag (formerly at the Bank Information Center), with whom I collaborated closely on the Cuiabá case.

I am sincerely appreciative of many other individuals who agreed to be interviewed for this project, including representatives from Bolivian state institutions (especially the National Service for Protected Areas, the hydrocarbons ministry, the environmental ministry, the land and rural development ministry, and the state oil company), Enron/Ashmore and Shell's subsidiaries (GasOriente Boliviano, Gas Transboliviano, Transredes), Empresa Minera Paititi, numerous nongovernmental organizations, US government agencies (US Agency for International Development, US State Department, US Embassy in La Paz, Overseas Private Investment Corporation), and international financial institutions (World Bank, Inter-American Development Bank).

This book has genuinely been a labor of love ever since I began conducting research on the Cuiabá conflict during my doctoral studies in the Department of Geography at the University of California, Los Angeles (UCLA). My initial fieldwork in 1999–2000 was generously funded by grants from the Inter-American Foundation, the Tinker Foundation, the Ford Foundation, the UCLA Latin American Center, and the UCLA International Studies and Overseas Program. Subsequent research funding came from various sources at the University of Oregon, including the Office of Research and Faculty Development and the university's College of Arts and Sciences, Department of International Studies, and Department of Geography.

Both the Andrew W. Mellon Foundation and the University of Arizona Press contributed generous funding toward the writing of this book as part of the First Peoples, New Directions in Indigenous Studies publishing initiative. This included support to attend a valuable mentoring workshop in May 2011 at the Native American and Indigenous Studies Association annual meeting in Sacramento, California. While there, I benefited tremendously from the detailed feedback my editor, Allyson Carter, and my mentor, Amy Den Ouden (associate professor of anthropology, University of Massachusetts, Boston), provided me. I am also grateful to the editors and authors from the other three university presses who participated in the workshop. Finally, I give special thanks to Julia Heydon and Barbara Altmann of the Oregon Humanities Center for providing a faculty subvention grant for this book.

A number of colleagues gave me thoughtful and careful feedback on the manuscript. First and foremost, I would like to thank Dennis Galvan for his close read on an early first draft and for his instructive guidance in organizing the book. I am deeply indebted to the anonymous reviewers who meticulously read earlier versions of the manuscript and who provided such thoughtful guidance on revising the text. I give special thanks to Leslie Kriesel for her helpful editorial comments and suggestions. Since the very beginning, my editor at University of Arizona Press, Allyson Carter, has been extremely supportive in many ways, in imparting her insights, in describing my work to the publishing committee, and in spending so many hours communicating with me. I am grateful to Editorial Assistant Scott Herrera for being so diligent and responsive in handling the logistics involved in coordinating the review process. I thank Stephen Cote for his constructive feedback on the history of hydrocarbons in Bolivia. Special thanks also to Patricia Watson, who did a phenomenal job with copyediting, and Nancy Arora and Lisa Stallings, who supervised the production process. I am most grateful to Rachel Shaw for developing a superb index and for meticulously reviewing the page proofs. Finally, I thank Natasha Varner, Lela Scott MacNeil, and Abby Mogollon for so diligently publicizing this book.

At the University of Oregon, I am deeply grateful to faculty members of the Department of International Studies and the Department of Geography for the various ways they have supported my work. I thank those members of the human geography writing group that reviewed a portion of one chapter: Lise Nelson, Alec Murphy, Susan Hardwick, Shaul Cohen, Xiaobo Su, and Amy Lobben. Thanks also to Mark Carey, Carlos Aguirre, and Katharine Meehan for their very thoughtful and constructive feedback. Lynn Stephen and Analisa Taylor were instrumental in encouraging me to write this book and urged me to submit it to University of Arizona Press.

Librarian Megan Henning threw her heart into this project and was immensely helpful in completing formatting. A big thanks to her for meticulously combing through the text to convert citations and references into American Sociological Association format. Many thanks also to my dear friend and colleague, Annie Zeidman-Karpinski, the science and technology services librarian at the University of Oregon, for her wizardry with Zotero, for her unending support, and for connecting me with Megan. I thank Ashley Blazinski, as well, for her earlier formatting work.

Over the years, many colleagues have inspired me intellectually and have contributed to this book through discussions and exchanges. Special conference sessions on Indigenous peoples, extractive industries, and political ecology were particularly formative during conferences held by the Association of American Geographers, the Latin American Studies Association, and the Second Conference on Ethnicity, Race and Indigenous Peoples in Latin America. Thanks to Jessica Budds, Leonith Hinojosa-Valencia, and Tom Perreault for organizing and participating in influential sessions on geographies of extractive industries at the 2012 meeting of the Association of American Geographers. Thanks also to Matthew Himley, Denisse Roca Servat, and Emily Billo for organizing and chairing sessions on resource extraction in Latin America at the 2012 Latin American Studies Association Conference. I thank Jeffrey Bury, Anthony Bebbington, and Kenneth Young for putting together groundbreaking sessions on "Subterranean Struggles" at the 2008 Association of American Geographers conference. Finally, I thank the various discussants that have commented on papers I presented at different conferences, including Tom Perreault, Gerardo Hector Damonte Valencia, Anthony Bebbington, and Vandana Wadhwa.

Many thanks to my various colleagues from the Bolivian Studies Association and the Bolivia and Environment sections of the Latin American Studies Association. Thanks also to my colleagues who are members of the Cultural and Political Ecology Specialty Group, the Indigenous Peoples Specialty Group, and the Latin America Specialty Group of the Association of American Geographers. Finally, I thank my colleagues from the editorial collective of the journal *Latin American Perspectives*.

I am very fortunate to have worked with such brilliant and inspiring graduate students at the University of Oregon. Special thanks to those students whose research has been so helpful to my own, particularly Meche Lu, Nate Bellinger, Marie Javdani, Sue Dockstader, Elias Meyer, Evan Shenkin, Paul Lauermann, Joshua West, Patrick Jones, Dustin Foskett, Elizabeth Miskell, Lindsay Ramirez, Michelle Platt Bassi, Ignacio Krell Rivera, Chris Thomas, Wen Lee, Kate Faris, Heather Wolford, Julie Bacon, Devon Bonady, Tim Myers, Thomas Mason, Bridget Sharry, Shannan Stoll, Lexi Stickel, Kelsey Provo, Courtney Toch, Susie Grimes, Maguette Diame, Jean Faye, Lindsey Foltz, Lia Frederiksen, and Jason Schnoor. Thanks also to all the undergraduate students who so kindly provided feedback on chapter drafts.

During my graduate studies in the Department of Geography at UCLA, I benefited tremendously from the close guidance provided by the members of my dissertation committee: Joshua Muldavin, John Agnew, Stephen Bell, and Carlos Torres. I am especially grateful to my dear friend and colleague Joshua Muldavin, who has continued to provide sage advice and support to me throughout my tenure at the University of Oregon. I also owe special thanks to Susanna Hecht, Judy Carney, and Melissa Savage for the seminal courses they taught and for their deep dedication in serving on my master's committee. Susanna Hecht's pioneering research on deforestation dynamics in the Amazon inspired me to pursue my graduate studies at UCLA and triggered me to begin examining connections between structural adjustment, stabilization, and deforestation.

I thank Jesse Nichols for the many hours he spent reviewing and editing video footage at the request of Chiquitano and Ayoreo organizations. Daniel Redo very kindly allowed me to use a fabulous map he made of the Chiquitano region. He also was a tremendous help in cochairing two inspiring sessions at the 2010 Association of American Geographers Conference on Leftward Politics and Implications for Latin American Peoples and Landscapes.

I am extremely grateful to my family and friends for their ongoing support and love. Above all, I thank my wife, who has supported me in so many ways since we first met in Santa Cruz, Bolivia, at a consultation meeting regarding the Inter-American Development Bank–financed bioceanic corridor. Heartfelt thanks as well to my two dear children, who have been a continual source of inspiration and joy. I thank my parents, Sheila and Roderick Hindery, for their tireless moral support, for their scholarly insights, and for the time they spent reading the manuscript at various stages. My sister's love and generosity has also been essential in carrying me through this project. I have been humbled by the gracious commitment my Bolivian family has given me since the beginning. I am particularly grateful to my father-in-law, whose engineering background and many years of experience in rural areas proved invaluable, particularly during some testing vehicle breakdowns in the middle of the Chiquitano forest. I am deeply indebted to my Bolivian family and the Chiquitanos for nursing me through two bouts of dengue fever, and salmonella to boot. Finally, I am grateful to my former housemates in Santa Cruz, Bolivia, Jordi Benería-Surkin and anthropologist Enrique Herrera, for many constructive debates about Indigenous political mobilization, development, and the environment.

Abbreviations

ADN	Acción Democrática Nacionalista (Nationalist Democratic Action), the Bolivian political party formerly led by General Hugo Banzer Suárez
AFP	Administradoras de Fondos de Pensiones (Pension Fund Administrators)
ASL	Asociaciónes Sociales del Lugar (Local Social Associations), community logging organizations
BCF	billion cubic feet
CANOB	Central Ayorea Nativa del Oriente Boliviano (Ayoreo Native Center of Eastern Bolivia)
CARE	Cooperative for Assistance and Relief Everywhere
CCICH-Turubó	Central de Comunidades Indígenas de Chiquitos-Turubó (Center for Indigenous Communities of Chiquitos-Turubó), a community-based organization located in the Department of Santa Cruz, Bolivia
CEADES	Colectivo de Estudios Aplicados y Desarrollo Social (Collective for Applied Studies and Social Development), a small Indigenous rights organization based in Santa Cruz
CEDIB	Centro de Documentación e Información Bolivia (Bolivian Documentation and Information Center)

CEDLA	Centro de Estudios Para el Desarrollo Laboral y Agrario (Center for Studies of Labor and Agrarian Development), a small NGO based in La Paz
CEJIS	Centro de Estudios Jurídicos e Investigación Social (Center for Juridical Studies and Social Investigation), an NGO and law collective that defends Indigenous rights in Bolivia
CICOL	Central Indígena de Comunidades Originarias de Lomerío (Indigenous Center for Native Communities of Lomerío), a Chiquitano organization based in Lomerío
CIDOB	Confederación de Pueblos Indígenas de Bolivia (Federation of Indigenous Peoples of Bolivia), the Santa Cruz–based national federation of Indigenous peoples
CIMAL	Compañía Industrial Maderera Ltda., a Santa Cruz–based logging corporation
CIPABA	Central Indígena Bajo Paraguá (Indigenous Center of Bajo Paraguá)
CIPSJ	Central Indígena Paikoneka de San Javier (Paikoneka Indigenous Center of San Javier)
CIRPAS	Central Indígena Reivindicativa de la Provincia Ángel Sandoval (Indigenous Center for the Reclamation of Rights of Angel Sandoval Province), a regional Chiquitano Indigenous organization based in San Matías, Bolivia (at the northern end of the Cuiabá pipeline)
CITES	Convention on International Trade in Endangered Species of Wild Fauna and Flora
COICA	Coordinadora de las Organizaciones Indígenas de la Cuenca Amazónica (Coordinator of Indigenous Organizations of the Amazon River Basin)
COMIBOL	Corporación Minera de Bolivia (Mining Corporation of Bolivia)
COMSUR	Compañía Minera del Sur (Mining Company of the South), founded by Gonzalo Sánchez de Lozada in 1962; owned the Don Mario gold mine
CONAMAQ	Consejo Nacional de Ayllus y Markas del Qullasuyu (National Council of Ayllus and Markas of Qullasuyu), Bolivia's main highland Indigenous federation

CORDECRUZ	Corporación Regional de Desarrollo de Santa Cruz (Regional Development Corporation of Santa Cruz)
CPESC	Coordinadora de Pueblos Étnicos de Santa Cruz (Council of Ethnic Peoples of Santa Cruz), a Santa Cruz–based regional Indigenous federation
CPILAP	Central de Pueblos Indígenas de La Paz (Center for Indigenous Peoples of La Paz), a regional organization representing eight Indigenous peoples and their organizations
CSUTCB	Confederación Sindical Única de Trabajadores Campesinos de Bolivia (Sole Confederation of Peasant Workers of Bolivia)
ECA	export credit agency
EFE	a Spanish language news agency
EMIPA	Empresa Minera Paititi, a subsidiary of Canadian-based corporation Orvana Minerals, in turn controlled by Sánchez de Lozada's Bolivian company, COMSUR
ENSR	a global environmental remediation firm
ERBOL	Educación Radiofónica de Bolivia
FAN	Fundación Amigos de la Naturaleza (Friends of Nature Foundation)
FCBC	La Fundación para la Conservación del Bosque Chiquitano (Foundation for the Conservation of the Chiquitano Forest)
FOBOMADE	Foro Boliviano sobre Medio Ambiente y Desarrollo (Bolivian Forum on Environment and Development)
FPIC	Free, prior, and informed consent
FPICon	Free, prior, and informed consultation
GasOriente Boliviano	Owner and operator of the Bolivian segment of the Cuiabá pipeline. Originally a subsidiary of Enron and Shell, and subsequently a subsidiary of Ashmore Energy International.
GASYRG	Gasoducto Yacuiba–Río Grande (Yacuiba–Río Grande Gas Pipeline), a pipeline that runs parallel to the Yabog pipeline
GMO	genetically modified organism

IDB	Inter-American Development Bank
IDH	Impuesto directo a los hidrocarburos (direct tax on hydrocarbons)
IDP	Indigenous development plan; the Cuiabá IDP was a program financed by Enron and Shell (later Ashmore Energy International) to compensate affected communities for impacts caused by the Cuiabá pipeline
ILO	International Labor Organization, a specialized agency of the United Nations that promotes social justice and internationally recognized human and labor rights
IPS	Institute for Policy Studies
LIL	Learning and Innovation Loan, a type of loan granted by the World Bank aimed at sparking innovation and flexibility in use of funds
MAS	Movimiento al Socialismo (Movement Toward Socialism)
MNR	Movimiento Nacionalista Revolucionario (National Revolutionary Movement), the Bolivian political party that led the 1952 revolution but later implemented neoliberal reforms
MST	Movimiento Sin Tierra (Movement of People Without Land)
MTPA	million tons per annum
NGO	nongovernmental organization
OAS	Brazil-based construction firm contracted to build the Villa Tunari–San Ignacio de Moxos interdepartmental highway (that had been proposed to run through TIPNIS)
OICH	Organización Indígena Chiquitana (Chiquitano Indigenous Organization), a regional Indigenous organization
OPIC	Overseas Private Investment Corporation, a US government export credit agency that provides political risk insurance, low-interest loans, and loan guarantees to US businesses
PROBIOMA	Productividad Biosfera y Medio Ambiente (Biosphere Productivity and Environment), an NGO that helped organize non-Indigenous populations affected by the Cuiabá pipeline

TCF	trillion cubic feet
TCO	tierras comunitarias de origen (native communal lands), lands given in collective title to Indigenous groups
TIPNIS	Territorio Indígena y Parque Nacional Isiboro-Sécure (Isiboro-Sécure Indigenous Territory and National Park)
Transredes	Capitalized company operating Bolivia's pipeline network. During the neoliberal era Enron and Shell purchased a 50 percent share in the company. Subsequently nationalized under Morales.
UCLA	University of California, Los Angeles
UMA	Unidad del Medio Ambiente (Environmental Unit), an environmental office housed within the hydrocarbons ministry
UNDRIP	UN Declaration on the Rights of Indigenous Peoples
UNECLAC	UN Economic Commission for Latin America and the Caribbean
UNODC	UN Office on Drugs and Crime
USAID	US Agency for International Development
VAIPO	Viceministerio de Asuntos Indígenas y Pueblos Originarios (Vice Ministry of Indigenous and Native Peoples' Affairs)
WWF	World Wildlife Fund
YABOG	Gasoducto Yacuiba–Río Grande (Yacimientos-Bolivian Gulf pipeline)
YPF	Yacimientos Petrolíferos Fiscales (Fiscal Petroleum Fields)
YPFB	Yacimientos Petrolíferos Fiscales Bolivianos, the state oil and gas company of Bolivia

CHAPTER ONE

Political Ecology, Pipelines, and the Conduits of Resistance

Disputing "Development"

Disgruntled over the Bolivian government's renewed support for a controversial road through the Isiboro-Sécure Indigenous Territory and National Park (Territorio Indígena y Parque Nacional Isiboro-Sécure, TIPNIS), in January 2012 a block of Indigenous legislators from President Evo Morales's political party, Movement Toward Socialism (Movimiento al Socialismo, MAS), formed a caucus to defend Indigenous rights and keep the project at bay. Although the representatives retained their party affiliations, the act spoke to a broader rift forming between the MAS and some Indigenous groups. The move came as a long-promised countermarch of coca-dependent communities supportive of the highway[1] approached the highland capital of La Paz, without police repression and without much press coverage. During the previous year, Bolivia's main Indigenous organizations had joined Yuracaré, Mojeño, and Chimane Indigenous peoples from TIPNIS in a two-month-long march—the Eighth Indigenous March—from the Amazon Basin to La Paz in opposition to the project. They feared the road would bring development activities that would undercut the livelihood of communities dependent on hunting, fishing, and subsistence agriculture. Several weeks before this seminal march took place, Morales made it clear that he supported the highway when he urged men from the coca-producing Chapare region to woo Yuracaré females into accepting the road: "If I had time, I would go to enamor the Yuracaré comrades and convince them to not be opposed; so, young men, you have instructions from the president

1

to win over the Trinitarian Yuracaré comrades so they don't oppose construction of the road" (qtd. in Chipana 2011, translation by author). The
TIPNIS conflict was seen as a litmus test of whether Morales's reputedly
pro-Indigenous government would respect the rights that Indigenous groups
had won since the first March for Territory and Dignity in 1990, and whether
Morales would comply with his own proposal to adopt the Indigenous doctrine of "Living Well" (*Vivir Bien*) over the capitalist, modernist ideology
of living better (*vivir mejor*):

> As long as we do not change the capitalist system for a system based on
> complementarity, solidarity, and harmony among peoples and nature,
> the measures we adopt will be palliatives that will have a limited and
> precarious character. For us, what has failed is the model of "living bet-
> ter" [*vivir mejor*], of unlimited development, of industrialization without
> borders, of modernity that disregards history, of increasing accumulation
> of goods at the expense of others and nature. That is why we propose the
> idea of "living well" [*Vivir Bien*], in harmony with other human beings
> and with our Mother Earth. (Evo Morales, November 28, 2008, qtd. in
> Ministerio de Medio Ambiente y Agua 2008, translation by author)

In contrast to the countermarch, the high-profile Eighth Indigenous
March garnered wide coverage in the domestic and international press.
The marchers, who were hampered by violent police repression and resistance from coca growers, eventually arrived in La Paz and prompted passage of a law declaring TIPNIS an untouchable area, off limits to highways
and other development activities. A statement from a Chiquitano, Isabel
García Ipamo, who marched against the highway, captures a feeling of be-
trayal shared by Indigenous groups and supporters who had grown increasingly weary of Morales's policies:

> The president is the president of the coca growers. He is not representing
> all of the country. He has always resented the Indigenous peoples of the
> eastern lowlands of Bolivia. Now we have seen how he is discriminating
> against this mobilization that we are undertaking, even though we had
> complete faith in him because he is Indigenous, and even though he is
> now president because of our support. We thought that he was going to
> be more sensitive toward Indigenous peoples, but we were mistaken
> because now we are marching once again. We believed that there were
> not going to be more marches asking for our demands, but that is not
> the case: we continue marching, we continue worse than before, because

at least the previous governments respected protected areas. Our constitution establishes that protected areas are untouchable, but in an instant
this president wants to undo the TCOs [native communal lands] and
protected areas, which we care for extensively. What will happen to the
other TCOs if this protected area is not cared for? We have taken great
care to ensure that the TCOs are not violated or colonized by the same
people that the president now wants to place in all of the TCOs and protected areas. (qtd. in *Bolpress* 2011a, translation by author)

This individual, a law student who suspended her studies to participate
in the march, came from a Chiquitano community located in a large-scale,
collective Indigenous territory (tierras comunitarias de origen, or TCO) in
the Chiquitano forest. The Chiquitanos, like the Guaraní and many other
Indigenous groups located across the country, had sent contingents to support the march in solidarity with TIPNIS communities opposing the road.
They knew that the TCOs they had struggled long and hard for during the
1990s were under threat, as was their inclusion in a reputedly "Indigenous"
government. For more than a decade, the Chiquitanos, Bolivia's most numerous Indigenous group in the lowlands,[2] had battled boldly against
cattle ranchers, farmers, loggers, mining companies, and transnational
energy giants to reclaim ancestral lands through the new mechanism of
TCOs.

How could it be that Bolivia's first Indigenous president, who vowed to
"refound" Bolivia as a twenty-first-century intercultural, plurinational,
socialist state (Kohl and Bresnahan 2010a:5), was now being targeted by
some of the very groups that had brought him to power? How could a head
of state with the most radical proposal to address global climate change[3] be
simultaneously pursuing an extraction-oriented development model that
harmed the marginalized populations he was supposedly defending? How
could an administration that implemented a new constitution guaranteeing
Indigenous people's rights to land, self-determination, and a healthy environment pursue such a contradictory agenda? And how could a government
that was the first to adopt the UN Declaration on the Rights of Indigenous
Peoples as national law advance development projects in violation of Indigenous peoples' right to free, prior, and informed consent?

In this book, I assert that to understand such contradictions, it is necessary to comprehend the nature of the Morales administration's development
model, what Vice President Álvaro García Linera has termed "Andean-
Amazonian" capitalism.[4] At its core, the model is a form of state capitalism predicated on using profits from oil, gas, minerals, and other natural

resources to drive domestic development. I contend that it privileges a Western view of modernization and industrialization over Indigenous cosmologies of respect for Mother Earth and living well (*Vivir Bien*) that are ironically enshrined in the new constitution (see chapter 8). And in practice, the state's rights and the pretext of collective societal interest often trump Indigenous rights and environmental protection. The government's relentless pursuits to extract and industrialize minerals and hydrocarbons with transnational partners inevitably result in degradation and dispossession of Indigenous peoples located atop deposits (Webber 2011:234) or in the path of pipelines.

Although development under Morales shares many features of economic nationalism (see chapters 7 and 8), it carries forward various elements of the preceding neoliberal model of development, which I detail in chapter 2 (Bebbington and Humphreys Bebbington 2011; Kaup 2010; Webber 2011). I argue that although the Morales administration has boosted the state's share of profits from the oil and gas sector and channeled them into industrialization and social spending, on the ground extraction continues to take a toll on affected communities and environments, much like during the neoliberal era.

Throughout this book I refer to *neoliberalism* as a set of political and economic ideologies that aim to liberalize trade, privatize state enterprises and services, introduce market-oriented management practices to the public sector, and reduce certain state functions (e.g., regulating corporations and providing social services) (Jessop 2002; see also Webber 2011:227). Neoliberal policies and projects often enclose the environmental commons, facilitating capital accumulation while simultaneously generating opposition (Perreault 2009). While neoliberalism tends to have these common goals and effects, it is not monolithic, but rather multifaceted, with diverse forms that vary geographically and historically (Jessop 2002; Larner 2003; Peck and Tickell 2002; Peck 2004; Brenner et al. 2010; Kim and Wainwright 2010). Compared with neoliberalism, *Andean-Amazonian capitalism* under Morales discards some features of neoliberal orthodoxy yet preserves its core reliance on the capitalist market as the main driver of growth and industrialization (Webber 2011:232). Although so-called nationalization by the Morales administration obligated foreign companies to pay greater royalties and taxes, it has left transnational corporations still extracting and exporting most of the country's natural gas. I argue that to better understand rising discontent among Indigenous groups that brought Morales to power, it is necessary to grasp the limits of reform within the logic of global capitalism. With this goal in mind, I trace the history of the neoliberalism in Bolivia as it relates to Indigenous peoples and their environment (chapter 2). I then move on to the principle case examined in this book, Enron and Shell's Cuiabá pipeline (see figures 1.1 and 1.2), which is particularly instructive because the Chiquitano and Ayoreo peoples affected by the pipeline struggled over the project's consequences from the height of the neoliberal era through the reputedly anti-neoliberal administration of Evo Morales. Guarayo congressman Bienvenido Sacu, a member of the newly formed Indigenous caucus who served as Morales's director of TCOs in the Vice Ministry of Lands (Viceministerio de Tierras), invoked historical memories of the Cuiabá case to warn against the potential effects of the road through TIPNIS: "We have to remember that when the Santa Cruz–Trinidad highway was constructed it cut through Guarayo territory and brought a series of problems such as deforestation and effects on our rivers and waters. And there are other examples, such as the Santa Cruz–Cuiabá pipeline, which affects the Chiquitano dry forest. Our Indigenous brothers and sisters do not want to repeat these experiences" (qtd. in CIDOB 2011, translation by author).

The Cuiabá case helps us understand not only the constraints imposed by the neoliberal reforms but also the ways in which Indigenous groups mobilized during and after the neoliberal era (1985–2005) in defense of their rights to land, consultation, and consent over development and conservation

Figure 1.1 Construction of the Cuiabá pipeline through the Chiquitano forest. Author's photo.

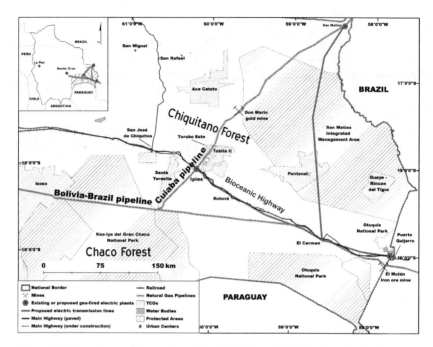

Figure 1.2 Locations of the routes of the Cuiabá and Bolivia-Brazil pipelines, Don Mario gold mine, El Mutún iron ore mine, Indigenous territories, Chiquitano dry forest, Pantanal wetlands, Chaco forest, protected areas, urban centers, proposed power transmission lines, and Santa Cruz–Puerto Suárez bioceanic highway (a project of the Initiative for the Integration of Regional Infrastructure in South America). Map by Daniel Redo.

activities that affect them. Chiquitanos and Ayoreos affected by the Cuiabá pipeline demanded genuine consultation and a just compensation program after Enron and Shell met with just a few affected communities, offering an insignificant amount of funding. And under Morales, despite new constitutional guarantees regarding free, prior, and informed consultation, the administration pressed ahead with conflictive projects. Just weeks before Indigenous groups marched against the controversial highway through TIPNIS, Morales infamously warned: "Whether they like it or not, we will build that road" (qtd. in Lazcano 2011b).

On a broader level, the major conflicts analyzed in this book—the Cuiabá pipeline, oil exploration in the northern La Paz Department, road development in TIPNIS—offer important insights for understanding how Indigenous peoples are advancing the emergent Indigenous rights regime—namely, International Labor Organization (ILO) Convention 169 and the

UN Declaration on the Rights of Indigenous Peoples—on the ground. Sawyer and Gomez (2012:2) have maintained that despite the proliferation of such new legal instruments to safeguard the rights of Indigenous peoples, paradoxically, Indigenous peoples have experienced increased discrimination, exploitation, dispossession, and racism because of an unprecedented surge in extractive development. This book emphasizes that while this extractive boom has certainly hindered implementation of new legal tools, Indigenous peoples have nonetheless used them in strategic ways to compel governments, corporations, and international financial institutions to comply with their rights. In a pragmatic manner, Indigenous groups affected by the above projects simultaneously embraced Western law as a tool to consolidate rights, while at the same time working outside of it, whether through direct actions (marches, blockades, strikes) or electoral politics. During an inspection of the Cuiabá pipeline in 2008, I accompanied a Chiquitano leader who was enthusiastically memorizing the newly adopted UN declaration so he could share it with other Chiquitanos. He knew the Chiquitanos had already successfully used ILO Convention 169 to demand adequate consultation, fair compensation, and political inclusion. His optimism reflected a broader, fundamental belief that in order for legally recognized rights to be respected, Indigenous peoples must continue to actively exercise and defend them on the ground. These are lessons that resonate with similar cases of resource extraction and Indigenous mobilization in other parts of Latin America and abroad.

Fallout on the Frontier

The central conflicts examined in this book are located on the fringes of the Amazon Basin; the Cuiabá pipeline cuts through the middle of the Chiquitano forest (see figures 1.3 and 1.4), perhaps "the largest remaining tract of relatively undisturbed tall dry forest in the Neotropics, if not the entire world" (Parker 1993). TIPNIS and the world-renowned Madidi National Park, located on the Andean-Amazonian region, are among the most biodiverse places on Earth. Yet all are objects of oil and gas development by transnational oil corporations, and home to Indigenous communities mobilizing against affronts on their livelihood. As transnational oil giants scour remote ecoregions of the planet for new deposits to fill their coffers, Indigenous peoples living in the world's remaining forests struggle to assert their rights in the face of encroaching "development" (Gedicks 2001:41). Few places appear to be immune from the advance of the energy

Figure 1.3 The Chiquitano dry forest. Author's photo

Figure 1.4 Black howler monkey. Author's photo

frontier in what Michael Klare (2010) has called an "era of extreme energy." Across the globe, from the Niger Delta to the cloud forests of the Colombian Amazon, rural Indigenous peoples who depend directly on the environment for their livelihoods are particularly vulnerable to the impacts of oil and gas extraction.

Throughout the Americas, recent booms in oil, gas, and mining development have sent shockwaves across affected Indigenous communities as they struggle for cultural survival and the ecosystems upon which they depend (see Sawyer and Gomez 2012; Bebbington and Bury in press-a). As oil corporations flaunt the alleged benefits of gas as a supposedly "clean" fuel (Peet et al. 2011), tribes in the United States and Canada are contending with water contamination caused by hydraulic fracturing (fracking), a controversial technology that pumps a mixture of water, chemicals, and sand into shale rock formations at high pressures to extract gas and oil; while some groups, seeing economic benefits, have half-heartedly embraced the boom, others have banned the process altogether. Discoveries of new shale megafields in Argentina have lured oil giants Chevron (US), Exxon (US), Apache (US), and Total (French) into a frantic new rush in the region, triggering opposition among Mapuche communities already affected by gas development and aware of fallout in North America (Scandizzo 2012); in November 2011, members of a Mapuche community occupied one of Apache's gas-processing plants, demanding an end to drilling because of water pollution (EFE 2011).

In the Amazon, since the oil boom of the 1970s, Indigenous groups and supporters in Bolivia, Ecuador, Peru, Colombia, and elsewhere have mobilized as oil and gas development has penetrated remote ecosystems (witness the twenty-year-long legal battle against Chevron-Texaco in Ecuador and the struggle over the Camisea gas pipeline in Peru) (Finer et al. 2008; Finer and Orta-Martínez 2010; Gavaldá 1999; Gerlach 2003; O'Rourke and Connolly 2003; San Sebastián and Hurtig 2004; Sawyer 2004); a more recent boom in oil, gas, and mining throughout the more intact, exceptionally biodiverse forests of the western Amazon (Bolivia, western Brazil, Colombia, Ecuador, Peru, Venezuela) has generated sharp conflicts among affected Indigenous peoples (Bebbington 2012; Bebbington and Bury in press-a; Bebbington and Humphreys Bebbington 2011; Finer et al. 2008; Finer and Orta-Martínez 2010; Griffiths 2007). Government support for extractive development and associated unrest has persisted across ideological divides (Bebbington and Humphreys Bebbington 2011). Even in Ecuador and Bolivia, where left-leaning, populist administrations claiming environmental credentials have adopted progressive constitutions and laws, they have steadily drifted away from the Indigenous base that helped bring them to power.

With noted exceptions, research on the consequences of this recent expansion is scant (Hecht 2011:214–215). Further, very few studies focus on the Chiquitano region, the site of the Cuiabá conflict. Existing literature related to the hydrocarbons sector in Bolivia has focused primarily on the political economy of natural gas and oil in relation to dynamics of social change and conflict over distribution of revenues (Humphreys Bebbington and Bebbington 2010; Hodges 2007; Kaup 2008; Kohl and Farthing 2006; Postero 2007; Schroeder 2007; Webber 2011). Much of this work centers either on the 2003 "gas war" in La Paz or on the Chaco region, where many of the major gas fields are located. This book complements these important contributions by offering insights into Indigenous mobilization in relation to Bolivia's recent extractive boom, linking it with environmental considerations, the neoliberal economic reforms, and subsequent state capitalism under Morales.

Though the particularities of the cases explored in this book vary, as do their historical contexts, they provide valuable insights that are applicable elsewhere, especially given the substantial rise in socioenvironmental conflicts in Latin America over the last decade linked to natural resource extraction and development (Clara Galvis 2011; Gudynas and Acosta 2011b). A 2011 report on extractive industries and Indigenous peoples produced by James Anaya, the UN Special Rapporteur on the rights of Indigenous peoples, identified "natural resource extraction and other major development projects in or near indigenous territories as one of the most significant sources of abuse of the rights of indigenous peoples worldwide. In its prevailing form, the model for advancing with natural resource extraction within the territories of indigenous peoples appears to run counter to the self-determination of indigenous peoples in the political, social and economic spheres" (Anaya 2011).

Organization of the Book

In the remainder of this chapter I describe the methods and approach I used in conducting this research, noting unique considerations that emerged because of my simultaneous role as an academic and advocate. Subsequently, I provide a brief synopsis of historical developments in the Chiquitano region, underscoring how the Chiquitanos and Ayoreos repeatedly struggled against external actors for control over natural resources, livelihood, and identity. I describe how I employ a political ecology framework to analyze the Cuiabá conflict in relation to shifting patterns of control and access to natural resources (Bryant 1992; Martinez-Alier 2002). Finally, I give a historical overview of oil and gas development in Bolivia, providing background necessary for the subsequent chapters.

Chapter 2 sets the stage for the primary empirical account of resistance and protagonism surrounding the Cuiabá pipeline (chapters 3–6 and 9). Drawing heavily on primary documents, I trace how the World Bank, working in alliance with the US government, transnational corporations, and neoliberal regimes, triggered partial privatization of Bolivia's oil and gas sector, creating the structural conditions necessary for Enron, Shell, and other transnational oil corporations to enter Bolivia. Such pressure encouraged neoliberal administrations beholden to transnationals to rewrite laws and regulations to lure foreign investment, create corporate-dominated, World Bank–funded regulatory agencies, and reduce government royalties and taxes. I argue that neoliberal advocates pushed the reforms using a deceptive discourse that foreign corporations would outperform defunct state companies, expand output, be better stewards of the environment, and alleviate poverty. Instead, by the World Bank's own accounts, extreme poverty increased significantly and state budgets were depleted. Internal documents showed that the reforms were largely self-serving policies pushed to aid US investors, open new markets, and create jobs in the United States, and extractive industries were prioritized in direct contradiction with the World Bank's mandate of sustainable development and poverty alleviation.

I argue that the reforms fueled unparalleled expansion of oil and gas projects (including the key cases explored in the book), generating substantial impacts across Indigenous territories and prized ecosystems (mirroring similar patterns in Peru, Ecuador, and elsewhere)—a consequence acknowledged by the World Bank itself. This, in turn, triggered rising resistance and protagonism among affected Indigenous peoples, who advanced their interests using newly won rights to recognition, territory, consultation, compensation, and political participation (Postero 2007). By highlighting the profound transformations the reforms brought about, chapter 2 helps us better understand the contradictions of Morales's development agenda—a form of state capitalism incorporating many elements of neoliberalism—as it relates to Indigenous peoples and their environment.

Chapter 3 explains how Enron and Shell planned the Cuiabá pipeline in cahoots with the US government and Bolivia's neoliberal champion, Gonzalo Sánchez de Lozada, who was ousted in the gas war of 2003 and currently lives in exile in the United States. It details how, in order to cut costs and supply Sánchez de Lozada's gold mine, the companies built the pipeline directly through the heart of the Chiquitano forest. The chapter centers on the dramatic story of how conservation organizations were used by Enron and Shell to justify the project. Five US and Bolivian conservation groups negotiated a $20 million conservation program with the oil giants behind closed doors. The program created just enough appearance of environmental sensitivity for the US government to finance the pipeline. Chapter 3 highlights the ethical ambiguity of conservationists and companies secretly negotiating a multimillion-dollar conservation program that both greenwashed a destructive pipeline and excluded Indigenous organizations and the Bolivian government from negotiations and management of the program board.

Drawing on some of the case history, chapter 3 addresses the events leading up to the creation of the conservation program and US government funding of the pipeline, including conflicts over Enron's and Shell's substandard environmental impact studies, the pipeline route, and complicities between the Bolivian government and the oil companies. The chapter culminates with the description of the US government's vote to lend Enron $200 million to build the pipeline directly through the middle of the Chiquitano forest—a decision made immediately after Enron leaked news about the conservation program, in violation of an agreement it made with World Wildlife Fund. Chapter 3 shows how the controversial conservation program, used to greenwash adverse impacts of the Cuiabá pipeline, was a "fortress conservation"[5] initiative disguised as community-based conservation. Conflict over the pipeline and the exclusionary conservation program would mark the beginning of rising mobilization during the country's 2000–2005 anti-neoliberal rebellion.

Chapter 4 tells the explosive saga of how Indigenous groups, allied organizations, and the Bolivian government reacted to the exclusionary conservation program and US government funding of the pipeline along the controversial route. It recounts the Chiquitanos' and Ayoreos' struggle to democratize a program that granted private corporations and conservation organizations control over their ancestral lands—a blatant form of accumulation by dispossession (Harvey 2003).[6] I assert that the conservationists' exclusion of Indigenous peoples and devaluation of Indigenous knowledge stemmed from a Western environmentalist worldview privileging "wild" nature over peopled landscapes (see Hecht 1993).

In this and subsequent chapters, I argue that the Chiquitanos and Ayoreos employed what I call *dynamic pragmatism*, a flexible decision-making approach that considers practical consequences in light of changing social, historical, and environmental circumstances. I build on what Scott Pratt (2002:19–20) has termed "native pragmatism," a concept that underscores the Native American roots of key tenets in classical pragmatism, including "the principles of interaction, pluralism, community, and growth." In this book, I elaborate on the concept in the context of social mobilization, showing how the Chiquitanos and Ayoreos worked with supporting organizations cooperatively, pragmatically, and at times in contradiction, forming flexible and shifting coalitions, with changing tactics and fluid identities. In their quest for control over territory and natural resources, the Chiquitanos and Ayoreos exercised a mix of insurgent citizenship (Holston 1996; Holston and Appadurai 1996), resurgent identities (Bolanos 2011; Porro et al. 2011), and assertions over forest stewardship. In a reflection of broader trends elsewhere, the Chiquitanos embraced their Indigenous identity, converting their legal status from "peasant" (*campesino*) to "Indigenous," in part to secure land rights they helped win during the 1990s. Compared with the more interest-based aims of their international allies (e.g., stopping the US government's loan), the Chiquitanos and Ayoreos were more intent on securing a long-term, autonomous compensation program that supported their ways of living and guaranteed land tenure—a struggle rooted in self-determination, cultural identity, and livelihood. Sometimes they directed their claims through electoral channels, for example, through newly elected Indigenous representatives, while on other occasions they sidestepped the state altogether, engaging in radical actions or dealing directly with the companies, international financial institutions, and US government. They both carried out case-specific actions related to the pipeline and participated in nationwide mobilizations, for example, to defend national sovereignty over hydrocarbons, elect Morales, and write a new constitution. This strategy mirrored how the MAS political party oscillated between mass activism and electoral politicking (Postero 2010:31).

Chapter 5 turns to a fine-grained anatomy of Indigenous and allied mobilization that led to land titling, as well as to the creation, implementation, and extension of the Cuiabá pipeline's Indigenous Development Plan, a community development initiative funded by Enron and Shell as compensation for adverse pipeline impacts. It illustrates how, as the economic reforms deepened, Indigenous peoples engaged using what Arturo Escobar (2006) calls "place-based, yet transnationalized strategies" of resistance and protagonism to attain their aims.

Chapter 6 describes how Chiquitanos, Ayoreos, and supporters challenged the environmental injustices brought by the Cuiabá pipeline. While Enron and Shell made off with handsome profits, affected communities saw few benefits from the pipeline's compensation program and were disproportionately burdened with adverse social and environmental impacts. Once again, they employed *dynamic pragmatism*, prioritizing putting pressure on the companies to rectify those impacts that most directly threatened their livelihood, including water contamination, road degradation, increased conflict, and rising encroachment (e.g., by loggers, ranchers, colonists, and narcotraffickers). The Chiquitanos employed independent, community-based monitoring—syncretizing traditional ecological knowledge with expertise provided by a local nongovernmental organization (NGO)—to counterbalance distorted company reports and raise community awareness regarding legal rights.

With allied organizations, the Chiquitanos and Ayoreos used transnational boomerang advocacy (Keck and Sikkink 1998) to amplify their voice and target key corporate headquarters, Bolivian state actors, and US government agencies. Such actions triggered a front page story in the *Washington Post* and visits from the US State Department and Enron International's vice president for project finance. And a loose alliance with non-Indigenous grassroots organizations and NGOs helped compel the companies further to resolve outstanding issues.

Chapters 7–11 describe Indigenous mobilization, extractive development, and environmental struggle under the administration of Evo Morales. Chapter 7 gives an overview of the Morales administration's policies regarding resource extraction, primarily in relation to oil and gas development. In chapter 8, I contend that while the 2009 Bolivian Constitution provides significant new rights for Indigenous peoples and the environment, contradictions in the text and in practice present serious challenges. Evidence from the Cuiabá conflict and other cases (oil development in the northern La Paz Department, road development in TIPNIS) bring to light significant difficulties with application and enforcement. The chapter centers on struggles over consultation and consent, contextualizing them within the state's conflictive development model. It demonstrates how Indigenous peoples used an emergent Indigenous rights regime to oblige other actors to respect their rights.

Chapter 9 returns to the book's primary case, the Cuiabá pipeline, looking at new and continuing developments under the Morales administration. It describes how Enron's heir (Ashmore Energy International), Shell, the US government's Overseas Private Investment Corporation, and the World Bank distanced themselves from the project, shirking responsibility for ongoing impacts. Faced with ongoing issues, the Chiquitanos pragmatically employed both ILO Convention 169 and new legal instruments (e.g., the UN declaration and the 2009 constitution), in conjunction with other actions, to augment their claims. Mobilization to democratize Enron and Shell's exclusionary conservation program waned, and conflict increased as some communities opted to work with the initiative, yet another expression of *dynamic pragmatism*. I argue that the program's persistence to date speaks to a broader continuation of fortress-style programs worldwide. Like during the neoliberal era, direct actions, including a threat to close the pipeline valve, compelled the companies to continue the Indigenous compensation program; asserting their autonomy, the Chiquitanos and Ayoreos continued to restructure the initiative around their lifeways, but the program had mixed results, with persistent problems, new dependencies, and inequities.

Taking a broader perspective, chapter 9 analyzes how, while domestic and international legal decisions have advanced Indigenous rights regarding compensation, paradoxically, these changes incentivize communities to consent to development projects that have historically degraded their lands. And though the Morales administration recognized far more collective land titles (TCOs) for Indigenous groups than did previous neoliberal regimes, government support for extractive industries and infrastructure development threatens their integrity and violates Indigenous rights to consultation, consent, and self-determination.

I describe how under Morales, environmental and social impacts of the Cuiabá pipeline escalated as Enron's heir (Ashmore) and Shell still had not adequately reforested or controlled the pipeline route and access roads. Encroaching development—hunting, logging, farming, and mining—continued, and new synergistic impacts mushroomed in conjunction with the Don Mario gold mine and two new gas-fired power plants. I close chapter 9 by explaining how, although recent national unrest exemplifies diminishing patience among Indigenous groups who have supported Morales, the Chiquitanos are cognizant of the gains achieved under the administration and have faith that increasing government representation, in tandem with unrelenting insurgent citizenship, will uphold Indigenous rights.

Chapter 10 centers on the still unfolding TIPNIS case, arguably the most challenging conflict endured by the Morales administration thus far. It highlights parallels with the Cuiabá case, emphasizing that at the crux of both conflicts are struggles over consultation, consent, and self-determination.

Chapter 11 concludes by elaborating on the central arguments explored in the book, explaining the significance of the central cases for understanding what the shift from neoliberalism to state capitalism means for extractive industries, Indigenous peoples, and the environment. It assesses prospects for improved relations among Indigenous peoples, the state, transnationals, and international financial institutions.

On Methods and Political Ecology

I initially became interested in the Cuiabá case through volunteer work at Amazon Watch, a small US-based NGO with a mission to protect Amazonian forests and advance the rights of Indigenous peoples living in the Amazon Basin. I was intrigued by how the organization, unlike many conservation organizations, partnered directly with Indigenous groups confronting megadevelopment projects on their lands. Although I had planned to conduct dissertation research examining how the neoliberal economic reforms affected deforestation and Indigenous peoples' livelihood in the Chiquitano forest, I shifted to the Cuiabá case once I realized I could do a similar investigation surrounding the pipeline, which was of more immediate concern to the Chiquitano and Ayoreo Indigenous peoples living in the region.

While I did not formally work for the organization during my dissertation research (October 1999 to August 2000), I coauthored publications and subsequently worked for it for several months in 2002 and 2003. While this role aided my research in many regards (e.g., establishing contacts with Indigenous organizations, NGOs, and international financial institutions), it also raised important considerations about ethics, neutrality, and objectivity, which I elaborate on more fully elsewhere (Hindery 2003a; for an insightful reflection on issues related to positionality while conducting participatory action research, see Robertson 2010). Similarly, it placed this work in the midst of debates regarding the merits of political engagement within the field of political ecology, which has been criticized for not prioritizing reciprocity with research subjects (Walker 2007:366) and for having limited involvement in the policy realm (Walker 2006:383). Throughout the book, I discuss my role as an advocate and provide critical analysis about Amazon Watch and the effects of my interventions.

Over the years, at the request of Chiquitano and Ayoreo Indigenous organizations, I have translated various documents from the companies and US government agencies, reported the results of my research, produced reports in Spanish, and shared photos and video footage. Throughout the book, in an effort to highlight Indigenous voices, I incorporate a substantial amount of testimony but do not use actual names except in instances where the individuals are public figures or have been quoted in other sources. Although I make an effort to communicate testimony from a diverse cross section of Chiquitanos and Ayoreos living in communities affected by the Cuiabá pipeline, a substantial number of quotes come from leaders who were elected to monitor pipeline impacts. By including this testimony, I do not mean to privilege the voices of "elites" over other community members but have, in certain instances, opted to include such accounts since these individuals tended to have unique knowledge about the pipeline because they have traversed the right-of-way and frequently compared findings with other communities. In addition, many of them were elected by their communities to compile and aggregate testimony within and across communities. While such knowledge is, of course, situated and partial (see Haraway 1988), as I note throughout the text, the reports that pipeline monitors produced were reviewed and approved (or rejected) by each community.

While I draw on a variety of theoretical approaches, I primarily employ a political ecology framework,[7] which considers the interface between ecology and political economy (Blaikie et al. 1987:17). Political ecology centers on the interactions among political interests, social institutions, and human–environment relations across multiple scales and over time (Blaikie 1985; Blaikie et al. 1987; Robbins 2004; Zimmerer and Bassett 2003). It emphasizes the importance of subaltern—in this case, Indigenous—experiences and knowledge about culture, the environment, economy, and politics (Escobar 2006; see also Sawyer 2004; Kirsch 2006). In this book, I use the approach as an entry point to understanding the nexus of Indigenous politics, "development," and environment.

Despite the extractive boom sweeping across Latin America, until recently, research on conflicts related to extractive industries, social conflict, and the environment has been surprisingly sparse. Given the imminent need to address this gap, key scholars in the field of political ecology have begun to publish seminal volumes compiling evidence from various cases around the world (see, e.g., Bebbington 2012; Bebbington and Bury in press-a; Sawyer and Gomez 2012). Emerging scholarship has shown that even progressive governments in Latin America have continued to defend extractivist and conventional development strategies (Bebbington 2009; Gudynas and Acosta 2011a), at times even noting that environmental protection is a luxury that should be undertaken in the distant future (Gudynas 2010:54, 60–61). Bebbington, Bury, and Gallagher (in press-b) conclude that "resource extraction constitutes a vital domain of research that will push the frontiers of political ecology at the same time as political ecologists make important contributions to understanding its causes, its nature, and its consequences." Building on the work of Jamie Peck (2004), I use the approach to go beyond merely exploring the underlying principles of neoliberalism, instead showing the dialectical relationships between extractive-oriented development models (focusing on neoliberalism and state capitalism), their social and environmental impacts on the ground, and Indigenous social mobilization. In this regard, I contribute to a line of inquiry within the field that asks how specific social and environmental conditions are produced and how they are entangled with various facets of capitalism (Peet et al. 2011:29). Following Gavin Bridge (2011:316, 320–321), I delineate how the materialities of gas—particularly extraction and distribution (e.g., pipelines)—although not determinant, shape social relations and generate social and environmental contradictions (e.g., adverse effects on livelihood and the environment).

By focusing on conflict over natural resources that are the basis for Indigenous livelihood, the book also hinges on another critical area of inquiry within the framework (Wolf 1972; Bryant 1992; Blaikie 1994; Robbins 2004). I argue that political ecology must situate local and regional dynamics (e.g., Indigenous mobilization in response to oil, gas, and mining development) in the context of larger macroeconomic and political forces (e.g., Bolivia's neoliberal economic reforms and the subsequent turn toward resource nationalism). Throughout the book, I contend that Indigenous mobilization surrounding the Cuiabá pipeline underscores the importance of agency and identity in challenging the structural confines imposed by neoliberalism.

Another central theme in political ecology focuses on the relation between environmental conservation and struggles over environmental control (Robbins 2004:149–170). Research in the field has shown how conservation, despite its laudable goals, is often a means (or cover) for powerful actors to control natural resources and the value derived from them (Peet et al. 2011:27). In my account of the fortress-style Chiquitano Forest Conservation Program, I argue that conservationists, employing a neoliberal form of environmental governance, usurped control of natural resources from the Chiquitanos and Ayoreos, accumulating $20 million from Enron and Shell in the name of conservation. I analyze the Chiquitanos' and Ayoreos' dynamic and pragmatic strategies to democratize the program and rectify adverse social and environmental impacts from the pipeline.

This book is based on extensive ethnographic research (interviews, participant observation, and document analysis), combined with field investigations to analyze environmental impacts. It incorporates data collected for my dissertation research (1999–2000) and synthesizes information gathered during a series of several-week-long trips to Bolivia in 2002, 2004, 2005, 2006, 2007, 2008, 2010, and 2011. In covering the Cuiabá case, I focus more on the Chiquitanos than the Ayoreos since the pipeline affects thirty-four Chiquitano communities with an estimated 7,516 individuals, versus only two Ayoreo communities, with a population of 274 individuals (OICH and CEADES 2004:36). All translations of Bolivia's 2009 constitution are by Luis Francisco Valle V. (2010), with translation errors corrected by the author.

A Political Ecology of the Chiquitanía

Chiquitano and Ayoreo Indigenous peoples living in the Chiquitano region (or Chiquitanía, see figure 1.5) have repeatedly struggled against external actors for control over natural resources that are the source of their identity and livelihood. Driven by geopolitical, economic, and religious motivations, various actors entered their ancestral lands, including colonial and state authorities, merchants, missionaries, gold prospectors, rubber barons, cattle ranchers, commercial farmers, and, most recently, transnational oil corporations. In response to this intrusion, they have carried out diverse acts of resistance and protagonism. The exploits of invasive actors were

Figure 1.5 Chiquitano community affected by the Cuiabá pipeline. Author's photo

highly dependent on Indigenous labor and geographical knowledge. The congregation by Jesuits of more than fifty ethnic groups into missions substantially fragmented Indigenous cultures and increased vulnerability by fomenting dependence and diminishing subsistence activities. Although the majority of the Indigenous peoples living in the region were sedentary agriculturalists (albeit still heavily reliant on hunting and gathering), the Jesuits systematized communal agriculture and animal husbandry (Díez Astete 1993:119). They introduced cattle raising and agriculture as principle economic activities, displacing traditional practices of hunting, fishing, and gathering. In addition, they organized production of woodworks, textiles, musical instruments, buildings, soap, sugar, honey, and wax (Montaño Aragón 1989). In some ways, the mission regime protected the Chiquitanos from abuses by Spanish authorities. And religious conversion was not total, as the Chiquitanos syncretized their diverse spiritual beliefs with Catholicism.

Following expulsion of the Jesuits and the formation of the Republic of Bolivia in 1825, the state allocated Indigenous lands to whites and mestizos from Santa Cruz and the highlands, drawing Indigenous peoples of the Chiquitanía into various forms of indentured labor. Although the collapse of the rubber industry liberated thousands of Indigenous peoples of Bolivia, many in the Chiquitanía became rapidly enmeshed in dehumanizing patronage systems on ranches and farms. Others were enlisted in military exploits and development projects, resulting in further cultural transformation.

Paradoxically, in the Chiquitanía the agrarian reform of 1953 largely benefited the landed elite and overlooked ancestral boundaries and traditional systems of natural resource use. Furthermore, despite the reform, national development policies in the eastern lowlands from this moment on generally favored ranchers, commercial farmers, logging companies, and foreign oil companies over Indigenous peoples and peasants (*campesinos*), resulting in further concentration of land and other natural resources. Throughout the neoliberal era (1985–2005), international trade agreements, projects, and policies promoted by various international financial institutions (e.g., the World Bank, International Monetary Fund, Inter-American Development Bank, Overseas Private Investment Corporation, and the Andean Development Corporation) supported key agents of deforestation and environmental degradation in the region, limiting access to natural resources and sparking intense conflicts, for example, through the World Bank's Eastern Lowlands Natural Resource Management and Agricultural Production Project (Hecht 2005; Hindery 1997; Jones 1995; Kaimowitz et al.

1999; Redo, Millington, and Hindery 2011; World Bank 1993). Construction of Enron and Shell's Cuiabá pipeline, which was initially supported by a $200 million loan from the US government's Overseas Private Investment Corporation, is another prime example.

Although pressure from the Indigenous movement and international community led to implementation of a new agrarian law in 1996 that allowed Indigenous groups to obtain collective titles (TCOs), it enshrined the private property rights of landowners and was plagued with issues during implementation (see chapters 2 and 5). Under Morales, TCO titling would accelerate, but a new agrarian reform would have limited impact (chapter 9); encroaching development activities would continue, in some cases accelerating, further jeopardizing Indigenous lands.

Currently, the Chiquitanos primarily practice community-based subsistence agriculture, small-scale animal husbandry (e.g., raising cattle), hunting, fishing, gathering, and handicrafts (Díez Astete 1993:119; McDaniel et al. 2005:923). Some community members are integrated with the cash economy to a limited extent for supplemental income (e.g., men working as laborers for cattle ranches or logging companies, or women working in domestic service in urban areas) (Birk 2000:178; McDaniel 2002:391; OICH and CEADES 2004:47). Principal crops include rice, corn, yucca, and plantains, while secondary crops include peanuts, sugarcane, kidney beans, and sweet potatoes. Some Chiquitanos have cattle as a source of income, and many raise poultry for daily consumption.

Chiquitanos depend on the natural resources of the forest for a wide range of materials, including medicine, building materials, household supplies, fuelwood, and tools; most rely on hunting and fishing for protein and medicine. Natural resource use is informed by spiritual beliefs; for example, the spirits of the forest (*jichis*) oversee human exploitation of the environment, ensure that families only take what is necessary for subsistence, and punish violators (Birk 2000:191).

With a long history of common property resource management, Ayoreo settlements and lands are organized communally, while production is typically split among two or three related families (Díez Astete 1993:119). Ayoreos practice shifting cultivation of various crops, including corn, rice, manioc, and plantains, and their secondary crops include squash and beans. Although previously significant, hunting has become less prevalent among community members as logging and other development activities (e.g., commercial farming and ranching) have diminished wildlife populations. In general, decline in natural resources caused by such development activities is a factor that has caused Ayoreos to enter the cash economy to survive. Their social relations have also changed as a result of the establishment of large-scale farms and cattle ranches, which impede their itinerant lifestyle and intraethnic communication.

In an attempt to proactively address threats to their livelihood, Ayoreo leaders deviated from previously tribal social structures and formed an intercommunity, regional Ayoreo Indigenous organization, the Ayoreo Native Center of the Bolivian Oriente, which is affiliated with the main lowland Federation of Indigenous Peoples of Bolivia (Confederación de Pueblos Indígenas de Bolivia, CIDOB). Similarly, the Chiquitanos organized themselves into local and regional Indigenous organizations that are affiliated with CIDOB, including the Chiquitano Indigenous Organization (Organización Indígena Chiquitana, OICH); the Center for Indigenous Communities of Chiquitos, located near the southern end of the Cuiabá pipeline; and the Indigenous Center for the Reclamation of Rights of Angel Sandoval Province, located at the northern end of the pipeline. In addition, the Coordinator of Ethnic Peoples of Santa Cruz represents Indigenous peoples of the Department of Santa Cruz, which includes Chiquitano and Ayoreo communities.

A Brief Hydrocarbons History: The Privatization/ Nationalization Pendulum

Over the past hundred years, intense power struggles emerged over Bolivia's hydrocarbons, with control shifting back and forth between the state and foreign oil companies. Oil production began in the early 1900s and intensified when the state transferred all concessions to John D. Rockefeller's Standard Oil Company in 1921 (Gavaldá 1999:25). The move marked the onset of US-led neocolonialism, based on privatization and extraction of Bolivia's hydrocarbon resources.

By 1920, vast areas had been ceded to foreign oil companies, some of which sold oil to Paraguay during the 1932–1935 Chaco War between Paraguay and Bolivia (Molina 1999b:71). Marc Gavaldá (1999:25) argues that Standard Oil and Royal Dutch Shell caused the war, because both companies desired the oil reserves that existed in the Chaco region, along the border of Bolivia and Paraguay. He claims that while Standard Oil financed the war on the Bolivian side, Royal Dutch Shell financed it in Paraguay. Emerging historical evidence, however, casts doubt on whether the companies in fact fueled the war.[8]

During the Chaco War, some several thousand Chiquitanos were recruited, many of whom perished—a fate shared by thousands of Guaraní,

Quechuas, and Aymaras who also fought in defense of Bolivian oil (OICH and CEADES 2004:42). After Bolivia lost the war, the state broke its contract with Standard Oil, relegated the company to exploration, and regained control through the creation of the state oil company, Yacimientos Petrolíferos Fiscales Bolivianos (YPFB), in 1936 (Gavaldá 1999:25; Molina 1999b:71). The following year, the government nationalized the industry (Gordon and Luoma 2008:82). Standard Oil's properties were expropriated as Standard Oil was found guilty of illegally transporting oil to Argentina and selling it to Paraguay during the conflict. In response, Standard Oil and the US government pressured the Bolivian government to indemnify the company. Consequently, in 1943, the company reached an agreement with the Bolivian government in which Bolivia paid Standard Oil $1.5 million in exchange for Standard Oil leaving the country and handing over its exploration data (Gavaldá 1999:26). The government agreed to the deal because the United States threatened to discourage investment in Bolivia if the company was not compensated (Royuela Comboni 1996).

As an outgrowth of the Bolivian revolution of 1952, Victor Paz Estenssoro's leftist Revolutionary Nationalist Movement (Movimiento Nacionalista Revolucionario, MNR) party implemented agrarian reform and nationalized the mining sector (Molina 1999b:71). Nationalization had the unintended consequence of devastating the Bolivian economy because the United States responded by sanctioning mineral imports, a vital source of revenue (Gavaldá 1999:26); approximately 50% of the tin produced in Bolivia was exported to the United States. The MNR's actions worried financiers and government officials in the United States and Europe, because they were seen as moves toward communism and protectionism (Royuela Comboni 1996:109; Conduru 2001:15). To stifle these tendencies, the administrations of US presidents Truman, Eisenhower, and Kennedy granted a substantial amount of aid to Bolivia (Conduru 2001:15; Rabe 1988:77–78). Between 1953 and 1961 Bolivia received, on a per capita basis, more economic aid from the United States than any other country in the world (Rabe 1988:77–78). Faced with the threat of economic sanctions, domestic food shortages, and international and domestic political pressures, in 1956 the Estenssoro administration opened Bolivia to foreign investment in hydrocarbons (Royuela Comboni 1996:109; Conduru 2001:16). US president Dwight D. Eisenhower reached an agreement with Estenssoro in which the United States gave support on condition that Bolivia grant concessions to US oil interests, including Gulf Oil, Tesoro, and Occidental. To this end, with US financial support, the Bolivian government contracted the US law firm Davenport and Schuster to develop a new hydrocarbons code (Royuela Comboni 1996:109). Despite widespread waves of protest from various sectors of Bolivian society, the Davenport Code was promoted and implemented as law in 1956 (Royuela Comboni 1996:109). The law enabled foreign investments in hydrocarbons and forbade state companies from extracting Bolivian oil (Conduru 2001:17). Nationalist uproar emerged as Gulf Oil invested in Bolivia's oil fields and, in 1967, signed a contract with Argentine parastatal corporation Gas del Estado to export Bolivian gas for twenty years (Mares 2006). The Bolivian populace was outraged because this placed Bolivian state company YPFB in direct competition with Gulf Oil to supply gas to Argentine markets. The response foreshadowed what would become a predictable pattern of popular protest over foreign control over hydrocarbons and export that favored transnationals above public interest.

Public pressure pushed Gulf Oil into negotiations with the administration of General René Barrientos over an increase in royalty payments, but discussions failed, and in 1969 the sector was nationalized yet again under the leftist military regime of Alfredo Ovando Candía (Mares 2006; Royuela Comboni 1996:141). The Davenport Code was repealed, Gulf Oil was expelled from Bolivia with an indemnification agreement, and the state once again gained control of Bolivia's oil reserves. In 1972 the pendulum swung back again toward privatization when the administration of General Hugo Banzer Suárez enacted a new hydrocarbons law that permitted joint operation contracts and concessions (Gavaldá 1999:27). Bolivia granted concessions of thirty years to eighteen new companies. In the 1970s, YPFB recovered after the indemnification of Gulf Oil,[9] and two private companies, Occidental Petroleum and Tesoro Petroleum, performed particularly well (Vargas Salgueiro 1996:104). In 1972, with financing from the World Bank and US private firms, YPFB and Gulf Oil inaugurated Bolivia's first major gas pipeline to Argentina, known as Yacimientos-Bolivian Gulf, or YABOG (Calvo Mirabal 1996). In doing so, the World Bank both underwrote the cost of the investment and increased the Bolivian government's credibility in committing to exporting gas and integrating the region economically (Mares 2006).

Vying to keep Bolivian gas as a potential reserve, in 1974 and 1978 Brazil signed accords with Bolivia to open Brazilian markets to steel, petrochemicals, fertilizer, and cement produced at a proposed industrial complex located in Bolivia near the Brazilian border, atop the El Mutún iron deposit. In exchange, Bolivia agreed to sell Brazil 4.1 billion cubic meters of gas per year over the next twenty years (Mares 2006). Popular unrest exploded over the deal because little development had resulted from YABOG; in addition, Argentina tried to reduce the price and volume of gas imports from Bolivia (Vargas Salgueiro 1996). Based on their experience with YABOG,

Bolivians who objected to the agreement with Brazil therefore worried the proposed industrial complex would not serve the public interest. Against this backdrop, the Mutún project fell apart and would not be revived until the administration of Morales.

By 1979 oil exports declined drastically, largely because the amount of time in which Gulf Oil was to be indemnified was reduced from twenty to six years (Vargas Salgueiro 1996). This acceleration of payments, which occurred during the dictatorship of General Banzer (1971–1978), significantly increased YPFB's debt, amounting to an estimated loss of $58 million (Molina 1999b:72). More generally, Banzer's policy of achieving economic growth by accruing debt sowed the seeds of severe economic decline in the early 1980s, which justified the adoption of neoliberal economic "reforms." Ironically, Banzer increased debt fivefold, masked by rising oil and tin prices, which increased export earnings (Bailey and Knutsen 1987:47). Although the sector was negatively affected during the early 1980s, high international petroleum prices helped compensate for YPFB's production problems (Molina 1999b:72; Vargas Salgueiro 1996:73). However, during this period, while YPFB's production diminished, the private sector's relative contribution to national production of oil and gas increased, which fueled neoliberal arguments to privatize the state company (Molina 1999b:73).

By 1985, a number of factors, including debt, falling tin prices, high interest rates, and a decline in foreign aid, led to hyperinflation (Bailey and Knutsen 1987:47). The crisis ushered in the election of Victor Paz Estenssoro (MNR), who had been president during the agrarian reforms of the 1950s. Estenssoro's administration sought to contain inflation and attract foreign investment through "shock therapy" measures advised by Harvard economist Jeffrey Sachs (Hylton et al. 2007:95). These entailed radical structural adjustment and stabilization policies prescribed by the World Bank and the International Monetary Fund. The neoliberal era had officially begun. It was an ironic about-face from Paz Estenssoro's first term in office (1952–1956), when the government granted universal suffrage (including Indigenous peoples), nationalized the three largest tin companies, and carried out an unprecedented agrarian reform. In 1985, the government reversed course, dismantled the state Mining Corporation of Bolivia (Corporación Minera de Bolivia), and stopped participating in hydrocarbons production. Instead, it became a cheerleader for international capital, shifting its duties to policy making and promoting private investment (Viceministerio de Energía e Hidrocarburos 2002).

Until 1992, YPFB benefited from the policies since inflation was contained and international prices of hydrocarbon derivatives stabilized (Molina 1999b:73), but subsequently successive neoliberal governments debilitated the company's financial condition, paving the way for its partial privatization, or "capitalization." In 1985, as a condition of an agreement with the International Monetary Fund, the Bolivian state ceased to invest in new capital goods, such as equipment and facilities (Bolivian Government 1985). Consequently, since the state was unable to fund and maintain the capital-intensive state oil company, the agreement undermined YPFB's ability to turn a profit (Kaup 2010). This sowed the seeds of YPFB's financial deterioration, making it a prime target for future privatization. Carlos Villegas Quiroga, who would serve as Bolivia's hydrocarbons minister under Morales, described how neoliberal policy makers and business interests debilitated the company: "They de-capitalized the company. . . . It didn't have funds to invest in exploration, development, production, or other types of activities" (qtd. in Gordon 2005).

As the subsequent chapters of this book reveal, these neoliberal reforms, especially capitalization, would generate tremendous investment in the hydrocarbons sector and would spark intense conflict with Indigenous peoples living in the path of "development."

CHAPTER TWO

The Neoliberal Turn and the Rise of Resistance

Pipeline Precursors: Building a Neoliberal Paradise

The neoliberal economic "reforms" adopted in the early 1980s and thereafter defined a new era in which multilateral aid and political pressure (mostly from the United States) encouraged Bolivian president Gonzalo Sánchez de Lozada to partially privatize the national oil company, rewrite laws and regulations in favor of transnationals, create corporate-friendly regulatory agencies, and cut royalties and taxes on new fields from 50% to 18% (Dussan 2004:37; see World Bank 1994b, 2006). The goals were clear: eliminate the state monopoly, promote private investment in the sector, and offer transnationals incentives to explore and develop reserves. To a certain degree, history had repeated itself and hearkened back to periods when the United States obligated Bolivia to privatize the sector and surrender its domestic reserves to Standard Oil and Gulf Oil. Yet the economic, legal, and institutional reforms adopted in the neoliberal era transformed the state and economy much more profoundly and catalyzed unprecedented expansion of oil, gas, and mining development across Indigenous territories and fragile ecosystems. Attracted to the reforms, by the 1990s various oil giants seeking lucrative markets trained their sights on Bolivia, which at the time was considered the second-largest gas reserve holder in South America, after Venezuela.

In this chapter, I argue that the coordinated efforts of the World Bank, US government, Bolivian government, and transnational corporations led to partial privatization of Bolivia's hydrocarbons sector, facilitating the entrance of Enron, Shell, and other transnational oil corporations. I claim this had significant effects on Indigenous peoples and ecosystems located in the midst of expanding oil and gas activities. I assert that Indigenous peoples responded by employing fundamental rights gained as a result of their mobilization in the 1990s. In this and subsequent chapters, I show how the agency of Indigenous peoples and supporters was evident in their efforts to negotiate, challenge, and shape the way the neoliberal reforms were implemented on the ground.

In the opinion of the World Bank, a "breakthrough" occurred in 1993 when University of Chicago–schooled Sánchez de Lozada assumed the presidency with a commitment to downsize government through privatization and dedicated to drafting new laws and regulations to attract foreign investment (World Bank 2006:3). Sánchez de Lozada had gained the World Bank's credibility while serving as Bolivia's economic planning minister from 1985 to 1989, when he oversaw implementation of the first round of neoliberal reforms. Seizing the day, the World Bank swiftly shifted its strategy from merely limiting the role of the state in hydrocarbons to an all-out crusade for privatization. The benefits brought to transnationals would be unparalleled: during the neoliberal era, foreign oil corporations reaped a full 82% of the value of gas produced through various taxes, while the state received only 18%—a tax regime that would be subsequently reversed with the 2005 hydrocarbons law and 2006 nationalization (Webber 2006). According to an estimate from the Barrows Company, an international reference library for oil, gas and mineral laws, Bolivia had the lowest royalty and tax rates in South America (Hylton et al. 2007:102). Transnational corporations would be further favored by new laws that permitted foreign ownership in border regions and created tax-exempt areas for energy-export projects (Mares 2006:20).

In 1996, Sánchez de Lozada implemented the so-called Energy Triangle to kick-start foreign investment in the sector. The triangle was anchored around three crucial points: (1) capitalizing, or partially privatizing, the state oil company, Yacimientos Petrolíferos Fiscales Bolivianos (YPFB), (2) enacting a new hydrocarbons law, and (3) building the country's first major pipeline to export gas to Brazil—a project that would inaugurate Enron's official entrance into Bolivia (Gavaldá 1999:27). All three were premised on the creation of favorable economic conditions for transnational oil corporations, buttressed by substantial support from a cadre of neoliberal international financial institutions.

Capitalization: A Pseudonym for "Privatization"

The linchpin of Sánchez de Lozada's Energy Triangle was the World Bank–financed capitalization law (1994), which authorized private investments in state-owned enterprises, including YPFB (World Bank 1994b). With the introduction of capitalization, the World Bank shifted its focus from macroeconomic stabilization (e.g., containing inflation) to deeper structural reforms (e.g., privatizing state companies and backing laws and regulations favoring transnationals) aimed at wooing private investment (World Bank 2006:1). The bank loaned the Bolivian government $65 million, complemented by another $82 million from the Inter-American Development Bank (World Bank 2006:8). Funding was contingent upon a long list of conditions, including approval of the capitalization law, creation of a new regulatory agency, and presentation to Congress of a new hydrocarbons law (World Bank 2006:8).

Through what seemed a technocratic, reputedly apolitical exercise, capitalization and its accompanying reforms would transfer control over hydrocarbons, along with the lion's share of its economic benefits, from the Bolivian state and citizens to foreign oil corporations. This is not to romanticize accumulation prior to the neoliberal era, because even nationalized enterprises were not democratically controlled by Bolivia's popular classes during the post-1952 period. Yet capitalization, which was a form of partial privatization and takeover of state-owned hydrocarbons assets by transnational capital in the United States and other core economies, epitomized what David Harvey (2003) has called "accumulation by dispossession" (see Spronk and Webber 2007). With the stroke of a pen, each state company became a corporation as shares were sold to interested workers for an amount not greater than their retirement benefits. In addition, the state's stake was transferred to Bolivian citizens of legal age (by December 31, 1995), to be held in trust by newly created pension fund administrators (Administradoras de Fondos de Pensiones, AFPs) (World Bank 2006:2). The move made pension fund contributors dependent on the profitability of oil and gas development, causing them to inadvertently finance activities that were destructive to the country's Indigenous peoples and sensitive ecosystems.

Through capitalization the state oil company was divided into two exploration and production companies, a transport company, a refining company, and several service companies (Dussan 2004:40). In 1997 Amoco (now British Petroleum), Argentina's state oil company Yacimientos Petrolíferos Fiscales (Fiscal Petroleum Fields, YPF [now Repsol]), Perez Companc (acquired by Petrobras), and Pluspetrol (acquired by Repsol) bought 50% of the equity in the two exploration and production companies (Chaco and Andina) for $571 million (Dussan 2004:41). Enron and Shell purchased a 50% share in transport company Transredes for $263.5 million, gaining control over virtually the entire pipeline network for the domestic market. Capitalization differed from privatization in that the money gained from the sale of YPFB did not go to the state but, rather, stayed with the transnationals to finance future investment (Ewing and Goldmark 1994). The World Bank claimed that foreign investment would upgrade defunct state companies and expand output (World Bank 2006:2), ironically the same companies that the World Bank and the International Monetary Fund had eviscerated since the mid-1980s. Transnationals agreed to invest their contributions over an eight-year period (Dussan 2004:41), yet critics claimed they did not comply with their promises. Over a decade later, the administration of Evo Morales would file charges claiming that Enron failed to invest $260 million in the Bolivia-Brazil pipeline as it had agreed to do in a contract with YPFB, and would maintain that the corporation's heir—at the time, Prisma Energy International, subsequently Ashmore Energy International—owed the government $130 million (Embassy La Paz 2006a). A 2004 audit by the Bolivian government found that Enron and Shell had invested only about one-fourth of what they had committed to in their agreement (Fernández Terán 2009).

Besides supporting laws that more visibly wooed foreign oil corporations, the World Bank backed a dizzying array of other reforms to create an optimal "enabling environment" for transnationals: legal reforms related to regulatory and commercial disputes (creation of an arbitration law, administrative procedures law, and secured transactions law); financial reforms including modification of regulations for securities, insurance, and deposit-taking institutions, as well as contractual savings and pension mechanisms; restructuring of the Central Bank; and creation of the Organic Central Bank Law and the Superintendence of Banks and Financial Entities Law (World Bank 1994a, 1994b).

Bolivia was not alone in the capitalization of its state oil company. As a result of various pressures, such as those from multilateral development banks (including the World Bank and the Inter-American Development Bank), by the late 1990s a number of other countries in Latin America had privatized state oil and gas companies to varying degrees, including Argentina, Brazil, Colombia, Ecuador, and Peru (Gavaldá 1999:23). Yet the neoliberal purity and purported success of the Bolivian program in attracting foreign investment made it a "model for privatization worldwide" (International Energy Agency 2003).

A Deceptive Discourse

International financial institutions made a discursive case for capitalization by arguing that Bolivia's state enterprises were not sufficiently productive, were corrupt and bureaucratic. While such claims were not unwarranted, ironically, within the first seven years of capitalization, although hydrocarbons production was 135% greater, revenues accrued by the state grew by a mere 10% (Gordon and Luoma 2008:89). Moreover, corruption under the privatization experiment was rampant, exemplified by the meddling of a company that would come to epitomize corporate corruption the world over—Enron. The Cuiabá pipeline project, the key case for this book, would gain international notoriety as one of Enron's elaborate accounting shell games—games that would ultimately bring Enron down. Enron used a fictional investment company named LJM1 to perform an accounting trick to list projected revenue on the books as current profits—even though the pipeline had not even delivered any gas yet and therefore had generated no revenue (Grimaldi 2002). Before Enron's collapse, rosy earning reports had fueled Enron's mushrooming stock price, and the Cuiabá revenues were worth about 15% of what was listed in Enron's late 1999 reports.

Neoliberal proponents further claimed the state oil company had caused significant environmental impacts and insisted that capitalized companies would do better (Molina 1999b:81)—a claim this book questions. Finally, the World Bank contended that capitalization would alleviate poverty (World Bank 1994b), a point that would later be challenged given that profits from capitalized oil companies went primarily to parent transnationals, state revenues were unevenly distributed geographically, and the projects generated little employment, with few linkages to the rest of the economy (Andersen and Meza 2001). Newly capitalized companies brought in less than half the revenue that the state oil company had (García Linera 2004a:232; see also Gordon and Luoma 2008:89). The World Bank itself found that "despite a broad range of reforms, growth performance and poverty reduction have been disappointing" (World Bank 2000a). By the World Bank's own accounts, extreme poverty increased from 36.5% in 1997—when capitalization occurred—to 41.3% in 2002 (World Bank 2004:2). As the reforms were implemented, foreign investment exploded, but trickle-down benefits were illusory (Kaup 2010:128), and the state budget was left in shambles (Shultz et al. 2005:16–17).

Vested Interest

From behind the deceptive neoliberal discourse emerged a body of evidence that the reforms were not a humanitarian endeavor but rather self-serving policies that would bring substantial economic benefits to the United States, the World Bank, and Sánchez de Lozada himself. Vested interests abounded. US economic gain was a key driver of capitalization. CORE International Inc., a management consulting firm that assessed the funding prospects for capitalization for the US Trade and Development Agency, indicated that funding capitalization would benefit US investors, create demand for American equipment and services, open new markets, and create jobs in the United States:

> CORE International recommends that these projects be financed by TDA [US Trade and Development Agency]. These projects will assist Bolivia in its capitalization process and provide enhanced opportunities for American businesses to invest in and benefit from the restructuring of these government owned businesses into the private sector. . . . The capitalization process will result in transfer of funds to finance the rehabilitation of the power, petroleum, and telecommunications sectors, including purchase of equipment, spare parts and provision of training. No adverse environmental impacts are anticipated. Also, the effect on U.S. jobs will be positive as the U.S. vendors will need to increase their production of the equipment required to rehabilitate the system in Bolivia. . . . The minimum potential for exports to achieve the proposed rehabilitation, modernization, and expansion of the three sectors is estimated at $562.5 million. Assuming that approximately 80% of this amount will be needed for imports by the Bolivians, the total potential for import of foreign-source equipment and services will be $450 million. (CORE International 1994)

The company was also candid about the need for the US government to provide support to US firms in order to give them an advantage over foreign competitors (particularly from Europe and Japan) that were expected to compete in the sale of technology and equipment for the power, petroleum, and telecommunications sectors.

Internal documents from the World Bank suggest that it funded oil, gas, and mining projects over other initiatives because of their high returns: "By sector, Oil, Gas and Mining had by far the highest equity return after specific provisions (26.6%)" (Wysham 2001). Further, they showed that the

World Bank knew its investments contradicted its mandate of sustainable development and poverty alleviation. One document stated that the World Bank's role as a leading source of fossil fuel financing posed a "clear and present danger" to its reputation and the global environment (Wysham 2001). Between 1992 and 2002, the World Bank invested $15.7 billion in oil, gas, coal, and fossil fuel–power projects versus only $1 billion in renewable energy and energy efficiency (IPS 2002). A study ranking oil corporations that benefited from World Bank financing during the same period listed Shell third ($1.9 billion), Enron eleventh ($967 million), and British Petroleum–Amoco twelfth ($939 million) (IPS 2002).

Banking on Goni

Vested interests were not only evident at the World Bank but also apparent with President Gonzalo Sánchez de Lozada—familiarly known as "Goni." As founder and head of the private mining company Mining Company of the South (Compañía Minera del Sur, COMSUR), and Bolivia's wealthiest mine owner in 1993, Sánchez de Lozada had an enormous economic stake in the mining sector (Conaghan et al. 1990; Gordon and Luoma 2008:86). He therefore stood to gain from privatization of the state mining company, Mining Corporation of Bolivia (Corporación Minera de Bolivia, COMIBOL). COMSUR, which, ironically, was a holding company incorporated in Panama (International Finance Corporation 2004:2), was the largest zinc producer in Bolivia and Argentina. As Bolivia's economic planning minister, Sánchez de Lozada oversaw the 1985 closing of COMIBOL, one of the government's most controversial austerity measures (Albro 2005:438). The move would ironically drive many of the approximately 25,000 laid-off miners into cultivating coca in the Chapare region, where Evo Morales would rise to power as a leader of the coca-grower movement. Subsequently, in 1989, the Bolivian government and the World Bank decided to privatize COMIBOL rather than modernize it (World Bank 1997:7). Then, after the World Bank–proclaimed "breakthrough" election of Sánchez de Lozada in 1993, the government swiftly enacted the capitalization law, which, besides capitalizing the state oil company and other enterprises, aimed at capitalizing the state's tin-antimony smelter, Vinto. Vinto was offered together with the option of joint venture or lease contracts for the country's two largest tin mines, Huanuni and Colquiri. However, because of intense domestic resistance, privatization was delayed and did not occur until 1999, under the administration of General Hugo Banzer Suárez (*Economist* 2007). Sánchez de Lozada would quickly become implicated in irregularities surrounding COMSUR's acquisition and the subsequent sale of Vinto. After several years of heated controversy, in 2007 Morales seized and rationalized the smelter, claiming that it had been sold fraudulently to COMSUR (BBC 2007; Business News Americas 2007).

Late in his first term, Sánchez de Lozada's conflict of interest as champion of capitalization and majority owner of COMSUR was thrust into the international spotlight when a tailings dam collapsed at COMSUR's Porco mine—at the time the largest producer of zinc in Bolivia—near the city of Potosí (Garcia-Guinea and Harffy 1998). In August 1996, more than 235,000 tons of toxic tailings, including arsenic, cyanide, lead, and zinc, flowed into a tributary of the Pilcomayo River, affecting 8,000 Weenhayek and Guaraní Indigenous people in Bolivia near the city of Tarija, as well as 15,000 Guaraní living as far as eight hundred kilometers downstream in the Chaco region of Paraguay and Argentina. Experts at the University of Tarija labeled the event the country's worst ecological disaster (Carlos Rocha 1996). Britain's *New Scientist* magazine denounced the rupture as one of the worst environmental disasters in Latin America (Edwards 1996; Farthing 2009). A study from the University of Tarija alleged that arsenic released from the failure caused the death of three minors who drank water and ate fish from the Pilcomayo (Carlos Rocha 1996). Local groups from Tarija organized a protest march "in defense of life and the environment" to pressure COMSUR to shoulder the cost of crop damage. Guaraní Indigenous communities soon encountered dead fish with symptoms of heavy metal poisoning (Garcia-Guinea and Harffy 1998). Many local populations ceased to fish and drink from the Pilcomayo, increasing malnutrition and risk of cholera. The environmental organization League for the Defense of the Environment (Liga de Defensa del Medio Ambiente) blasted Sánchez de Lozada's administration and COMSUR for downplaying the incident and covering up evidence (Carlos Rocha 1996). Local residents had reported small leaks in the dam long before the failure, but COMSUR took no preventive measures.

In one of his final offerings to transnationals, Sánchez de Lozada, once again with World Bank support, ushered in a new mining code in March 1997 that assured the consolidation and expansion of foreign investment in Bolivian mining (World Bank 1997:11). Owing to his diligent implementation of these neoliberal reforms, by 1997 twenty-four private lease or joint venture contracts totaling $140 million had been signed for mining on 1 million hectares of mining concessions on COMIBOL properties.

The World Bank's ties to Sánchez de Lozada were even more apparent in its direct investments in COMSUR. The bank's private arm, the International Finance Corporation, not only was an 11.1% shareholder in the company but also approved loans totaling $36 million, a full 36% of the projects' total cost (International Finance Corporation 2002:1). Among these projects were the Puquio Norte and Don Mario gold mines, both of which generated tremendous conflict with Chiquitano Indigenous communities.

The saga surrounding the Don Mario mine began in March 2002, when Sánchez de Lozada was appointed chairman of the board of the Canadian mining corporation Orvana Minerals Corporation because his company, COMSUR, bought majority control. Tipped off by a press release suggesting that Orvana's subsidiary, Empresa Minera Paititi (EMIPA), would reactivate the Don Mario gold mine in the middle of the Chiquitano forest, in September 2002 I notified Chiquitano organizations and traveled to the mine with a group of leaders and a visiting delegation from the Amazon Alliance, a coalition of Amazon Basin Indigenous groups and a variety of northern and southern nongovernmental organizations (NGOs). At the mine, we witnessed EMIPA building an unauthorized four-kilometer pipeline to tap gas from Enron and Shell's Cuiabá pipeline. Interviews with officials from the mine and oil companies, along with other documentation, would confirm that Enron and Shell knowingly left a valve behind precisely where the mine was located (see figure 2.1) and that a key reason that the

Figure 2.1 Valve that Enron and Shell placed where the Cuiabá pipeline passes the Don Mario gold mine. Author's photo

pipeline was routed through the middle of the forest was to supply Sánchez de Lozada's mine (see chapter 5; Hindery in press). Nowhere was this
disclosed in the pipeline's environmental impact studies. Further, COMSUR
itself arranged financing for gas-fired plants at the mine. Even during times
when no gas was exported to Cuiabá, Brazil—the alleged purpose of the
Cuiabá pipeline—gas was still supplied to the mine. Outraged at these violations and frustrated that they were not consulted or compensated, Chiquitano communities engaged in intense mobilizations directed at EMIPA
and the bank (see chapter 5).

Conniving for Control

Sánchez de Lozada had initially argued that capitalization would create a
win-win situation in which the government would maintain control of its
hydrocarbons resources while increased foreign investment would spur
greater revenues, jobs, and economic growth (Gordon and Luoma 2008:87).
He publicly promised Bolivians that the state would maintain a 51% stake
in capitalized companies, yielding only 49% to foreign corporations (Calle
Quiñonez 2001:48), yet World Bank documents reveal that the program
intended to transfer 50% of YPFB's shares to private investors and reserve
the remaining 50% for the Bolivian people through private pension fund
administrators (AFPs) (US Department of Energy 2002). Ultimately the
state's share would be significantly smaller, with private companies gaining
administrative control (Dussan 2004:37). As the World Bank itself noted,
"An investor agreement assigned full management responsibilities to the
new investors" (2006:10). A letter from the Bolivian government to the World
Bank requesting the capitalization loan echoed that "management control
of the new company will be in the hands of the private investor" (Minister of
Finance of Bolivia 1994). Enrique Menacho Roca, former president of Bolivia's Chamber of Hydrocarbons, was initially convinced of capitalization
but later felt deceived because the government had no real participation
(Gordon and Luoma 2008:89). A report to the World Bank on capitalization candidly clarifies the significance of control and how it was craftily
wrestled from the hands of the government through a management contract, done at the bidding of foreign investors: "Originally, the government
had based its capitalization plan on a 49–51% split between private investors
and the public. Potential foreign investors balked at this arrangement, however, fearing the inability to effectively manage the enterprises under a sce-
nario where the majority control is in the hands of the public. Therefore, the
government changed the law to a 50–50 formula, and the private investor

will be given assurance of control of the capitalized enterprise through a management contract" (CORE International 1994).

The significance of administrative control became even more apparent through cables sent by the US Embassy in La Paz in June 2006, published by the whistleblower website Wikileaks. The cables, which show Transredes's concern about maintaining control after the Morales administration's May 2006 nationalization of the hydrocarbons sector, states: "Transredes shareholders are negotiating directly with the GOB [government of Bolivia] regarding the GOB's plans to acquire ownership control over the company and the terms of its new contract, per the GOB's May 1 nationalization decree. . . . The negotiations are going well, say Transredes executives, and Transredes will continue to negotiate as long as it is able to maintain administrative control over the company's operations" (Embassy La Paz 2006b). The cables vividly underscore the US government's keen interest in ensuring that transnationals maintain control over Bolivia's oil and gas reserves, particularly given the country's leftward turn.

In the cases of Enron and Shell's Bolivia-Brazil and Cuiabá pipelines, private capital overwhelmingly predominated, again wielding control. Although capitalized company Transredes had a share in each project, giving the appearance that the state had control, in reality the state only owned 25% of the former and 20% of the latter (Hindery 2004). And soon after the Cuiabá pipeline was built, Transredes sold its shares, yielding Enron and Shell absolute control. Moreover, foreign corporations not only had management control over Transredes but also held four out of seven seats on the company's board. A contract between Enron and Shell specified that Enron would appoint the board's president and secretary, while Shell held the right to name the board's manager and financial director (OICH and CEADES 2004:86). The financial fallout for the Bolivian government was severe. In the case of the Bolivia-Brazil pipeline, it was estimated that the 17.2% of total revenues that were obtained by the two Bolivian pension funds, which had a 34% share in Transredes (AFPs), would generate only $97 million by 2005, compared with $400 million that foreign companies would earn (Molina 1999b:75; Lohman 1999).

Despite significant protests and criticisms, capitalization was conducted with little transparency, with lack of consultation, and with censorship, which obstructed public scrutiny and accountability (Molina 1999b:75; Vargas Salgueiro 1996). Bolivian citizens and Congress lacked access to contracts classified as confidential (Gordon and Luoma 2008:89). In 1999 pressure from labor unions opposed to capitalization persuaded the government to transfer some of YPFB's assets to employees, whereby the Petroleum

Labor Company (Empresa Laboral Petrolera) gained control of thirty-three service stations, six storage facilities, four bottling plants, and approximately 13% of YPFB's refining capacity (Lynch 2002). In a retrospective assessment of capitalization, the World Bank conceded that despite Sánchez de Lozada's "strong commitment" to the program's "bold initiatives," it had underestimated popular opposition and should have garnered wider support by focusing its "communications campaign on the advantages and the 'why' of capitalization" to quell opposition and lamented not involving the public earlier in the process and trying a softer, "phased approach" (World Bank 2006:17, 18, 32).

Revolving Doors

Over the decade following capitalization, frustrated government officials began speaking out about a bewildering web of conflicting interests, aided by well-oiled, revolving doors between capitalized companies and state institutions. Andrés Soliz Rada, who became minister of hydrocarbons under Morales and was previously a member of the investigatory commission for the Enron case, made a series of damning allegations about such links. According to evidence he amassed, Carlos Kempff Bruno gave up his post at Enron and Shell's capitalized company, Transredes, to assume a position as minister of economic development under the administration of Jorge Fernando "Tuto" Quiroga Ramírez (August 2001 to August 2002) (Soliz Rada 2002). He subsequently returned to work at Transredes. Juan Ascui, who served as an executive at Transredes, worked simultaneously for Bechtel Corporation, which not only pushed privatization of water delivery in the city of Cochabamba—provoking the water war of 2000—but also produced a study for a controversial gas export project (Pacific Liquefied Natural Gas [LNG]) that would lead to the ouster of Sánchez de Lozada during the 2003 gas war. Carlos Alberto Lopez, former vice minister of hydrocarbons under Quiroga, subsequently worked for the capitalized company Chaco (British Gas–Amoco). Herbert Muller, who was Bolivian minister of finance under Quiroga, was an executive at US-based oil company Maxus and later worked at French oil giant Total-Bolivia.

The Price Isn't Right

Through the neoliberal reforms, transnationals were granted the rights to commercialize oil and gas and could pursue higher prices in more profitable markets (Kaup 2010:128). They gained the power to choose sellers and determine volumes. Through Presidential Decree 24806, Sánchez de Lozada gave investors control of the country's hydrocarbons at the point of extraction. The state relinquished its inalienable control of hydrocarbons and yielded its power to determine prices and locations of sale. Under the new neoliberal regime, regardless of public need, transnationals could opt to keep hydrocarbons in the ground until more profitable outlets were found.

Thanks to the reforms, the transnational oil corporations that took part in capitalization could sell petroleum to YPFB at prices greater than available internationally. Between 1997 and 1999, this caused the state to lose an estimated $36 million (Molina 1999b:74). Moreover, a double standard existed regarding regulation of gasoline prices. Although the Superintendence of Hydrocarbons could raise prices immediately when there was a 5% increase in international prices of oil and its derivatives, it could lower prices only when there was a 20% reduction in international prices (Molina 1999b:75). As a result, this policy reduced state revenues, as buyers opted to not purchase more expensive Bolivian oil.

The 1996 Hydrocarbons Law

The hydrocarbons law of 1996 defined the neoliberal framework for the hydrocarbons sector, giving transnationals free entry to build and operate pipelines, as well as nondiscriminatory access to transport (Dussan 2004:39, 48). It deregulated petroleum product prices, freed hydrocarbons trade, and carved out separate roles for the state and private companies. Foreign corporations were authorized to import, export, and market hydrocarbons freely and were permitted to engage in distribution, transportation, industrialization, and refining (Gavaldá 1999:43).

The law, supported by the World Bank, gave an instructive glimpse into US influence on Sánchez de Lozada's administration. It was drafted using a translation of an English version that was written entirely in the United States (Gavaldá 1999:43). The law authorized risk-sharing contracts (joint ventures) between the state and private companies, granted for a maximum of forty years (Dussan 2004:39). Additionally, it created a concession-based system that had no spatial limits to exploration (Gavaldá 1999:43). In 1997, the Bolivian government's national secretary of energy distributed 10.2 million hectares among twenty-one foreign hydrocarbons consortiums.

In order to promote private investment in hydrocarbons exploration and production, the law established an "attractive and competitive tax system," reducing state royalties and taxes from 50% to 18% in all "new" fields (Dussan

2004:37; Kaup 2010:127). This reward was supposed to entice investors to discover reserves in areas where exploration and extraction were more challenging (Kaup 2010:127). It was a radical departure from Bolivia's past— for the previous six decades foreign companies had split benefits 50/50 with the Bolivian government (Shultz et al. 2005:16).

Proponents of capitalization argued that increased foreign investment led to the discovery of massive new reserves, yet most "new" fields had already been discovered and simply had not been certified (García Linera 2004a:227). All probable fields were classified as new, even if they were located in existing areas of extraction, whereas all proven fields were classified as existing and therefore subject to the higher taxation rate of 50% (Molina 1999b:74). However, two months after introduction of the 1996 hydrocarbons law, another law was issued that stipulated only proven fields in production at the time of YPFB's sale would earn the 50% taxation rate (Kaup 2010:127). These distinctions were extremely significant given the vast amount of new reserves declared since capitalization. According to a report from YPFB, as of May 2002, 97% of hydrocarbons reserves in the country were considered new (*Los Tiempos* 2002). Although existing oil reserves totaled only 27.8 million barrels, new reserves amounted to 901.3 million barrels (*Los Tiempos* 2002). Similarly, whereas existing gas reserves (provable and estimated) totaled only 1.5 trillion cubic feet (TCF), new reserves were estimated at 50.7 TCF. The seemingly mundane distinction was also crucial because it reclassified the natural gas megafields of San Alberto and San Antonio from existing to new and thus subject to the 18% rate (Quiroga 2004:84–85). This represented "a giveaway that could cost the nation hundreds of millions, if not billions, of dollars over the next 40 years" (Kohl 2004:904). Within the first two years of capitalization, new fields had been recognized for eighteen out of twenty-two capitalized companies, illustrating how swiftly the country's hydrocarbons were being handed over to foreign corporations (Molina 1999b:74).

The World Bank's self-assessment of capitalization hailed the development of natural gas reserves as possibly the greatest benefit to Bolivia arising from the program. It boastfully cited data that proven reserves had increased from 4 TCF in 1997 to 28 TCF in 2004 and that probable reserves had risen from 2 TCF to 25 TCF during the same period (World Bank 2006:12). Yet recent data suggests that transnational oil corporations and previous administrations inflated estimates and that, as of 2010, Bolivia's proven gas reserves had fallen to 9.9 TCF (Energy Information Administration 2011). YPFB's former president, Carlos Villegas Quiroga, charged that boosters of the controversial Pacific Project circulated erroneous figures.

Critics were outraged that the state conceded gas and oil reserves based on provable reserves only—as opposed to being based on estimated reserves— which in 1999 amounted to more than $60 billion but of which Bolivia was to receive only 10% (Molina 1999b:74; *El Diario* 1999). Furthermore, transnational corporations that gained control of YPFB paid only minimal taxes based on volume exported, not based on brute production or at the wellhead (Molina 1999b:74).

Short of writing Bolivia's laws itself, the World Bank went as far as to provide the government with substantial funding, advice, and technical support to craft regulations promoting "competitive market conditions that would attract new entrants seeking to exploit profitable opportunities" (World Bank 2006:2). The World Bank made its loans conditional on passage of various laws and regulations, including the capitalization law and the hydrocarbons law (World Bank 1994b; Minister of Finance of Bolivia 1994). The 1994 Law of the Sectoral Regulation System (Ley del Sistema de Regulación Sectorial) claimed to create an independent, professional regulatory agency for the market and prohibited the state from engaging in business activities (Dussan 2004:37, 42). Instead, the state was relegated to making policy, enticing foreign investment, and negotiating contracts, along with regulating tariffs and calling out anticompetitive practices (World Bank 1994a).

What emerged were highly centralized, undemocratic regulatory agencies (Crespo 2000), such as the Superintendence of Hydrocarbons. These agencies illustrated how the neoliberal reforms paradoxically centralized resource governance while simultaneously decentralizing administrative governance and political participation through the creation and funding of municipalities and various multicultural initiatives (Perreault 2009:141). Financed by the World Bank and transnational oil corporations, the Superintendence of Hydrocarbons was anything but independent (Gavaldá 1999:43).

The hydrocarbons law assigned various functions to the Superintendence of Hydrocarbons that eroded state control, such as the power to grant concessions for transportation and distribution of gas, determine the volume of gas to be distributed nationally versus exported, establish and monitor transportation tariffs, and impose prices of petroleum derivatives based on international prices (Molina 1999b:76). Consequently, both the hydrocarbons law and the Law of the Sectoral Regulation System substantially shifted control over territory and natural resources from the state to transnational oil corporations.

Enter Enron: The Bolivia-Brazil Pipeline

By the 1990s, development in the eastern lowlands had shifted increasingly toward extracting and exporting natural gas, prompted by increased demand in Brazil, the discovery of vast reserves in southern Bolivia, and construction of the historic Bolivia-Brazil pipeline. In 1999, gas exports soared upon completion of the $2.15 billion megaproject, which was championed by Enron and Shell, with substantial support from an assemblage of neoliberal financial institutions. Enron and Shell took the lead in ownership, each with 30% shares, followed by Bolivian pension funds (25.5%), Brazil's state oil company, Petrobras (9%), British Gas (2%), El Paso (2%), and Total-FinaElf (2%) (British Gas Group 2001). Tenneco Gas and Australia's Broken Hill Proprietary also became involved as minor investors. Financed by loans from Brazil's National Bank for Economic and Social Development ($333M), the World Bank ($310M: a $130M direct loan and a $180M credit guarantee), Petrobras ($280M), the Inter-American Development Bank ($240M), the Export Import Bank of Japan ($104M), the Andean Development Corporation ($80M), and the European Investment Bank ($60M), the 3,056-kilometer-long pipeline was constructed from near the city of Santa Cruz, Bolivia, to the border town of Puerto Suárez, and then on to the distant coastal city of Porto Alegre, located in southern Brazil (Hamerschlag 1999; Pató 2000).

Had it not been for this multilateral financing, the project, and all of its resultant effects on local peoples and the environment, probably would not have come to fruition. Without such support, alternative commercial loans would have resulted in a price for gas that would have severely hindered its ability to penetrate the market (de Franco 2001). Private investors hesitated until multilateral financing was obtained and Petrobras agreed to bear the financial risks (de Franco and Law 1998). And this financing cemented Brazil's own decision to commit to the project (Mares 2003). Both World Bank and Brazilian involvement helped the project beat out Argentine competitors vying to supply gas to Brazil (Mares 2006).

The World Bank, and other international financiers, viewed the pipeline as an integral component in energy integration and economic liberalization of the hydrocarbons sector in the Southern Cone—the southern region of South America, composed of Argentina, Chile, Paraguay, and Uruguay (de Franco 2001; Salles Abreu Passos 1998; Mares 2003; Energy Sector Management Assistance Programme 2003). It was part of broader neoliberal efforts to geographically shift power over Latin America's natural resources and labor supplies from states and communities to international capital. Brazil's desire to boost the Southern Common Market (Mercado Común del Sur, Mercosur) regional trade agreement and its own regional prominence helped propel the project (Mares 2006).

The pipeline represented the third vertex of Sánchez de Lozada's so-called Energy Triangle, which hinged upon establishing a secure market in Brazil, which was achieved through a series of bilateral negotiations between Bolivia and Brazil (Gavaldá 1999:27). It became a hallmark example of predatory extractive development designed to maximize benefit for transnationals while returning little for the Bolivian people.

Geopolitical interests drove Brazil's pursuit of Bolivian gas, as Brazil looked to extend its influence in the region and secure an energy alternative that fit best in its energy matrix, which depended heavily on hydropower, petroleum, and wood/sugarcane derivatives (Mares 2006). The Bolivian government viewed the project favorably because of problems exporting gas to Argentina. Negotiations related to the pipeline began as early as 1988, when the presidents of Bolivia and Brazil signed the Treaty of Energy Integration, which led to Brazil signing a twenty-year contract to purchase gas from Bolivia in 1993 (followed by a series of amendments regarding the volume to be exported, price, and partners) (Pató 2000). To sweeten the deal, Petrobras also won exploration rights in some of Bolivia's largest fields (Mares 2006). At last, YPFB was on the brink of completing a final contract for the pipeline, a project that could have increased its profits by at least $50 million per year for forty years (Kohl 2004:904). Instead, earnings would be redirected to foreign firms that would acquire loans from many of the same multilateral institutions that had previously offered YPFB loans.

This fate was sealed in 1994, when Enron won the bid to invest in, construct, and operate the pipeline. Critics complained that the deal made a mockery of the public bidding process that the World Bank had supposedly required. Appalled that the government proposed to yield as much as 55% of the project to Enron, YPFB leaders engaged in strikes and alleged that the government had personal ties with Enron representatives (Pató 2000). On March 22, 1996, Sánchez de Lozada defended his neoliberal scheme, sending in Bolivian Army to occupy refineries and natural gas facilities to prevent workers from sabotaging them (Mares 2006). To quell opposition, Enron invited Shell to purchase some of the disputed shares, which reduced Enron's stake (Pató 2000). The controversial deal would later serve as fodder for the ouster of Sánchez de Lozada during the 2003 gas war and would become the subject of a revealing lawsuit against Enron under the administration of Evo Morales. Morales would reopen a 2004 case against Enron, claiming it improperly acquired shares in the pipeline through a dubious contract signed by Sánchez de Lozada. His administration would file charges that the US-exiled president and ex-Enron officials falsified contracts that damaged the state and violated the Bolivian Constitution (Flores 2006). A comment in a cable sent by the US Embassy in La Paz in July 2006 candidly suggests that to some extent the contract probably did favor Enron unfairly to the detriment of the Bolivian government: "Some analysts suggest that the subject contract unfairly favored Enron, giving the company more than it merited at the GOB's [government of Bolivia's] expense. Others argue that the charges are a political mechanism through which the GOB seeks to gain majority ownership of Transredes without having to provide compensation. The truth likely lies somewhere in between" (Embassy La Paz 2006a).

Enron's shady entrance into Bolivia was set in motion on July 13, 1994, when then president of YPFB, Mauricio Gonzales, and Enron executive Rebecca Mark signed a memorandum of understanding to form a joint venture that stipulated the development, financing, construction, and operation of the Bolivia-Brazil pipeline (CEDIB 2001). Under the agreement, YPFB was to have a 60% share in the project, leaving Enron with a 40% stake. Yet, reportedly, Sánchez de Lozada instructed then minister of capitalization, Alfonso Revollo, to yield YPFB's share to Enron and Shell's capitalized company, Transredes (Aramayo Montes 2002). Supposedly giving the "appearance" of a public bidding process, one week after the agreement was signed, international consulting company Crown Agents allegedly issued a report recommending Enron be selected (Cortés 2003). A few months later, Sánchez de Lozada signed a contract with Enron on December 9, 1994, at the first Summit of the Americas in Miami (CEDIB 2001). The contract solidified the previous memorandum of understanding, gave Enron exclusive rights to construction of pipelines in Bolivia, and guaranteed staggering annual returns of 18.5% on investments (CEDIB 2001; Baeza 2002). Additionally, it permitted Enron to set up the joint venture as an international offshore company free of Bolivian taxation (Langman 2002). Enron agreed to obtain financing to bring the project to fruition.

The deal was suspect on a number of grounds. Andrés Soliz Rada, a former member of the government's commission investigating the Enron case, stated that while Sánchez de Lozada requested permission from Congress to travel to the summit, he never mentioned signing an agreement with Enron (CEDIB 2001). YPFB's board did not authorize the contract until December 14, 1994, five days after it had been signed. Government sources complained that until 1996 the legal department of YPFB did not even have the original contract, which only surfaced after political pressure was applied. Even though Enron had already landed the deal, YPFB and the Ministry of Capitalization opened bidding in February 1995 (Baeza 2002). Holding the agreement in secrecy for more than a year, only in February 1996 did Sánchez de Lozada officially acknowledge that Enron had been picked from three prospective companies. Armando de la Parra, a former congressman and president of the commission investigating Enron, called the so-called public bid "a sham to mask a secret deal between Sánchez de Lozada and Enron" (qtd. in Langman 2002).

In 2004, Juan Carlos Virreira, then presidential appointee investigating capitalization, presented evidence that Enron obtained its 40% share in the project without paying anything since Petrobras financed construction through a "turnkey" contract—putting financing in place and assuming most of the project's risk (*La Razón* 2006; de Franco and Law 1998). Thus, Enron failed to comply with the 1994 contract that stipulated the company would acquire financing (CEDIB 2001).

From Greenwashing Gas to Environmental Conflict

The World Bank argued that gas from the Bolivia-Brazil pipeline would bring significant environmental benefits on the Brazilian side by reducing deforestation for fuelwood and displacing high-pollution fuel sources in the industrial city of São Paulo, plagued by pollution from fuel oil with high sulfur content (de Franco 2001). Yet the project's environmental impact study was extremely inadequate in its analysis of secondary impacts, for instance, in failing to examine how the pipeline would trigger increased extraction in southern Bolivia and construction of additional pipelines that feed into it (e.g., the Cuiabá, YABOG, and GASYRG pipelines) (Hamerschlag 1999). Nor did it disclose how it would supply Sánchez de Lozada's Don Mario gold mine (financed by the World Bank) and the El Mutún iron ore mine.

The pipeline was built through several sensitive ecosystems, including the Bolivian Kaa-Iya del Gran Chaco National Park (managed by the Guaraní); the Chiquitano forest; the Izozog, Chiquitos, and Utoquis wetlands (Bolivia); the Brazilian Protected Areas of Ibitinga and Corumbatati; the Brazilian National Forest of Ipanema; the Brazilian Pantanal National Park; and the endangered remnants of the Mata Atlântica rainforest (Pató 2000; Hamerschlag 1999; Soltani, Hamerschlag, and Hindery 1997). Environmental organizations found that the pipeline right-of-way—the path that was cleared through the forest to construct the pipeline—and illegal service roads increased access to sensitive areas (Hamerschlag 1999). The independent supplemental environmental assessment for the Cuiabá pipeline shows an aerial photo of a section of forest that was cleared by settlers who gained access through the Bolivia-Brazil pipeline's right-of-way (FAN et al. 1999). Conservation groups joked that the right-of-way had become a road, which I verified by driving along it at high speeds in September 2002. Subsequently, barriers and guards controlled access better, but the right-of-way was not properly reforested.

The Bolivia-Brazil pipeline directly affected Guaraní, Chiquitano, and Ayoreo Indigenous communities living along its path (Soltani, Hamerschlag, and Hindery 1997). The companies did not provide affected communities with adequate information about the project and failed to consult with them about compensation until late in the project cycle, in violation of International Labor Organization Convention 169 (Hamerschlag 1999). The Chiquitanos complained that they were completely excluded from the final compensation program, a fact they would remember and later use to leverage compensation for Enron and Shell's Cuiabá pipeline. Lawyers from the Bolivian legal organization Center for Juridical Studies and Social Investigation (Centro de Estudios Jurídicos e Investigación Social) denounced the companies for not fulfilling their land-titling commitments. The civic committee of the town of El Carmen and the Bolivian organization Biosphere Productivity and Environment (Productividad Biosfera y Medio Ambiente) called attention to worker misconduct, sexual abuse of women, and reduced access to food and medicine.

Neoliberalism and Its Snowballing Synergies

The Bolivia-Brazil project is a classic example of networks of oil and gas pipelines that increasingly connect Latin American countries with abundant supply (e.g., Argentina, Bolivia, Colombia, Ecuador, Venezuela) to those with deficits (e.g., Brazil, Chile, Uruguay). Such "arteries for global trade" (Soltani and Osborne 1997) are now linked to key ports that bleed hydrocarbons through the region's "open veins" (Galeano 1971). Carving their way through Indigenous territories and threatened ecoregions, new geographies of extraction have unfolded as neoliberalism has taken hold in the region (Hindery in press). Although distinctive histories have shaped diverse outcomes within and across Latin America (Perreault and Martin 2005), the Bolivian experience has had parallels elsewhere. In adjacent Peru, neoliberal development ushered in massive investment in mining under President Alberto Fujimori, with little state oversight (Bury 2005). Subsequently, the administration of Alan García Pérez advanced an extractive model of economic development by formalizing private property rights and luring foreign capital into mining and hydrocarbons (Bebbington 2009; see also Bury and Norris in press). In Peru, Honduras, and Guatemala, as economic liberalization fueled a mining boom, concern over rising social and environmental impacts fed growing social movements (Slack 2009:117). In Ecuador, the neoliberal reforms pressured the debt-burdened government to authorize increased oil development in the Amazon, causing significant harm to Indigenous peoples and the environment and generating intense social mobilization (Gerlach 2003; Sawyer 2004; Watts 2005; Weiss 1997).

On a global scale, environmental conflicts proliferated with the spread of neoliberalism, as dominant models of economic development introduced environmentally destructive practices into sensitive landscapes, where communities often rose in defense of the places that were the source of their cultural identity and livelihood (Escobar 2006). Multilateral development agencies and export credit agencies emerged as key "brokers" in hydrocarbon-producing states, simultaneously engaging in the contradictory role of enforcing transparency among petroleum-dependent governments and oil corporations (Watts 2005). The significance of their financing was crucial to fossil fuel projects that otherwise would not have come to fruition. For instance, as with the Bolivia-Brazil and Cuiabá pipelines, the Chad-Cameroon oil pipeline and the West Africa gas pipeline would not have been built had it not been for support from international financial institutions—including the World Bank, the US government's Overseas Private Investment Corporation (OPIC), the European Investment Bank, and the Inter-American Development Bank (Lowman 2011:25). Such patterns exemplify how, over the past three decades, international financial institutions have increasingly promoted and financed the liberalization of extractive industries around the world (Sawyer and Terence Gomez 2012:1).

Within Latin America, although neoliberalism has been a powerful force over the last three decades, it must be understood as embedded within other historical processes (e.g., colonialism and liberalism). As described in chapter 1, in the Chiquitano region, the Cuiabá conflict, although centered around the Cuiabá pipeline (a neoliberal infrastructure project), is but the latest series of struggles over extractive forms of development in which the Chiquitanos and Ayoreos have engaged. Conflicts around natural gas in other parts of the country are also situated with a long history of territorial loss for Indigenous peoples (Bebbington et al. in press).

Throughout the world, neoliberalism has been implemented in a geographically differentiated manner, characterized by distinctive, local forms and varying historical dynamics (Jessop 2002; Larner 2003; Peck and Tickell 2002; Peck 2004; Brenner et al. 2010; Kim and Wainwright 2010). Such heterogeneity is perhaps most evident in Latin America, where neoliberalism has unfolded in some of the most hybrid configurations, differing ideationally, ideologically, and institutionally (see Peck 2010). As described previously, in Bolivia this was exemplified by Sánchez de Lozada's Energy Triangle, a scheme designed to boost foreign investment through partial privatization of the state oil company, a new hydrocarbons law, and the Bolivia-Brazil pipeline. Many Latin American governments, including the administration of Bolivian president Sánchez de Lozada, implemented "soft" policies that supported environmental protection and management, such as community-based resource management and expansion of national protected areas (Zimmerer 2009:157). Paradoxically, in Bolivia, some practitioners of this form of neoliberalism were in fact opposed to "harder" policies, such as privatization, trade liberalization, and cuts in social services. Such soft initiatives arose in part due to claims made by Indigenous peoples, reflecting a more general pattern of how populist movements tweaked neoliberal policies into various hybrid forms (Peck 2004). Although in some cases such enterprises legitimated and stabilized neoliberal policies, in others, including the Cuiabá pipeline case, they undermined them. As the subsequent chapters demonstrate, in the Cuiabá case, top-down neoliberal governance of the environment prevailed, despite Indigenous mobilization and resistance from a few sympathetic actors within Bolivian state institutions. Enron, Shell, and international conservation organizations implemented a $20 million conservation program, touting it as a success story in community-based conservation. Yet, ironically, since the companies and conservationists governed the program, the program symbolized a move "back to the barriers" (Hutton et al. 2005), instead epitomizing fortress-style conservation (chapters 3 and 4). The Chiquitanos and Ayoreos would forcefully rebel against the initiative for excluding them from the management board.

Indigenous peoples have responded to neoliberalism in complex and varied ways (Lucero 2008:122), building upon a protracted history of resistance and accommodation (Stern 1982, 1987; see Postero 2007; Sawyer 2004). In Bolivia, as implementation of the neoliberal reforms progressed, increasing dispossession by commercial agriculture, logging, hydrocarbon production, and mining encouraged Indigenous groups in the country's eastern lowlands to organize and demand greater political participation and land rights (see Healey 2009:90; see also Hylton et al. 2007:96; Postero 2007; Redo, Millington, and Hindery 2011; Valdivia 2010:72). Whereas highland Indigenous peoples had been organized more around class, lowland Indigenous peoples had more freedom to construct distinct political identities and organizations using ethnic (i.e., Indigenous) and environmental discourses because of weak state presence in what Richard Chase Smith (1985) calls the "myth of vast Amazonian emptiness," and because of the environmental significance of the Amazon in transnational environmental networks (Lucero 2008:109). In debates about possible terms for self-identification, leaders from the chief lowland Indigenous organization Federation of Indigenous Peoples of Bolivia (Confederación de Pueblos Indígenas de Bolivia, CIDOB), expressed preference for using the term *Indigenous* because it resonated with international supporters (Healey 2009:94). Support from international development organizations and NGOs was crucial to the formation of CIDOB and other lowland Indigenous organizations (Lucero 2008:91).

Two seminal marches in 1990 and 1996 led to recognition of Indigenous peoples in the lowlands, ratification of International Labor Organization Convention 169—also known as the Indigenous and Tribal Peoples Convention, supporting territorial and communal rights to natural resources—and approval of a new agrarian law recognizing collective titles for thirty-three native communal lands (tierras comunitarias de origen, TCOs) (Healey 2009:90–91). Mobilization also led to adoption of the 1994 Law of Popular Participation, which devolved funds and responsibilities to municipalities and required local participatory budgeting and oversight (Kohl 2003:153; Centellas 2000). Besides decentralizing resources and political power, it recognized some 15,000 grassroots territorial organizations, including traditional Indigenous organizations, urban neighborhood organizations, and modern peasant unions (Kohl 2003:156). In the Chiquitano region, the law devolved five small-scale cattle projects from a regional development agency (Regional Development Corporation of Santa Cruz [Corporación Regional de Desarrollo de Santa Cruz]) to the Chiquitanos, empowering them to manage the enterprises autonomously (OICH and CEADES 2004:117).

The Law of Popular Participation was one of several softer "neoliberal multicultural" reforms (Hale 2002:487) that reflected compromises neoliberal proponents made because of intense resistance from Indigenous and other popular movements. Its passage illustrated how, although neoliberalism often threatened Indigenous peoples' livelihoods and was frequently challenged, it also opened pathways to pressure state elites into redrafting constitutions and laws to reflect multicultural demands, what José Antonio Lucero (2008:122) calls a "surprising compatibility of neoliberalism and multiculturalism." In Bolivia, neoliberal multiculturalism was reflected by University of Chicago–schooled Sánchez de Lozada's choice of Victor Hugo Cárdenas, the Aymara leader of the Revolutionary Liberation Movement Tupaq Katari (Movimiento Revolucionario Túpac Katari de Liberación) party, to run as vice president (Lucero 2008:133). This alliance projected a multicultural agenda, giving neoliberalism "a human, even Aymara face" (Hylton et al. 2007:99). As a result of such pressure, in 1994 the constitution was amended to redefine the state as multicultural and pluriethnic (Kohl and Farthing 2006:90).

Paradoxically, in the 1990s, when highland labor-based groups were under attack by the neoliberal project, the rise of Indigenous mobilization in the lowlands was made possible, in part, because of the softer multicultural reforms Sánchez de Lozada implemented in tandem with harder structural reforms (Lucero 2008:125). It is perhaps not surprising from a "Gramscian view that hegemonic systems, to remedy their own deficiencies and placate groups they disadvantage, incorporate or promote processes whose logic is partially antithetical to their own basic tenets" (Buechler 2009:84). Besides the popular participation law, other significant multicultural reforms included the 1996 agrarian reform law recognizing communal land titling (TCOs) for Indigenous peoples, administrative decentralization, and bilingual, intercultural education.

This softer underbelly of neoliberalism lent a "participatory democratic profile to a government fundamentally set on liquidating remaining state enterprises and opening up the country to foreign capital" (Hylton et al. 2007:98). Though Indigenous peoples made some gains, the reforms marginalized radical voices in the 1990s (Lucero 2008:141) and did not substantively transform "political, institutional, or territorial configurations linked to the state's colonial legacies," possibly even worsening "the persistence of racism and coloniality in everyday discourse and state structure" (Gustafson 2009:993–994). Paradoxically, the seemingly progressive multicultural reforms, especially popular participation, often excluded Indigenous groups and ensured continued dominance of political elites, but they also paved the way for "postmulticultural" resistance to neoliberalism, a new potent protagonism exemplified by the rise of Morales's Movement Toward Socialism (Movimiento al Socialismo, MAS) political party and the 2003 gas war (Postero 2007:218–219). Decentralization generated openings in municipal-level political spaces that in some cases cultivated Indigenous leaders who helped build MAS (Healey 2009:84). It had the unintended consequence of

fueling the rise of the coca-growers movement and their leader, Evo Morales, an ironic turn of events given that neoliberalism had driven laid-off
miners into coca growing in the first place (Lucero 2008:141, 183). Taken
together, neoliberal multiculturalism sowed the seeds of a radical anti-
neoliberal rebellion that would occur during the 2000–2005 period. Grassroots territorial organizations, the state-based communitarian organizations
that emerged out of the popular participation law, would help organize
protests during the gas war and would later facilitate public teach-ins about
the 2004 referendum over gas nationalization (Postero 2007:218–219).

Clashes between Indigenous peoples and transnational oil giants that
arose under neoliberalism illustrated tensions between the softer multicultural reforms—especially land titling and decentralization—and harder
policies, such as the capitalization law, the hydrocarbons law, and the heart
law (described subsequently), which brought the transnationals in the first
place. The Bolivia-Brazil pipeline was the first among a number of gas
pipelines built to supply gas to Brazil. Its existence snowballed into a series
of synergistic side effects and triggered rising resistance. The pipeline enabled the construction of a number of other pipelines in the lowlands that
affected Indigenous peoples and the sensitive ecosystems in which they
live. These included the Yacimientos-Bolivian Gulf (YABOG), Yacuiba–
Río Grande (Gasoducto Yacuiba–Río Grande, GASYRG), and Cuiabá
pipelines—the latter of which is the primary case for this book. All were
made possible by financing from multilateral development agencies and
export credit agencies. For instance, the Bolivia-Brazil project would not
have advanced had the World Bank and other multilaterals not subsidized
it through preferential financing and contract guarantees (Mares 2006).
Taking the long view, they funded the pipeline because they considered it
a crucial lever to pressure Bolivia and Brazil to implement the neoliberal
reforms and accelerate hydrocarbons development in the Southern Cone.
Similarly, a $200 million loan from the US government's OPIC was critical
in pushing the Cuiabá project forward.

Neoliberalization of the hydrocarbons sector in Bolivia aided private
(mostly foreign) capital and international financial institutions while marginalizing Indigenous peoples (Perreault 2012:100). The neoliberal reforms,
especially capitalization and the 1996 hydrocarbons law, triggered a substantial increase in investment from transnational oil corporations and international financial institutions (Viceministerio de Energía e Hidrocarburos
2002). This, in turn, sparked an unprecedented level of exploration, production, and pipeline building (Dussan 2004:42), affecting Indigenous peoples
and fragile ecosystems (Hindery 2004). Three years into capitalization, the

World Bank itself acknowledged these effects: "With the increase in investment in hydrocarbons after capitalization and, consequently, in social and environmental impacts, the Vice-Ministry of Energy and Hydrocarbons identified the need to reinforce its response in strengthening the capacity of the sector to monitor social and environmental impacts" (World Bank 2000b).

Between 1997 and 2001, during the height of the neoliberal era, investment in hydrocarbons increased from $296 million to $401 million (Economist Intelligence Unit 2002). In 1995, two years before YPFB was capitalized, gas export volumes were 70 billion cubic feet (BCF) (Energy Information Administration 2011). By 2005, at the close of the neoliberal era, exports had expanded fivefold to 362 BCF. Gas production rose by a factor of four, from 113 BCF in 1995 to 436 BCF in 2005. These increases in investment and production quickly translated into on-the-ground impacts for communities and environments located where oil and gas development was occurring.

The economic reforms also included specific incentives that promoted hydrocarbons development. In the case of the 1996 hydrocarbons law, once a new field was declared commercially viable, the contractor was obligated to drill at least one producing well within the first five years (Dussan 2004:39). Oil corporations could also take substantial tax deductions for spending on exploration, development, extraction, and environmental protection (Kaup 2010:128).

The Bolivian experience of mushrooming resource extraction amidst a neoliberal boom had unique features but paralleled broader processes occurring at a global scale. At the same time, intensified assaults against Indigenous peoples and their environments for minerals and hydrocarbons occurred in West Papua, Indonesia, Papua New Guinea, Colombia, Peru, Ecuador, Brazil, Nigeria, and elsewhere (Gedicks 2001). These conflicts arose as neoliberal reforms deepened, as there was what mining expert Roger Moody calls a "radical shift" in financing sources (Bosshard and Moody 1997). Projects that had previously been financed by shareholders and state enterprises were increasingly backed by multilateral development agencies and regional banks. Export credit agencies (ECAs) would play an increasing role, as with the Cuiabá project in Bolivia (financed by the US government's OPIC) and the Camisea Gas Project in adjacent Peru (considered for financing by the US government's Export-Import Bank). In both of these cases, however, the ECAs rejected financing after significant pressure from Indigenous peoples and environmental organizations.

Banking on Dependency

World Bank funding of the Ministry of Sustainable Development, the Superintendence of Hydrocarbons, and the environmental office of the hydrocarbons ministry not only made these agencies dependent on World Bank loans but also created conflicts of interest since these were the bodies charged with regulating the social and environmental impacts caused by the World Bank's reforms (e.g., capitalization) and projects (e.g., the Bolivia-Brazil pipeline and the Don Mario gold mine) (Hindery 2004). While the World Bank loaned the Bolivian government hundreds of millions of dollars for the Bolivia-Brazil pipeline and its neoliberal reforms, it doled out a measly $5.5 million to address the adverse social and environmental effects caused by the hydrocarbons boom the reforms had brought. Yet, ironically, this so-called Learning and Innovation Loan (LIL) project would prove an ineffective bandage for a burgeoning wound. It largely greenwashed the bank's failure to prevent and address adverse impacts it predicted could stem from the reforms: "The capitalization of the hydrocarbons, power, and mining sector companies as well as the adoption of new sectoral laws designed to promote investment and competition in these sectors could have detrimental environmental effects if expansion activities are not adequately regulated and monitored" (World Bank 1994b).

The LIL project was problematic in that the World Bank funded an environmental office housed within the hydrocarbons ministry—the Environmental Unit (Unidad del Medio Ambiente, UMA)[1]—an inherent conflict of interest highlighted by officials I interviewed at the Ministry of Sustainable Development. One individual accused the hydrocarbons ministry of neglecting environmental issues under the pretext that national interest excused adverse impacts. Compounding this conflict, financing for the office came from both the World Bank and hydrocarbons revenues, making it difficult for UMA to objectively regulate adverse impacts of hydrocarbons projects triggered by the World Bank's reforms. Moreover, the office was heavily influenced by transnationals (FOBOMADE 2000). The environmental NGO Foro Boliviano sobre Medio Ambiente y Desarrollo (FOBOMADE) decried revolving doors between capitalized oil companies and the ministry, implicating the former head of the environmental office as well as the former vice minister, who worked for Chaco (British Gas–Amoco). One of the specialists the office proposed to hire was the environmental head of Enron and Shell's capitalized company Transredes. FOBOMADE insisted that such ties reduced the agency's will to enforce existing laws.

Indigenous groups and NGOs denounced the World Bank for designing an ineffective and exclusionary project, for spending inordinate amounts of money on consultants, and for co-opting civil society groups. Ironically, the World Bank repeatedly refused their demand to fund affected communities to monitor and regulate hydrocarbons projects, flagrantly contradicting the rhetorical aims of the World Bank's decentralization reforms. FOBOMADE lambasted the World Bank for spending $1 million out of $5.5 million to hire specialists rather than funding local communities. Existing examples of monitoring by Chiquitano, Ayoreo, and Guaraní communities affected by the Bolivia-Brazil and Cuiabá pipelines were disregarded. World Bank staff expressed appreciation for this plea but admitted that existing agreements and loan conditions obligated them to channel funds to the environmental office of the hydrocarbons ministry. In fact, funding of the office had been predetermined four years earlier in the World Bank's project document for the capitalization program (World Bank 1994a:2). This meant that consultations gave civil society groups the illusion that democratic input could modify the project, when in fact the outcome was predetermined.

Project documents consistently reflected the World Bank's reluctance to grant local communities decision-making power in monitoring hydrocarbons projects. Rather, words such as *participation* and *consultation* served as a veneer, obscuring the World Bank's primary aim to concentrate funding and decision-making power in the office. This was apparent in one of the project's specific objectives, which were modified slightly based on feedback from civil society groups: "Strengthen the capacity of institutions and communities involved or affected by activities in the hydrocarbons sector to participate in the regulation and mitigation of social and environmental impacts" (World Bank 2000b).

Indigenous rights organization CEADES condemned the World Bank and foreign oil corporations for manipulating the lowland Indigenous federation CIDOB to legitimate an undemocratic consultation mechanism that excluded affected communities and thwarted their ability to monitor the companies. FOBOMADE staff were concerned that some of the organizations involved in the project were functionaries of the World Bank. They accused the environmental organization League for the Defense of the Environment (Liga de Defensa del Medio Ambiente) of having a significant conflict of interest, since it both worked closely on the project and accepted a contract with Enron and Shell's capitalized company Transredes to monitor mitigation of the notorious Río Desaguadero oil spill, which I describe later.

Despite the LIL project's initiatives, pernicious effects of hydrocarbons activities on communities and ecosystems persisted, attesting to the project's shortcomings. In the Cuiabá case, the Bolivian government approved the project's environmental license with a controversial route bisecting the Chiquitano forest based on a positive recommendation from the LIL-funded environmental office of the hydrocarbons ministry (*La Prensa* 2002).

Ridiculing Regulation

Rhetorically, international financial institutions and transnational oil corporations made the case that the neoliberal reforms and the foreign investment they brought would improve the state's ability to regulate the environment. Yet, they championed the very laws—the capitalization law, hydrocarbons law, and heart law—that would overwhelm agencies' regulatory capacities due to the resulting boom in hydrocarbons activities, a point acknowledged by the World Bank itself (World Bank 2000b). Moreover, as newly capitalized companies began to operate in Bolivia, they used their tremendous clout to pressure regulatory bodies to not enforce existing laws. Bolivian agencies imposed minimal sanctions and did not suspend pipeline construction or operation, even though such actions were supported by existing laws.

As detailed subsequently, in the case of the Cuiabá pipeline, representatives from the Ministry of Sustainable Development acknowledged that Enron and Shell placed immense pressure on the Bolivian government to issue the environmental license rapidly and to approve a controversial route cutting through the heart of the Chiquitano forest. In July 1999, speaking before the conservative Santa Cruz civic committee (Comité Cívico Pro-Santa Cruz), Enron executive Abraham Moreno proudly exclaimed that his "company had achieved approval of the 'Heart Law'" (Ley Corazon, approved March 23, 1999), which made it legal for foreign corporations to own property in border regions—previously prohibited by the constitution (Molina 1999a:199). Consistent with neoliberal plans to integrate Latin America economically, the law intended to make Bolivia the "heart" of energy and telecommunications infrastructure in South America. It designated eleven projects, including Enron and Shell's Cuiabá pipeline, to attract foreign investment to accelerate the export of gas and electricity to neighboring countries. Suspiciously, just hours before the law was approved, President Banzer's administration accepted a $10 million donation to the country's rural electrification program, Proner, from Enron and Shell's capitalized company Transredes, allegedly as compensation for costs the state company had incurred during the privatization process (CEDIB 2001; Baeza 2002). According to analysts from Bolivian think-tank Bolivian Documentation and Information Center (Centro de Documentación e Información Bolivia, CEDIB), through this contribution the companies quelled opposition from local populations living in the Chiquitano who had demanded the Cuiabá pipeline bring electricity to the region.

Enron lobbied the US government for the Cuiabá project as well, desperate to ensure that the US government's OPIC granted it a $200 million loan. In the words of *Washington Post* writer James Grimaldi (2002), the story of the Cuiabá project offered "a case study of symbiotic relationship. While Enron was seeking billions in OPIC loans and insurance, the company lobbied Congress to save OPIC from extinction." A former OPIC employee stated that Enron lobbyist John Hardy, Jr., visited OPIC so often that coworkers joked he had moved into the office of Harvey Himberg, OPIC's environmental director. Enron became one of OPIC's top clients. Between 1992 and 2001 OPIC was the leader in public financing for Enron, approving approximately $2.6 billion in finance and risk insurance for fourteen fossil-fuel projects (Vallette and Wysham 2002:4, 18). A press release OPIC issued on the day it approved Enron's loan praised the project's unprecedented environmental requirements and boasted it was the first project under Bolivia's heart law—a law Enron had lobbied hard for (OPIC 1999c).

Within the first three years of capitalization, Enron and Shell were responsible for seven oil and gas spills (OICH and CEADES 2004:87) and caused significant impacts to Indigenous peoples and ecosystems through construction of the Bolivia-Brazil and Cuiabá gas pipelines. The most serious spill occurred in January 2000 when Transredes's OSSA II oil pipeline, which runs from Arica, Chile to Santa Cruz, Bolivia, ruptured in the Andean highlands near the town of Sica Sica, leaking 29,000 barrels of crude oil into Río Desaguadero, Lake Uru Uru, and Lake Poopó (*La Razón* 2000d). The spill, which stretched for at least 250 kilometers (Transredes 2000), was the worst in Bolivia's history, yet it barely made a blip in the international press. Domestically, however, it served as a wake-up call, alerting Bolivians to the perils of privatization. The livelihoods of Quechua, Aymara, and Uru farmers and fishers were devastated as the oil contaminated more than a million acres of crops, pasture, and native prairies on which their sheep and llamas depended—in addition to polluting water sources containing fish and birds they caught (Getter et al. 2000; Haglund 2008:51).

While Transredes flatly rejected claims that there were any adverse health effects, community members complained of immediate illnesses triggered by oil exposure. A study carried out by Bolivian biochemistry professor Roger Carvajal found that the spill could cause leukemia, tumors, and immune system deficiencies in affected communities and livestock (2001:38–39). Even an audit paid for by the company itself estimated that about 40% of animals diagnosed had fallen ill or died because they consumed oil toxins—refuting the company's repeated statements that there were no such links (ENSR International Corp. 2001:11).

Affected communities and their advocates accused Transredes of negligence, because it had disregarded three separate warnings from Bolivian officials and the company's own technicians to repair the pipeline prior to the spill (Haglund 2008:52). Officials from the Ministry of Sustainable Development called Transredes negligent for allowing the oil to flow out of the pipeline for more than twenty-three hours before closing shutoff valves (Langman 2002). In flagrant disregard for an order issued by the Ministry of Sustainable Development, Transredes did not provide clean water, medicine, and uncontaminated pasture to affected communities (*La Razón* 2000f). Outraged at the company's abysmal response, the communities and supporting organizations engaged in legal action, protests, marches, lobbying, and press outreach, which ultimately pressured the company to pay a paltry $1.2 million as compensation to 127 communities (Haglund 2008:54). The amount equated to what Transredes paid parent companies Enron and Shell for "professional services" and did not include long-term effects.

Two communities, Chuquiña and Japo, opted for legal action and filed a $14 million civil suit against Transredes with the aid of the La Paz–based Center for Public Interest Law. After a two-year struggle, they ultimately settled for $450,000 (Chuquiña) and $476,000 (Japo), an amount they considered grossly inadequate but that was, tragically, far greater than what was awarded to other communities (Haglund 2008:66).

The company deployed an elaborate damage control scheme, carrying out an aggressive public relations and legal campaign, manipulating data to minimize evidence of damage, pressuring communities one by one to sign minimal compensation agreements—a tactic previously employed in the Cuiabá pipeline case (the principal case examined in this book)—and using the image of the aid organization Cooperative for Assistance and Relief Everywhere (CARE) to put a compassionate spin on a shoddy compensation program (Haglund 2008:53). The Bolivian NGO FOBOMADE criticized a destructive web of nepotism that arose among the state,

Transredes, and the various NGOs and consultants the company con-tracted (FOBOMADE 2001b). FOBOMADE's former president, Hans Moëller, claimed he received threatening phone calls from Transredes and was followed (Haglund 2008:68). He said the company scared off or paid off those responsible for defending affected populations.

Regulatory authorities favored modest administrative actions over crimi-nal proceedings against the company because of pressure from the com-pany and the US government. Transredes's clout was well known. One well-respected head of a national newspaper told me his publication was the only one that had the integrity to refuse to attend a black-tie event put on by Transredes. The vice minister of sustainable development said one of the reasons she did not press criminal charges against Transredes was that the legal system was tilted in the company's favor (*La Prensa* 2000). She further went on record stating that Transredes repeatedly pressured her through her relatives and acquaintances to treat the company favorably (Sánchez-Moreno and Higgins 2004:1669). Both the vice minister and an-other official claimed that visits from the US Embassy increased this pres-sure. According to a legal adviser to the ministry, representatives from the embassies of the United States, United Kingdom, and possibly the Nether-lands urged the vice minister to consider the importance of Transredes's investment in her decisions regarding the spill. Analysts from CEDIB al-leged that a single visit from US ambassador Donna Hrinak to then minis-ter of sustainable development José Luis Carvajal convinced him to not enforce a $1.9 million fine that Transredes refused to pay (CEDIB 2001; Baeza 2002; Langman 2002). Carvajal said the government had "its hands tied" with regards to imposing penal sanctions on Transredes (*El Deber* 2000). The company declared it was convinced it would not be sanctioned for the successive oil spills since it was "a Bolivian company" with national capital. It boldly stated that the government would not dare to apply a severe punishment.

Rising Resistance to Structural Chains

Bolivia's neoliberal reforms created an unlevel playing field, pitting trans-national oil giants against Indigenous peoples living in the path of develop-ment and funding state institutions that often inhibited mobilization. For instance, in July 2000, a local reporter and I observed an official from the Ministry of Peasant, Indigenous and First Peoples Affairs—partly funded by the World Bank—offer money to Indigenous peoples and peasant peoples to dissuade them from participating in a march. The representative was operating in tandem with another official from the National Institute of Agrarian Reform, also backed by the World Bank. More broadly, structural conditions such as laws, regulations, contracts, and institutions favoring transnationals dampened prospects for opposition to hydrocarbons projects like the Bolivia-Brazil and Cuiabá pipelines. The 1993 gas purchase contract signed between Bolivia and Brazil (Pató 2000), followed by the 1994 contract Sánchez de Lozada signed with Enron, created momentum for the project that was difficult to stop four years later when so-called consultations with affected populations began. Similarly, the 1999 heart law solidified Enron and Shell's Cuiabá pipeline. Both projects were economically viable only because of multilateral financing—for example, from the World Bank and OPIC—and otherwise would not have been supported by private commercial banks.

Struggles by Guaraní, Chiquitano, and Ayoreo Indigenous peoples over the Bolivia-Brazil and Cuiabá pipelines in the late 1990s would be followed by violent clashes over predatory foreign investment projects during the 2000–2005 anti-neoliberal rebellion. Such projects aimed to transfer the economic benefits derived from natural resources to transnational corporations—a form of what Harvey (2003) calls "accumulation by dispossession" (see Spronk and Webber 2007:32). In response, mobilization arose to reclaim the commons. A burgeoning wave of Indigenous and popular resistance to neoliberalism would take the form of place-based struggles over natural resources that either provided the basis for livelihood (e.g., water and land) or could generate revenues for social spending (e.g., oil, gas, and minerals). These movements would demand radical change to the existing political and economic order, much of which was centered on a call to return control over natural resources from foreign corporations to the state and marginalized communities (Webber 2011:99; Hylton et al. 2007:144; Gordon and Luoma 2008:99). The rebellion marked the end of "neoliberal multiculturalism," ushering in a new era of insurgent "post-multicultural citizenship" in which Indigenous peoples—along with workers, peasants, and marginalized urban dwellers—equipped with new rights that had, ironically, been provided during the neoliberal period, challenged neoliberalism itself (Postero 2007).

The 2000–2005 cycle of insurgency exploded in February 2000 when residents of Cochabamba battled Aguas del Tunari, a subsidiary of the US-based Bechtel Corporation, Italy's Edison, and Spain's Abengoa Corporation, which took private control over water delivery. Mirroring a familiar story in the hydrocarbons sector, World Bank and International Monetary

Fund reforms had eased Bechtel's entrance into Bolivia. In July 1997, World Bank officials had forced privatization of the city's water system when they told President Sánchez de Lozada that it was a precondition for receiving $600 million in debt relief (*El Diario* 1997; Shultz and Kruse 2000; Shultz 2003). The World Bank included specific loan conditions requiring privatization of the water companies in La Paz and Cochabamba (World Bank 1998). After widespread mobilization and violent repression, the company's contract was canceled, and the state utility was restored. In the end, neoliberal efforts for the most part did not materialize because water was available in nature in a variety of forms and because "highly simple, localized, and autonomous" systems, such as hand-dug wells, were readily implemented (Perreault 2009:151). Furthermore, popular movements in Cochabamba (2000) and in El Alto and La Paz (2005) defied privatization and commodification, using arguments that water was a social good and human right. Peasant (*campesino*) irrigators challenged standardization inherent in neoliberalism by advocating for customary uses "which are inherently place- and group-specific, idiosyncratic, and variable in time and space" (Perreault 2009:152).

Resistance to privatization of water delivery was followed by more generalized protests over the neoliberal reforms, including those objecting to the eradication of coca (Lucero 2008:171). In February 2003, an International Monetary Fund–backed tax increase and austerity measures fueled riots that left approximately thirty people dead (Mekay 2003; Kohl and Farthing 2009). The violent event hurt Sánchez de Lozada's legitimacy and contributed to his ouster in October of the same year (Kohl and Bresnahan 2010a:8).

Over the next several months, a series of uprisings occurred across the country from an array of groups with wide-ranging demands, including rejection of the Free Trade Agreement of the Americas, abrogation of a law criminalizing blockades, public university autonomy, and respect for communal justice (Hylton et al. 2007:110–111). Violent government repression solidified and emboldened growing mobilizations (Gordon and Luoma 2008:91). Ultimately, splintered movements would unite and oust President Sánchez de Lozada in October 2003 over a controversial plan to ship liquefied natural gas to California. By early 2003, gas had become a locus of intense struggle at the national level for Indigenous and popular movements seeking an alternative to the neoliberal state and accumulation by dispossession (Harvey 2003; Spronk and Webber 2007; see also Kaup 2010:128). Ironically, the budget shortfall resulting from capitalization of the state oil company and other neoliberal reforms (Kohl 2003:346; Shultz et al. 2005:16–17) had fueled widespread unrest calling for rejection of the neoliberal model and nationalization of hydrocarbons. Natural gas became what Jan Selby (2005) calls a "structurally significant" resource in Bolivia since it is both a crucial input in industrial capitalist economies and a principle source of revenue for the state and its populace (see Perreault 2012:75).

During the months leading up to the conflict, Sánchez de Lozada was implicated in conspiring with the Pacific LNG consortium[2] to export gas to California through historic rival Chile rather than Peru. Deep-rooted tensions had flared up as Bolivians viewed the project as a means by which to regain access to the Pacific, which had been lost in 1879 when Chile annexed Bolivia's coastal territory during the War of the Pacific. Furthermore, the project would have generated significant profits for Pacific LNG but only a relatively small proportion of revenues for the Bolivian government. Facing pressure from the US ambassador to Bolivia, Sánchez de Lozada agreed to accept a mere half of what Brazil was paying for Bolivian gas (Orgáz García 2002; see Gordon and Luoma 2008:91). Under the arrangement, the Bolivian government would have received a meager $190 million annually while the consortium would have profited nearly $1.9 billion per year (Gómez 2004).

Mobilization culminated in a broad coalition of Indigenous and popular movements from various sectors descending upon the government in La Paz and carrying out solidarity protests throughout the country. In the lowlands, the Chiquitanos and other Indigenous groups joined others engaging in a hunger strike (Hylton et al. 2007:116). Key demands of the social movements that led the rebellion included resignation of Sánchez de Lozada and his ministers, trial for those responsible for killings, the repeal of the 1996 hydrocarbons law, a constituent assembly to rewrite the constitution, and nationalization and industrialization of gas (Hylton et al., 2007:114; Gordon and Luoma 2008:91). Up through the final days of "Black October," the administration of US president George W. Bush praised Sánchez de Lozada's efforts and made it clear that the US government would not recognize any other government (Gordon and Luoma 2008:93). On October 17, 2003, Sánchez de Lozada resigned and boarded a plane to Miami, leaving a legacy of sixty-seven people dead in the final two months of his second term. The event would pave the way for a 2004 referendum that overwhelmingly supported state ownership over oil and gas, followed by a greater revenue-generating hydrocarbons law (2005) and nationalization of the sector under Morales in 2006.

In this chapter I have argued that the World Bank, working in cahoots with the US government, transnational corporations, and neoliberal regimes, promoted partial privatization of Bolivia's oil and gas sector, enabling

Enron, Shell, and other foreign oil corporations to enter the country. This, in turn, had unprecedented consequences for Indigenous peoples and environments located where extraction ensued. In response, the burgeoning lowland Indigenous movement began to exercise newly won rights to address escalating impacts. Having provided this critical context, chapter 3 turns to the key case examined in this book, Enron and Shell's Cuiabá pipeline, which was one of the key infrastructure projects built as a result of the neoliberal reforms.

CHAPTER THREE

Green-stamping a Pipeline

Of Enron Corp.'s many political maneuvers in Washington before its fall into bankruptcy, winning the promise of federal financing for a 390-mile pipeline from Bolivia to Brazil through the Chiquitano Dry Tropical Forest may have the most enduring consequences.

—JAMES GRIMALDI,
"ENRON PIPELINE LEAVES SCAR ON SOUTH AMERICA"

Planning a Pipeline

Thus read the headline of a front page story in the *Washington Post* that momentarily catapulted the story of Enron and Shell's Cuiabá pipeline into the international spotlight. Planning for the pipeline took place in 1998, when the companies began conspiring with the Bolivian and US governments to build a 626-kilometer-long natural gas pipeline from the main Bolivia-Brazil pipeline (at Rio San Miguel, Bolivia) to Cuiabá, Brazil (see figure 1.2). In sync with neoliberal doctrine, the companies aspired to export nearly all of the gas to their very own power plant in Cuiabá, which would produce electricity for industrial development in Mato Grosso, Brazil. Benefits on the Bolivian side would be few and far between, yet the Bolivian government touted the pipeline as a vital megaproject because it was expected to generate $50 million annually, with estimated exports of 2.5 million cubic meters of gas per day (*El Deber* 1999). Declaring the project a national priority, the government discouraged opposition from the outset. As they had done with the main Bolivia-Brazil pipeline, Enron and Shell flaunted the Cuiabá project as a model for Bolivia's integration with the Southern Common Market (Mercado Común del Sur, Mercosur) countries of Argentina, Paraguay, Uruguay, and Brazil. They boasted that it demonstrated "that responsible economic development can go hand-in-hand with progressive environmental policy."[1]

In this chapter, I argue that despite progressive environmental rhetoric, the companies green-stamped the Cuiabá project by funding a $20 million

63

conservation program that convinced the US government to authorize a $200 million loan to the companies to build the pipeline directly through middle of the Chiquitano forest and Pantanal wetlands. I explain the environmental significance of these ecoregions and highlight the diverse aims of the Indigenous and allied nongovernmental organizations (NGOs) that organized in response to the pipeline. I then show how a competing independent environmental study conducted by the conservation groups that were initially opposed to the pipeline's contentious route ultimately served only to increase Enron and Shell's funding for the conservation initiative. This persuaded the conservationists to accept the controversial route and convinced them to privately sign off on a program that excluded the Chiquitanos, Ayoreos, and Bolivian government from governance. I claim that the program, touted by the companies and conservationists as a model for community-based conservation, in fact is a contemporary form of "fortress conservation," one that epitomizes green imperialism and green neoliberalism.

The route that Enron and Shell proposed crossed directly through Chiquitano and Ayoreo Indigenous territories—affecting thirty-six communities with a population of about 8,000—as well as four critical ecoregions: the Gran Chaco and Cerrado (a mixture of grasslands and scattered trees), the Chiquitano dry forest, and the Pantanal wetlands (Dinerstein et al. 1995; FAN et al. 1999; OICH and CEADES 2004:84). Of particular concern to environmental groups was the 142,941-square-kilometer Chiquitano dry forest (as estimated by Portillo-Quintero and Sanchez-Azofeifa 2010)—approximately the size of Nicaragua (which is 129,494 km^2). The Chiquitano forest is classified in terms of biological distinctiveness as "globally outstanding," the highest ranking category in a study that evaluated more than two hundred terrestrial ecoregions in Latin America (Dinerstein et al. 1995). In species richness the forest is second only to the dry forests of Mexico (Gentry 1995). A Conservation International rapid assessment program team called it "what may well be the largest remaining tract of relatively undisturbed tall dry forest in the Neotropics, if not the entire world" (Parker 1993). Approximately ninety species living in the forest are listed in the Convention on International Trade in Endangered Species of Wild Fauna and Flora (CITES), including twenty-four mammals, fifty-nine birds, and eight reptiles (Ergueta and Morales 1996; FAN et al. 1999). A variety of important vertebrate species inhabit the forest, including vulnerable species (jaguar, ocelot, river otter), rare and vulnerable species (maned wolf, giant armadillo, giant anteater, black howler monkey, spider monkey, and several eagles), rare species (bush dog, margay cat, and several arma-

dillos), and at-risk species (red and gray brocket deer and paca). Other vertebrate species include the marsh deer, lowland tapir, blue and gold macaw,
tree porcupine, white lipped and collared peccaries, greater rhea, and land
tortoise. The forest is not only a center of plant diversity but also one of the
most threatened ecosystems in the neotropics and the most endangered
ecoregion in Bolivia.

The proposed route also crossed the world-renowned Pantanal wetlands (see figure 3.1), which lie in Brazil and Bolivia. In 2001, Bolivia's Pantanal wetlands were included on the Ramsar Convention's list of wetlands
of international importance because of their crucial role in regulating
floods and droughts in eastern Bolivia and because of their high biodiversity,
supporting approximately 197 species of fish, 70 species of amphibians and
reptiles, 300 species of birds, and 50 species of large animals.

In order to finance the pipeline, Enron and Shell sought a $200 million
loan from the US government's Overseas Private Investment Corporation
(OPIC), an export credit agency that provides political risk insurance, low-
interest loans, and loan guarantees to US businesses, with clients including
Enron, Citibank, and Bechtel Corporation. On its website, OPIC indicates
that it operates on behalf of "America's economic and strategic interest" by
promoting investment and creating markets in "less developed countries"

Figure 3.1 Pantanal wetlands near the Cuiabá pipeline, in the vicinity of the
Brazilian border. Author's photo

and "countries in transition from non-market to market economies, thereby complementing the development assistance objectives of the United States." In addition, the agency alludes to having a hand in shaping host countries' laws in the interest of US businesses by working with "governments to help create economic climates that attract U.S. investment"—witness Bolivia's 1999 heart law, which legalized the Cuiabá pipeline (see chapter 2).

It was telling that the companies had to resort to OPIC for financing rather than the World Bank or other multilateral development agencies. Their move was emblematic of a global shift in aid toward export credit agencies, which have used taxpayers' money to back projects multilaterals deem too risky and damaging to the environment and affected populations, such as the Ok Tedi Mine in Papua New Guinea (Cray 2000; Environmental Defense Fund 1999; Retallack 2000). Export credit agencies have been criticized for having weak public disclosure policies and poor social and environmental standards and for frequently supporting projects associated with large-scale corruption and mismanagement (Retallack 2000). They have directly funded a substantial number of fossil fuel projects and have indirectly leveraged considerable cofinancing through public and private institutions (Rich 2009:10). Between 1992 and 1998, the US export credit agencies OPIC and Export-Import Bank provided $23 billion to coal, oil, and gas projects. Only after intense pressure from affected populations and NGOs did standards improve somewhat during the 2000s.

Indigenous organizations and allied NGOs (CEADES, Friends of the Earth, and Amazon Watch) rallied to defend the rights of the Indigenous communities affected by the pipeline and to avert likely long-term social and environmental consequences. Such secondary impacts included development activities that were encroaching on the forest, including logging, mining, large-scale commercial farming and cattle ranching, small farmer colonization, hunting, and bioprospecting. Although these supporting organizations carried out some unified actions with the Chiquitanos, their interests and presence were varied. Operating from the premise that the Chiquitanos ought to be the protagonists in the conflict, the Collective for Applied Studies and Social Development (Colectivo de Estudios Aplicados y Desarrollo Social, CEADES) worked intimately with communities and parent organizations to identify needs and devise an elaborate plan of action aimed at pressuring the companies to comply with legal requirements to title lands, fund community development projects, and address adverse social and environmental impacts caused by the pipeline. The organization's overarching mission was to advance Chiquitano autonomy and to nurture self-sustaining initiatives that were deeply rooted in Chiquitano culture.

It provided technical and educational support, helping the Chiquitanos to understand and exercise their rights, document violations, and channel demands. CEADES had a sustained presence on the ground, working on the project from 1998 to 2008, when staff shifted and the headquarters of the organization moved from Santa Cruz to Cochabamba. Although it stayed out of the spotlight, international organization Oxfam was a key funder of CEADES and provided essential support to the campaign. As is common with donors in northern countries, Oxfam viewed CEADES as a legitimate vertical intermediary interfacing with Indigenous groups, the state, and the private sector (McDaniel 2002; see Macdonald 1995; Meyer 1993).

In contrast to CEADES, US-based NGOs Friends of the Earth and Amazon Watch—the latter where I worked formally for several months—intervened on a more sporadic basis and ceased to formally engage in the case after 2002. With the exception of a couple of short trips to Bolivia, Friends of the Earth primarily worked in the United States, garnering attention in the press and engaging in high-level meetings with OPIC, OPIC's oversight agencies (US State Department, USAID, and the Treasury), and Enron. The case was relevant to the organization's mission because it fell into its campaign to monitor export credit agencies such as OPIC. Soon after OPIC canceled its loan to Enron in 2002, Friends of the Earth's interventions in the case ended, despite the fact that environmental impacts and community conflicts loomed large and were increasing. Like Friends of the Earth, Amazon Watch representatives worked within the United States to discourage OPIC from financing the pipeline and, subsequently, to ensure that OPIC and the companies addressed adverse impacts, titled Indigenous lands, and democratized a controversial conservation program. In Bolivia, I collaborated with Amazon Watch to monitor the aforementioned issues on a local level and did fieldwork that formed the basis of reports and letters on unresolved issues. Because of funding allocation issues and strategic choices, Amazon Watch's leadership effectively terminated its Bolivia program in 2002, which brought an end to its involvement in the Cuiabá case. Subsequently, I continued supporting Chiquitanos independently, albeit sporadically. In part, Amazon Watch's decision reflected a problem common among donor-driven northern NGOs, which often have life cycles determined by funding (Markowitz 2001; Price 1994). The move also reflected the NGO's tendency to shift to other campaigns after it did what it could to stop megaprojects from happening, or to at least ameliorate what it perceived to be the worst impacts on Indigenous groups and the environment; this was partly because of its limited resources.

Moreover, its involvement in the case had been questioned internally given the pipeline crossed the outer fringes of the Amazon, casting doubt on whether the campaign fell within the organization's geographic scope. Such abrupt changes raise serious issues common to NGOs that support Indigenous groups, including long-term accountability, legitimacy, and dependency, particularly given that impacts of the Cuiabá pipeline on the Chiquitanos continue to this day. They remind us that Indigenous–environmentalist alliances can be unstable and that transnational political mobilization as a vehicle for Indigenous activism has limitations (Conklin and Graham 1995).

Months before the former groups had mobilized, Enron and Shell had already begun preliminary work on the pipeline, prior to receiving an environmental license from the Bolivian government (OICH and CEADES 2004). In November 1998, the companies began clearing forest and transporting and storing construction materials in the community of Taperas, located at the southern end of the pipeline route. The act was a flagrant disregard for Bolivian law, an audacious display of confidence that the project would be approved—a tactic not uncommon in the region and mirrored by the case of the Heavy Crude Pipeline (Oleoducto de Crudos Pesados, OCP) in Ecuador, which transports crude oil from the Amazon, over the Andes, to a terminal on the Pacific Ocean. Bowing early on to corporate power, in December 1998 the Ministry of Sustainable Development approved the companies' deficient environmental impact study and granted them permission to build the pipeline. It did so in violation of International Labor Organization Convention 169, which protects the rights of Indigenous peoples, as well as Bolivia's 1992 environment law, because affected communities had not even been consulted and a compensation program had not been established (OICH and CEADES 2004:154).

News that the companies had begun work and were seeking OPIC financing triggered diverse reactions. CEADES and the Chiquitanos mobilized but were concerned primarily with negotiating a community compensation program that would advance endogenous ways of living and secure land tenure—a struggle rooted in identity and livelihood. Recognizing that OPIC financing required implementation of a compensation program, they pressured the companies and the Bolivian government to do so and did not rescind opposition to the pipeline until a $2 million agreement was reached (see chapter 5). Amazon Watch and Friends of the Earth, along with conservation organization World Wildlife Fund (WWF), mobilized more over concern that the pipeline would cut through the heart of the Chiquitano forest, paving the way for development activities

that would degrade the environment upon which the Chiquitanos depended. Although WWF was involved in some community-based conservation initiatives in the region (not directed exclusively at Chiquitanos), its
interests were more oriented toward biodiversity conservation—as its subsequent involvement in an exclusionary conservation program demonstrates. In contrast, Amazon Watch and Friends of the Earth simultaneously
objected to OPIC's financing of the pipeline altogether while backing and
amplifying the Chiquitanos' demands.

A retrospective analysis of the case conducted by the Chiquitanos and
CEADES concluded that their mobilization was weakened when the
companies drove a wedge between them and the environmental groups
(OICH and CEADES 2004:113). When the Chiquitanos and CEADES
rejected the project and demanded the companies address both social and
environmental issues in a new study, the companies insisted on a compromise in which they would address the social issues through an indigenous
compensation fund but would leave environmental issues to the domain
of the Bolivian government—which had already issued the license. The
companies thereby managed to divide social and environmental concerns,
weakening possibilities for more unified opposition and ensuring that separate negotiations would ensue.

In December 1998, Amazon Watch and Bank Information Center—a
Washington, DC–based watchdog of international financial institutions—
visited Bolivia and briefed WWF on how to deliver comments to OPIC
(WWF 2000). WWF then sent a scathing evaluation of the pipeline's environmental impact study to the agency, criticizing it on a number of
grounds, including its failure to consider long-term impacts and alternate
routes around the forest. OPIC personnel were acutely concerned with the
issues WWF raised, particularly given WWF's international clout—then
the world's largest conservation organization, boasting a membership of
4.7 million—and considering its prior boisterous criticisms of Shell's egre-
gious practices in Nigeria. This was arguably the single most significant
factor that would ultimately lead to the creation of a controversial conservation program for the Chiquitano forest. In January 1999, representatives
from OPIC visited Bolivia and flew over the proposed pipeline route with
WWF and the Santa Cruz–based Noel Kempff Mercado Museum of Natural History. Representatives from these two conservation organizations
had the opportunity to point out ecological concerns related to the pipeline
and the need to conserve the Chiquitano forest and Pantanal wetlands—
opening the case for a multimillion-dollar conservation program.

Dueling Studies and Rumblings over a Conservation Program

In February 1999, WWF and the Noel Kempff Mercado Museum of Natural History wrote a letter to OPIC calling on it to fund independent scientific studies before financing the pipeline (WWF 2000). Similarly, WWF, Amazon Watch, and Friends of the Earth wrote a letter to OPIC's board of directors urging OPIC to postpone funding until adequate studies were carried out. These NGOs opposed OPIC financing of the pipeline through the Chiquitano forest based on the argument that US tax dollars should not be spent to fund the destruction of rare tropical forests (Soltani and Hindery 1999). Furthermore, they claimed that the project violated not only US president Bill Clinton's 1997 pledge that US export credit agencies would safeguard tropical forests but also the US Foreign Assistance Act and OPIC's own policies, which prohibited it from financing projects in "primary tropical forests" (Soltani and Hindery 1999).

The debate over whether the Chiquitano forest was "primary" was central in deliberations by OPIC's board of directors on the financing of the project. OPIC defined "primary forest" as a "relatively intact forest that has been essentially unmodified by human activity for the past 60 to 80 years," distinguished by an abundance of mature trees and limited "artisanal" or subsistence levels of hunting, fishing, logging, and migratory farming (Grimaldi 2002). NGOs argued that Enron had a heavy hand in crafting the definition, given that Enron executives lobbied OPIC in its formulation of environmental policies. Atossa Soltani, executive director of Amazon Watch, stated: "At every step OPIC sided with Enron, finding every way possible to circumvent its primary forest policy. OPIC management put on an all-out effort to defend its largest business client" (qtd. in Langman 2002).

OPIC, under Enron's influence, made a concerted effort to amass "scientific" data proving the forest was not primary. Nevertheless, three out of fifteen board members—Undersecretary of Treasury Timothy Geithner, Undersecretary of State Stuart Eizenstat, and US Agency for International Development (USAID) administrator J. Brian Atwood—felt that the Cuiabá project violated OPIC's environmental policy. Renowned conservation biologist Thomas Lovejoy, who was the World Bank's chief biodiversity adviser at the time, said that OPIC's definition was so restrictive that no forest in the world could be classified as "primary" and that the World Bank, by contrast, would have considered the Chiquitano primary and therefore not funded the pipeline.

William Denevan (1992), renowned for his research in the Bolivian lowlands, has argued that the notion of "primary" forests has little validity because the Americas were heavily populated prior to European contact and Indigenous peoples had significantly affected the areas thought to be primary. In the case of the Chiquitano forest, artifacts found along the route of the pipeline during excavation of the pipeline trench confirmed Indigenous peoples lived throughout the forest (FAN et al. 1999). This suggests that the Indigenous peoples living in the forest had minimal adverse impacts on it and that, to the contrary, their management practices helped conserve it. A letter the main lowland Indigenous federation, Federation of Indigenous Peoples of Bolivia (Confederación de Pueblos Indígenas de Bolivia, CIDOB) sent to OPIC's president argued that Indigenous management practices themselves had conserved the Chiquitano forest and that Indigenous peoples, not outside groups, had the right to continue doing so:

> Mr. Munoz, is it ethical that the problems that affect us be defined outside of our territory and without our consent? Does OPIC also think that the Chiquitano Forest, recognized as "one of the most extensive, least disturbed and well preserved dry tropical forests" exists because of conservation organizations? NO. Definitely not. If tropical forests still exist it is because Indigenous people exist. The forests have been conserved because of the traditional forms of management that we still practice. But projects such as the pipeline and others alter our habitat, our forms of life; these alterations cannot be "compensated" because they are irreversible damages. We can avoid impacts (for example through the alternative route proposed) or minimize them, but the damage exists. (CIDOB 1999)

While the impacts of the Chiquitanos' contemporary practices on the environment are not nil—for example, community forestry and small-scale cattle ranching—and vary significantly within and across communities, they pale in comparison with those of other actors in the region: large-scale commercial farmers, cattle ranchers, logging companies, mining companies, and oil corporations. Moreover, research has demonstrated that inhabited forests like the Chiquitano can be even more effective than protected areas for curtailing deforestation (Hecht 2011; Pedlowski et al. 2005; Merry et al. 2008; Nepstad et al. 2006). As the literature in political ecology has shown, the landscape management practices of local peoples have frequently created habitat or protected species (Peet et al. 2011). Increasingly, conservation initiatives have been carried out in and adjacent to areas long inhabited by humans (Zimmerer 2006; Parks and Harcourt 2002).

Meetings held between OPIC, WWF, and the Noel Kempff Mercado Museum of Natural History, coupled with letters written by WWF, Amazon Watch, and Friends of the Earth, prompted OPIC to require additional studies and moved the date on which OPIC's board was to vote on the pipeline from March 9 to June 15, 1999. On March 15, OPIC declared it would not finance the project until it completed a more adequate study that, among other things, addressed potential long-term secondary impacts. The decision ridiculed Bolivian state institutions that had already issued the environmental license for the project. Over the next several weeks, although these agencies would remain involved in a back-and-forth battle over competing studies, their role would be largely symbolic.

To address deficiencies in the first environmental study, Enron and OPIC organized a second supplemental study (FAN et al. 1999:1). In March 1999, Enron attempted to convince several conservation organizations to carry out the study but failed because they considered Enron's deadline unattainable. Executives from OPIC and Enron then visited WWF's office in Bolivia that March, and WWF recommended they consider an alternative route for the pipeline that would avoid the Chiquitano forest (WWF 2000). To echo this concern, representatives from WWF's office in the United Kingdom met with executives from Shell in London. In April 1999, Enron and Shell went against the recommendations of WWF, Amazon Watch, and Friends of the Earth to contract an independent organization, Entrix-PCA, to undertake the supplementary study—the same private consulting firm that had botched the original study. The NGOs argued that besides this conflict of interest it was absurd that the study was to be undertaken in a period of only ten days in order to cater to the timeline of the companies and OPIC (Molina 1999a:202). Convinced that Entrix-PCA would produce yet another inadequate report concluding the forest was not primary, five international and Bolivian conservation organizations— WWF, Wildlife Conservation Society, Missouri Botanical Garden, Noel Kempff Mercado Museum of Natural History, and Fundación Amigos de la Naturaleza—obtained a small amount of financing from Enron to conduct an independent study (Molina 1999a:202). Ironically, given the rushed time frame, the study was also undertaken in just a few days.

Over the following few weeks, a high-powered technical battle ensued between the conservationists and oil corporations over whether the forest was primary—one that excluded the Chiquitanos from having any meaningful voice. Given the history of the Bolivia-Brazil pipeline, the Chiquitanos understood how the Cuiabá pipeline might affect their livelihood, yet potential social effects took a back seat to Western environmental concerns. Western scientific knowledge about biodiversity conservation and ecosystem functionality counted most, while Indigenous knowledge was relegated to an inferior position.

In May 1999, a pivotal meeting was held in which the conservation organizations and Entrix-PCA presented the results of their two competing studies (WWF 2000). The event proved to be a high-power showdown, attended by company executives, representatives from the conservation NGOs and Entrix-PCA, scientists who contributed to the studies, and observers from the Bolivian government's National Service for Protected Areas, Bolivia Sustainable Forest Management Project (a USAID forest protection project), and USAID. Predictably, while Entrix-PCA consultants concluded that its study proved the Chiquitano forest was secondary, the conservation organizations claimed their study proved that it was primary, which signified that by financing the pipeline OPIC would violate its statutory regulation approved by the US Congress that forbids it from financing development projects that negatively affect "primary tropical forests" (FAN et al. 1999:10). The conservation groups predicted the pipeline would open the forest to development and therefore recommended it be rerouted around the forest, along existing roads. They further made a formal call for a long-term, regional conservation program to be developed to compensate for "the inevitable impact that the pipeline will have on the ecoregions, regardless of the route that is eventually chosen" (FAN et al. 1999:2). They blasted the Entrix-PCA study for not adequately addressing secondary impacts, for failing to provide a long enough time frame and large enough scale to measure conservation data, and for not being objective, given the relationship between Enron and Entrix-PCA.

Although respected independent scientists were contracted to provide data for the supplemental study, Entrix-PCA staff wrote and edited the report, even going so far as to write a conclusion that distorted the scientists' findings. The conservation groups argued that Entrix-PCA staff was biased because Enron paid them and because they had an interest in supporting the conclusions of the original environmental study they had conducted. Ultimately, the companies accepted the conclusions of Entrix-PCA over those of the conservation organizations (WWF 2000). Ironically, one of the key independent scientists who analyzed whether the Chiquitano forest was primary had reportedly been told not to overly criticize a key scientist who contributed to the supplemental study because it could make the companies reluctant to finance the proposed conservation program. Nonetheless, the production of the independent study triggered OPIC, Enron, and Shell to engage in a series of negotiations with the conservation groups in

Washington, DC, and Bolivia over the creation of what would prove to be a controversial conservation program (Molina 1999a:202).

Enron and Shell rejected the proposed alternative route on economic grounds, arguing they would incur cost overruns and needed to construct the pipeline during the dry season of 1999 (WWF 2000). They stated that the Brazilian government could fine them $1 million per day if the pipeline was not operating by March 1, 2000. Enron lobbyist John Hardy, Jr., told the head of the environment team in Bolivia for USAID that the company chose the most direct route (through the forest) because it wanted to build the pipeline quickly and keep costs competitive (Grimaldi 2002). On its website, OPIC claimed that the alternative route around the Chiquitano forest was 70% longer than the route that bisected the forest. It argued this would have increased construction costs alone by $120 million (excluding other possible increased costs due to delay penalties, operating for an extended period on diesel fuel, cost escalations, and financing), thereby making the project financially unviable and unfundable by OPIC or other lenders.

Considering additional costs that the companies accrued because they constructed the pipeline through the forest—a $20 million conservation program, delay penalties, financing charges, additional studies—in hindsight it might have been cheaper for them to construct it along the alternative route, around the forest. Enron's bankruptcy disclosure statement in fact states that although the original projected aggregate capital cost of the Cuiabá project was $505 million, significant delays and cost overruns pushed the actual cost up to $740 million (Weil, Gotshal, and Manges LLP 2004:519).

As the date on which OPIC was to vote approached, it became increasingly clear that the agency would grant Enron financing regardless of public pressure and that, like many other neoliberal projects (see chapter 2), the deal was predetermined. Amazon Watch alleged that when OPIC approved financing for the companies' Cuiabá power plant in Brazil during fall 1998, it also agreed to finance the pipeline; if OPIC backed out it could face a legal battle with Enron: "OPIC staff at times have admitted that the project could not be denied financing because OPIC had made an initial commitment to Enron when it approved the Cuiabá power plant project and that OPIC could face lawsuits from Enron for backing out of its commitment. In other words, regardless of the forest type, this project must go forward due to bureaucratic misjudgments" (Soltani and Hindery 1999).

If this assessment is correct, then the whole public process soliciting input about the project was a sham, giving the mere illusion of democratic participation without any real possibility of stopping OPIC financing or

rerouting the pipeline—paralleling the World Bank's Learning and Innovation Loan project (see chapter 2) and the World Bank–financed Bolivia-
Brazil pipeline (completed in 1998) (see chapter 2). In the latter case, a
former president of the regional Guaraní organization Asamblea del Pueblo
Guaraní protested that the Guaraní had pressured to alter the pipeline's
route in vain because the decision had already been made (Griffiths 2000).[2]
As chapter 2 describes, an investigation I carried out in 2002 with Chiquitano organizations suggested that Enron and Shell conspired with Bolivian president Gonzalo Sánchez de Lozada to route the pipeline through the
middle of the forest to supply his gold mine (financed by the World Bank).
Dissent within fractured Bolivian state institutions pointed to a mire of
vested interests. Vice Minister of Sustainable Development Neisa Roca stated
that she wanted the pipeline to be built along the alternative route but that
the vice president's office instructed her to issue the environmental license
for the route bisecting the forest. Commenting on why the ministry did not
heed recommendations from NGOs and Indigenous groups but instead
granted the environmental license accepting the controversial route, she
stated: "Such are the risks of development. We cannot impede, for example, the construction of the Santa Cruz–Puerto Suárez highway [financed
by the Inter-American Development Bank], which also cuts through forests"
(qtd. in *El Deber* 2002, translation by author). Ministry officials acknowledged that Enron and Shell lobbied intensely to obtain the environmental
license rapidly and to approve the route that bisected the Chiquitano forest. They also admitted that the ministry granted the license based on
both a positive recommendation from the World Bank–financed environmental office of the hydrocarbons ministry (chapter 2) and Enron's shoddy
environmental study (*La Prensa* 2002).

Dealing with the Devil

By June 1999, Friends of the Earth, WWF, and Amazon Watch were applying an increasing amount of pressure on OPIC's board of directors in
opposition to its financing of the pipeline. They all sent letters and lobbied
both OPIC and its board of directors. The NGOs helped organize letters
signed by dozens of other NGOs from around the world, as well as a letter
to the executive director of OPIC, signed by various members of the US
Congress. The central argument against OPIC financing remained constant: OPIC was prohibited from financing extractive and infrastructure
projects in primary forests (Molina 1999a:203).

During May and June 1999, the five conservation groups that authored the independent study, led by WWF, entered into closed-door negotiations with the companies and OPIC, excluding the Bolivian government, Indigenous groups, and other local actors (Molina 1999a:202). During the final talks, the US ambassador to Bolivia also helped broker an agreement (Molina 1999a:202). WWF continued to lead separate negotiations with the companies in an effort to create a conservation program for the Chiquitano region (WWF 2000).

Given that OPIC was to vote on whether to finance the pipeline on June 15, the conservation organizations intensified negotiations with the companies and OPIC during the final week (Molina 1999a:203). Then, suddenly, just a few hours after WWF issued a press release opposing OPIC financing, rejecting routing the pipeline through the forest, and declaring the forest primary, WWF executives held a pivotal private meeting with the companies in Washington, DC (WWF 2000). Months of pressure paid off, as the companies pledged to invest $20 million for conservation of the Chiquitano forest. The agreement was formalized on June 11, when the companies and the five conservation organizations that undertook the independent study signed a protocol agreement to invest up to $30 million in a long-term conservation program for the Chiquitano forest, called the Chiquitano Forest Conservation Program. Enron was to invest $20 million, and the conservation organizations were to raise $10 million in matching funds. Instantly privatizing control over the Chiquitano forest, the companies and conservationists appointed themselves members of the program's board, excluding the Bolivian government and Indigenous organizations.

The agreement specified that OPIC could not put conditions on the conservation initiative and that the signatories to the protocol could not disclose its content until there was mutual agreement on how it should be disseminated (WWF 2000). However, both OPIC and company representatives flagrantly violated this clause and shared it with the OPIC board, officially giving the project the "green stamp" necessary to justify financing (WWF 2000). The companies argued to OPIC that the program had alleviated environmental concerns and that the pipeline could be built along the controversial route (Molina 1999a:203). WWF had been used by Enron and Shell to greenwash a destructive pipeline that would pave the way for encroaching development. The conservation program created just enough appearance of environmental sensitivity for OPIC to defend funding the pipeline. Through entirely separate negotiation processes with the Chiquitanos and the conservationists—a divide-and-conquer approach— the companies had cleared two major hurdles to winning OPIC's financing of the pipeline: establishing a compensation program for the Chiquitanos and funding a conservation program for the conservationists. On June 15, just four days after the conservation agreement was signed, OPIC's board of directors approved financing the pipeline along the controversial route bisecting the Chiquitano forest. OPIC wrote a nonbinding stipulation that the companies must implement the conservation program and Indigenous compensation program. Following suit, the next month Bolivia's Ministry of Sustainable Development authorized the companies to begin construction, officially inaugurating the pipeline (OICH and CEADES 2004:217).

Representatives from the OPIC board later confirmed that the conservation program persuaded them to approve financing. A US State Department representative informed me that when the vote was being decided, she gave her consent for the project on condition that the debate about forest definitions as they relate to OPIC's guidelines be reopened. This individual suggested to me that the conservation program convinced her to approve the route through the Chiquitano forest, clarifying that her initial position was to follow the alternative route. Other officials from the US State Department also told me that the consensus in Washington, DC, was that the conservation program was a quid pro quo for OPIC's financing of the pipeline. According to a representative from Friends of the Earth, one representative from one of the conservation organizations shifted from opposing OPIC's financing of the pipeline to endorsing the project as environmentally beneficial once the conservation program was funded, and because the individual was deemed a board member. Amazon Watch alleged that company representatives used the creation of the conservation program to gain political support for OPIC financing of the pipeline as a quid pro quo agreement. It claimed that on the eve of OPIC's vote, Enron and OPIC lobbyists showed the agreement to their congressional allies and oversight agencies that had been encouraging OPIC to alter the route or reject financing the project. This, then, convinced the latter that the conservation organizations supported OPIC financing and that the conservation program had alleviated the conservationists' concerns.

Representatives from Biosphere Productivity and Environment (Productividad Biosfera y Medio Ambiente, PROBIOMA), a Bolivian organization that aided non-Indigenous populations affected by the pipeline, echoed the sentiment expressed by Friends of the Earth and Amazon Watch: "The conservationist current, which defends flora and fauna with a great degree of insistence, little by little is unmasking itself and showing its true face: capitalism. . . . They are only concerned with money, and little by little are becoming the guarantors of devastation. Hasn't the defense of the

Chiquitano Forest become this? Haven't they used 'scientific' concepts as a pretext to negotiate millions?" (PROBIOMA 2000d). The relationship between the conservation organizations and transnational capital would become increasingly clear after the pipeline was built. On March 23, 2000, Enron and individuals from the conservation organizations signed an agreement, which included the companies financing $324,407 to reforest "sensitive" places along the pipeline route. One of the organizations, the Noel Kempff Mercado Museum of Natural History, was contracted to reforest a four-kilometer pipeline route leading from the Cuiabá pipeline to Sánchez de Lozada's Don Mario gold mine—which in and of itself would generate tremendous controversy. And in 2004, the museum would be contracted to conduct a study on reforestation of the Cuiabá pipeline route. Taken together, these incidents would lucidly illustrate how, as neoliberal policies enclosed the commons, in this case the Chiquitano forest and Pantanal wetlands through the exclusionary conservation program, "they simultaneously create opportunities for capital accumulation and generate the social conditions necessary for opposing such processes" (Perreault and Martin 2005:193–194)—the subject of chapter 4.

Creation of the conservation program reflected a broader trend in Bolivia in which neoliberal institutions directed some of their financial and administrative support to enforcement activities under what Dan Brockington (2002) calls "fortress conservation" (Zimmerer 2009). Discursively, this shift stemmed from a Western wilderness preservationist current that devalued inhabited landscapes, yet materially, the change was related to political and economic schemes to obtain "valuation of the sources of biological or genetic raw materials and the environmental and ecosystem services in which they are housed" (Zimmerer 2009:172). Since the 1980s, environmental governance has devolved (though not entirely) from the central government to NGOs, aid agencies (often operating in collaboration with state institutions), and local municipalities (Perreault and Martin 2005; Perreault 2009:138). In the Chiquitano case, the conservationists and corporations usurped control over the forest from the Chiquitanos, appointing themselves "global" managers of a biodiversity bastion of the world—a contemporary form of "green imperialism" (Sachs 1993; Shiva 1993).

Establishment of the conservation program demonstrated that despite the reputed rise of community-based conservation in the 1980s and 1990s (Adams and Hulme 2001), fortress-style conservation had triumphed once again, representing a shift "back to the barriers" (Hutton et al. 2005; Lauermann 2011). Transnational oil corporations and conservation organizations had created an initiative that excluded the Chiquitanos from deciding the "fate of the forest" (Hecht and Cockburn 1990). Ironically, in the process, the conservationists became Enron's pawns, and green-stamped a project that would give rise to the impacts they decried. Furthermore, the conservation program would reflect what Michael Goldman (2005) calls "green neoliberalism," a form of global environmentalism that supports and legitimates the practices of corporations (Perreault 2009:139).

OPIC boldly announced its decision to approve the pipeline along the controversial route by issuing a press release boasting that it had required the multimillion-dollar conservation initiative along with unprecedented environmental standards (OPIC 1999b). Little did the agency know that its decision to back the project would unleash a fury of potent protagonism that would parallel rising discontent across the country over failure of the neoliberal model. As chapter 4 explains, conflict over the Cuiabá pipeline and exclusionary conservation program would mark the leading edge of rising mobilization during the country's 2000–2005 anti-neoliberal rebellion.

CHAPTER FOUR

Struggling for Transparency and Fairness

Rescaling Resistance Through *Dynamic Pragmatism*

The neoliberal economic reforms implemented in Bolivia since 1985—particularly structural adjustment, capitalization of the state oil company, the hydrocarbons law, and the heart law—brought transnational oil corporations like Enron and Shell into Bolivia, sparking intense mobilization by affected Indigenous peoples. As the reforms deepened, Indigenous peoples engaged by using "place-based, yet transnationalized strategies" of resistance and protagonism (Escobar 2006), or acts of "place-based globalism" (Osterweil 2005), to counter impacts caused by the hydrocarbons boom. In this and the next two chapters I show how, in the case of the Cuiabá pipeline, mobilization to democratize the Chiquitano Forest Conservation Program (this chapter), compensate communities (chapter 5), and resolve environmental and social impacts (chapter 6) took diverse forms across multiple geographic scales, including national and international press outreach, lobbying international financial institutions and the Bolivian and US governments, negotiating with Enron and Shell and their Bolivian subsidiaries, and direct actions such as blockades and takeovers of company camps. I contend that such actions are expressions of what I term *dynamic pragmatism* (defined in chapter 1) and highlight the importance of agency in challenging the structural confines imposed by neoliberalism. During the Cuiabá conflict, the Chiquitanos and Ayoreos often pragmatically bypassed the state and scaled up their actions, directly engaging with neoliberal champions at an international level, including the pipeline financier (OPIC) and the World Bank. They also amplified their voice by selectively and strategically engaging with allied nongovernmental organizations (NGOs) savvy at garnering international press attention and pressuring transnational corporations and international financial institutions. This exemplified a high-stakes struggle over voice (i.e., representation) and nuanced ways in which Indigenous people navigate local-global networks and discourses in the creation of political subjectivity (Lucero 2008:155). Such identity construction is often achieved in conjunction with other actors, with specific political purposes in mind (Jackson 1995). For instance, Alcida Rita Ramos (1998) has shown how in Brazil indigenous groups have publicized conflicts to make broader political claims to the state and other actors. In the Cuiabá case, the Chiquitanos and Ayoreos articulated broader political aims—for example, enforcement of new rights to territory, consultation, and compensation—through specific claims related to the pipeline as well as through participation in larger national mobilizations.

In some respects, the sort of transnational activism displayed by the Chiquitanos and Ayoreos mirrored Indigenous mobilization against transnational oil corporations abroad, such as Occidental Petroleum in Colombia, Chevron/Texaco in Ecuador, and Shell in Nigeria (Gedicks 2001:81). In all of these cases, Indigenous groups found that because states were heavily dependent on international financing, they were more vulnerable to pressure for human rights reform. Indigenous engagement in the Cuiabá case also echoed a form of globalized politics emerging throughout the Brazilian Amazon, where influential national associations—for example, human rights groups, forest peoples' federations, and the Workers' Party (Partido dos Trabalhadores, PT)—formed alliances with international environmental organizations to chart a more ecologically, socially, and economically sound path for Amazonian forests (Hecht and Cockburn 1990; Conklin and Graham 1995; Schmink and Wood 1992; Nugent 1993; Harris and Nugent 2004; Hecht 2011).

The Chiquitanos' and Ayoreos' responses must be contextualized around what Jeffery Webber (2011:2) has characterized as a "revolutionary epoch" against neoliberalism that occurred in Bolivia between 2000 and 2005. This period was characterized by mass mobilization from below and state crisis from above that together enabled transformative structural change. The Cuiabá conflict began at the forefront of broader resistance to neoliberal reforms across Bolivia, including the water wars of 2000 and 2005, the gas wars of 2003 and 2005, and the 2003 riots against a tax hike driven by the Washington, DC–based International Monetary Fund. In response to being marginalized by powerful transnational oil corporations, international financial institutions, and the governments of Bolivia and the United States, the Chiquitanos and Ayoreos engaged in a range of actions to assert their moral claims over natural resources in the region, thereby reaffirming their cultural identity and attachment to a place that was the source of their livelihood.

The Cuiabá case highlights dynamic and contradictory relations between identity-based movements and interest-based movements. The effectiveness of mobilization often depended on the degree to which the Chiquitanos' and Ayoreos' primarily identity-based actions (e.g., to secure land tenure) coincided with interest-based actions of allied NGOs (e.g., to stop OPIC financing of the pipeline). They worked with supporting organizations cooperatively, pragmatically, and at times in contradiction, forming flexible and shifting coalitions. They strategically constructed a dynamic, shifting political identity, at times appropriating environmental narratives espoused by allies to advance their own agenda (see Zimmerer 2009:171). In part, their engagement with supporting organizations reflected the sort of pragmatic "middle grounds" Richard White (1991:ix, 50–51) has described, in which Indigenous and non-Indigenous peoples develop systems of communication and exchange through which both sides perceive their goals can be met through debate, negotiation, and creative innovation. Such an intermediary cultural space is dynamic and often characterized by mutual accommodation and new forms of communication and cooperation (Conklin and Graham 1995:705).

The Chiquitanos' *dynamic pragmatism* has had a long tradition since European contact, characterized by varying practices of avoidance, resistance, and accommodation under Jesuit occupation, during the rubber boom and ranching expansion in the 1800s and early 1900s, and throughout the development of unions and Chiquitano organizations since the 1950s (McDaniel 2003:347). Chiquitano organizations emerged in the 1980s in response to encroachment by logging and mining companies in the 1970s, responding with a radical reaction, including direct confrontation and roadblocks (McDaniel 2003:353). The Chiquitano organization Indigenous Center for Native Communities of Lomerío (Central Indígena de Comunidades Originarias de Lomerío, CICOL) was organized in part by Chiquitanos who had built agrarian unions in the early 1960s to resist ranching patrons and end service requirements. Chiquitano identity based on defiance and resistance is proudly remembered and reprojected to outsiders as new development activities unfold in the region. Identity construction is also related to other pragmatic ends. Chiquitano leaders at CICOL are chosen based on how well they are perceived to interact with outside agencies and represent community interests; they are expected to embody Chiquitano values and secure projects that advance economic development (McDaniel 2002:375). Such a pragmatic construction of syncretic identities parallels how the Shuar Federation in Ecuador simultaneously formed a resistance movement critical of state policies yet upheld a strong sense of hybrid identity, blending traditional Shuar beliefs with Western-style models of political organization (Hendricks 1991).

While a generally recognized distinction between "pragmatic Amazonians" and "radical Andeans" (Lucero 2008:140) may have some merit, nuanced patterns emerged in the Cuiabá case. The Chiquitanos' and Ayoreos' actions were taken strategically and ranged from those that were more accommodating, such as negotiations, lobbying, press outreach, to those that were more radical, for example, direct actions taking over company camps, protests, and threats to close pipeline valves. In contrast, the Federation of Indigenous Peoples of Bolivia (Confederación de Pueblos Indígenas de Bolivia, CIDOB), the main lowland Indigenous federation, had a more conciliatory reputation than did more radical highland federations (Lucero 2008:171–172), including Chiquitano organizations. On various occasions, Chiquitano leaders from the Council of Ethnic Peoples of Santa Cruz (Coordinadora de Pueblos Étnicos de Santa Cruz, CPESC), a regional Indigenous organization that included the Chiquitanos, balked at CIDOB's suspension of marches to negotiate with neoliberal governments. In fact, a rift between the two organizations was well known among lowland Indigenous groups and supporters (Cáceres 2008b:2). In 2000, at a negotiation located at the offices of CIDOB, I observed CPESC leaders and representatives from legal support organization Center for Juridical Studies and Social Investigation (Centro de Estudios Jurídicos e Investigación Social, CEJIS) storm away as CIDOB leaders and government officials settled on agreements that CPESC deemed too modest.

In the early 2000s, the Chiquitanos pursued change through both electoral politics and more radical actions, sometimes blurring the lines between them. They simultaneously ran candidates for congressional office while participating in national marches confronting the state, pressuring state institutions, and bringing legal actions, for example, pushing for a new constitution and hydrocarbons law. In some respects, this political path paralleled the rise of Evo Morales, and a shift in the Movement Toward Socialism (Movimiento al Socialismo) political party from more radical resistance to more reformist governance (Webber 2011:98–99). Chiquitano congressional deputy José Bailaba and Chiquitano senator Carlos Cuasace, among others, worked to unify the highland and lowland Indigenous movements and in

2003 helped to organize a pivotal march to remake the constitution—a goal that would eventually be realized under Morales:

> First, we marched as Indigenous peoples from the lowlands. I remember it well. We marched for 37 days—not only because of the hydrocarbons issue, but also because we were demanding a new constitution and a constituent assembly. When we were fighting we realized that we wouldn't achieve anything alone and, of course, the traditional political parties saw that it was good for us to continue divided. They said to us "Why join forces with those from the highlands?" And then we realized the great interests they had. So I remember it well. We met with one of the leaders from the highlands and said: "Look brother, you have the same problems that we have, the same needs." So then it resulted in the agreement we made not only for the hydrocarbons law but also to defend the rights of both the Indigenous peoples of the highlands and lowlands, those who are most discriminated against. We not only defended the sovereignty of our state, of our natural resources, but also realized we needed a change within the framework of the constitution . . . and that's when we demanded a constituent assembly. We made this agreement, we held a press conference and we joined forces, the highlands and the lowlands. (qtd. in Cáceres 2008a, with translation corrections by the author)

Following the 2003 gas war, Chiquitano leader Justo Seoane served as Indigenous affairs minister under the government of Bolivian president Carlos Diego Mesa Gisbert. Similar patterns of political mobilization arose among the Guaraní as well. When avenues created by the neoliberal multicultural reforms such as the Law of Popular Participation were inadequate, young Guaraní leaders also took part in broader democratic mobilizations, such as the movement for a constituent assembly (Postero 2007:218). In the Cuiabá case, outrage over the fortress-style Chiquitano Forest Conservation Program quickly spread from localized actions in the region to a transnational campaign to democratize the controversial initiative.

Fortress Fallout

News that OPIC had approved a $200 million loan for the pipeline after the conservation organizations secretly negotiated a $20 million conservation program triggered an outburst of opposition. Indigenous groups, allied organizations (CEADES, FOBOMADE, Amazon Watch, Friends of the Earth), non-Indigenous communities, and some Bolivian state institutions lambasted the companies (Enron and Shell) and five conservation organizations (WWF, Wildlife Conservation Society, Missouri Botanical Garden, Noel Kempff Mercado Museum of Natural History, and Fundación Amigos de la Naturaleza) for brokering a private agreement that usurped control over natural resources in the Chiquitano region from local communities and the state and that gave OPIC the green light to approve financing of the pipeline along the controversial route through the middle of the Chiquitano forest:

> The negotiations of these five conservation institutions . . . were carried out behind the back of the country, not only without ethical considerations, but also in violation of every principle regarding the rights of people to control their own resources. We believe that the public and the governmental authorities ought to know about this violation by these five institutions that don't represent anyone, as well as the issue of negotiating for environmental compensation. We believe that the time has come to stop those who use the environment as a form of profit. (PROBIOMA et al. 1999, translation by author)

The Bolivian organization Biosphere Productivity and Environment (Productividad Biosfera y Medio Ambiente, PROBIOMA), which spearheaded organizing non-Indigenous communities impacted by the pipeline, condemned the conservation organizations for green-stamping the pipeline and selling out to the companies:

> [We] denounce the so-called "green stamp" that five "conservation" NGOs gave in exchange for $20 million, thereby guaranteeing that Enron and Shell would enter the Chiquitano Dry Forest. PROBIOMA initiated the process of informing the region and country, and subsequently issued a public condemnation, which enabled investigation of the "conservationists" who took advantage of defending the Dry Forest in order to appropriate 20 million dollars for themselves. (PROBIOMA 2001, translation by author)

The Bolivian environmental organization Bolivian Forum on Environment and Development (Foro Boliviano sobre Medio Ambiente y Desarrollo, FOBOMADE) issued a statement about the creation of the conservation program titled "The Cuiabá Project: How to Buy Conservationists," which suggested the conservation organizations sold out to the companies by accepting the program in exchange for allowing the pipeline to be constructed through the forest. FOBOMADE and Amazon Watch criticized the conservation groups for taking advantage of pressure FOBOMADE and Amazon Watch had created by opposing OPIC financing to convince the companies to contribute more money to the conservation program (Molina 1999a:203).

The Chiquitanos and Ayoreos vehemently rejected the program because it gave private corporations and conservation organizations control over their ancestral lands—an overt form of "accumulation by dispossession" (Harvey 2003; see also Peet et al. 2011:27):

> We told them "You may not come inside here. You must go outside because we live in the forest. We have cared for the forest for hundreds of years, like our ancestors." . . . Why should others have the right to come and make themselves owners? I think this is illegal. They don't even have legal status. The state doesn't recognize them either, and I don't know how they have given them this kind of work so they can take over this [forest] and do whatever they want with the money. (Chiquitano community member, interview by author)

Foreign conservationists had accumulated $20 million in exchange for pledging to privately conserve natural resources already claimed and managed by Indigenous groups. The private agreement gave the companies and conservationists the power to conserve an area totaling 80,000 square kilometers—1.6 times the size of Holland—in which approximately 135,000 Chiquitanos lived in 180 communities, along with 274 Ayoreos in two communities (OICH and CEADES 2004:84). In the stroke of a pen, the Chiquitano region would join the ranks of other rural areas around the world that had been transformed into sites of neoliberal governmentality as nonstate or quasi-state actors rose to govern regions peripheral to state control (Watts 2003; Perreault and Martin 2005).

Oddly enough, during the period in which the Chiquitano Forest Conservation Program was formed and operated, comanagement arrangements between Indigenous peoples and the state, while problematic, had been enacted under neoliberal regimes. Such was the case with the Sirionó people of Isiboro-Secure Indigenous Territory and National Park (Territorio Indígena y Parque Nacional Isiboro-Sécure, TIPNIS), which was deemed an Indigenous territory under the administration of Bolivian president Gonzalo Sánchez de Lozada (Zimmerer 2009:167). Ironically, even Kaa-Iya

National Park—adjacent to the Chiquitano forest and the Bolivia-Brazil pipeline—was comanaged by the Guaraní, in collaboration with the Wildlife Conservation Society. Yet in the case of the conflictive Chiquitano Forest Conservation Program, the Wildlife Conservation Society was unwilling to permit Indigenous representatives to serve in a management role. And to add insult to injury, through the guise of "conservation," the program justified a pipeline—facilitated by aggressive neoliberal capitalism—that would push degrading development activities onto the Indigenous commons (Harvey 2005).

The agreement excluded Indigenous peoples from the governing board, in violation of their right to "participate in the use, management and conservation of natural resources," specified in International Labor Organization (ILO) Convention 169 (Bolivian Law 1257). Using this legal argument, over the next several years the Chiquitanos and Ayoreos would engage in various actions to gain control of the program and remove the companies and conservation groups from the governing board. As struggles against neoliberalism spread across Bolivia, the Chiquitano case offered insights into Indigenous groups reclaiming commons claimed by neocolonial agents operating in neoliberalized landscapes. In some respects the struggle over the conservation program would parallel Bolivia's water and gas wars, which centered on issues of resource governance and distributive justice (Perreault 2008:243).

At its core, the ensuing conflict was a struggle over control of natural resources, a central focus within the field of political ecology (Bryant 1992; Robbins 2004). Indigenous communities from the Chiquitano region contended that the fortress-style conservation program diminished their access and control over natural resources in the Chiquitano forest because they were excluded from the board. They based their claim to govern the program on grounds they had conserved and lived in the forest historically, were its rightful stewards, and were most capable of conserving it. As the conflict played out, ancestral claims of territory and belonging helped the Chiquitanos strengthen a shared sense of intercommunity identity (Lovell 1998) but would eventually give way to divisions between communities that opted to participate in the program and those that did not (chapter 9).

In one of Latin America's most neoliberalized countries, the case would illustrate how different interest groups attempt to control rule making over natural resources amid conflicting normative frameworks (Boelens and Doornbos 2001). While economically powerful oil corporations and conservationists defined the rules and procedures that usurped Indigenous communities' control over natural resources, the latter engaged in various forms of resistance and protagonism to modify the program in accordance with their rights, for example, by proposing the forest be conserved through an autonomous Indigenous conservation program. Through such assertions, the case shows how rights over natural resources are defined not only by lawyers and technocrats but also in grassroots struggles.

Entrenched in Eden

With the exception of World Wildlife Fund (WWF)—which would soon repent, withdraw from the program, and renew its objection to OPIC financing—the conservation organizations all dropped their opposition to OPIC's financing of the pipeline after the companies agreed to finance their $20 million initiative. Unshaken by opposition, the groups audaciously proceeded to implement the program, with little regard for the legal and moral objections raised by Indigenous groups and others.

A representative from one of the conservation groups who was party to the program went so far as to tell me he did not think there was a problem that representatives from the Bolivian government and civil society were not included during negotiations. He maintained that Indigenous and peasant (*campesino*) communities could not effectively manage the forest and that the existing governance structure of the program was adequate (composed of representatives from the five conservation organizations and the companies). Like other board members, he argued that Indigenous representatives should not serve on the board because it would cause a conflict of interest—that is, Indigenous peoples would be funding themselves to carry out conservation. This was a peculiar argument given the existence of other conservation programs autonomously governed or comanaged by Indigenous peoples, not to mention the reputedly autonomous Indigenous compensation program. This individual further added that the end (conservation) justified the means (alluding to the controversial negotiation process and governance structure). Additionally, he suggested that his organization was one of the few good conservation groups working in the country.

While the Chiquitanos and Ayoreos were by no means perfect stewards of the forest—a point they acknowledged themselves in a self-assessment (OICH and CEADES 2004)—they contended that overall their management practices had preserved the forest over time, particularly compared with other actors in the region (e.g., large-scale commercial farmers, cattle ranchers, logging companies, and mining companies). Over subsequent years, the conservation organizations would remain intransigent, rejecting even a compromise proposal to fuse Scientific Ecological Knowledge with the Chiquitanos' and Ayoreos' Traditional Ecological Knowledge (Berkes 1999; Kimmerer 2002). This plan would have placed Indigenous representatives on the board while moving the conservation groups and companies to a technical advisory committee. Instead, the conservationists insisted that a consultative body they had created would give Indigenous groups sufficient power to make decisions and propose programs—a body the Chiquitanos and Ayoreos rejected entirely.

Similar to other cases in which Western science has marginalized Indigenous knowledge systems (Agarwal 1992; Haraway 1988), in the Chiquitano case the conservationists devalued the Chiquitanos' and Ayoreos' Traditional Ecological Knowledge, driven by a racialized imaginary that justified an antidemocratic, authoritarian form of conservation (Sundberg 2008:578–579). And by prioritizing Scientific Ecological Knowledge over Indigenous knowledge, the conservationists, companies, and OPIC disempowered and dispossessed the Chiquitanos and Ayoreos (see Berkes 2008; Gedicks 2001:17; see also Peet et al. 2011:37). Their debasement of Indigenous knowledge was rooted in a Western environmentalist worldview that saw nature as wilderness—what Hecht (1993) has called a "Lost Eden"—and Indigenous peoples as separate, rather than recognizing the Chiquitano forest as an inhabited landscape. This separation was enshrined in the governance structure of the program itself as Indigenous groups were excluded from the board. As the conflict unfolded, whereas the conservationists would promote Western-style initiatives, Indigenous groups would propose projects to improve livelihood while sustaining the forest—a struggle for environmental justice that bridged the human–environment divide. In this context, conflict over the conservation program underscores how hegemonic control of knowledge about the environment can marginalize subaltern peoples—a key theme in emerging scholarship within the field of political ecology (Peet et al. 2011:31). This is not to reject science as a useful form of knowledge but rather to emphasize how specific types of ecological knowledge are chosen and validated, how problems are narrated and structured, and how particular assumptions and practices become normal and internalized (Peet et al. 2011:40).

Like the conservation organizations, OPIC too remained entrenched in its position. To calm critics, the agency published a list of loan conditions that required the companies to comply with OPIC's environmental requirements, alter the route of the pipeline to avoid any areas of critical habitat or primary forest (according to its own disputed definition), and implement both the conservation program and the Indigenous compensation program. However, the Chiquitanos, Ayoreos, and organizations critical of OPIC and the conservation program (the Bolivian NGOs CEADES, PROBIOMA, and FOBOMADE and the international NGOs Amazon Watch and Friends of the Earth) steadfastly rejected the conservation program and maintained their position that the pipeline would cross primary forest and therefore violate OPIC's own lending policies.

When Amazon Watch and Friends of the Earth wrote letters to OPIC criticizing the program, OPIC responded that it was a private agreement between the companies and the conservation NGOs and that it was not a compensation program for the impacts of the pipeline—despite the fact that WWF, which had devised the program, stated that its purpose was precisely to compensate for the inevitable impact that the pipeline will have on the ecoregion (WWF 2000). OPIC used these arguments to distance itself from the conservation program and to excuse itself of any duty to resolve the conflict it had exacerbated. Indigenous organizations and the other critical groups argued to the contrary, claiming that OPIC had the moral and legal obligation to require the companies to democratize the program.

Ascending Antagonism: Indigenous and Allied Responses to Fortress Conservation

Over the next several years, Indigenous groups and allied organizations employed a suite of different measures—including direct actions, letter writing, negotiations, and press outreach—to pressure the conservation organizations and companies to step down from the board and allow Indigenous peoples to govern the program. While some of these efforts persuaded state institutions to take action, the state response would prove weak and fractured. At the surface, the environmental ministry initially issued strong statements condemning the program in defense of national sovereignty, but in practice it never used its authority to stop the program from operating: "They did their business amongst themselves. They are going to use the land to put the pipeline in. They are going to see that the environment will not be hurt. They are judge and jury. . . . This is my country, those are my natural resources, and I am in charge of them. And now we are going to give responsibility to third parties?" (Langman 2000).

Despite some damning declarations issued by supportive state authorities— the congressional Commission on Sustainable Development, Indigenous congressmen, and the national ombudsman, Ana Maria Campero—the

Indigenous groups' efforts to democratize the conservation program would be thwarted by an elite-dominated prefecture in Santa Cruz and a debilitated environmental ministry that was largely beholden to the companies.

The struggle over the conservation program began with a divided decision among Indigenous groups and technical advisers. Without consulting with Chiquitano and Ayoreo organizations—which would soon reject the program altogether—the main lowland Indigenous federation (CIDOB) and its technical arm (Center for Indigenous Territorial Planning) asked the companies to grant Indigenous groups three spots on the board; on June 23, 1999, CIDOB sent a letter to OPIC demanding respect for rights established in ILO Convention 169 and demanded that it require the companies to include two Indigenous representatives and one technical adviser on the program board (one Indigenous representative and one non-Indigenous technical adviser from CIDOB, and one Indigenous representative from CPESC representing Indigenous peoples in the Department of Santa Cruz). Although neither OPIC nor the companies heeded the request, CIDOB would go on to participate with the program before eventually capitulating to the Chiquitanos' request to withdraw and cease any affiliation. While CIDOB's move was driven by good intentions to increase Indigenous participation in the program, it would tragically deepen an existing divide between CIDOB and the Chiquitanos.

The next month environmental organizations stepped up their campaign to democratize the program. Amazon Watch and FOBOMADE spearheaded a sign-on letter (signed by Rios Vivos Coalition, International Rivers, Rainforest Action Network, and Project Underground) to the conservation organizations lambasting them for (1) encouraging OPIC to finance the pipeline along the controversial route through the forest; (2) setting a bad precedent that corporations can buy conservation organizations to greenstamp destructive development projects, undermining the efforts of NGOs and communities opposed to them; (3) blatantly excluding peoples of the Chiquitano and Bolivian environmental groups from negotiations; (4) taking advantage of environmental groups opposing the loan (i.e., the signatories) to increase funding for the conservation program; and (5) agreeing to the controversial route because the companies gave them $20 million. Under intense pressure, on September 11, 1999, an embattled WWF withdrew from the program, citing conflicts of interest and lack of transparency, as well as lack of local participation in governance (WWF 2000). WWF's reputation in Bolivia and abroad was clearly at stake. The organization was reeling from criticism that Enron and Shell had used it to green-stamp a destructive pipeline that would ironically degrade one of the most prized ecoregions that WWF claimed to defend.

After several weeks of attempting to reform the conservation program from within, WWF recognized that the companies and other conservation organizations were unwilling to yield decision-making power to Indigenous groups and other local actors. According to its own public account, WWF proposed that local actors serve on the governing board, but certain individuals from the companies and conservation organizations resisted. Representatives from Shell and the Wildlife Conservation Society even explored the possibility of administering the program by creating an NGO based in the United States, which would have reduced legal risks and secured control by the conservation organizations and companies—a form of offshore evasion. In the ensuing weeks, representatives from the other conservation organizations, the US State Department, and Shell tried to convince WWF to rejoin the conservation program, but it never did because the program was not fundamentally changed. However, it would subsequently maintain a collaborative role with the conflictive initiative, even going so far as to state that it hoped the money it had raised independently could be used as matching funds.

In an apparent attempt to control damage from the organization's controversial involvement in the program, a few weeks later the president of WWF-US wrote a letter to the vice president of the United States, Al Gore, calling on the government to prohibit OPIC from financing the pipeline because the Chiquitano forest was primary. While symbolically important, the move would not accomplish this goal, although it added to pressure that would eventually lead OPIC to cancel the loan for the pipeline after Enron's bankruptcy in 2002.

Over the course of the next year, Indigenous leaders and allied organizations educated affected communities about the controversial conservation program. This led to an increasingly organized front across the region. In April 2000, as a result of concerted lobbying, the environmental ministry sent a letter to the conservation organizations opposing the program. The agency stated the program was operating illegally and demanded the sponsors provide information about its constitution and activities (OICH and CEADES 2004). Mirroring the past, the action raised expectations that the ministry would force the program to comply with the law, to little avail. Frustrated over several months of inaction, in August 2000 the Chiquitanos, Ayoreos, and the Collective for Applied Studies and Social Development (Colectivo de Estudios Aplicados y Desarrollo Social, CEADES) bypassed the environmental ministry altogether. They invited the companies to negotiate while simultaneously lobbying sympathetic regional state institutions—the environmental division of the Santa Cruz prefecture and the departmental council. The next month the environmental division of the prefecture, one of the few regional institutions supportive of Indigenous demands, sent a report to the sympathetic departmental council, denouncing the companies and conservationists for violating human rights, allegedly committing biopiracy, and illegally negotiating natural resources of the Chiquitano forest. In response, the council issued a resolution calling on the state authorities in La Paz—including the environmental ministry—to stop the program from violating national sovereignty. It denounced the companies and conservation organizations for supplanting the Bolivian state and municipal authorities in the management and administration of the Chiquitano forest (in violation of the Bolivian Constitution and environmental law). The council demanded that Enron and Shell democratize the governance structure of the program. Chiquitano and Ayoreo organizations also presented a forceful letter to the prefecture requesting that it not grant the program legal status (*personería jurídica*). In response, the prefecture's legal division conducted a review and submitted a report to the prefecture confirming that the program was indeed operating without legal status (OICH 2000).

Using a carrot-and-stick approach, on September 4, 2000, CPESC, the umbrella organization representing Indigenous peoples of Santa Cruz (including the Chiquitanos), sent a proposal to the conservation organizations and companies that included seven programs to be managed through the Indigenous compensation program—an effort to create an autonomous Indigenous conservation program. Three days later the main Chiquitano organization, Organización Indígena Chiquitana (OICH), issued a resolution stating that it would expel parties representing the conservation program from the Chiquitanos' territory. The Chiquitanos voted that they would detain the vehicles used by the conservation program authorities whenever they entered Chiquitano communities. By mid-September the Chiquitanos and Ayoreos lost patience that the companies had not disbursed funds for the Indigenous compensation program. Mainly because of this issue and partly out of frustration over the exclusionary conservation program, they made a pragmatic choice to carry out radical direct actions to pressure the companies (detailed further below). On September 17, communities at the southern end of the pipeline peacefully took over a worker camp for the pipeline. Simultaneously, communities at the northern end of the pipeline erected blockades, took over worker camps, and confiscated company equipment. Compelled by these actions, the companies agreed to disburse compensation funds but rejected the Indigenous proposal for an autonomous conservation program, maintaining their position that the existing program was a legitimate and legal private agreement. They invited the Indigenous groups to apply to the existing program to fund separate conservation projects but insisted they would not step down from the board or permit Indigenous representatives to serve on it. The Chiquitanos and Ayoreos rejected this invitation, standing firm in their position that they should control the program, contending that the interests of the companies and conservation groups were at odds with their own. They reaffirmed that the program must be restructured in accordance with their rights as established under ILO Convention 169. Yet because the companies conceded to their chief demands regarding the compensation funds, they suspended direct actions on September 24, making no gains on the conservation program. While at the time this was a pragmatic decision to gain what they perceived was feasible, in retrospect it was likely a missed opportunity because the companies were significantly harmed by work stoppage on the pipeline.

Not until March 2001 did any further significant developments occur. At this time, the Chiquitanos and Ayoreos—with support from CEADES and legal support organization CEJIS—presented a legal claim to the Santa Cruz ombudsman. They argued that the conservation program had violated Indigenous rights and asserted that government authorities at the national level had not heeded their various denunciations. The principal peasant federation of Santa Cruz (Federación Sindical Única de Trabajadores Campesinos) and PROBIOMA supported this claim and sent letters to the national ombudsman and environmental ministry, urging the institutions to take action. The action was indicative of broader convergence between campesino and Indigenous groups that was occurring in the lead-up to the election of Evo Morales. Once again under pressure, the ministry sent the conservation program a warning letter asking it to comply with the law. But when the program sponsors refused to heed the ministry's request, claiming its activities were legitimate, the agency did not enforce its action.

Two months later, several Chiquitano and Ayoreo organizations (OICH, CANOB, CIPSJ, CIPABA, and CICOL), along with parent organization CPESC, presented yet another legal petition to the prefecture of Santa Cruz asking it not to grant the conservation program legal status. Unsure if it would act in their favor, they submitted a legal complaint to the national ombudsman, citing the fact that the prefecture had not even acted on its own resolutions condemning the program. Pushed to respond, the prefecture declared that it would not decide whether to grant the program legal status and deferred the decision to the environmental ministry. Non-Indigenous civic committees from the region then followed suit, sending requests to deny legal status to the Santa Cruz ombudsman and prefecture. In addition, they adopted more radical measures, voting to reject the conservation program outright and expel it from the region.

In July 2001 WWF-UK evaluated the conservation program and released a report concluding that it had increased social and environmental conflicts, constituting a risk for the sustainability of the forest and Indigenous peoples living within it. This finding resonates with an emerging body of research on conservation that pragmatically recognizes effective conservation must consider social justice, emancipation, and cultural integrity (Robinson 2011). A 2004 self-evaluation produced by CEADES and the Chiquitanos (OICH and CEADES 2004) would later reach a similar conclusion, that by excluding Indigenous peoples from "using, administering and conserving natural resources" the program had violated Bolivian and international laws and threatened the forest's long-term integrity. More broadly, the case would corroborate research showing that when centralized authorities significantly alter local institutions managing natural resources, widespread resistance and conflict over management often ensues (Robbins et al. 2009; Brockington 2002).

Frustrated that the Santa Cruz prefecture and the environmental ministry did not take action, in September 2001 the national ombudsman, Ana Maria Campero—a highly respected defender of Indigenous rights in Bolivia (a rarity under neoliberal regimes)—sent a letter to the ministry threatening to take the matter to the president and other state institutions if it did not modify the conservation program in compliance with Indigenous rights outlined in ILO Convention 169 and other pertinent laws. This would prove to be the most significant action taken by any state institution yet would cause the ministry to take only limited action several months later.

Finally, after three years of pressure, in July 2002 the ministry issued the conservation organizations a formal warning and gave them sixty days to comply with the law. Nonetheless, almost predictably, they did not heed this directive, and the ministry did not enforce its order. Consequently, Indigenous groups and allied organizations called upon the agency to carry out a full environmental audit of the pipeline—as specified in the environmental law—based on this and various other violations (detailed in subsequent chapters). But capitulating once again to the companies, the ministry rejected this demand, agreeing to only a superficial field inspection in April 2003, accompanied by a small contingent of representatives from other state institutions. To the dismay of the Chiquitanos, Ayoreos, and their supporters, this lip-service inspection proved to have little effect because the conservation program continued operating. Worse yet, the inspection revealed that in January 2003 the elite-dominated Prefecture of Santa Cruz had gone back on its previous decision and granted the program legal status. Further, CEADES and the Santa Cruz Indigenous organization CPESC published a letter to the prefecture written by a representative of the conservation program that threatened to cancel a forthcoming donation the program was going to make to the prefecture if it did not grant the program legal status and tax-exempt status (CPESC and CEADES 2003). Once again, neoliberal state institutions at the national and regional level had shown a lack of political will stemming from their complicity with transnational capital. José Bailaba, a Chiquitano member of Congress, stated: "It is concerning in this initial phase that government authorities responsible for the inspection, who should be enforcing national laws and defending the public interest, are being hosted, and apparently assisted financially, by the corporations. While this sort of dependence exists transparency in the process is unlikely" (Hindery 2003b).

Anticipating this might be the case, the Indigenous groups and CEADES conducted a simultaneous "shadow" audit, which concluded that the conservation groups were ignoring the ministry's warning and had even tried to buy support from communities by offering medical services. Frustrated that four years of pressure had not changed the program, in 2004 the Chiquitanos used newly elected Indigenous congressional leaders to convince the congressional Commission on Sustainable Development to hold a hearing in the region to resolve the conflict and to address lack of compliance with the Indigenous compensation agreement and impacts caused by the pipeline. This effort succeeded, and in April 2004 the commission interrogated representatives from the companies and conservation organizations for possible violations of the environmental law, forestry law, constitution, and civil code, as well as for committing biopiracy, falsifying public documents, operating without legal status, and distributing expired medicine to community members in exchange for their consent to the conservation program (*El Deber* 2004). The commission also criticized the manner in which the forest was classified as secondary rather than primary. After the hearing concluded, the commission instructed the ministry to initiate a full-fledged environmental audit (as specified under the environmental law). Yet even this supportive action would not be sufficient to persuade neoliberal authorities at the national level to act, and it would be the last major event to democratize the program during the neoliberal era. At least the Indigenous compensation program, while fraught with its own issues, would bring more tangible benefits to affected communities.

At the international level, Enron's 2002 bankruptcy made virtually no difference on the ground, particularly because OPIC washed its hands of liability after canceling the infamous $200 million loan for the Cuiabá pipeline. In 2004 the US Bankruptcy Court for the Southern District of New York ruled that Enron's heirs in Bolivia (first Prisma Energy International, subsequently Ashmore Energy International) had to continue funding the conservation program and respond to alleged violations. But the governance structure of the program remained unchanged, and social and environmental impacts continued to be generated by the pipeline.

In this chapter, I have sketched the broad contours of Indigenous mobilization surrounding the Cuiabá case, situating it within broader mobilization occurring throughout the country, particularly in relation to neoliberal projects and policies. I have contended that the conservationists' marginalization of Indigenous peoples and subordination of their knowledge reflected a Western environmentalist worldview that prioritizes "wild" nature over peopled landscapes. I have claimed that Indigenous mobilization to restructure the fortress-style conservation program was a struggle for access and control over natural resources, identity, and livelihood—key areas of inquiry within the field of political ecology. And I have argued that the Chiquitanos' and Ayoreos' strategic use of Indigeneity, their judicious engagement with allies, and their careful selection of mobilization tactics reflect what I call *dynamic pragmatism*. I elaborate more on this concept in the subsequent chapters, first in the context of struggle over consultation, compensation, and territory.

CHAPTER FIVE

Struggling for Consultation, Compensation, and Territory

Calling for Compensation

To obtain an environmental license from the Bolivian government and a $200 million loan from the US government's Overseas Private Investment Corporation (OPIC), Enron and Shell were obligated to carry out consultations and fund a community compensation program, known as the Indigenous Development Plan, for Chiquitano and Ayoreo Indigenous peoples affected by the Cuiabá pipeline, as described in chapter 3. Creation of the program was not, then, a humanitarian gesture of corporate goodwill but rather a self-serving act to gain financing and authorization for the project. Moreover, it was required by the Bolivian environmental law, International Labor Organization (ILO) Convention 169 on Indigenous and tribal peoples and the internal directives of the World Bank (which were followed by OPIC). The program's stated goals were to avoid and mitigate adverse social and environmental consequences on communities and to promote equitable and sustainable development (Entrix-Bolivia 1999:1), yet from the outset, it was clear that the companies and OPIC had merely reduced Indigenous rights to "compensation," which they considered an unavoidable cost of the project (OICH and CEADES 2004:114). In this chapter, I show how the Chiquitanos and Ayoreos struggled against this myopic view, instead advocating for a long-term, self-sustaining, autonomous program that genuinely improved living conditions, secured control over land and other natural resources, and ensured cultural survival. I show how, whereas the alternatives proposed by the Chiquitanos and Ayoreos had cultural underpinnings, the community development initiatives designed by the companies reflected neoliberal and modernist ideologies. I argue that the Chiquitanos and Ayoreos persuaded other actors to respect their rights by reclaiming their Indigenous identity and by using a dynamic and pragmatic mix of direct actions, lobbying, negotiations, and press outreach at multiple geographic scales.

Between September 1997 and December 1998, Entrix-PCA, the consulting firm hired by Enron and Shell, carried out consultations and drafted a compensation program for Chiquitano and Ayoreo communities affected by the Cuiabá pipeline as part of the project's environmental impact assessment process (Entrix-Bolivia 1999:2; GasOriente Boliviano et al. 1999:4). Initially, the company consulted with only five Chiquitano communities and two Ayoreo communities, excluding twenty-nine other communities located in the pipeline's area of influence (OICH and CEADES 2004:37). It merely consulted with the Federation of Indigenous Peoples of Bolivia (Confederación de Pueblos Indígenas de Bolivia, CIDOB), the main lowland Indigenous federation, and two regional Chiquitano organizations, bypassing the more radical Chiquitano Indigenous Organization (Organización Indígena Chiquitana, OICH)—the parent organization representing the Chiquitanos—and the Council of Ethnic Peoples of Santa Cruz (Coordinadora de Pueblos Étnicos de Santa Cruz, CPESC), the regional umbrella organization representing Indigenous peoples of the Department of Santa Cruz, which included the Chiquitanos. After consulting with the seven communities, Entrix-PCA spent a full seven months (from November 1997 to May 1998) negotiating exclusively with one non-Indigenous technical adviser from CIDOB without informing the Chiquitano and Ayoreo organizations or the communities. The Chiquitanos and legal support organization Center for Juridical Studies and Social Investigation (Centro de Estudios Jurídicos e Investigación Social, CEJIS) criticized this person for being a functionary of transnational oil corporations and the World Bank. A first draft of a compensation program was developed by the companies and this individual, with no Indigenous participation. It largely reflected the technocratic vision of the document's architects, with little resonance with Chiquitano and Ayoreo reality.

Chiquitano leaders condemned Entrix-PCA for carrying out a consultation process that was undemocratic, incomplete, and not transparent. They accused the company of bypassing community members altogether, instead "buying off" uninformed community authorities by paying them $100 in exchange for signing agreements that transferred the communities' easement rights to the company (OICH and CEADES 2004:147).

Entrix-PCA simply informed the communities that the pipeline was a project of national interest, without providing adequate information and without asking them whether they wanted the project. This had the effect of building momentum for project approval and repressing potential opposition early on. Ultimately, Enron and Shell circumvented the Chiquitano organizations and signed an umbrella agreement with CIDOB in which the companies paid a mere $1,000 for easement rights along the entire pipeline route.

Outraged that the companies were running roughshod over their rights, between May and June 1998 the Chiquitanos began to build a more unified movement aimed at developing a compensation program that would truly improve the livelihood of affected communities. The main Chiquitano organization, OICH, demanded a series of workshops be held in which the Chiquitanos would review the existing draft of the compensation program (OICH and CEADES 2004:152). In these meetings, the Chiquitanos made some significant gains. First, they managed to separate the Indigenous compensation program from a separate non-Indigenous compensation fund for local municipalities. This was a significant assertion of autonomy over the administration of "development" projects in their territories, with land tenure being the chief demand. Moreover, the Chiquitanos felt it was essential they administer funds rather than elite-dominated municipalities vying to control the resources and negotiations. In addition, the Chiquitanos helped to convince the companies to include two Ayoreo communities that had been excluded, along with Ayoreo Native Center of Eastern Bolivia (Central Ayorea Nativa del Oriente Boliviano, CANOB), the regional Ayoreo organization. Finally, recognizing that Entrix-PCA had no real decision-making power, the Chiquitanos insisted that Enron and Shell send representatives to negotiate.

Based on these slightly improved but still superficial consultations, in December 1998 Entrix-PCA finalized a draft proposal for the compensation program—as part of the project's environmental impact study—totaling $600,000 and consisting of four key projects: agricultural and livestock production, land titling, organizational strengthening, and handicrafts. Inspiration for some of these projects came from a compensation program previously developed for Guaraní and Ayoreo communities affected by the main Bolivia-Brazil pipeline—a program that had excluded the Chiquitanos. Later that same month, unbeknownst to the Chiquitanos and Ayoreos—and without their consent—the companies presented the draft compensation program to the Ministry of Sustainable Development as part of the pipeline's environmental impact study. On December 17, 1998, the agency approved the deficient study—which did not adequately evaluate long-term impacts—and granted the companies a license to build the pipeline, disregarding that the communities had not agreed to the compensation plan.

Appalled by what happened, in January 1999 the Chiquitanos organized across communities and organizations and developed a unified front with a more radical agenda. Radicalization deepened further when the companies committed yet another audacious act in violation of the Chiquitanos' rights: in the beginning of January, the companies attempted to reach an agreement with old leaders from the lowland indigenous federation, CIDOB, excluding newly elected leaders who had expressed solidarity with the Chiquitanos' demands. This prompted the Chiquitanos, along with the new leaders at CIDOB, to declare their opposition to the pipeline because their rights had been violated, particularly the right to free, prior, and informed consultation, the right to just compensation, and the right to benefit from development projects. They demanded full participatory review of the environmental impact study, including the compensation program. Looking for new pressure points, the Chiquitanos and allied organizations learned that although the environmental license had been granted, the companies still needed to secure financing from OPIC before they could begin construction. With a new tool in hand, they began to use this hurdle as leverage to negotiate a more inclusive and better funded compensation program:

> When we learned the environmental impact study for the Cuiabá pipeline was approved and that the company had already received the license from the government to begin construction we thought all that remained was to obligate the company to comply strictly with the environmental impact study; then we discovered that there are laws that defend Indigenous rights and also some directives outside of Bolivian law: OPIC required an Indigenous compensation program . . . this was an opportunity for the communities to demand and exercise their rights. (OICH and CEADES 2004:143)

At the Chiquitanos' request, on January 22 the new leaders at CIDOB sent a letter to OPIC officially stating that CIDOB would oppose the pipeline until there was agreement on a compensation program (OICH and CEADES 2004:156). This marked the beginning of a period of intense negotiations with company representatives over the compensation program, which continued until May 1999, when a final agreement was reached. As a result of the Chiquitanos' forceful demands, negotiations during the period were more transparent and participatory than before. Because of the pressure, the companies agreed to include all Chiquitano organizations in all subsequent meetings.

Recalling the divisive manner in which Entrix-PCA had elaborated the original compensation proposal, in February 1999 the Chiquitanos developed a set of ground rules about how negotiation would be conducted and regarding compensation itself. They made an interregional agreement across communities that compensation should be proportional to the number of individuals and communities affected in each area, and they established a principle that negotiation be carried out jointly so as to avoid division and uneven distribution of benefits. Negotiation was to be conducted directly with official representatives from Enron and Shell, not with consultants or intermediaries: "We only realized the role Entrix played after months of negotiation . . . so we said 'We want to talk to the pig's owner, not its caretaker'" (OICH and CEADES 2004:126).

The negotiating team was to be composed purely of Indigenous leaders, limiting the role of technical advisers. Legal actions were deemed to be used only as a last resort. Finally, the compensation program was to be self-governed by the Chiquitanos and Ayoreos and was to generate self-sustaining community projects that would endure for as long as possible. While in practice these guidelines were not always met, they functioned as laudable ideals and improved interactions and benefits to some degree.

Reenergized with greater solidarity and a clearer political path, in mid-February Chiquitano and Ayoreo communities and organizations reviewed Entrix-PCA's draft compensation proposal. At the end of the month, pivotal, three-day-long negotiations were held among the Indigenous organizations (the Chiquitano and Ayoreo organizations CPESC and CIDOB), the Collective for Applied Studies and Social Development (Colectivo de Estudios Aplicados y Desarrollo Social, CEADES), and the companies. Indigenous representatives signed a memorandum of intention to agree to a $1.5 million compensation program and consented to sign a final document by March 16. The tentative agreement granted the Chiquitanos and Ayoreos the authority to govern the compensation program, provided land titling support for all affected communities, and funded drinking water systems in three communities.

Chiquitano and Ayoreo leaders then relayed the potential agreement to the communities and reviewed the offer more carefully. After a series of internal meetings, consensus emerged to reject the proposal because the amount was insufficient, the consultation process had been shoddy, and the program imposed a short-term development vision at odds with the

Chiquitanos' and Ayoreos' social and cultural realities (OICH and CEADES 2004:111). The Chiquitanos and Ayoreos immediately developed a counterproposal with technical support from CEADES. This began with a direct democratic process in which community members and leaders identified community needs and priorities. CEADES helped to systematize and write the results in the form of a technical document but maintained its philosophy that the Chiquitanos and Ayoreos should be the protagonists driving the process. Based on this information, leaders from OICH, in collaboration with CEADES, drafted the alternative document and then revised it with members of a negotiating team composed of representatives from OICH, CPESC, CIDOB, CANOB (the main Ayoreo organization), and two regional Chiquitano organizations. The final version was then circulated and approved by affected community members in community and regional meetings.

Alarmed that opposition could jeopardize the project, Enron and Shell agreed to engage more directly with the Indigenous organizations, displacing Entrix-PCA to a secondary, more secretarial role. Asserting their autonomy, the Chiquitanos rebuffed Entrix-PCA's assessment that only seven communities were affected by the pipeline. They argued the company had based its conclusion on a flawed criterion that affected communities were only those located in the pipeline route or crossed by access roads. To the contrary, they argued that the pipeline affected a much larger part of the Chiquitanos' territory, including water bodies and traditional hunting, fishing, farming, and gathering grounds that were vital for subsistence and cultural identity. Based on these additional criteria, the Chiquitanos proposed that Enron and Shell compensate a total of thirty-four communities: twenty-four affected directly, where settlements were located within ten kilometers of the proposed route, and ten affected indirectly, where areas used for subsistence were affected. An estimated 5,233 Chiquitanos were affected directly, and 2,283 were affected indirectly (OICH and CEADES 2004:36). Two Ayoreo communities were affected by the pipeline, totaling 274 individuals.

The counterproposal that the Chiquitanos and Ayoreos ultimately produced retained the four key projects Entrix-PCA had proposed—agricultural and livestock production, land titling, organizational strengthening, and handicrafts—but differed in many respects. It demanded potable water systems in three communities as well as funding for office headquarters, office equipment, educational scholarships, training, and vehicles. It also included a project for archaeological, cultural, and tourist development, as well as support for the management of the San Matías Natural Reserve

(FAN et al. 1999:64). Besides these material demands, it requested funding for twenty-six "Indigenous environmental monitors" (one from each community directly affected by the pipeline) to independently monitor impacts caused by the pipeline (OICH and CEADES 2004:197). It called for an additional $2 million to compensate a larger number of communities and to make the proposed projects more robust.

While the counterproposal still bore the imprint of a technocratic, production-oriented model of development imposed by the companies, the new "hybrid" version to some extent articulated the Chiquitanos' and Ayoreos' own visions for the future. It was a significant departure from Entrix-PCA's original proposal. But in hindsight the Chiquitanos concluded that their position was weakened because they were inexperienced in negotiating with transnational corporations and because they feared the companies would build the pipeline along an alternative route that would exclude the Chiquitanos from the "opportunity" to be compensated (OICH and CEADES 2004: 49). Company representatives threatened community members they would begin construction whether or not there was a compensation program and stated they would request whatever "support" was necessary from the government. Some Chiquitano leaders also regretted that the communities prioritized mostly short-term needs because they felt compelled to come up with funding as soon as possible. Enron and Shell preyed on this anxiety by pressuring the Chiquitanos to accept the least amount of compensation possible and finish negotiations quickly—to avoid fines the companies alleged the Brazilian government would impose if gas was not delivered on time. This was but one of many pressures that emerged during negotiations:

> Our immediate goal was to defend the space where the company was going to build the pipeline: land titling was urgent. . . . There was fear that the pipeline would be built without our lands being titled. We wanted to defend the territory and receive just compensation. We wanted benefits to be distributed according to the communities' needs and we wanted to govern. With the main Bolivia-Brazil pipeline we didn't participate in anything. Now we wanted to change the conditions. . . . There was a history of communities being walked over in the case of this previous pipeline. So we wanted to defend the communities from being walked over during construction. The situation wasn't easy. The government pressured us. The company never told us how much it was going to profit. . . . There were various pressures. We were in front of a monster of a company. With the power it had, it could do whatever it wanted. (OICH and CEADES 2004:146)

This powerful account vividly illustrates the Chiquitanos' struggle over fundamental rights that had been won in the 1990s, particularly the right to territory, consultation, compensation, self-determination, and autonomy (e.g., governance of the compensation program). As the subsequent chapters demonstrate, these very same rights would lie at the heart of resource conflicts under the administration of Evo Morales, and the lessons learned from the Cuiabá case would prove instrumental in encouraging the government and transnationals to respect them. The statement also makes it very clear that the Chiquitanos' historical memory of their experiences with the main Bolivia-Brazil pipeline strongly influenced the actions they undertook in conjunction with the Cuiabá pipeline. This was a pattern that occurred in other sites of gas extraction and distribution in Bolivia as well, such as in Tarija, where the struggles of the Guaraní and Ween-hayek were informed by pervasive memories of territorial loss (Bebbington et al. in press). Such memories were transmitted within and among Indigenous peoples in Bolivia through "lessons learned" workshops organized by CEADES, CEJIS, and other nongovernmental organizations (NGOs).

Looking back, the Chiquitanos deplored that the companies marginalized discussion about potential environmental impacts by artificially dividing social and environmental assessment. Curiously, in their May 1999 independent study of the pipeline, the same conservation organizations that would exclude the Chiquitanos from a $20 million conservation program a month later reached a similar conclusion—that it was lamentable and erroneous that the companies divided negotiations regarding the conservation program and the Indigenous compensation program (FAN et al. 1999:65).

On March 23, 1999, another significant meeting occurred in which the companies raised their offer to $1.6 million, while the Chiquitanos lowered their demand to $2.2 million. Adding yet more pressure, the companies threatened to take the case to arbitration to resolve the conflict, which the Chiquitanos strongly opposed. The Chiquitanos and CEADES knew that the private arbiters were beholden to the companies and landowners. Over the next several weeks, Chiquitano and Ayoreo leaders consulted with affected communities, which decided to carry out direct actions—for example, blockades or strikes—if the companies did not accept the Indigenous offer. Meanwhile, despite the lack of agreement on the compensation program, on March 28 the companies requested that the state's Superintendence of Hydrocarbons grant a concession for the construction and operation of the pipeline. The agency published the request in the press, inviting the public to present any opposition within thirty days. Learning of this new leverage point, on May 7 the Chiquitanos and Ayoreos, in collaboration with legal support organization CEJIS, took legal action and presented the agency a statement of opposition to the project (OICH and CEADES 2004:216). They argued that the companies had violated ILO Convention 169 (Bolivian Law 1257) because the affected communities had not agreed to the proposed compensation. To their astonishment, the Superintendence of Hydrocarbons approved their petition, which obligated the companies to go back to the negotiating table, this time with higher-level representatives. Redoubling their efforts, the Indigenous groups threatened to erect blockades if the companies did not come through with an adequate compensation program. And back in the United States, Amazon Watch, Friends of the Earth, and the Bank Information Center (a watchdog of international financial institutions, based in Washington, DC) went as far as bringing two Chiquitano leaders to Washington, DC, to put more direct pressure on OPIC.

The three-pronged approach (threatening blockades and presenting opposition to OPIC and the superintendence) was a success. It compelled the companies to sign a compensation agreement less than a week later, on May 12, 1999. The following day, CPESC officially dropped its opposition in a joint letter to the superintendence that was written and signed by both Chiquitano leaders and company representatives. The act was yet another pragmatic decision the Chiquitanos made to prioritize the compensation agreement—which they perceived would immediately benefit their livelihood—over the perhaps riskier goals of stopping the pipeline or routing it around the forest. They remembered being excluded from compensation for the Bolivia-Brazil pipeline and, under great pressure from the companies to close a deal, opted to do so lest they lose the opportunity. But the move weakened the relatively unified front that the Chiquitanos and allied organizations (Amazon Watch, Friends of the Earth) had formed against OPIC's financing of the pipeline through the forest. For the following several weeks the latter would embark on a more solitary quest to paralyze the project while the conservation organizations (WWF, Wildlife Conservation Society, Missouri Botanical Garden, Noel Kempff Mercado Museum of Natural History, and Fundación Amigos de la Naturaleza) would engage the companies and OPIC in a dueling battle over competing studies—in search of a lucrative conservation program (see chapter 3).

During the final days of negotiations, company representatives relentlessly tried to diminish the amount of compensation, while Indigenous representatives fought to increase it over a longer time period. Ultimately, an agreement was reached in which the companies approved a two-year-long, $2 million program. Although the amount only equaled 2% of the pipeline's estimated revenues over the same period, it was triple what the companies had offered in the beginning. Mobilization had clearly paid off, yet in hindsight, the Chiquitanos regretted not pushing for a greater amount and for dropping a demand that the companies finance a long-term trust fund (included in the original counterproposal). In retrospect, they realized they had the upper hand since the companies were desperate for OPIC's loan and authorization from the superintendence.

The program that the companies and the Chiquitanos and Ayoreos ultimately secured incorporated most of demands made in the counter-proposal—agricultural and livestock production,[1] land titling, organizational strengthening, and handicrafts—plus funding for potable water systems in three communities, office headquarters, office equipment, and three pickup trucks. The organizational strengthening project included funding for twenty-six "Indigenous environmental monitors" (one from each community directly affected by the pipeline) to independently monitor impacts caused by the pipeline (OICH and CEADES 2004:197). But other demands were not met, such as educational scholarships, support for archaeological, cultural, and tourist development, or funding for the management of the San Matías Nature Reserve. Instead, the companies merely agreed to compile information and studies on the potential for tourist development in the region (GasOriente Boliviano et al. 1999:10). With respect to the archaeological initiative, they circumvented the Chiquitanos and funded a program through the government's Vice Ministry of Culture.

Although the program would have significant flaws, the Chiquitanos celebrated the fact that the conflict strengthened unification during negotiation and implementation and perceived it to be a significant improvement from previous projects that had completely excluded them, like the Bolivia-Brazil pipeline (OICH and CEADES 2004:141). And it necessitated a sort of crash course on Indigenous rights, particularly those that had been won since the rise of the lowland Indigenous movement, generating increased awareness from the community level on upward. These would prove to be powerful tools in larger mobilizations leading to the election of the country's first Indigenous president.

Compensation in Practice

Implementing the compensation program proved to be as challenging as negotiating it, and the issue of governance proved particularly problematic.

For the Chiquitanos and Ayoreos, securing a program that gave them autonomy had been a must—a lesson they had learned from the flawed compensation program for the Bolivia-Brazil pipeline (which compensated only Guaraní and Ayoreo communities). The program's governing body included representatives from two regional Chiquitano organizations, one Ayoreo organization, the umbrella Indigenous organization for Santa Cruz (CPESC), the main Chiquitano Indigenous organization (OICH), and the lowland Indigenous federation (CIDOB), as well as one company representative and one independent representative elected by Indigenous communities and the companies (Entrix-Bolivia 1999).

The composition of the body suggested Indigenous groups had control over decision making, but in practice they were significantly constrained because the companies held the power of the purse and pressured Indigenous representatives to vote the company line. The Chiquitanos' and Ayoreos' struggles for autonomous governance had won significant representation, but economic power concentrated in the hands of the companies thwarted Indigenous efforts to implement their visions. Company representatives claimed that decisions were reached through consensus and therefore rarely required a vote. However, the executive coordinator of the program maintained that company representatives directed negotiations and led Indigenous representatives to reach agreements that served the companies' interests. Similarly, although company representatives asserted that the program was governed by Indigenous leaders, the Board of Evaluation of Programs and Funds, which approved the disbursement of funds, was composed of two company representatives and only one Indigenous representative. The board froze funds when the companies disagreed with how money was spent, which limited the Chiquitanos and Ayoreos from adapting projects to their shifting needs and priorities. Indigenous representatives from the governing body reported that on numerous occasions they had to aggressively demand that funds be disbursed. Most notable was a sixteen-day-long action in September 2000 when communities at both ends of the pipeline erected blockades, took over worker camps, and confiscated equipment and vehicles to force the companies to immediately disburse the $1,020,000 that was already due (after failed negotiations). They alleged that the companies' sporadic and partial payments constituted illegal retention. They also demanded the conservation program be restructured (as detailed in the preceding chapter) and insisted the companies fulfill commitments to support land titling.

Under financial duress since construction was stopped, high-level executives from Enron and Shell entered the scene and invited Indigenous representatives to dialogue, requesting that the actions be suspended. The

Indigenous groups conceded, and two delegations of Indigenous leaders and their technical advisers met with company representatives to reach a solution. The Indigenous team persuaded the companies to disburse the compensation funds and convinced them to restore damaged roads, install potable water systems, and complete construction of offices.

The mobilization served as a reminder to the Chiquitanos and Ayoreos that even in a David-and-Goliath battle, they still had considerable power. With a weak state wedded to transnational capital, they realized that direct actions or even threats of direct actions—strikes, blockades, equipment confiscation, takeovers of worker camps—were highly effective in forcing the companies to comply with their contractual and legal requirements. Yet they often did not deploy such tactics at will but guarded them as a last resort after other measures failed. This lesson would resonate with other struggles occurring throughout Bolivia during the neoliberal era and would later prove valuable in checking the developmentalist agenda of the Morales administration. Guarayo leader Bienvenido Sacu, who served as secretary for land and territory in the lowland Indigenous federation (CIDOB) and was a key ally for the Chiquitanos and Ayoreos during the Cuiabá conflict, contended that Indigenous groups had no choice but to engage in strikes and blockades to compel the companies to comply with their commitments (Langman 2002). He would later be elected to congress and went on to serve as director of native communal lands (tierras comunitarias de origen, TCOs) in the Vice Ministry of Lands (Viceministerio de Tierras) under Morales. Yet even under an administration that was reputedly more favorable toward Indigenous peoples, he would ironically go on to criticize the Morales administration when he became a spokesperson during the historic 2011 march to stop a highway from cutting through the Isiboro-Sécure Indigenous Territory and National Park, known as TIPNIS (see chapter 10). In 2002, a Chiquitano leader who would later run for congress as a member of the Movement Toward Socialism (Movimiento al Socialismo) political party called for unification and radicalization in order to pressure the companies: "We have many desires to be able to join together hand to hand in order to confront this situation, because this, companions, is a war of rifles against sling-shots, but those of us who are using the sling-shots are not backing up one step, and we are ready to shoot the rifles" (interview by author).

Struggling for Sustainability

After Enron and Shell began building the Cuiabá pipeline, the Chiquitanos and Ayoreos renewed their demand for a long-term, self-sustaining, autonomous compensation program as they began to experience adverse social and environmental impacts (see chapter 6). They argued that the companies should extend the program longer than the initial period agreed on (two years) because the amount was insufficient and because they believed they should be compensated for long-term impacts that were emerging (e.g., those mentioned in reports produced by OICH, CEADES, and Amazon Watch).[2] They demanded the companies only extend the program not just for as long as the pipeline operated (estimated at forty years) but for as long as social and environmental impacts occurred, a right supported by ILO Convention 169, particularly the right to participate in the economic benefits of projects that affect Indigenous peoples and the right to receive reparations for damages. One Chiquitano community member expressed hope that with combined pressure from allied organizations the Chiquitanos might succeed in this goal: "With their support [allies] perhaps we will be able to recuperate something for 40 years. If not, it will show that our rights are not respected. We have every right since the pipeline crosses through our province, near our communities and even affects some peoples' houses" (interview by author).

Over the next few years, allied pressure would help extend the program multiple times. Friends of the Earth and Amazon Watch garnered international press coverage and lobbied key decision makers in OPIC, the agencies overseeing OPIC (USAID, the US Treasury, and the US State Department), and Enron and Shell. The NGOs pointed out central problems with the program and urged company executives to finance its extension. Friends of the Earth initiated a campaign involving a number of "socially and environmentally conscious" shareholders who worked to improve Enron's practices. This was critical in encouraging John Hardy, Jr., Enron International's vice president for project finance, to visit Bolivia and listen to issues expressed by Friends of the Earth, Amazon Watch, and Indigenous groups (see chapter 6).

Because they feared more protests and were under pressure from allied organizations, a few months before financing for the program expired company representatives entered into negotiations with Indigenous groups and agreed to extend the original two-year program for an additional ten months, until October 2001. The extension provided further support for land titling, Indigenous monitoring of the process, technical and legal training for a legal adviser, and independent studies on the potential for local economic development activities, such as tourism. Subsequent mobilizations forced the companies to extend the program again until 2006 and then again through 2010 (see chapter 9).

During these negotiations, Indigenous leaders persuaded the companies to modify community projects, which they felt were still culturally inappropriate and poorly designed—a relic of the Entrix-PCA consultants. As the program was implemented, communities exerted autonomy and were selective about which projects they prioritized and how they were put into practice—albeit with resistance from company monitors. Chiquitanos in one community decided to have a fish farm instead of cattle ranching because their territory was small: "What failed us is that the community is very small. The people didn't want the cattle project due to a lack of land. . . . Therefore, we didn't implement it, but instead used the money to build a fish farm" (Chiquitano community member, interview by author).

Chiquitanos in one community complained that they had not received enough cattle. In another community, the chicken and agriculture projects had been only partially implemented. Chiquitano women lamented that the chicken projects were failing because they lacked funding for feed and transportation. In October 2001, Chiquitano leaders sent a scathing letter to an Enron official in charge of social and corporate responsibility. They criticized Enron for designing problematic initiatives, such as the farming and livestock projects, which did not achieve the results promised in the initial agreement.

In evaluating the program overall during the first few years, the Chiquitanos and Ayoreos had mixed impressions. The program—a hybrid of mixed modern and "traditional" practices—had, to a certain extent, met some subsistence needs and brought more income into communities. But the scattered projects lacked an overarching vision of Indigenous autonomy and had not genuinely brought about community-based governance (OICH and CEADES 2004:810). Although the program brought some modest material benefits to the Indigenous organizations (e.g., office equipment, vehicles, and computers), in retrospect the Chiquitanos felt it should have done more to train leaders. They cautioned that they should not lose sight of the more significant goal of making their organizations sustainable without relying on funding from the program: "Organization strengthening should not be reduced to the computers and vehicles we received through the compensation program. Our organizations should continue standing when compensation ceases. We want what we started to be sustainable" (OICH and CEADES 2004:181).

The Chiquitanos were pleased that the program had curbed emigration to cities from the communities, a result paralleling communities elsewhere that have slowed emigration by fusing modern and traditional practices (Bebbington 1993). Yet they were concerned that some of the programs (e.g., small-scale cattle ranching) might not be environmentally sustainable in the long term. They expressed a desire to reorient the program such that it more adequately ensured the forest be conserved based on Traditional Ecological Knowledge.

Regarding equity, income and material differences within and across communities emerged over time. Even though the Chiquitanos and Ayoreos negotiated an umbrella compensation program for all affected communities, some communities negotiated separate, add-on agreements for varying amounts (including schools, hand-held radios, road improvements, and wells). This was a legacy of Entrix-PCA's "divide and conquer" consultation approach. Since the total compensation amount for the program was insufficient, Chiquitano and Ayoreo communities created a rotating fund so that all families would eventually participate in successive rounds, yet not all families took part.

Engendering Inequality

Of the $2 million designated for the compensation program, only $100,000 was destined for handicrafts production (e.g., bags, baskets, necklaces), a project that had been demanded by Chiquitano and Ayoreo women seeking income-generating activities. While the project's purported aim was laudable—to support activities practiced by Chiquitano and Ayoreo women and revitalize cultural traditions—the amount of funding allocated to the endeavor was disproportionate compared with other projects. Funding for agricultural and livestock production—primarily oriented toward male Chiquitanos—made up the lion's share of the budget, totaling $1,232,004, followed by organizational strengthening ($558,067) and administration and management ($81,616) (GasOriente Boliviano et al. 1999:8).

Chiquitano and Ayoreo women complained about disproportionate funding and pointed out that in some communities it was never implemented and in others disbursement of funds was delayed. The project also focused only on producing goods for the market, instead of improving subsistence activities—for example, subsistence farming and collecting medicinal plants. These issues provided a window into broader gender asymmetries in the program, which in part reflected the fact that negotiations were primarily led by male leaders. These patterns were similar to those exhibited in the cases of the Chad-Cameroon oil pipeline and the West Africa pipelines, which "exacerbated existing gender discriminations and inequalities by depriving women of their critical livelihoods and favoring men in consultation, hiring and compensation schemes" (Lowman 2011:25). Looking back at implementation over the first few years, the Chiquitanos concluded that besides creating gender inequities, the program had not sufficiently benefited children (e.g., through educational support) or elderly community members (OICH and CEADES 2004:180).

From Conspiracy to Compensation

In 2002 a high-profile scandal gave the Chiquitanos and Ayoreos a new tool with which to demand an additional compensation program for social and environmental impacts caused by Bolivian president Gonzalo Sánchez de Lozada's Don Mario gold mine, located in the heart of the Chiquitano forest (chapter 2). The conspiracy, which involved Enron and Shell, the World Bank, and Sánchez de Lozada, would illustrate how concerted mobilization between the Chiquitanos and allied organizations could work past an unsympathetic neoliberal regime to pressure the World Bank and companies to comply with laws requiring compensation. A chain reaction ensued after I received a press release suggesting the mine—cofinanced by the World Bank—was going to reactivate by illegally tapping natural gas from Enron and Shell's Cuiabá pipeline.[3] After notifying the Chiquitanos and Ayoreos, I visited the mine with Indigenous leaders, CEADES, and a visiting delegation from the Amazon Alliance[4] in September 2002. We witnessed the mine company Empresa Minera Paititi (EMIPA), a subsidiary of Canada's Orvana Minerals Corporation, which in turn was controlled by Sánchez de Lozada's Bolivian company, Mining Company of the South (Compañía Minera del Sur, COMSUR), building an unauthorized four-kilometer pipeline to tap the Cuiabá pipeline from a gas outtake valve that Enron and Shell had secretly left behind. Infuriated that EMIPA did not obtain their free, prior, and informed consent or offer a compensation program—violating ILO Convention 169, Bolivia's environmental law, and World Bank directives—the Chiquitanos and Ayoreos presented a legal petition to the World Bank compliance adviser/ombudsman (CPESC 2003). They cited various violations of their rights and demanded compensation, arguing that the World Bank had a duty to persuade the companies to act because it was an 11.1% shareholder in COMSUR.

Simultaneously, Amazon Watch, Friends of the Earth, CEADES, the Chiquitanos, and the Ayoreos all engaged in domestic and international press outreach to gain additional leverage, which led to highly visible coverage in the tumultuous months leading up to Sánchez de Lozada's ouster (during the October 2003 gas war). In response, the ombudsman conducted an investigation from August 24 to September 3, 2003, which found that consultation was inadequate (International Finance Corporation 2003:15). Despite this apparent victory for the Indigenous groups, both the World Bank and EMIPA questioned the Indigeneity of the five communities affected by the mine, essentially seeing "Indigenous identities as anachronistic" (Lucero 2008:189). The Indigenous organizations thus continued concerted pressure, most notably during a seminal march in Potosi, Bolivia, where approximately one hundred Indigenous people from twenty-two communities affected by COMSUR's highland mines joined Chiquitanos affected by the Puquio Norte and Don Mario gold mines. The action, supported by CEADES, was held in July 2004, on the World Bank's sixtieth birthday, at the close of the bank's extractive industries review. Marchers held banners stating "COMSUR + World Bank make more poverty" and "COMSUR and World Bank: no to the violation of human rights," demanding compensation for social and environmental damage (Friends of the Earth International 2004). Ultimately, as a result of combined pressure, the Chiquitanos and Ayoreos won a battle of identity politics and negotiated a five-year, $620,000 Indigenous compensation program in 2006. Although issues would arise during implementation that paralleled outcomes of the compensation program for the pipeline, overall it was viewed as an improvement (see chapter 9).

Struggling for Territory

Recognizing that the Cuiabá pipeline would induce destructive development activities in the Chiquitano forest and Pantanal wetlands, the Chiquitanos made land titling one of the central components of the Indigenous compensation program. Given the imminent threats to their lands—large-scale ranching, farming, logging, and mining—they viewed it as essential for cultural survival. For the Chiquitanos, the struggle to receive land titles was about defense of livelihood, an assertion of identity, autonomy, and resource control (Offen 2003:47). Territories they demanded contained the natural resources necessary for subsistence and market activities and were intimately intertwined with cultural practices. The Ayoreos did not participate because the two communities affected by the pipeline had already received titling support from other sources (including the compensation program for the main Bolivia-Brazil pipeline).

At the time when the Indigenous compensation program was being negotiated, Chiquitano communities held title to an extremely small proportion of land compared with large-scale landowners. Their deep-seated demand for land rights echoed other Indigenous groups mobilizing throughout the country to regain ancestral lands. Historically, land distribution policies in the Bolivian lowlands had benefited medium- and large-scale landowners at the expense of Indigenous and peasant populations. When Sánchez de Lozada assumed the presidency in 1993, 78,000 medium- and large-scale landowners had been granted 22.8 million hectares of economically productive land (87%), while 77,000 small-scale landowners had been granted only 3.2 million hectares of land (12.4%) (Pacheco 1998). This concentration of land was largely a function of political favoritism and corruption, which resulted from the influence of large-scale landowners (e.g., cattle ranchers, commercial farmers, and logging companies) (Bonifaz 1999:134). During the military dictatorships of General Hugo Banzer Suárez (1971–1978) and others (1980–1982), hundreds of thousands of hectares of land were fraudulently distributed to political cronies for free (some up to 50,000 hectares) (Urioste 2010:2). Indigenous lands often contained concessions or development activities with titles that were fraudulent or obtained through improper or illegal procedures (Bonifaz 1999). Multiple overlapping titles were common. Consequently, by the time Indigenous groups won the right to apply for titles, they had difficulty asserting their traditional territorial claims in the face of these conflicting claims (Paz 1999).

In the 1990s, the growing Indigenous movement in the lowlands mobilized around land as territory, blending the concepts of autonomy, alternative development, and environmental protection (Lucero 2008:92). This in turn drew upon the experience of the Iroquois Nation in North America (Healy 2001; Lucero 2006a). In 1996, Indigenous mobilization was hybridized with neoliberalism in the form of the 1996 agrarian law (Law 1715, the National Service of Agrarian Reform Law [Ley del Servicio Nacional de Reforma Agraria, commonly known as Ley INRA]). This World Bank–sponsored law aptly represented the two-headed nature of neoliberal multiculturalism in that it simultaneously enabled Indigenous groups to acquire large-scale collective land titles (TCOs) and enshrined private property rights of agribusiness (Gustafson 2002; Kohl and Farthing 2006; Lucero 2008:134). One of the most important features of the law was the creation of large-scale native communal lands (TCOs), defined as "the geographic spaces that constitute the habitat of Indigenous and native peoples and communities, to which they have traditionally had access and where they maintain and develop their own forms of economic, social, and cultural organization, so as to ensure their survival and development. They are inalienable, unseizable and imprescriptible" (Article 41) (qtd. in Garzón 2010:28, translation errors corrected by author). In this regard, TCOs represented a spatial mobilization strategy that Indigenous groups could use within the confines of neoliberal multiculturalism to secure land tenure over large tracts of land, with greater access and control over natural resources and lifeways.

Indigenous groups that applied for land titling had to decide whether to apply for simple land titles or larger TCOs. In making this decision, the former were quicker but usually resulted in smaller, fragmented land titles compared with TCOs, which were collectively owned and managed by Indigenous groups, indivisible, and could not revert back to the state. While certainly a move toward autonomy, TCOs did not grant Indigenous peoples living in the territories the right to self-government (Birk 2000:156).

As in many other cases throughout Latin America, for the Chiquitanos the right to communal land was central to autonomy and a cornerstone for collective identities formed through language, cosmology, and environmental practices (Sundberg 2008:573). Compared with the 1953 agrarian reform, which had divided lands into parcels, the new law recognized lands over a continuous space. Nonetheless, TCOs had the effect of creating "archipelagos of land" as opposed to continuous, unified tracts (Gustafson 2009:995). Within TCOs, legal existing private property was respected, but new development activity was prohibited, except for mining and hydrocarbons development, since the state retained rights to the subsoil (Birk 2000:142). During negotiations for the 1996 agrarian law, Indigenous groups managed to change the original law so that forestry concessions were not allowed on TCOs (Birk 2000:156). In cases in which forestry concessions overlapped with TCOs, TCOs were supposed to take precedence—though often not in practice. TCOs were vulnerable to state expropriation for conservation purposes and cases of national interest, such as the Cuiabá pipeline. Despite these drawbacks, by the inception of the Cuiabá pipeline they were used to bring legal actions in response to fraudulent claims against landowners and transnational oil corporations and were the basis for planning natural resource use (Gustafson 2009:995)

During the neoliberal era, state institutions responsible for land titling[5] often delayed, rejected, or obstructed Indigenous and peasant land claims for political and economic reasons (see Birk 2000:158). Some representatives had ties to landowners located on Indigenous lands or were landowners themselves. Although the new agrarian law of 1996 called for the titling of sixteen requests for TCOs within ten months, as of 1999 only four of the sixteen had been titled (Birk 2000:157).

In the Chiquitano region, politicians from various political parties, including Acción Democrática Nacionalista (ADN) and Movimiento Nacionalista Revolucionario, owned large tracts of land. According to representatives from Enron and Shell, members of the ADN claimed more than 60,000 hectares. They alleged that the companies' efforts to fulfill their land titling obligations depended on the political will of leaders of the megacoalition of political parties in the provinces of Chiquitos and Ángel Sandoval.

Favoritism and corruption in state institutions also confounded Indigenous peoples' efforts in securing land tenure. In June 2000, prior to the third national Indigenous march from the lowlands (March for the Earth, Territory, and Natural Resources), a representative from the Bolivian newspaper *El Deber* and I witnessed an official from the Vice Ministry of Indigenous and Native Peoples' Affairs (Viceministerio de Asuntos Indígenas y Pueblos Originarios, VAIPO) offering to pay rural Indigenous peoples who had congregated in Santa Cruz to travel back to their communities. In October 2001, various NGOs reported that the Agricultural Chamber of Eastern Bolivia (Cámara Agropecuaria del Oriente), which represents large-scale farmers and cattle ranchers, reached an agreement with the government to legalize lands that had been granted during the infamous dictatorship of General Luis García Meza Tejada.[6] In addition, this agreement enabled the government to reconsider Indigenous territories, recognize development activities within protected areas, and change a rule on the number of cattle necessary per unit of land.

During the neoliberal era, state institutions often did not evict third parties who were illegally residing on Indigenous and peasant territories that were already titled or immobilized because they were pressured by powerful interests such as cattle ranchers, large-scale farmers, and logging companies. Immobilization refers to a process under which the state admits areas claimed by Indigenous groups in order to initiate land regularization, which in turn defines the areas to be granted to third parties and Indigenous peoples (Pacheco et al. 2008:6). In some instances, the National Institute of Agrarian Reform authorized third-party properties within TCOs, creating a "Swiss-cheese" effect that jeopardized their integrity and sustainability (Griffiths 2000:52). Landowners also acquired properties that surrounded and isolated communities. At times, the state went as far as to take administrative and legal action against Indigenous leaders, communities, and organizations. Indigenous communities lost access to natural resources and became engaged in intense conflicts with third parties. In 2001, a notoriously violent attack occurred against a Chiquitano leader and two representatives from the legal support organization CEJIS who were working to solidify a Chiquitano TCO called Monteverde, where the forestry superintendence had granted more than 120,000 hectares of concessions despite declarations from the ILO and a verdict from the Supreme Court of Justice in favor of the Chiquitanos (FOBOMADE 2001a; Parellada et al. 2010). According to CEJIS, several men assaulted and kidnapped one of the CEJIS representatives, holding him in the office of a cattle ranching organization for several hours until he was released. National marches of 2000, 2002, and 2004, in which the Chiquitanos and Ayoreos participated, pushed to resolve such conflicts and were critical in expediting land titling for Indigenous groups (Parellada et al. 2010:65–66).

During the neoliberal period, political and economic influences on state institutions involved in land titling were also disguised as technical debates. To determine the spatial needs of Indigenous communities, the VAIPO assessed access and use of natural resources and territorial needs (Birk 2000:158). Ironically, although VAIPO's alleged purpose was to support Indigenous peoples, its role was heavily criticized by Indigenous groups and NGOs for consistently underestimating the amount of land needed and for using questionable calculation methods. To demonstrate the need for a particular quantity of land, a landholder had to demonstrate the land was being "actively worked," which was measured by the "socioeconomic function" requirement. This standard was not applied equally to Indigenous peoples and large-scale landowners. The latter could meet the requirement by simply paying taxes (Pacheco 1998). Although the 1996 agrarian law stated that the concept was allegedly meant to foster sustainable land management through agriculture, forestry, and conservation, landowners understood they needed to clear forests in order to show they were "working" the land (Gomez Wichtendahl 2009:138; Robertson and Wunder 2005:40; see also Redo, Millington, and Hindery 2011).

Titling amid Transnationals: From Identity to Territory

Against this backdrop, the Chiquitanos clearly faced an uphill battle in securing land titles in the Cuiabá case. Thanks to all the actions they and their allies had carried out, Enron and Shell agreed to support land titling for thirty-eight Indigenous communities located in the pipeline's area of influence as part of the Indigenous compensation program. The companies were to provide technical assistance and undertake the legal work necessary to obtain land titles, with the stated goal of guaranteeing land tenure in the medium and long term (GasOriente Boliviano et al. 1999). The agreement specified that company representatives had to ensure that Indigenous communities had legal status (*personería jurídica*), carry out legal and technical review of existing titles and delineate boundaries (*saneamiento*, also known as land regularization or "retitling"),[7] fund the process, and present a formal petition to the government's National Institute of Agrarian Reform (Urioste 2010).

Many of the communities affected by the pipeline lacked legal status (*personería jurídica*) or were legally classified as *campesinos* rather than as Indigenous peoples. This was a legacy of political shifts that occurred decades earlier. With the 1952 revolution the corporatist state had replaced the derogatory word "Indian" (*Indio*) with "peasant" (*campesino*), thereby replacing an ethnic category with one rooted in a class-based union identity (Andersson 2002:5; Malloy 1970; Guzmán-Ríos 2007). Like elsewhere in Latin America, historically the term *Indio* had been used to legalize abuse and race-based social and political exclusion (Sundberg 2008:573; Brysk 2000). Use of the term *campesino* was a political attempt to construct a monocultural national identity based on the slogan "We are all of mixed descent" ("Todos somos mestizos") (Molina Barrios and Albó 2006:17). In order to receive state recognition and land, campesinos were grouped into an agrarian union structure that fused traditional Indigenous institutions with trade union models (Healey 2009:89). In the 1970s Chiquitanos began to identify themselves as campesinos in order to obtain land titles (Republica de Bolivia 2006). With the rise of the Indigenous movement in the 1980s and 1990s, many Chiquitanos, along with other lowland peoples, reclaimed their identity as Indigenous, revaluing their culture and recuperating their collective rights. Xavier Albó (1991) has referred to this transition as the "return of the Indian," which was coupled with a swing back from the language of class to that of ethnicity—an act of negotiating the politics of Indigenous authenticity (Lucero 2008:78,91). While the benefits of this switch were perhaps more clear to lowland groups, in the highlands confusion and conflict emerged over whether to retain local class-based models of unions or reconstruct ancestral *Ayllus*—fundamental units of social organization of Andean communities, based on kinship groups and communally held territory (Fabricant 2010:90)—based on ethnicity (Lucero 2008:137). The 1994 Law of Popular Participation, one of the multicultural reforms of the 1990s, provided a means to formally legalize such reclassifications because it allowed Indigenous, peasant, and urban collectivities to obtain legal status. Under the 1996 agrarian law, applications for individual or collective land titles could not be processed until legal status had been obtained (Laurie et al. 2002:255). And since the law granted only Indigenous peoples, not campesinos, the right to form TCOs (Lucero 2006b:46), it gave communities classified as campesinos a powerful incentive to convert their legal status to Indigenous. With such legal changes, Chiquitano organizations saw the benefits they could gain by reclaiming their Indigenous identity and ceasing to identify as *campesino*. Grassroots organization CICOL did this in 1998 when it changed its name from Central Intercomunal Campesina del Oriente Lomerío to Central Indígena de Comunidades Originarias de Lomerío (McDaniel 2002:375).

In the case of the Cuiabá pipeline, the Chiquitanos made a pragmatic judgment to secure the territory of affected communities by obligating the companies to provide financial, legal, and technical support to make this conversion. While instrumental in some regards, it reflected their desire to reclaim their cultural identity, using it to gain legal rights to ancestral lands and resources. The Chiquitanos' assertion of identity, authenticity, and rights in defense of territory and lifeways echoed new patterns emerging throughout the Amazon (Hecht 2011). In their quest for territory, they exercised a mix of insurgent citizenship (Holston and Appadurai 1996), resurgent identities (Bolanos 2011; Porro et al. 2011), and assertions over forest stewardship (Minzenberg and Wallace 2011; Sundberg 2006). Their view of Indigeneity as a dynamic process mirrored what Marisol de la Cadena and Orin Starn (2007:3) have described as "an open-ended historical process, inevitably marked by past and present colonialisms and yet also unfolding along as yet undetermined pathways."

As was the case with the compensation program in general, the Chiquitanos, Ayoreos, and allied organizations had to exert intense pressure to force the companies to comply with land titling commitments. Negotiations were frequent, and representatives from the program's directive committee, in collaboration with CEADES, negotiated selection of extension agents, approval of purchases, and approval of the annual operating plan. Concerns emerged for a number of reasons, including delays in disbursement of money for the program and failure to pay for legal personnel (an underlying cause of the September 2000 blockades and camp takeovers).

Lobbying the US government to pressure the companies and Bolivian government—what Margaret E. Keck and Kathryn Sikkink (1998) have called the "boomerang effect"—proved instrumental. In February 2000, Indigenous leaders and allied organizations lobbied representatives from the US Agency for International Development and the US State Department who traveled to the Chiquitano to investigate the heated conflict. Also learning that the Inter-American Development Bank (IDB) was about to finance Enron and Shell's Yacimientos-Bolivian Gulf (YABOG) pipeline, Indigenous groups, CEADES, Friends of the Earth, Bank Information

Center, and Amazon Watch gained a new leverage point. They lobbied the IDB to pressure the companies to fulfill land titling commitments and resolve other issues before granting a loan.

Friends of the Earth demanded that the IDB pressure OPIC to withdraw its loan to the companies, promote an investigation of issues related to the pipeline, and require Enron and Shell to withdraw from the governing board of the Chiquitano Forest Conservation Program. The organization warned that if the IDB did not do so, Friends of the Earth and other NGOs would publicize that the IDB gave a "green stamp" to the pipeline. Representatives from CIDOB also sent a letter to the US State Department, which they copied to the IDB. IDB officials expressed concern, not only conceding that OPIC had erred but also indicating that they would require the companies to consult with stakeholders about unresolved issues before authorizing a loan.

In March 2000, Amazon Watch participated in the annual meeting of the IDB and met with key officials about Enron and Shell's practices in Bolivia. The executive director of Amazon Watch interrupted an interview that the president of OPIC was conducting with the press in order to discuss unresolved issues. As a result, the representative secured a meeting later that day with the OPIC president in which both an Indigenous representative and representatives from Amazon Watch participated. In addition, during the IDB conference, Amazon Watch representatives issued a press release titled "IDB Should Not Finance Enron, Shell in Bolivia." Subsequently, IDB staff communicated to Enron and Shell that they must address outstanding issues before the bank would consider financing new projects. In August 2001, Transredes, a consortium that includes Enron and Shell, contacted Amazon Watch to have an urgent meeting about the YABOG pipeline, an indication of the effect of lobbying.

Conflict over Communal Lands

The Chiquitanos viewed the land titling program as a means to support an existing claim for a communal territory at the southern end of the pipeline (TCO Turubó Este, a 101,120-hectare demand presented in 1997), as well as a new claim for a communal territory to the east of the pipeline (TCO Pantanal, a 1,820,153-hectare demand presented in September 2000) (Tribunal Agrario Nacional 2007; Equipo Nizkor and Derechos Human Rights 2004). In November, regional Indigenous leaders engaged in heated negotiations with the companies because they refused to pay the total amount required for land titling and would not provide sufficient legal, technical, and financial support for TCOs. Indigenous representatives argued the compensation agreement established that the companies were required to cover all costs associated with land titling, whether or not communities opted for simple land titles or TCOs. They also pointed out that the OPIC web page stated that the companies were to pay an additional $1.6 million for land titling. The companies claimed this was an error and stood firm in their decision to not fully support TCOs. In hindsight, the Chiquitanos lamented they did not press the companies to designate a specific amount and regretted not establishing an agreement directly with the government (OICH and CEADES 2004:178). Concerned about insufficient funding, some communities pragmatically conceded to small-scale private property titles rather than TCOs (OICH and CEADES 2004:159). CPESC, the regional Indigenous organization of Santa Cruz, complained that the companies' legal consultant discouraged communities from applying for TCOs. Instead, the individual encouraged them to apply for simple land titles under the pretext that this would avoid conflict with large-scale landowners. Yet behind the scenes the companies were befriending landowners in the area to use their properties to access the pipeline and knew of their strong ties to the neoliberal regimes in power.

In response to the various actions the Chiquitanos and Ayoreos carried out during the first several months (described in the preceding section), the companies requested they resolve the matter through arbitration. Company letters indicated they would neither support titling of TCOs nor lands greater than 10,000 hectares. CEADES was particularly concerned that the arbitrators the companies chose were private companies opposed to Indigenous demands and partial to the companies and landowners organizations (e.g., the Agricultural Chamber of Eastern Bolivia). Ultimately, in December 2000, when Indigenous groups negotiated an addendum with the companies to extend the compensation program, they secured additional financing and support for land titling, as well as Indigenous monitoring of the land titling process. But the companies bypassed parent organizations and negotiated a side deal with regional Chiquitano organization Indigenous Center for the Reclamation of Rights of Angel Sandoval Province (Central Indígena Reivindicativa de la Provincia Ángel Sandoval, CIRPAS). To the dismay of parent Chiquitano organizations, who suspected the companies influenced CIRPAS leaders, the agreement specified the companies would contribute only $40,000 toward TCO Pantanal. A clause stated the amount could not be increased under any circumstances and stipulated the companies would not fund anything else related to land titling in the area (GasOriente Boliviano et al. 2000; CCICH-Turubó 2008).

In the end, this would thwart progress on titling the TCO, and even TCO Turubó Este would have to seek funding through other sources, including the controversial conservation program and the Don Mario mine compensation program (see chapter 9).

By October 2001, two years after construction on the pipeline had begun, none of the affected communities had received titles to their land. A letter Indigenous organizations sent to Enron that month complained that although the compensation program had effectively ended (although it was subsequently extended), the companies had not complied with the agreement (Chiquitano Indigenous Organization 2000). They were unconvinced by the companies' response that the Bolivian government had just begun to issue simple land titles. They further complained that the companies still had not complied with supporting TCOs. Moreover, they maintained that the opening of access roads into communities made them vulnerable to encroaching development since they lacked titles. Finally, after three more years of concerted pressure, entailing negotiations, press outreach, lobbying, direct actions, and national marches, the government granted twenty-eight communities simple land titles, amounting to 136,503 hectares. Five communities received title to a communal property (Propiedad Comunal Turubó Este), which would eventually be converted to a TCO under the administration of Evo Morales (see chapter 9). Progress on titling TCO Pantanal would prove much slower.

This chapter has focused on Indigenous and allied mobilization over consultation, compensation, and territory, all fundamental rights that are enshrined in international and domestic law. I argued that the Chiquitanos and Ayoreos encouraged other actors—the companies, the Bolivian government, OPIC—to respect their rights using a pragmatic combination of direct actions, lobbying, negotiations, and press outreach at the local, regional, national, and international scales. In one of the most striking displays of such *dynamic pragmatism*, the Chiquitanos initially opposed the pipeline and threatened direct actions to leverage a better-funded and more equitable compensation program. Similarly, they used a conspiracy involving the World Bank, Sánchez de Lozada, and Enron to secure a compensation program for the Don Mario gold mine, which tapped gas from the Cuiabá pipeline. To achieve this end, many communities had to pragmatically participate in a political battle over identity, asserting and reclaiming their Indigeneity. And in their struggle for territory, some communities opted for the calculated risk of applying for large-scale, collective TCOs over small-scale titles. Finally, I contrasted the companies' utilitarian view of compensation as "the cost of business" against that of the Chiquitanos and Ayoreos, which, although obviously not monolithic, tended to prioritize an inclusive, long-term, culturally appropriate, and autonomous program that genuinely improved living conditions and ensured control over natural resources necessary for livelihood and cultural survival. In chapter 6 I extend further the concept of *dynamic pragmatism* in the context of environmental justice, describing how the Chiquitanos and Ayoreos shrewdly utilized transnational advocacy and focused on addressing those effects of the pipeline that impinged on their livelihood.

CHAPTER SIX

Struggling for Environmental Justice

Challenging Environmental Injustice

The case of the Cuiabá pipeline is a classic story of environmental injustice, an outgrowth of a neocolonial form of development based on neoliberal ideology (Wolford 2008). Facilitated by the neoliberal economic policies they had championed themselves, Enron, Shell, and locally allied elites accrued the lion's share of the pipeline's profits. Little was left for the Bolivian state, and much less for the Chiquitano and Ayoreo communities affected by the project. Their $2 million compensation program paled in comparison with the exclusionary $20 million conservation program that had green-stamped the pipeline. Until the election of Evo Morales, gas from the pipeline was transported directly to Bolivian president Gonzalo Sánchez de Lozada's gold mine and then straight to Brazil, where it was largely destined to power large-scale agribusiness. In a highly uneven playing field, Indigenous groups struggled to gain fair compensation, land tenure, and control over an exclusionary conservation program. Much of this conflict stemmed from a lack of political participation and a series of "procedural injustices" (Carruthers 2007:398; Byrne et al. 2002:8; Perreault 2008:243; see Newell 2008) that arose because the Chiquitanos and Ayoreos were excluded from decisions regarding the siting and risks of the pipeline and the conservation program; moreover, they had only limited say in the design of the Indigenous compensation program. And to add insult to injury, communities lying in the path of the pipeline bore the brunt of the human and environmental consequences brought by construction,

Figure 6.1 Soil degradation during construction of the Cuiabá pipeline. Author's photo

including water contamination, road degradation, and increased conflict (see figure 6.1). It was a pattern that paralleled other cases around the world in which marginalized communities affected by oil and gas activities suffered a disproportionate share of adverse environmental effects yet gained relatively meager benefits (see, e.g., Sawyer 2004; Watts 2005; Martinez-Alier 2002). As Bebbington and Bury (in press) suggest, given the acute inequities and environmental impacts generated by extractive industries, it is unsurprising that heightened conflicts involving environmental (in)justice occur in the sector. Based on the case of the Cuiabá pipeline, this chapter recounts how the Chiquitanos, Ayoreos, and allies mobilized to rectify such injustices. It demonstrates how their strategic use of transnational advocacy and their prioritization of impacts that most directly affected their livelihood were expressions of *dynamic pragmatism.*

Within the first couple of years after construction of the Cuiabá pipeline, indirect impacts began to affect livelihood as well, since the pipeline route and new roads provided access to the forest for loggers, hunters, and cattle ranchers. Although often disparate and sporadic, lobbying by Indigenous organizations and allies (particularly CEADES, Amazon Watch, and Friends of the Earth) was pivotal in influencing the companies, as described in chapter 5. Leveraging the press to add weight to their voice, they targeted key Bolivian state institutions (the environmental and hydrocarbons ministries, sympathetic lawmakers), the Overseas Private Investment Corporation (OPIC), and OPIC's oversight agencies (USAID, the US Treasury, and the US State Department). The World Wildlife Fund (WWF), though recovering from a damaged reputation, was still able to use its international clout and history criticizing Shell in Nigeria to secure high-level meetings with the corporation and state institutions in the United States and Bolivia. But while concerted actions by Indigenous groups and allies proved critical in compelling the companies to mitigate adverse environmental and community impacts, pressure from non-Indigenous monitoring committees— organized by the Bolivian organization Biosphere Productivity and Environment (Productividad Biosfera y Medio Ambiente, PROBIOMA)— and from other organizations was also important. And the basis for much of this mobilization was evidence gathered by Indigenous environmental monitors and other actors that challenged the rosy picture painted by the companies' public relations team.

When the Chiquitanos negotiated the Indigenous compensation program, they pragmatically succeeded in pressuring the companies to fund twenty-six Indigenous representatives, one elected from each community directly affected by the pipeline, to monitor environmental and social impacts caused by the pipeline and participate in conflict resolution (OICH and CEADES 2004:197). This was to check the monitoring of consulting company Dames & Moore, which communities generally distrusted given its complicity with Enron and Shell (and given its poor past record in monitoring the main Bolivia-Brazil pipeline). The Chiquitanos complained that the company never shared its own monitoring reports and did not inform the government of impacts condemned by Indigenous organizations. In one instance the Chiquitanos denounced the companies for producing a "counterreport" that used false information and photos that supposedly came from the Indigenous environmental monitors (OICH and CEADES 2004:206); the companies indicated that a particular monitor was from a community he was actually not from and claimed that he was satisfied with the condition of the damaged roads. That the company reports were not objective was not a surprise and was an outgrowth of a problematic provision in the environmental law that required companies to produce their own compliance reports rather than delegating this duty to an independent body.

Although government inspectors produced periodic reports, state institutions charged with regulating the environment and safeguarding Indigenous rights were relatively ineffective in attending to impacts because they were weak, fractured, and heavily influenced by the companies (see chapter 2). As with its dealings with the conservation program and Indigenous compensation program, the environmental ministry's meager efforts to address pipeline impacts reflected the fact that it was a relatively weak agency, compromised by corruption and controlled by factions that prioritized putting the pipeline into operation over protecting the environment. While some staff welcomed collaboration and were appreciative of issues raised by Indigenous groups and nongovernmental organizations (NGOs), their efforts were overshadowed by the aforementioned issues. Lower-level personnel alleged that corruption stemmed in part from competition over limited resources. Some wished international donors had imposed stricter conditions with greater oversight. But more damning allegations concerning complicity in government crackdowns, corruption, and inadequate training also surfaced. It was widely reported that one of the environmental ministers, Erick Reyes Villa[1]—appointed under Sánchez de Lozada—was a gynecologist by training and that the vice minister, Neisa Roca, was notorious for accumulating an unusually large sum of money (*Los Tiempos* 2002). In 2011, Reyes Villa would receive a suspended sentence of three years in prison for complicity in genocide during the gas war of October 2003 (*Bolpress* 2011c; Human Rights Watch 2012).

For the first several months of pipeline construction, the vice minister of sustainable development had more power than the minister himself because the former was a member of Acción Democrática Nacionalista, the political party of the Bolivian president, General Hugo Banzer Suárez. Frequent political changes also took a toll. From the beginning of pipeline construction until 2001, there were four different ministers. Scarce resources and dependence on the companies plagued the ministry, too. A ministry official acknowledged that it could afford only one monitor to focus on the pipeline, an individual who allegedly did not interact enough with communities and who was largely controlled by the companies. According to this account, during occasional field inspections the monitor had to work quickly because he depended on the companies for accommodations and transportation—and the companies gave him only limited information.

During construction of the pipeline, officials from the environmental ministry were aware that the companies had violated the environmental law by building or improving unauthorized roads but had to balance competing interests from civil society while under pressure from other state actors and the companies. Although Indigenous groups and other organizations (CEADES, FOBOMADE, PROBIOMA, Amazon Watch, and WWF) had lobbied the ministry to enforce the law, the companies influenced local actors to win the agency's approval. The companies were particularly keen on improving the Las Petas-Candelaria road at the northern end of the pipeline route in order to penetrate the forest to build the pipeline. During the first few months of construction, they worked quickly to complete as much as possible before the beginning of the rainy season (December to March). Company spokesmen continued to warn that the Brazilian government could fine them $1 million per day if the pipeline was not operating by March 1, 2000. To further their cause, they helped form a "pro-road committee," composed of representatives from a regional Chiquitano organization, landowners, the companies, the municipal government of San Matías, and even the environmental ministry, and encouraged members to send letters to the ministry, the Santa Cruz Prefect, and the Superintendence of Forestry in support of the road. The companies even forwarded requests from local Indigenous leaders. The companies, landowners, and local politicians argued the road would help the communities since they were isolated for several months each year during the rainy season. Chiquitano communities in the vicinity felt torn because they desired easier transit (e.g., to bring goods to market, access medical care, attend school) yet feared the perils of encroaching development. In November 1999, local actors in support of the road threatened to stop pipeline construction and erect blockades if their demand was not met. Watchdog groups speculated that the companies may have been behind this threat, in an underhanded attempt to stifle critics and win the ministry's authorization. Under intense pressure from multiple parties, the ministry ultimately approved the road with the condition that the companies, through their consultants, Dames & Moore, comply with existing environmental laws and regulations by monitoring, preventing, and mitigating the adverse impacts (e.g., by controlling erosion and avoiding impacts on wetlands).

Aware of the ministry's compromised condition, the Collective for Applied Studies and Social Development (Colectivo de Estudios Aplicados y Desarrollo Social, CEADES), with funding from Oxfam, organized intensive training of Indigenous environmental monitors and closely coordinated their efforts over the next several years. Although Chiquitano and Ayoreo community members drew upon Traditional Ecological Knowledge and were generally aware of the pipeline's consequences, CEADES educated monitors to systematically assess impacts, emphasizing immediate and long-term secondary effects (e.g., illustrating how the pipeline was part of broader national and hemispheric infrastructure development plans). It maintained its philosophy that the Chiquitanos and Ayoreos should be the protagonists and, in contrast to other allied organizations, insisted

Indigenous authorities take the lead in conducting assessments, lobbying, and negotiating. Indigenous monitors regularly attended workshops hosted by CEADES on evaluating and documenting impacts. They reviewed legal rights won since the mobilizations of the 1990s and shared this knowledge with fellow community members. Monitors circulated throughout their communities, gathering and organizing complaints. They verified allegations, made their own observations, and assembled evidence in the form of testimony, documentation, and photographs. The monitors produced weekly reports, which were shared with community leaders, CEADES, and parent organizations. In collaboration with CEADES, they synthesized this information into three major reports detailing impacts and legal violations, each of which was reviewed and approved by the communities. Chiquitanos and allied organizations used these reports to garner press coverage, lobby the Bolivian and US governments, and pressure the companies.

Speaking Truth to Power

A November 1999 report produced by Chiquitano Indigenous Organization (Organización Indígena Chiquitana, OICH), the main Chiquitano organization, and CEADES elaborated on a number of impacts that significantly affected community livelihood (OICH 1999). One key conflict occurred at a community located at the northern end of the pipeline, where Enron and Shell's subcontractors contaminated a water source used by community members and their animals. According to the Chiquitanos, an estimated 5,000 liters of diesel was spilled. They accused the companies of not paying compensation for a calf and a horse that died from ingesting the contaminated water. In addition, to transport materials over the water body the companies cut trees from the surrounding habitat and placed them in the water so that heavy machinery could transit; the trees were not removed and were decomposing. The report further criticized the companies for contaminating the air, degrading roads, building an unauthorized air strip 500 meters from a community, using trees cleared from the pipeline route to build worker camps, and not treating solid waste. One community complained that settlers had entered along the pipeline route, threatening land tenure and access to natural resources. Communities located near the Brazilian border testified that individuals were transporting stolen vehicles along the pipeline route, endangering the lives of community members. Another community accused the company of not building a well as promised and for building a camp on the property of a cattle rancher located only 500 meters away. Members of yet another community were furious that the companies built the pipeline directly through the middle of their soccer field, ironically one that had been built with funding from the 1994 Law of Popular Participation (one of the neoliberal multicultural reforms).

Looking for quick resolution, the Chiquitanos issued a series of specific recommendations, including laboratory analysis of affected water bodies (with samples taken with the participation of community members), compensation for lost animals and degraded agricultural fields, weekly meetings, watering of roads to minimize dust, better worker training, and improved treatment of solid waste. While some of these demands were met, many issues were not settled, as evidenced by subsequent reports. The report also included a veiled threat that the Chiquitanos would undertake direct actions if conflicts were not resolved: "The majority of the communities have a tendency to carry out pressure tactics in order to be heard and to obtain solutions to socio-environmental conflicts. Such measures have already been taken in two communities and have led to favorable results" (OICH 1999:31, translation by author).

The same suite of direct actions that communities carried out to secure compensation, land titles, and control of the conservation program (e.g., blockades, strikes, takeovers of worker camps) were used to compel the companies to attend to adverse impacts. Company representatives maintained that they had to be concerned about the extent to which they responded to these measures, because they feared that if they conceded too much they would stimulate further actions. Yet in practice, they usually responded swiftly, cognizant that each day construction was delayed meant additional costs. At times, threats alone were sufficient. During pipeline construction, communities at the northern end of the pipeline threatened to paralyze construction and confiscate company vehicles if the companies did not repair damaged roads. Letters the companies sent to the environmental ministry illustrated how they addressed impacts to avoid conflict: "Despite having initiated the repair of the last 1200 meters of the road between the community and its camp on December 13, 1999, CONDUTO [a subcontractor] has not completed this work. It is recommended that the Contracted company assign personnel and machinery immediately to finish this work to avoid additional conflicts in this community" (GasOriente Boliviano et al. 2000).

Dissatisfied by the companies' response, the Chiquitanos cast their November 1999 report far and wide to key decision makers in Bolivia and the United States, copying the environmental ministry, the energy super-intendence, and OPIC's consulting company, AATA International. To further amplify their voice, they persuaded the lowland Federation of Indigenous Peoples of Bolivia (Confederación de Pueblos Indígenas de Bolivia, CIDOB) to send an open letter to President Banzer (CIDOB 1999) and gained coverage in the Santa Cruz–based newspaper *El Deber*. The letter demanded the government carry out an immediate inspection and make the companies comply with the environmental law. Referring to evidence compiled by the Indigenous environmental monitors, it highlighted those impacts that were perceived to be most damaging to community livelihood: contamination of water bodies, intoxication of livestock that consumed polluted water, and degradation of community roads.

During the same month, Amazon Watch discovered that one of OPIC's board members, Secretary of the Treasury Larry Summers, was going to visit Bolivia and suggested that the parent Indigenous organizations Council of Ethnic Peoples of Santa Cruz (Coordinadora de Pueblos Étnicos de Santa Cruz, CPESC) and CIDOB send a sign-on letter inviting him to meet with affected communities and fly over the pipeline route. Consequently, CIDOB did so, emphasizing the fact that the US government had a responsibility to resolve issues since it had funded Enron and Shell's pipeline through OPIC. The letter further complained that despite having sent various letters to OPIC, the only response the Indigenous organizations received was a 20-page letter, written in English, sent only to CIDOB (not the other Indigenous organizations). CIDOB argued that this showed a lack of respect for Indigenous cultures and requested a more transparent relationship. Although Summers did not travel to the region himself, this and other measures would trigger a visit from the US State Department several months later.

A forceful report produced the same month by Bolivian NGO PROBIOMA added even more weight to the demands put forth by Indigenous groups and supporters; it also underscored significant impacts felt by non-Indigenous populations affected by the pipeline. In the case of the Cuiabá pipeline, PROBIOMA repeated the role it had played with the main Bolivia-Brazil pipeline, monitoring impacts and compensation programs, organizing non-Indigenous monitoring organizations, and lobbying the companies, governments, and international financial institutions. In this regard, it acted as both a direct stakeholder and an intermediary organization that channeled community concerns. One of PROBIOMA's key goals was to alleviate poverty by advocating for local control of natural resources and non-monetary compensation. It helped organize and train local socioenvironmental monitoring committees (comités de fiscalización socioambiental) at various towns in the region, which in turn were fused into a coalition called the Natural Resource Defense Committee of the Great Chiquitano (Comité de Defensa de los Recursos Naturales de la Gran Chiquitanía). PROBIOMA also worked with sympathetic individuals in elite-dominated civic committees, albeit to a lesser degree. Construction of the Bolivia-Brazil and Cuiabá gas pipelines had prompted the organization to form local monitoring committees when it saw the need for affected communities to organize themselves to receive fair compensation, monitor impacts independently, and interface with the companies, governments, press, and supranational institutions (PROBIOMA 2009:1). Although not formally an outgrowth of the neoliberal multicultural reforms of the 1990s (particularly the Law of Popular Participation), as the grassroots territorial organizations were, these committees were born out of the same vein of decentralized governance. According to PROBIOMA's website, "The monitoring committee is an organization that is born from the heart of local populations, as a need that these populations have to monitor, denounce, and fight for the rights of citizens and natural resources" (translation by author).

The composition of monitoring and civic committees varied, with diverse representation from various groups ranging from cattle ranchers to individuals who had worked for oil companies. The groups also exhibited different degrees of mobilization; according to PROBIOMA, some were better organized and more effective in influencing the companies than others. The committees engaged in activities that paralleled those of the Indigenous environmental monitors: gathering community complaints, observing degradation along the pipeline route, producing reports, and pressuring decision makers.

PROBIOMA's confrontational engagements with the companies, conservationists, and the Bolivian government were often effective in pressuring for change, yet at the same time, the organization forged a cordial relationship with the vice minister of sustainable development, which gave it a direct conduit through which to channel its concerns. And besides working through formal channels inside the state, it spearheaded a grassroots campaign to raise awareness in the Chiquitano region and helped organize protests on the ground. The monitoring committees and coalition it forged facilitated mobilizations in three separate towns along the pipeline route within the first year (Guardia 1999:89).

PROBIOMA worked with local monitoring committees to produce several reports on pipeline impacts, compensation programs, and the Chiquitano Forest Conservation Program. Its first major report, also released in

November 1999, bolstered many of the Chiquitanos' claims, even though it focused more on the experiences of non-Indigenous populations. PRO-BIOMA documented road and bridge degradation, increased traffic and dust, disruption caused by drunken workers, placement of camps too close to communities, improper disposal of solid and liquid waste, failure to distribute the worker code of conduct, construction of unauthorized roads and airstrips, issues with the compensation programs, improper routing of the pipeline through sensitive areas, and use of wood from the pipeline route for camp construction (PROBIOMA 1999b). The following month it sent a letter to the vice minister of sustainable development, along with the report, requesting it to suspend the project's environmental license because of violations of the environmental impact assessment (PROBIOMA 1999a).

A report I wrote for Amazon Watch in December 1999 corroborated the major allegations raised in reports produced by the Chiquitanos and PROBIOMA. It detailed environmental and community impacts as well as issues with the Indigenous compensation program and the Chiquitano Forest Conservation Program (Amazon Watch 1999). Like the Chiquitano report, it highlighted legal and contractual violations but also emphasized breaches of OPIC's loan conditions and World Bank directives. It also differed by focusing on how the pipeline would trigger upstream and downstream gas development, such as plans that surfaced indicating the regional rural electric cooperative might tap into it. Noted impacts included water contamination, road deterioration, soil degradation, air pollution, inadequate control of the pipeline right-of-way, lack of reforestation, wetland degradation, construction of unauthorized access roads, and disruption of local towns near workers' camps. Based on these findings, Amazon Watch called on OPIC to withdraw financing and urged the companies to suspend pipeline construction and resolve outstanding problems. It recommended independent monitoring with adequate involvement of indigenous organizations and affected communities. I disseminated the report to a variety of actors, including the press, OPIC, and Bolivian state institutions (the Ministry of Sustainable Development, the National Service for Protected Areas, the Commission on Sustainable Development, and the Vice Ministry of Energy and Hydrocarbons). In response, on December 15, 1999, Enron and Shell created a section on the company website about the report, titled "GasOriente Boliviano Response to Amazon Watch Allegations," that stated: "We appreciate and share the interest of Amazon Watch and others in ensuring that the Cuiabá pipeline project is carried out in an environmentally sensitive and responsible manner. For this reason, we feel it is important to respond to the recent report distributed by Amazon Watch and to provide an update on the progress GasOriente Boliviano Ltda. . . . and the Project sponsors are making with regard to the commercial, social and environmental programs" (Enron and Shell 1999). The website noted some measures that the companies had taken to address concerns and indicated that they would heed some suggestions: "Amazon Watch provided a good suggestion that local communities be involved in monitoring/controlling access. We will investigate ways to implement this suggestion ensuring that any recommendation/decision comply with Bolivian law, and include the participation of pertinent Bolivian authorities."

Nonetheless, in the majority of their response, the companies created and answered a set of questions that supposedly summed up the key issues mentioned in the report but that actually skirted many of them. For instance, in response to the allegation that additional pipelines might tap into the Cuiabá pipeline, the companies stated that the Santa Cruz electric cooperative had approached them about the possibility of building a gas-fired power plant (subsequently built in Ipias; see chapter 9) but did not divulge the fact that they had left behind an outtake valve at Sánchez de Lozada's Don Mario gold mine, which would tap the pipeline in 2002. Overall, their response illustrated how the website functioned as a public relations tool to justify the project and subdue criticism. That they went to such efforts illustrated the impact of publishing the report in English (though it was also translated into Spanish), press outreach, dissemination on the Internet, and meetings with key decision makers—particularly considering that other actors (the Chiquitanos, CEADES, and PROBIOMA) had produced comprehensive reports that were not addressed on the site. Ironically, the reports produced by these groups contained far more detailed information on the pipeline's impacts and issues related to land titling and the compensation programs.

Mirroring Enron and Shell, of the four hundred projects OPIC funded, it chose to create a special section on its website for the Cuiabá pipeline in response to pressure from civil society, under the heading "OPIC & the Environment." While OPIC touted the project as its poster child for environmental stewardship, representatives from Indigenous groups and NGO watchdogs balked at how inaccurate the website was and criticized that it supported the companies' perspective. Despite the numerous violations these groups documented, OPIC presented only the social and environmental benefits of the pipeline.

During a meeting at the environmental office of the hydrocarbons ministry (Unidad del Medio Ambiente, UMA), staff criticized the Amazon Watch report but acknowledged that it was generally accurate. Several weeks later, in February 2000, UMA sent me a detailed, several-page-long response.

Though largely a point-by-point rebuttal in line with the companies' position, it revealed that they had carried out actions to address some of the issues raised. Representatives from the environmental office of the US Agency for International Development (USAID) and the US State Department also expressed concern. A USAID representative stated that the report was a significant influence in persuading the companies to mitigate impacts. An official from the Bolivian National Service for Protected Areas ordered a field inspection to investigate the allegations, forwarded the report to the environmental ministry, and requested that it resolve the problems. The ministry gave a copy of the report to their field inspector, who in turn investigated the claims. On February 24, 2000, an article appeared in a national newspaper in which the vice minister of sustainable development explained the results of their investigation, which revealed various impacts and instances of noncompliance and largely confirmed the report's allegations (*Presencia* 2000). The next day, a company representative admitted that the companies had cowritten UMA's response and conceded that it was biased.

Boomerang Advocacy and Amplifying Demands

In February 2000, representatives from the US State Department visited Bolivia to reconcile problems related to the pipeline. The trip was largely sparked by a representative from USAID Bolivia who had been lobbied by WWF, Amazon Watch, and other organizations. Moreover, by that time, the "boomerang effect" (Keck and Sikkink 1998) of transnational advocacy had made the Cuiabá case notorious in Washington, DC, among OPIC's oversight agencies and placed it front and center at the US Embassy office in Bolivia as well. State Department representatives themselves stated that they had conducted the investigation to protect US business interests and because the agency had been bombarded by competing complaints from communities, NGOs, industry, OPIC, and the press (namely, a critical article that appeared in the *Washington Times*). They further remarked that the pipeline was a significant development initiative given Bolivia's immense natural gas reserves. One representative asserted that the companies would heed the agency's recommendations because they wanted to maintain their image and sustain continuous support for the project.

Although the investigation did encourage Enron and Shell to mitigate a few direct impacts, overall the agency's ability to persuade OPIC and the companies to comply with the law was limited. The investigation itself was flawed because of its short time frame (one day at the pipeline), narrow scope, and lack of independence. When the State Department representatives surveyed pipeline impacts, staff from Enron and Shell escorted them without the participation of affected communities. They met with various NGOs but met with only one (non-Indigenous) technical adviser from the lowland Indigenous federation (CIDOB). Unfortunately, because there was little advance notice, key Indigenous representatives could not attend because they had prior commitments. The representatives visited only a couple of worker camps and focused on public health issues, such as solid and liquid waste disposal, while largely avoiding other social and environmental impacts. They did not meet with affected communities and never visited the stretch of the pipeline that crosses the Pantanal wetlands. In part, the narrow scope of the investigation reflected the fact that one of the representatives was a specialist in environmental health (hence the focus on waste issues), and lacked understanding of relationships between environment and development. For example, the representative expressed concern that the conservation program not be a social program, without recognizing how conservation goals proposed by Indigenous groups—for example, land titling and environmental education—were interconnected.

State Department representatives disagreed as to whether it was important to examine "social" issues, demonstrating how the agency was fractured. While one representative argued that to do so was beyond the State Department's mandate, another contended that social concerns were paramount and fell under OPIC's mandate and guidelines as a US government agency (as evidenced by OPIC's loan condition requiring implementation of the Indigenous compensation program). When the former representative stated the investigation would focus on Indigenous issues more than secondary environmental impacts, the other representative disagreed adamantly, claiming that the latter was a primary concern—once again showing how they dichotomized social and environmental issues. After the investigation was completed, the non-Indigenous technical adviser from the lowland Indigenous federation sent a follow-up letter to the State Department asking for more equitable relationships:

> There is a history of large companies that implement megaprojects that never improve the lives of Indigenous peoples who live in their ancestral spaces. These inequitable practices carried out by consultants, governments and multilateral organizations need to be changed. We must ask ourselves "Who is helping whom?" Are the projects helping Indigenous peoples or are the Indigenous peoples helping the projects?

Unequal Power Relations among Stakeholders
More global and equitable relations need to be created and improved upon. For example, OPIC communicates in a more direct manner to other NGOs and companies than to CIDOB. There is a complete lack of respect in its communications with Indigenous peoples in languages they do not understand (for example, the 20 page letter OPIC sent to CIDOB that was written in English). (CIDOB 2000, translation by author)

The letter also communicated many other demands, including land titling, a long-term trust fund, independent monitoring with community participation, democratization of the conservation program, and resolution of the impacts and issues described in the reports produced by the Chiquitanos and Amazon Watch. Ironically, the State Department never responded and did not share the outcome of the investigation. Affected communities and allied NGOs had to be content hoping their efforts were not in vain, trusting that the agency influenced the companies positively behind the scenes to address their concerns. Similarly, they were left wondering whether lobbying the Inter-American Development Bank to force the companies to rectify impacts before issuing them a loan for another pipeline had made any difference (see chapter 5).

During the same month, PROBIOMA conducted another field inspection and produced a second report, which cited many of the impacts it had noted previously but also leveled some new allegations: bribery of a local mayor, unauthorized use of access roads, increased prostitution, and inadequate control of the pipeline right-of-way to curtail hunting, biopiracy, and logging (PROBIOMA 2000b). Once again, the organization argued that the environmental ministry should suspend the project's environmental license. Finally, combined pressure from PROBIOMA, monitoring committees, Indigenous groups, and supporters triggered the ministry to conduct an investigation of the various allegations. As a result, it issued a legal warning to Enron and Shell on February 21, 2000, for not complying with the environmental impact assessment. The ministry noted poor management of solid waste, deficiencies in the areas of health, safety, and environment in one worker camp, and failure to properly oversee subcontracted companies. This was a far cry from the critics' demands to suspend construction and initiate a formal audit but was one of the strongest actions taken by the compromised agency—a testament to the power of mobilization in a neoliberal era.

In March 2000, frustrated that the companies had not complied with the non-Indigenous compensation program, residents from the border town of San Matías erected a blockade that stopped pipeline construction. The regional civic committee threatened to maintain the action until the companies disbursed the $1.5 million it had promised for community development projects. It also lambasted the companies, consultants, and OPIC for locating an airstrip too close to the pipeline (20 meters away), degrading roads, creating new roads instead of using the pipeline right-of-way, possessing dynamite, not paying for use of property, and threatening to solicit the Bolivian army. PROBIOMA assisted the committee in elaborating and disseminating their demands to the Bolivian press and decision makers. The companies tried to undermine the legitimacy of the mobilization by claiming that those who had incited it were drug traffickers interested in monetary gain. They lobbied the government and asked the Ministry of Interior to send the police and armed forces to contain the unrest. When civic leaders received threats that they would be arrested, townswomen created an emergency committee to lead future actions in case the companies did not comply with their agreements (PROBIOMA 2000c). Ultimately, the action succeeded in convincing the companies to disburse funds as stipulated, and the mobilization served as a template for future actions the Chiquitanos would undertake (see chapter 5).

In June 2000, Friends of the Earth succeeded using socially and environmentally conscious shareholders to oblige John Hardy, Jr., Enron International's vice president for project finance, to travel to Bolivia and hear complaints from affected Indigenous communities firsthand. It was a testament to the power of transnational advocacy in using local, national, and international connections to expand political influence (McDaniel 2002:380). During the two-day trip, representatives from Friends of the Earth, Amazon Watch (including the author), and Indigenous organizations did a flyover of the pipeline, surveyed direct impacts, and met with communities about problems with the compensation program and conservation program. They were accompanied by representatives from the companies, the hydrocarbons ministry, and consultants for the companies (Dames & Moore) and OPIC (AATA International). NGO and Indigenous representatives complained of being constrained because company officials guided the investigation and insisted on being present during all interviews and observations. This created an intimidating environment for community members who wished to testify anonymously, without fear of reprisal. Nonetheless, eventually, the trip culminated in an informal meeting among those present in which NGO and Indigenous representatives summarized key outstanding issues to the companies. Amazon Watch subsequently produced a video on unresolved issues and garnered substantial attention in the Bolivian and international press, including a story that aired on CNN Español featuring segments from the video. Working in conjunction with Friends of the Earth and Indigenous groups the organization also helped generate stories in the *Miami Herald, Washington Times, Financial Times, Oil Daily, San Francisco Chronicle, Latin Trade,* BBC Television, Reuters, the *Houston Chronicle,* CNN, the Associated Press, and various Bolivian newspapers and television stations. The companies' public relations team monitored this coverage and carried out press outreach and lobbying to counter criticism (see chapter 2). Although getting stories covered proved challenging in an elite-dominated press (Humphreys Bebbington and Bebbington 2010:53; Howard 2010:190), Amazon Watch, CEADES, and Indigenous organizations found some sympathetic reporters and took advantage of outlets affiliated with particular political parties that wanted to criticize other parties.

By July 2000, it became increasingly apparent that mobilization had led the companies to address some impacts. Documents from the companies and state institutions showed that the companies had agreed to compensate communities for use of well water, restore roads and bridges, control soil erosion, and mitigate contaminated water bodies. Leaking fuel tanks were removed along with contaminated soil. While many of the broader, long-term impacts endured, communities and advocates felt empowered that their efforts had some effect. Frequent negotiations with the companies, combined with persistent lobbying, protests, and press outreach, were the norm over the next couple of years, with efforts to gain fair compensation and control over the Chiquitano Forest Conservation Program remaining paramount.

In February 2002, two months after Enron filed for bankruptcy, OPIC canceled its $200 million loan to Enron and Shell, citing failed financial obligations. Amazon Watch and Friends of the Earth pointed out that pressure from Indigenous groups and NGOs had caused delays that factored into Enron's failure to meet its financial commitments. Moreover, they argued that OPIC recognized it had violated the agency's statute prohibiting it from financing infrastructure projects in primary forests. And it was aware of the various violations the companies had incurred. Indigenous groups and allies contended that with this move, OPIC had absolved itself from its liability for impacts that might not have happened had OPIC not initially authorized the loan, thereby enabling the project to occur in the first place.

In May 2002, Indigenous groups and supporters gained further momentum in pressuring the companies to address outstanding issues when the Cuiabá conflict made the front page of the *Washington Post.* Amazon Watch and Friends of the Earth helped generate the story, working behind the scenes for months to supply information for the article. This triggered a series of reactions on the part of Bolivian state institutions to reexamine how the environmental license was granted in the first place and to address the conflictive conservation program, increasing secondary impacts, land titling, and problematic compensation programs.

In September 2002, with news that President Sánchez de Lozada's Don Mario gold mine was going to illegally tap the Cuiabá pipeline, I accompanied Chiquitano Indigenous leaders, CEADES, and a visiting delegation from the Amazon Alliance to investigate and also participated in a broader survey across communities in the region affected by the pipeline (see chapters 2 and 5). Based on this visit, CEADES and the Chiquitanos produced a second major report on the pipeline in October 2002, followed by a report and video from Amazon Watch in December 2002 (OICH and CEADES 2002; Amazon Watch 2002). Experts from CEADES painstakingly enumerated dozens of violations of the project's environmental impact studies, as well as various domestic and international laws. Both reports revealed that the pipeline had caused secondary impacts at a regional scale, as predicted by these groups and the conservation organizations. A number of communities testified they had observed illegal loggers, hunters, land speculators, and cattle ranchers gaining access to the forest using new or improved access roads, as well as the pipeline route, which had not been sufficiently reforested or controlled as required by the environmental law. The relatively intact forest was difficult to penetrate before, but the new network of roads and the pipeline route served as arteries into the heart of the forest. The reports corroborated research showing that although moderate deforestation is typically associated with construction of pipeline rights-of-way, subsequent agricultural clearing, logging, and hunting along them can ensue (Dourojeanni et al. 2009:129). A representative of Enron and Shell's capitalized company Transredes stated, "We know, for example, that the right of way is almost like a road. We could use it to transport wood, contraband, or anything," and a community member noted, "Some people have complained and denounced that they [loggers] are engaging in contraband of timber. . . . With regards to hunting, they enter indiscriminately and kill five or six wild pigs. They [the companies] are not controlling this right of way as they had said, nor are they reforesting" (Amazon Watch 2002:9).

Once again, the Chiquitano report pragmatically underscored impacts that threatened community livelihood, including insecure safety valves and colonization along the road leading to the Don Mario gold mine. Community members feared potential gas explosions when they witnessed the pipeline subsiding in one location, as well as burned areas and increased dry vegetation along the pipeline route, which was poorly reforested and lacked adequate barriers: "There was some 'reforestation.' But now what do we have? Nothing. Contamination from logs that were cut and left there. Over time a lot is going to happen. If a fire enters it will run from one end of the pipeline to the other. It won't stop from here [southern end of pipeline] until San Matías [northern end of pipeline]. The fire won't stop" (Amazon Watch 2002).

Amazon Watch's report warned that the pipeline was leading to industrialization of the Chiquitano forest and Pantanal wetlands, noting plans for power plants, rural electrification, and provision of gas for domestic usage, which would increase encroaching development. Community members and company personnel indicated that valves had been left behind to supply future power plants in Ipias and San Matías—both of which were subsequently built under Morales's presidency (see chapter 9). The report also recommended that the government pursue small-scale, decentralized renewable energy alternatives rather than prioritizing developing energy corridors for export. It criticized the World Bank for considering financing the controversial liquefied natural gas project (Pacific LNG) that would lead to the overthrow of Sánchez de Lozada during the gas war one year later.

The Chiquitanos also denounced the Missouri Botanical Garden, Noel Kempff Mercado Museum of Natural History, and Fundación Amigos de la Naturaleza, which were board members of the controversial conservation program, for biopiracy: "People from the Noel Kempff Mercado Museum, who have a relationship with GasOriente Boliviano [Enron and Shell's subsidiary], took samples of seeds of paquió, almonds, cacha and 'varieties of wild peanuts.' The extraction of these resources was undertaken without authorization or awareness on the part of official authorities and the community. The community members suspect biopiracy" (OICH and CEADES 2002:20).

They further asserted that many of the community-specific issues they had pointed out two years earlier persisted. Ironically, although the companies had improved roads they needed to access the pipeline, they had not adequately restored many community roads and bridges. The improved road to the Don Mario mine, coupled with gas from the Cuiabá pipeline, facilitated its reactivation and led to a series of impacts at the mine (e.g., large dust clouds and deforestation for a tailing pond, reservoir, and facilities). The water source at one community was still contaminated, and the flow had diminished, despite company efforts to restore it. The report noted that in another community a potable water system was not completed, leaving behind an open water well and trench where a community member drowned; another person partially lost sight because of accidental contact with toxic paint left by the company. Elsewhere, the companies had not built a medical post as promised and had installed a broken electric generator. Worker camps had been abandoned and not properly dismantled.

The reports also confirmed findings in previous reports that although pipeline construction had generated some short-term employment and a rise in business in local towns, the impact was short-lived and the benefits were unevenly distributed across demographic and geographic lines: "Here in the center [of town] some taverns and snack stands benefited where they [the pipeline workers] came to serve themselves, but it wasn't like this in the communities where we live, because we are families that have scarce resources" (Amazon Watch 2002:13).

Community members resented that a number of workers remained after construction ended and generated conflict. More broadly, they were concerned about a perceived increase in migration into their territories as a result of the project and the access roads that were built or improved. Some individuals complained that prostitution and crime increased with the incursion of workers and immigrants—concerns that had been raised two years earlier. The Chiquitano report pointed to the creation of long-term dependencies and cultural alteration: "GasOriente Boliviano [Enron and Shell's subsidiary] employed various community members during construction of the gas pipeline who left their traditional activities, such as agriculture, hunting and fishing, in order to dedicate themselves completely to construction. Once construction concluded, community members were laid-off by the company and they had difficulty returning to their traditional activities" (OICH and CEADES 2002:8, translation by author).

As described in chapter 4, in April 2003, the Chiquitanos, Ayoreos, and allies convinced the environmental ministry to carry out a cursory field inspection—a far cry from the full-fledged audit they requested in 2002—along with other national and municipal authorities, company executives, Indigenous leaders,[2] and civic committee leaders. Also present was congressional representative Isaac Avalos, a well-known peasant (*campesino*) leader who had sporadically supported the Chiquitanos in the case since 1999. His involvement symbolized a broader, loose alliance that had formed between the Chiquitanos and campesino organizations in the region—albeit with persistent land conflicts.[3] It provided insight into how Indigenous politics became rearticulated during the period, illustrating relations between class-based and ethnic-based movements.

As a hedge against the likely outcome that the inspection would be merely lip service to their demands, Indigenous groups and CEADES conducted a simultaneous two-week-long "shadow" audit. They justified the audit by referring to the new legal rights they had won since Indigenous mobilization ignited in the 1990s: "This pipeline has caused systematic violations of Indigenous people's rights. It is provoking serious damage to biodiversity and is putting the sustainability of the communities at risk. The affected Indigenous communities are exercising constant vigilance of the actions of the corporations, international financial institutions and government, demanding respect for their rights as established in national and international laws, especially Convention 169 of the International Labor Organization, adopted as law 1257 in Bolivia" (CPESC et al. 2003:4).

The Chiquitanos and CEADES took great care to back their allegations with supporting evidence (mostly in the form of testimony or photographs). Their findings were also legitimated in a final agreement (*acta*) signed with government officials as well as in individual agreements signed at each affected community. The document confirmed many of the adverse impacts that Indigenous environmental monitors, Amazon Watch, and PROBIOMA had previously reported, including illegal logging and hunting, which limited communities' access to and use of the forest. It also recounted lingering problems with the Indigenous compensation program and conservation program. A number of new issues also surfaced. During the inspection, the Chiquitanos discovered additional access roads that the companies had built and observed a continued lack of reforestation (exacerbated by grazing livestock that had trampled tree saplings) (CPESC et al. 2003). Yet many community roads were still damaged from company vehicles. For the most part, participants witnessed the prevalence of dry bushes and grasses (increasing fire risk) but a lack of saplings. There were some small sections where assisted reforestation had succeeded—hailed as a good example—but these areas were threatened by livestock that entered the poorly controlled right-of-way.

The Chiquitano report also accused Enron and Shell of never consulting with communities about hidden gas outtake valves they left behind, such as the one that the Don Mario gold mine tapped. One community expressed heightened concern for safety because a tree landed on a nearby valve, causing a leak that the companies did not contain for four days; the community was particularly alarmed because there was evidence of fire along the adjacent pipeline route. Soil erosion and evidence of areas prone to landslides also stoked fears of a potential explosion. Near the border of Brazil, communities felt insecure because the pipeline route and access roads were being used for narcotrafficking and transport of stolen vehicles from the area and cattle from the communities. Backing the Chiquitanos, an official from the government's National Service for Protected Areas who worked in the region boldly denounced the occurrence of illegal hunting. Water bodies contaminated during construction had still not been remediated, as evidenced by persistent fuel contamination and decomposing vegetation that had been cleared during construction. Members of one community claimed this led to a rise in skin and gastrointestinal diseases. Additional degraded water bodies were also found, which communities claimed jeopardized their food security. In an attempt to allay concerns, in one community the companies drilled a well with a pump that did not function properly and was costly to operate, causing internal conflicts. A medical post was finally built in another community but without equipment and vehicles and reserved exclusively for emergencies. Similarly, an electrical generator was finally built but it provided only a small amount of power to the receiving community. The community whose soccer field was bisected by the pipeline still did not have a replacement field. And communities living near San Matías (bordering Brazil) complained of the emergence of three prostitution centers that did not exist prior to construction.

The exhaustive ninety-page report concluded with a concise summary of impacts and issues, detailing various legal and contractual obligations. It had one major demand: that the environmental ministry initiate a comprehensive environmental audit as prescribed by law. This illustrated how the Chiquitanos and Ayoreos held out hope that justice would prevail if they continued to exercise their rights and apply pressure. While from the outside this perhaps appeared naive, they knew that their efforts had produced some material improvements (e.g., the $2 million compensation program) and were important in safeguarding the rights gained during the previous two decades. And all of this had been possible amid powerful transnational corporations, international financial institutions, and a compromised government. Congressional representative Isaac Avalos summed up the investigation as follows: "This confirms that Enron has committed specific crimes, which should result in its ouster from Bolivia. . . . Now we hope that all irregularities will be investigated, that the social and environmental impacts of the project will be assessed, and that concrete solutions will be found to repair the damage suffered by the 31 Indigenous communities affected and to mitigate the destruction to the ecosystems of the Chiquitano Forest and Bolivian Pantanal" (qtd. in Hindery 2003b).

These strong words, which fittingly reflected Avalos's aggressive leadership style, spoke to a deeper animosity brewing throughout the country over the larger injustices that Enron and other capitalized (partially privatized) companies had committed during the neoliberal era. Indeed, the investigation occurred in the midst of the 2000–2005 anti-neoliberal rebellion, on the heels of the February 2003 tax riots driven by the Washington, D.C.– based International Monetary Fund, and soon followed by the gas war of 2003 and a second water war in 2005. His statement also attests to a broader convergence of social movements across class and ethnic lines that was afoot at the time. Just as Avalos had joined forces with the Chiquitanos at a regional level, at a national level in June 2005 ethnic groups in the highlands and lowlands united with the national labor union and the lowland landless movement to form the Unity Pact (Pacto de Unidad) in the lead-up to the election of Evo Morales (Buechler 2009:97). And in 2006 Avalos would be elected head of peasant organization Sole Confederation of Peasant Workers of Bolivia (Confederación Sindical Única de Trabajadores Campesinos de Bolivia), the first time an individual from the lowlands (Santa Cruz) led a traditionally highland organization, yet "another sign of the democratic rearticulations of Indigenous politics" (Lucero 2008:186).

To the dismay of the Chiquitanos and Ayoreos, neither the 2003 investigation nor a subsequent congressional hearing in 2004 (see chapter 4) would significantly alleviate impacts. Nor would the government ever heed their demand for a full-fledged audit. As the subsequent chapters demonstrate, although the reputed end of the neoliberal era would breathe new life and hope into the struggle, the Chiquitanos and Ayoreos would soon find that the election of the country's first Indigenous president would not be a panacea for the pipeline's problems, though it would bring some significant gains.

In this chapter I have claimed that the struggle over the Cuiabá pipeline can be viewed as a struggle for environmental justice. I illustrated how Chiquitano and Ayoreo communities experienced a disproportionate share of adverse environmental effects yet saw only modest benefits. I argued that their dynamic and pragmatic use of transnational advocacy, in conjunction with strategic direct actions (blockades, strikes, takeovers of worker camps), lobbying, negotiations, and press outreach, was essential to compelling the Bolivian government, US government, and companies to take action. I have shown that although dissent emerged within fractured state institutions, regulatory actions for the most part were limited in scope as a result of scarce resources, corruption, inadequate training, company influence, and a prevailing bias in favor of extraction. In an uphill battle, the Chiquitanos and Ayoreos prioritized impacts that affected their livelihood and persistently pursued the rationale that if they continued to exercise their newly won rights and apply pressure, injustices would be addressed. I argued that data on pipeline impacts that were collected by Indigenous monitors and NGOs proved pivotal in persuading external actors such as the environmental ministry and the companies to address these effects. This information, a fusion of Traditional Ecological Knowledge and expertise provided by CEADES, was instrumental in raising community awareness about legal rights and in countering the companies' distorted narrative that adverse impacts were minimal and under control. Non-Indigenous, decentralized monitoring committees spearheaded by the NGO PROBIOMA, as well as PROBIOMA's own mobilization efforts, were also crucial.

CHAPTER SEVEN

From Neoliberalism to Nationalism: Resource Extraction in the Age of Evo

In December 2005, Evo Morales Ayma became Bolivia's first self-declared Indigenous president. Winning an unprecedented 54% of the popular vote in a country where 66% of the population self-identifies as Indigenous,[1] his election dealt a "historic blow against informal apartheid race relations" (Webber 2011:231). Indigenous issues were propelled front and center in national politics as Morales promised to govern in favor of Bolivia's Indigenous majority. He vowed to "refound" Bolivia as a twenty-first-century intercultural, plurinational, socialist state (Kohl and Bresnahan 2010a:5).

Beyond raising the banner of Indigenous rights, the arrival of the Morales administration represented a rearticulation of Indigenous and popular movements (2000–2005) that had carried out a wave of intense popular protests in the later years of neoliberal hegemony (1985–2000) (Webber 2005). Morales's victory raised expectations that the neoliberal project was a relic of the past. In part, his election reflected widespread popular rejection of the model (Perreault 2009:135), which Morales codified by repealing the notorious Presidential Decree 21060, which Gonzalo Sánchez de Lozada (then planning minister) had helped craft during the beginning of the neoliberal period in 1985. The decree, which was based on the policy recommendations of Harvard economist Jeffrey Sachs and approved by the International Monetary Fund, included "shock therapy" measures such as currency devaluation, a floating currency, increases in prices charged by the public sector, a wage freeze and reductions in public sector employment, trade liberalization, the freeing up of prices, reform of labor laws, tax reform, and massive reduction in government spending in areas such as health and education (Mares et al. 2008:22; Gill 2000; Klein 2011). At a regional level, the Morales administration was situated on the crest of a rising "pink tide" of governments turning to the left across Latin America. Running on a center-left, populist platform that discursively syncretized Indigenous cosmologies with socialist ideologies, he vowed to uphold the demands of the social movements that brought him to power, including nationalization of hydrocarbons, land reform, and the election of a Constituent Assembly to draft a new constitution.

Now that a direct representative of Bolivia's historically marginalized Indigenous majority had been elected, expectations were raised that a new chapter had been opened for Indigenous peoples—that a new, meaningful relationship with the state, a state increasingly constituted of Indigenous representatives, could be forged. Indeed, under Morales, Indigenous peoples, previously excluded from citizenship and economic power, became a leading bloc in the state (Svampa et al. 2009a). Under his leadership, the UN Declaration on the Rights of Indigenous Peoples was adopted in 2007, followed by a new constitution in 2009 that promised unprecedented new rights for Indigenous peoples. Morales's vice president, Álvaro García Linera, a prominent Bolivian intellectual and former leader of the Tupac Katari Guerrilla Army, argued that Indigenous peoples must govern Bolivia. He insisted that this was the only way to end the colonial character of the republic and close the 180-year-old chasm between society and the state (Stefanoni 2005).

The administration overtly aimed to decolonize Bolivia politically, culturally, and economically (Svampa et al. 2009a) after centuries of imperialist exploitation. Morales himself characterized his political project as a decolonizing democratic revolution that modified power structures, expanded rights, and distributed wealth (Chávez and García Linera 2005). Discursively, the administration touted an image of communitarian socialism, yet under the ideology of "Evismo," Indigenous, democratic, and cultural "revolution" entailed merely modifications to existing political structures of power and elite rule, not "radical" economic change or transformative restructuring of political institutions (Webber 2011:65,176; see also Chávez and García Linera 2005). Although there were notable exceptions, in the months prior to the December 2005 elections Indigenous mobilization shifted from the streets to the core of state power (Lucero 2008:180). With the election of Morales, the Movement Toward Socialism (Movimiento al Socialismo, MAS) party departed from its anti-neoliberal and anti-imperialist ideology of the early 2000s and, for a variety of reasons (Svampa et al. 2009a), shifted to moderate reformism based on Andean-Amazonian capitalism (Webber 2011:98–99), a form of state capitalism.

In this chapter I provide an overview of the Morales administration's policies regarding resource extraction, particularly in relation to hydrocarbons development, Indigenous peoples, and the environment. I argue that profits from extraction have been increasingly aimed at industrialization, and that social spending, effects on communities, and environments largely parallel those that emerged under neoliberalism. I contend that rising discontent around extractive projects is related to the fact that the government's development model assumes Indigenous peoples must be incorporated as modern subjects. I point to dampened yet persistent influence from transnationals and international financial institutions and claim that the Morales administration is at risk because it has not sufficiently clarified how much responsibility for social and environmental impacts would be borne by transnationals that operated during the neoliberal period.

According to García Linera, the government's economic model entails forming a strong state to extract nationalized hydrocarbons and invest a portion of the surplus in modernizing Indigenous, family-based economies (Stefanoni 2005). During this "progressive" stage of capitalism, what Jeffrey Webber (2011:225) calls "reconstituted neoliberalism," a more numerous and politically significant proletariat would emerge, enabling the eventual transition to socialism. Indigenous peoples are seen as potential "proletariat" who must avail themselves to the imposition of "modern" ideals and to the continuation of resource extraction under the tutelage of the state. As with various cases in the Amazon, in the Bolivian case, the Andean-Amazonian model reduces Indigenous peoples and peasants (*campesinos*) to undifferentiated classes to be incorporated into a modernizing framework rather than recognizing them as distinct agents operating in particular political, cultural, economic, and environmental contexts (Nygren 2000; Brass 2002, 2005; De Souza Martins 2002; Bicker et al. 2003; Otero and Jugenitz 2003; Reed 2003; Rival 2003; Harris and Nugent 2004; Hecht 2010). While it is true that Indigenous peoples exercise rights of self-determination, and at times pragmatically choose "modern" or hybrid forms of development (Bebbington 1993; Kimmerer 2002), under Andean-Amazonian capitalism the state prescribed a universal template for modernization, with little chance to opt out.

A "Neoliberal" Nationalization

The Morales presidency began with a bang. On May 1, 2006, International Day of the Worker, Morales approved Presidential Decree 28701, announcing nationalization of the country's oil and gas reserves. He famously declared, "The time has come, the awaited day, a historic day in which Bolivia retakes absolute control of our natural resources. . . . The looting by the foreign companies has ended" (Prada 2006). The move sent shockwaves across the international press that Bolivia was moving forward with its leftward turn, in lock-step with Venezuelan President Hugo Chavez, who announced takeover of the last of the country's private oil fields on the same day. Morales famously sent troops to occupy fields ceded to transnational corporations during the neoliberal period. The nationalization process that followed solidified state ownership of hydrocarbons, with the administration taking credit for making good on a vote the Bolivian people had made in a 2004 national referendum to recuperate control from transnationals.[2] The government filed charges against former president Gonzalo Sánchez de Lozada and former officials of Enron for entering into contracts that damaged the state, for contravening the Bolivian Constitution, and for falsifying contracts (Flores 2006). Charges were also sought against former vice president Victor Hugo Cárdenas, ministers who served during Sánchez de Lozada's 1993–1997 presidency, and former executives of Bolivia's state oil company, Yacimientos Petrolíferos Fiscales Bolivianos (YPFB). The administration pushed ahead with trial in absentia of Sánchez de Lozada for crimes committed during the Gas War of October 2003. Meanwhile, Sánchez de Lozada declared that he would not return to Bolivia because he could not get a fair trial and remained in self-imposed exile in a suburb of Washington, DC, enjoying the protection of the US government. In 2008 the Morales administration formally asked the United States to extradite Sánchez de Lozada and two of his former ministers based on charges that included homicide, torture, and crimes against freedom of the press (Democracy Center 2009). At this writing, the United States had not replied to the government's request (Human Rights Watch 2012). In 2011, Bolivia's Supreme Court of Justice convicted five top military officers of genocide and two former cabinet ministers of complicity in the killings.

Although these actions met some of the demands made by the popular movements that propelled Morales into power, nationalization fell short because the government did not expropriate assets of any transnational corporations (Kohl 2010:117). Rather, it carried out what Brent Kaup (2010) calls a "neoliberal nationalization," which recuperated physical control of hydrocarbons for the state and obligated companies to sign contracts that paid greater royalties and taxes (Gordon and Luoma 2008:101). The state simply renegotiated contracts with foreign companies and purchased a minimum of 51% of their holdings. According to a representative from YPFB, the state did not nationalize the sector but, rather, conducted a "hostile takeover," or a free-market buyout (Gordon and Luoma 2008:130). "Nationalization" left transnational firms still extracting and exporting most of the country's natural gas. Foreign partners included Brazil's Petrobras, Venezuela's PDVSA, Spain's Repsol, the UK's BG Group, France's Total, China's Shengli, and Russia's Gazprom (Elliott 2011). In some respects, Morales's "nationalization" looked similar to the joint ventures spurred by the World Bank's "capitalization" of YPFB in the 1990s, whereby the state sold 50% of its equity to foreign companies (Hindery 2004; Gordon and Luoma 2008:103). Although the 2009 constitution solidified "nationalization," reaffirming that the Bolivian people have the inalienable and imprescriptible right to gas and oil, for all of its anti-neoliberal rhetoric it allows the state company to make contracts (Article 362) and form joint ventures with private, public, or mixed companies (Bolivian or foreign) (Articles 362, 363), as long as it has at least a 51% share (Article 363), specifying a determined amount of pay to contracted companies (Article 362).

Altogether, a political project that purported to warrant the term *post-neoliberal* turned out to be more a continuation of the neoliberal trajectory (Webber 2011:99). While it is certainly true that the influence of international financial institutions under Morales was significantly less than during the neoliberal period because of gas-fueled budget surpluses and regional alliances with Venezuela and Cuba (Kohl 2010:118), in its later years the government made some turns toward neoliberal champions. In 2011 Morales's ministerial cabinet approved a presidential decree establishing Bolivia as a shareholder in the Inter-American Development Bank, one of the chief architects of neoliberalism in Latin America (*El Deber* 2011). That same year, World Bank representative Óscar Avalle proudly proclaimed that the institution was a "partner" in Morales's platform for change and the fight against poverty (Agencia Boliviana de Información 2011a). Since Morales's election, although the World Bank did invest in projects in the areas of disaster management, climate resilience, health, and child development, between 2006 and 2011 a third of its investment ($110 million out of $337 million) went toward improving the San Buenaventura–Ixiamas road and Rurrenabaque Airport in the northern Bolivian Amazon, gateway to world-renowned Madidi National Park. A World Bank press release claimed the project would promote ecotourism and agroforestry, coupled with checkpoints to control illegal logging (World Bank 2011). Yet, as history has shown with other World Bank road investments in the Amazon (e.g., the Trans-Amazon highway), the road will likely spur extractive development in the form of logging, agriculture, mining, and oil drilling. Extractive industries remained king within Morales's overall development portfolio, and oil, gas, and mining development made up the lion's share of the pie.

Reslicing the Hydrocarbons Pie

Gas became paramount for the Morales administration to fund social programs and industrialization projects, to broaden its tax base, and to continue its political project of nationalization (Humphreys Bebbington and Bebbington 2010:154; Gordon and Luoma 2008). According to YPFB (2011), through the 2005 hydrocarbons law and 2006 nationalization, the state nearly doubled its revenues from $592 million in 2005 to more than $1 billion in 2006. Following nationalization, between 2006 and 2010, revenues averaged $1.4 billion, versus only $283 million between 2001 and 2005. Clearly, the state garnered significantly greater revenues under Morales than during the neoliberal period. On the day of nationalization, Vice President García Linera boasted that the state would receive 82% of the value of gas produced through various taxes, while transnational oil corporations would receive only 18%—exactly the opposite of the tax regime under neoliberal rule: 18% for the state and 82% for the transnationals (Webber 2006). Yet despite greater revenue gains, which were associated with high prices for natural gas internationally and a modified tax regime, social spending under Morales decreased as a proportion of gross domestic product, with little change in levels of inequality (Webber 2011:145, 232, 229). YPFB was plagued by corruption scandals and speculation over whether it had sufficient capital and competence to increase production (Gordon and Luoma 2008:106–107).

Passage and implementation of the 2005 hydrocarbons law gave all Bolivians the right to benefit from gas rents through the creation of a direct hydrocarbons tax (impuesto directo a los hidrocarburos, IDH), which increased regional governments' share of hydrocarbons revenue (Humphreys Bebbington and Bebbington 2010:145). Conflict between the central government and regions ensued over how revenues would be allocated (Hodges 2007), notwithstanding the fact that subnational governments probably garnered the greatest share of hydrocarbon revenues in the world, where hydrocarbons are a substantial share of national income and/or export earnings (Weisbrot and Sandoval 2008).

Tensions also arose among Indigenous people over the Development Fund for Indigenous Peoples and Peasant Communities that received 5% of the IDH, or 1.6% of net hydrocarbons revenues. The fund, which arose out of years of organizing by Indigenous groups and nongovernmental organizations (NGOs), including the Center for Juridical Studies and Social Investigation (Centro de Estudios Jurídicos e Investigación Social, CEJIS) and the Collective for Applied Studies and Social Development (Colectivo de Estudios Aplicados y Desarrollo Social, CEADES), was intended to fund projects created by Indigenous communities and parent organizations, including community development and land titling. One Chiquitano leader recounted this history in a nationalistic commentary that suggested the Indigenous movement, far from being separatist (Albro 2005), was concerned with reclaiming hydrocarbon rents taken by transnationals for the benefit of Bolivians:

> The Indigenous peoples marched to La Paz when there was a different government [prior to Morales] and we demanded that funds derived from hydrocarbons come directly to us. The transnational companies had previously negotiated so that money would go to other countries, because they were transnational companies that weren't Bolivian. All of the resources went out of the country and didn't leave anything. That was when the Indigenous movement mobilized to ensure that these funds, through the mechanism of the IDH, be directly managed by the state, the government. This was solved when the hydrocarbons law was modified so that funds would be distributed to Indigenous peoples, the subprefecture, the mayor and universities. The law designated 5% [for Indigenous peoples]. (interview by author)

Another Chiquitano leader related how radical action was needed to wrestle funds away from local and regional elites, suggesting that the critical pending task was to develop concrete proposals:

> We Indigenous peoples obtained these funds through our mobilizations, with marches, with strikes and a series of actions that we carried out. Now, who benefited from the money? First the prefecture, the mayor, the police, and others who were against us, those of us who marched to obtain the funds. But we haven't obtained anything yet. However, thanks to the national policy there is now a mechanism through which these funds can be accessed, an Indigenous fund. The Indigenous fund is supposed to directly support the needs of those communities that fought to create the fund. And this is about the fight between the group that has power and the policy of the state. The elite blame the state for being intransigent, stubborn, for not wanting to cede. That's not the

case. Where is the money going to go to? It will go to those who need it, but we have to propose projects so that we can access the funds. We have to organize ourselves, and this is the responsibility of our parent organizations. (interview by author)

Despite its lofty ambitions, under Morales, the Indigenous fund was plagued by problems over implementation, which was to be carried out by regional prefectures and municipal governments (Weisbrot and Sandoval 2008). One official from the hydrocarbons ministry told me very little of the money was spent due to bureaucratic inefficiency. News of the fund reinvigorated political struggles over identity as Indigenous peoples and peasants (*campesinos*) who had not been officially classified as "Indigenous" increasingly pressured for formal recognition in order to take advantage of new benefits and rights.

Differences of opinion within and across Indigenous groups emerged over control of hydrocarbons in general and over allocation of revenues. Looking at Guaraní and Weenhayek Indigenous groups in the Chaco region of Bolivia, Humphreys Bebbington and Bebbington (2010:155) found that some individuals were supportive of the MAS government yet contended that local Indigenous organizations should have greater control over gas and its revenues. In the Cuiabá case, Chiquitanos were frustrated that money from the Indigenous fund had not yet been disbursed but were cautiously optimistic that the resources would help foster autonomous and endogenous development. They viewed it as a mechanism to reclaim rights lost to Santa Cruz elites and expressed hope that the funds would not be siphoned off by departmental prefects and mayors, as had happened in the past.

Nationalization, Liability, and the Ghost of Enron

With the advent of nationalization, a great deal of uncertainty arose regarding how responsibility for social and environmental impacts caused by transnationals operating prior to nationalization would be shared (or not) with newly nationalized companies, YPFB, and joint ventures. Interviews I conducted with state officials, oil corporations, and Indigenous groups revealed additional confusion about whether community compensation agreements would be extended. As cases within and outside of Bolivia illustrate, assigning liability is a complex, highly politicized affair. Enron and Shell's OSSA II oil pipeline, from Sica Sica, Bolivia, to Arica, Chile, ruptured in January 2000, causing one of the worst oil spills in Bolivian history, and companies blamed YPFB for not maintaining the pipeline prior to capitalization (see chapter 2). Similarly, in nearby Ecuador, in what has been called the world's largest environmental lawsuit, attorneys representing Ecuadorian farmers and Indigenous groups have been battling Chevron-Texaco for nearly twenty years, countering the company's defense that liability for massive soil and water contamination rests with state company Petroecuador rather than Chevron-Texaco (Valdivia 2007; Klasfeld 2011b).

YPFB representatives I met with in 2008 issued a call for a baseline study to determine past liability for social and environmental impacts caused by transnational oil corporations prior to nationalization. However, the first phase of the study did not begin until early 2011. This made it difficult to gather accurate baseline data since nationalization occurred in 2006. Although wells and facilities were to be inspected, an official told me that pipelines were excluded because YPFB claimed that doing so would be too expensive. This claim may prove to be false if the case of the Cuiabá pipeline is any guide for the future. Enron, Ashmore Energy International, and Shell likely spent more than $30 million because of community compensation programs, environmental remediation, and the Chiquitano Forest Conservation Program. According to YPFB, as of 2006 at least four hundred wells had not been closed properly by the various transnational corporations that extracted oil and gas in recent decades. Depending on the results of the baseline study, these sites might also need to be remediated if soil and water contamination is found.

The 2009 constitution includes only weak language regarding past liability: it merely states that liability for historic environmental damages and crimes will be declared (Article 347), presumably by future legislation. It does, however, contain a provision that denies recognition of foreign court cases and foreign jurisdictions, prohibiting international arbitration (Article 366). Whether this prevents transnationals from taking international legal action regarding environmental liability remains to be seen.

Under Morales, division of social and environmental liability among joint ventures between YPFB and transnational corporations also proved messy. Bolivian state officials generally concurred that liability was simply divided in proportion to shares. However, they contended that operators (typically transnationals) would be entirely responsible for the costs of addressing social and environmental impacts. This view contrasted with what a representative from Gas Transboliviano informed me, that impact costs would be split proportionally.

Despite all the uproar over nationalization, ownership of the Cuiabá pipeline remained in private hands, untouched by the state. Although this placed liability squarely in the laps of Cuiabá's private-owners, the Chiquitanos were confused about whether they should direct complaints to YPFB or to GasOriente Boliviano (Enron and Shell's subsidiary, later purchased by Ashmore) and feared that compensation agreements would be terminated. Their concern was not unfounded. An official from YPFB informed me that he was unsure whether the company would issue new compensation agreements, noting that this could occur if warranted. In a 2009 case involving the Weenhayek peoples of the Chaco region, YPFB president Carlos Villegas came to the defense of transnational partner BG Bolivia, accusing the Weenhayek of obstructing investment by demanding excessive compensation (*La Razón* 2009). Weenhayek leaders and supporting attorneys from the NGO Bolivian Forum on Environment and Development (Foro Boliviano sobre Medio Ambiente y Desarrollo, FOBOMADE) argued that the Weenhayek demands were fair according to existing laws, particularly considering a historic debt owed to affected communities. Weenhayek leader Moisés Sapiranda stated, "Here, for over 100 years, we have never seen [economic benefits]. But thanks to God, with the new laws that exist in the country, now there is participatory consultation. . . . We absolutely do not think that our requests are excessive. That is not the case. They are consistent and proportional to the impacts [of oil exploitation]" (qtd. in *La Razón* 2009, translation by author).

Similar to the Cuiabá case, the Weenhayek had initially demanded a higher amount of compensation ($11 million) but after a series of negotiations agreed to $2 million over a twenty-two-year period. The arbitrary nature of compensation agreements adopted for extractive industries projects in Bolivia calls attention to the lack of regulations that clearly define procedures and requirements, a chief demand made by CEJIS, one of the principal legal organizations defending Indigenous rights in Bolivia (Bascopé Sanjinés 2010:31).

Enron's bankruptcy in 2002 exacerbated the confusing web of liability. In 2004, the US Bankruptcy Court for the Southern District of New York ruled that Ashmore, the corporation that had purchased Enron's shares in the Cuiabá pipeline, must address alleged violations of environmental laws and policies (Weil, Gotshal, and Manges LLP 2004). Yet, as this chapter shows, under Morales, significant impacts to Chiquitano communities and the environment persisted, and the Chiquitano Forest Conservation Program continued to exclude Indigenous representatives from the governing board. In apparent violation of Enron's bankruptcy ruling, an Ashmore official informed me in 2009 that no liability was transferred to Ashmore from Enron. After Ashmore purchased all of Shell's shares in the company's joint ventures in Bolivia and Brazil, including the Cuiabá pipeline (Reuters 2007), Shell distanced itself from assuming responsibility from ongoing impacts. The US government's Overseas Private Investment Corporation did the same after canceling Enron's loan in 2002, despite the fact that it violated its own internal environmental and social policies, as well as loan conditions for the Cuiabá project (see chapter 6). Similarly, the World Bank's International Finance Corporation withdrew its financing of the Don Mario gold mine, supplied by gas from the Cuiabá pipeline, effectively "washing its hands" of responsibility related to the scandal.

Development Contradictions under Evo

Throughout Latin America, governments across the political spectrum are intensively pursuing extractive models of development (Bebbington 2009; Bebbington and Humphreys Bebbington 2011; Gudynas and Acosta 2011a). A 2011 report released by Amnesty International warned that the expansion of agriculture, extractive industries, and megadevelopment projects into Indigenous lands was a significant and growing threat to Indigenous peoples across the Americas. It lambasted countries across the region— including Argentina, Brazil, Canada, Colombia, Ecuador, Guatemala, Mexico, Panama, and Peru—for carrying out development projects in Indigenous peoples' ancestral lands in violation of their right to give free, prior, and informed consent. Bolivia was conspicuously absent from criticism, perhaps unsurprisingly given the country's reputed advances in the area of Indigenous rights under Morales. Yet as the cases examined in the following chapters reveal, a deeper probe into practice reveals the persistence of a pernicious developmental model that jeopardizes the livelihoods of Indigenous peoples living in the path of extractive industries. Andean-Amazonian capitalism under Morales discards some features of neoliberal orthodoxy yet preserves "its core faith in the capitalist market as the principal engine of growth and industrialization" (Webber 2011:232). The government's economic vision entails modernization and industrialization guided by a strong state, using profits from natural resources exploited by the state in conjunction with its transnational partners. Although the state is fractured, with some dissenting voices, development under Morales has been primarily predicated on a modernist territorial imaginary based on extraction and economic nationalism. Such an agenda has butted up against strident resource regionalism (e.g., the regional autonomy movement in the gas-rich Department of Tarija), which itself is fragmented across social sectors and subregional scales (Humphreys Bebbington and Bebbington 2010:154).

Vice President García Linera, perhaps the most prominent architect and advocate of the Andean-Amazonian development model, has described the government's economic project as a process of economic decoloniza-tion, meaning stemming the outward flow of surplus—plugging Eduardo Galeano's (1971) "open veins of Latin America" (Svampa et al. 2009a)— and reinvesting it domestically. Paradoxically, however, the cases explored in this chapter suggest that such an agenda amounts to a new form of neo-colonialism, with resource extraction guided more by the state yet driven to a significant degree by the dictates of neoliberal capitalism.

García Linera argues for extraction of hydrocarbons to generate surplus to meet the basic needs of all Bolivians, including Indigenous peoples, whom he views as among those most in need. He recognizes a tension between expanding environmental protection and the need for large-scale production and expansive industrialization that generates a social surplus that can be redistributed and support Indigenous, peasant, communitar-ian, and small-scale modernization. Industrialization, then, is a part of the government's larger project of decolonization (Kaup 2010). García Linera believes that hydrocarbon production can be carried out in a way that does not destroy the environment and contends that surpluses can be used to strengthen and modernize community structures. In this context, it is clear that he ascribes to liberal notions of modernization and progress and does not see them at odds with Indigenous cultural survival or environ-mental protection. Such a view clashes directly with visions of many In-digenous peoples in Bolivia. Rafael Quispe, leader of the main Indigenous organization of the highlands, the National Council of Ayllus and Mar-kas of Qullasuyu (Consejo Nacional de Ayllus y Markas del Qullasuyu, CONAMAQ), while openly supportive of some of Morales's agenda for change, was also one of the most vocal critics of the administration's devel-opment model: "Capitalism or socialism is extractive, consumerist, devel-opmentalist. In this sense, they are the same. We have to speak of a new model of development, an alternative to this system. Because both capital-ism and socialism will go on changing the planet. And the development model of the Indigenous peoples is the Ayllu, the communitarian develop-ment model. We original Indigenous peoples for thousands and thousands and thousands of years have been living in equilibrium and respect for our Pachamama (Mother Earth), from whom we emerged" (qtd. in Weinberg

2010). Although it may be an exaggeration to claim that all of Bolivia's thirty-four Indigenous groups ascribe to the highland based "Ayllu" model and live in harmony with the environment, it can be said that they do not merely resist modern development; rather, they actively advance distinct place-based ways of living—what Mario Blaser (2004:26) has called "life projects"—as alternative paths to Indigenous futures.

The 2009 constitution contains a paradoxical mix of safeguards for Indigenous peoples and the environment combined with guarantees for the continuation of extractive development on Indigenous lands. On the one hand, the text insists that hydrocarbons must be developed both sustainably and equitably (Article 360) and notes that it is the "duty of the State and its residents to conserve, protect and use natural resources and biodiversity sustainably, as well as to maintain the environment's equilibrium" (Article 342). Yet as subsequent sections show, such prescriptions have thus far had little weight in practice and are thwarted by other provisions that undermine Indigenous rights.

Despite progressive discourse and legal advances, since Morales was elected Indigenous groups have increasingly expressed discontent with the development model, reflected by a rise of mobilization outside of the confines of what Webber (2011:100) has called the "Morales reform agenda." Frustration over the administration's project not only emerged among Indigenous peoples but also manifested in popular movements independent from the MAS that simultaneously defended the government against imperialism and the domestic right while challenging the administration and opting for more transformative change from below (Webber 2011:11, 176). As shown in subsequent chapters, this dual strategy was employed by Chiquitanos in the Cuiabá case and has been used by other groups, such as the Guaraní, as well (Humphreys Bebbington and Bebbington 2010). In May 2011, 350 Guaraní took over a processing plant of YPFB Andina Sociedad Anonima (SA), a joint venture of YPFB and Spanish transnational Repsol YPF Bolivia SA, demanding that the company return land allegedly taken from their native communal lands (tierras comunitarias de origen, TCOs) (Plataforma Energética 2011b). In 2011, neighborhood groups, students, and farmers living in the highland city of El Alto (formerly a suburb of La Paz) organized the Committee in Defense of the Popular Economy and Natural Resources, with the aim of growing into a national organization that would renew the October agenda of 2003, a platform that emerged from the coalition of popular movements that ousted Sánchez de Lozada that same year. The demands included (1) nationalization and industrialization of the hydrocarbons sector, including expulsion of transnational corporations, (2) establishment of a Constituent Assembly to advance Indigenous rights, (3) a trial of Sánchez de Lozada and others complicit for violence carried out during the 2003 gas war, (4) guarantees of workers' rights, (5) an end to coca eradication, and (6) an agrarian revolution that would expropriate estates and redistribute lands to smallholders.

Discursively, the Morales administration's shift toward domestic industrial development is reminiscent of the import substitution industrialization period in Latin America, in which domestic production of value-added import substitutes was prioritized. For instance, as described below, Morales opted to use gas to produce fertilizer and polyethylene, substituting these new domestically produced products for what had been imported previously. The 2009 constitution explicitly prioritizes industrialization (Article 355), energy sovereignty (Article 360), internal consumption (Article 379), and export of excess production incorporating the greatest quantity of value added possible (Article 367).

YPFB's 2009–2015 investment plan calls for aggressive growth in the hydrocarbons sector and aims for further industrialization (YPFB 2009). By 2015 YPFB anticipates increasing production of natural gas to 76 million cubic meters per day and liquids to 85 million barrels per day. Although the plan claims that exports will be vital to growth of the sector, it envisions substantial expansion of Bolivia's domestic market, as well as industrialization. Under Morales, pipelines have been built to urban areas, and gas is increasingly destined for commercial, domestic, and industrial consumption within the country. By 2015, YPFB expects natural gas to account for 48% of domestic energy supply, double what it was in 2010 (Agencia de Noticias Fides 2011). Gas lines are being built in urban centers throughout Bolivia, and by 2015 YPFB plans to increase the number of home connections from 150,000 to 900,000. Vehicles are increasingly being converted to use natural gas, and YPFB is developing gas stations and other related infrastructure. Striving to boost value-added commodities, YPFB plans to build two gas-powered fertilizer production plants,[3] a polyethylene plant, and a facility that would convert natural gas into diesel.[4] The company also envisions a $70 million joint venture with the Venezuelan government to produce prefabricated polyvinyl chloride (PVC) houses. The project, named Petrocasas, raised concern given adverse health effects associated with toxic chemicals found in the plastic. In the Chiquitano region, the Morales administration inaugurated two gas-fired power plants fueled by the Cuiabá pipeline, electrified the countryside, and reignited a project floated decades earlier to mine one of the world's largest iron ore deposits,

El Mutún, which borders Brazil near the town of Puerto Suárez (see chapter 9; see also figure 1.2).

Morales's moves toward industrialization and expansion of the domestic market have been met by a number of critical challenges. As Kaup (2010) points out, overcoming historical dependence on extractive industries through industrialization entails the painful task of diverting funds from social programs to invest substantially in exploration, production, and pipelines. Taken at face value, a review of YPFB documents suggests booming industrialization based on hydrocarbons, but whether it will have sufficient capital to carry out these projects is in question (*La Patria* 2010).[5] Whether gas reserves will be sufficient to meet the administration's lofty ambitions is also unclear. And even if these problems are managed, industrialized products will face challenges penetrating new markets, as in Brazil, which is developing fertilizer plants itself, using Bolivian gas (Muriel 2011).

YPFB greenwashes planned initiatives with references to the phrase *Vivir Bien*, an Aymara Indigenous concept used frequently by the Morales administration that signifies "to live well" and not at the expense of others or the environment. A similar pattern can be seen in the government's 2006–2010 National Development Plan (Borda and de la Barra 2007:80), which, while proposing such laudable aims as reducing poverty and creating a more inclusive society, still maintains extractive development as the engine of the economy (Gudynas and Acosta 2011a). Thus, the administration's development agenda is at odds with various provisions within the 2009 constitution, which states that industrialization of natural resources must safeguard Indigenous rights, territories, and the environment (Article 319). The document also asserts that Bolivia must further overcome dependence on export of raw materials and "achieve an economy with a productive base, within the framework of sustainable development, in harmony with nature" (Article 311).

In this chapter I have argued that although the model of development implemented under Morales has increased state profits from extractive industries and directed them toward industrialization and social spending, continued oil, gas, and mining development has affected Indigenous communities and environments in ways that are similar to the neoliberal period. I further contended that although state institutions are fractured, development has been based on a dominant modernist territorial imaginary rooted in extraction and resource nationalism. I suggested that in order to understand extractive development conflicts that have emerged under Morales, it is important to recognize that Indigenous peoples have been reduced to "proletariat" who must join the state's modernist project. I showed that while influence from international financial institutions and transnationals has waned to some degree, neoliberal players continue to wield significant power in advancing extractive development. Finally, I argued that through a "neoliberal nationalization" (Kaup 2010), the Morales administration has put itself in a vulnerable position because it has not carried out sufficient studies to delineate how liability for social and environmental impacts that accrued during the neoliberal era will be shared with transnationals.

As this chapter has shown, the domestic benefits produced by extractive development initiatives will need to be weighed in relation to potential adverse impacts to communities and the environment. The Morales administration's relentless pursuit to extract and industrialize minerals and hydrocarbons with transnational partners inevitably results in degradation and dispossession of Indigenous and *campesino* peoples located atop deposits (Webber 2011:234) or in the path of pipelines. As chapter 8 demonstrates, by the later years of the Morales presidency, clashes between the government and affected Indigenous groups intensified, with the latter calling into question contradictions in the constitution and on the ground.

CHAPTER EIGHT

Clashing Cosmologies and Constitutional Contradictions

The preamble to the 2009 Bolivian Constitution reads as follows:

In immemorial times mountains arose, rivers were displaced, lakes were formed. Our Amazonia, our Chaco, our highlands and our plains and valleys were covered by greenness and flowers. We populated this sacred Mother Earth with different faces, and since then we understood the current plurality of all things and our diversity as beings and cultures. This is how we formed our towns, and we never understood racism until we suffered it since the terrible times of colonization.

The Bolivian people, of plural composition, since the depth of history, inspired in the battles of the past, in the indigenous anticolonial uprising, in independence, in the popular liberation fights, in the Indigenous, social, and union marches, in the water and October wars [Gas War of October 2003], in the battles for land and territory, and with the memory of our martyrs, built a new State.

A State based in respect and equality among all, with principles of sovereignty, dignity, complementarity, solidarity, harmony, and equity within the distribution and redistribution of the social product, with the predomination of the search to live well; with respect to the economic, social, legal, political, and cultural plurality of the inhabitants of this land; in collective coexistence with access to water, work, education, health, and housing for everyone.

We left the colonial, republican, and neoliberal State in the past. We assumed the historical challenge to collectively build a Social Unitary

State of Plurinational Communitarian Law, which integrates and artic-
ulates the purposes of advancing toward a Bolivia that is democratic,
productive, carrier, and inspirer of peace, committed to integral development and with the free determination of its people.

We, men and women, through the Constituent Assembly and with
the original power of the people, manifest our commitment to the unity
and integrity of the country.

Complying with the mandate of our people, with the strength of our
Pachamama and giving thanks to God, we refound Bolivia.

Honor and glory for the martyrs of this constituent and liberating
feat that has made this new history possible. (translation by Valle V.
et al. 2010, with errors corrected by author)

As its preamble might suggest, Bolivia's 2009 constitution has been her-
alded as one of the most progressive charters in Latin America. In this
chapter, I explore the paradox that while the document grants important
new rights for Indigenous peoples and the environment, it has internal contradictions and has been violated by various extractive projects pursued
by the administration of President Evo Morales. I first look at some of the
historical origins of the constitution, highlighting the importance of mobilization during the 2000–2005 anti-neoliberal rebellion. I then review key
conflicts over consultation and consent, showing how Indigenous peoples
have proactively used International Labor Organization (ILO) Convention
169 and the UN Declaration on the Rights of Indigenous Peoples (UNDRIP)
to challenge the state's rights regarding development.

Passage of Bolivia's 2009 constitution resulted from many years of organizing on the part of Indigenous peoples and various social movements.
Intense mobilization to rewrite the constitution took place during the anti-
neoliberal rebellion from 2000 to 2005. In 2002, mirroring the Ecuadorian
experience, Bolivian Indigenous organizations, supported by the Center
for Juridical Studies and Social Investigation (Centro de Estudios Jurídicos e Investigación Social, CEJIS) and other organizations, demanded a
constituent assembly to rewrite the constitution, echoing a call made by
popular movements during the 2000 water war. Mobilization around this
end culminated in 2002 in the March for Popular Sovereignty, Territory,
and Natural Resources, which led to an agreement with the government
and political parties with parliamentary representation that a national constituent assembly was viable (CEJIS 2010). In the subsequent three years,
as the Movement Toward Socialism (Movimiento al Socialismo, MAS)
party consolidated power, election of a constituent assembly to draft a new

constitution became one of the central pillars of Morales's platform. Six months after Morales became president, 255 representatives (*constituyentes*) were elected to the Assembly, 137 of them from the MAS. Heated partisan conflict ensued between the government and the opposition over voting rules and document drafting. The process fell short of the transformative and participatory assembly envisioned by left and Indigenous groups during the revolutionary period of 2000–2005 (Webber 2011:99). Although the work of redrafting the constitution occurred between August 6, 2006, and December 15, 2007, it was not until January 25, 2009, that the Bolivian people ratified it with a 62% vote. Ostensibly, conclusion of the process solidified Morales's power and paralleled Bolivarian processes of political change carried out under other left-leaning regimes in Latin America: Venezuela (Hugo Chavez), Ecuador (Rafael Correa), Nicaragua (Daniel Ortega), and Honduras (Manuel Zelaya). It further provided the MAS a legal framework for advancing the reforms it had initiated since 2006.

Conservative political parties and pro-regional "autonomy" groups (Gustafson 2009:1007) seized upon the 2009 constitution as concrete evidence of how the Morales administration had advanced Indigenous rights to the detriment of non-Indigenous Bolivians. Juan Carlos Urenda Díaz, a corporate attorney and constitutional law scholar from Santa Cruz who supported the elite-driven regional autonomy movement, criticized the constitution for being racist toward non-Indigenous Bolivians (Urenda Díaz 2009). He contends that articles that grant privileges based on ethnicity are contrary to the principle of equality and the liberal democratic system. For instance, he claims that Indigenous peoples' right to participate in the benefits of natural resource exploitation (Article 30) is a racial privilege. Such an assertion neglects that this right is present in ILO Convention 169 (ratified in Bolivia in 1991) and UNDRIP (adopted identically as Bolivian Law 3760 in 2007). More broadly, his claim is emblematic of a discursive narrative present among lowland elite that now that Morales has come to power the tables have turned, with Indigenous groups now acting as hegemons, marginalizing the agroindustrial and business elite through land reform and other mechanisms (Gustafson 2009:1006).

The 2009 constitution, while not as transformative as the document envisioned by its proponents, is a significant departure from the previous charter. It gives Indigenous peoples the right to free existence; self-determination; cultural identity; a healthy environment; collective intellectual property; intracultural, intercultural, and plurilingual education; and exercise of their own political, legal, and economic systems according to their own cosmovisions. It further guarantees them the right to land, collective titling, and exclusive management of renewable natural resources located in their territories.

Discursively, the text is anti-neoliberal and decolonial, drawing heavily on Indigenous epistemologies and ontologies. Similar to its Ecuadorian counterpart, the document redefines Bolivia as a plurinational state, enshrining the doctrine of "Living Well" (*Vivir Bien*) and granting nature intrinsic rights. Yet, it reflects the "class-inflected vision of the left and the tensions that still mark the MAS-Indigenous alliance" (Gustafson 2009:1004).

While at the surface the constitution makes great strides toward a more harmonious relation between the state, Indigenous peoples, and the environment, contradictions within the text and development in practice reveal modest substantive change. The text has some strong provisions regarding Indigenous rights and environmental protection, but others that are directly at odds. Legislation to implement the constitution is still being developed, and early indications based on the Cuiabá case and others bring to light serious challenges with application and enforcement. Furthermore, the Morales administration's pursuit of development based on extractive industries contradicts the constitution's tenets regarding sustainable development, human rights, and the environment.

Similar to Ecuador's 2008 constitution, Bolivia's 2009 constitution invokes key tenets from various Indigenous cosmologies that clash with modern ideals: "Article 8. I. The State assumes and promotes as ethic-moral principles of the plural society: ama qhilla, ama llulla, ama suwa [don't be lazy, don't be a liar, don't be a thief (Quechua)], suma qamaña [to live well (Aymara)], ñandereko [harmonious life (Guaraní)], teko kavi [good life or new life (Guaraní)], ivi maraei [land without evil (Guaraní)], and qhapaj ñan [noble path or life (Quechua)]" (translation by Valle V. et al. 2010, with errors corrected by author).

Bolivian philosopher Javier Medina (2006), who has written extensively on the principle of "living well," contends that clashing ideals lie at the root of the divide between Bolivian elites and Indigenous peoples:

> The Bolivian problem is that its elites want an animist civilization (whose values are symbiosis, cooperation, equilibrium, upbringing, conversation, equivalence, agrocentrism) to function like a monotheistic civilization (whose values are the separation of God/Man/Nature, liberty, progress, development, individualism, accumulation, subjectivity, competition, domination, instrumental reason, carrying their truth to the ends of the world, and converting the infidels to their truth so that the world is one like you are One). (translation by author)

To live well (*Vivir Bien*) means "living comfortably and with dignity within one's means, without excess" (Johnson 2010:143) and privileges cultural identity based on ties to one's people and land (Medina 2006). The concept cannot be reduced simply to signify instrumental development alternatives but rather is an alternative paradigm to Western development altogether (Gudynas and Acosta 2011b). Bolivia's 2006 National Development Plan refers to the term as living with access and enjoyment of material goods as well as emotional, intellectual, and spiritual fulfillment in harmony with nature and fellow human beings. In this context, it is meant to be a guiding principle or paradigm for national development and, more broadly, for transforming the state and society. Yet, despite adoption of the principle in the constitution and various laws, recent struggles over the right to consultation illustrate how Bolivian Indigenous peoples continue to push for its genuine implementation as modern development under Morales proceeds in violation of the principle.

The Consultation Facade

Pressure from Indigenous, peasant and nongovernmental organizations (NGOs) led to the adoption of a series of significant legal measures related to consultation during the Morales presidency. These reforms grew out of previous measures adopted in the 1990s as a result of mobilization by the growing lowland Indigenous movement. In 1990, the first March for Territory and Dignity led to ratification of ILO Convention 169 in 1992 (Rivero Guzman 2007), which required the state to establish consultation procedures and grant fair compensation to Indigenous peoples for any damages (ILO 1991). Subsequent mobilization led to recognition of these rights in the 2005 hydrocarbons law and a 2007 presidential decree (President of Bolivia 2007) but did not include the concept of consent, thereby denying Indigenous groups the power to veto projects. A MAS-backed draft of the former had included veto rights for Indigenous peoples but was excised (Gordon and Luoma 2008:111). In September 2007, it appeared this would change when Evo Morales proudly announced approval of UNDRIP as Law 3760 before any other country had done so. UNDRIP does require free, prior, and informed consent (FPIC) prior to the approval of any project affecting Indigenous lands and other natural resources (Article 32). The document is now the primary international instrument on Indigenous rights. Rights listed in the agreement "constitute the minimum standards for the survival, dignity and well-being of the Indigenous peoples of the world" (Article 43). However, in apparent contradiction, the 2009 constitution merely requires the state to conduct free, prior, and informed consultation (FPICon).[1] This exclusion is very intentional and directly reflects a high-stakes battle over natural resource rights between the state and Indigenous peoples. In recent cases in which the Morales administration has pushed controversial development projects opposed by Indigenous peoples, the government has argued that consultation is not binding.

FPIC is a prerequisite for the fundamental right to self-determination and underpins Indigenous peoples' ability to exert sovereignty over their lands and natural resources (Carmen 2010:120; Westra 2008). Although 143 countries agreed to FPIC by voting in favor of UNDRIP, Canada, one of four countries that voted against it (along with the United States, Australia, and New Zealand) stated that inclusion of "consent" was one of the main reasons it opposed the covenant, fearing it would give Indigenous peoples veto power (Aboriginal Affairs and Northern Development Canada 2008). As with the Ecuadorian case, Bolivian Indigenous organizations and other groups that worked through the constituent assembly process to incorporate consent into the constitution ultimately failed. While the Morales administration's opposition was less overt, Ecuadorian president Rafael Correa emphatically opposed inclusion of FPIC in that country's 2008 constitution (Denvir and Riofrancos 2008). Although laws regarding consultation with Indigenous peoples have been on the rise throughout Latin America, exclusion of consent is a persistent problem. In Peru, the administration of Ollanta Humala finally adopted such a bill in 2011, after it had been repeatedly rejected by Peru's previous president, Alan Garcia; although the move marked a turning point in the country's policies on Indigenous rights, consent was visibly absent (Tegel 2011). Moreover, the state retains the right to subsurface resources and, if a dispute arises, has the right to make the final decision (Cabitza 2011b).

In practical terms, exclusion of consent means that the state and private sector can continue to merely consult with Indigenous peoples about hydrocarbons and mining projects occurring on their lands and then simply proceed with such development whether or not they agree. In this respect, the 2009 Bolivian Constitution is similar to Ecuador's new constitution, which also only recognizes the right to free, prior, and informed consultation, but not consent. The exclusion limits Indigenous peoples' ability to use legal means to challenge development projects that encroach upon their territories. However, in the Bolivian case, the fact that the government adopted UNDRIP as law means that Indigenous peoples could claim the right to consent since international treaties that grant more favorable rights than those contained in the constitution are superior (Article 256).

The Bolivian Constitution specifies that Indigenous peoples are guaranteed the right to obligatory consultation when nonrenewable natural resources (e.g. minerals and fossil fuels) are exploited within their territories (Article 30). However, this could be interpreted as excluding pipelines that pass through their territories but do not extract hydrocarbons from them. Along the same lines, the constitution grants Indigenous peoples the right to administer autonomous Indigenous territories and to exclusively use and manage renewable natural resources (Article 30) but does not grant such rights for nonrenewable natural resources. To the contrary, the state owns and is responsible for all mineral resources found in the soil and subsoil (Articles 348, 349, 359). The constitution designates all forms of energy as strategic resources and states that access to them is a fundamental right for development of the country (Article 378). Energy resources are to be governed based on the contradictory principles of efficiency, continuity, adaptability, and environmental preservation (Article 378).

Taken together, these constitutional provisions essentially require the state to promote extraction and transport of hydrocarbons on Indigenous lands regardless of whether or not affected populations consent but in a manner that meaningfully solicits input and minimizes adverse impacts. At the time of writing, Bolivian legislation regarding prior consultation is among the most complete and consistent in the region, but Indigenous groups have repeatedly complained about lack of application and enforcement (Garzón 2010:27).

In July 2010 a splintered assortment of Indigenous groups, including the lowland Federation of Indigenous Peoples of Bolivia, marched toward the highland city of La Paz, frustrated that, among other things, the Morales administration would not implement their proposed autonomy law (ley marco de autonomía), which they claimed was supported by the new constitution, ILO Convention 169, and UNDRIP. Supporters of the march, which included Chiquitano Indigenous peoples, claimed it would advance Indigenous rights to self-determination in native communal lands (tierras comunitarias de origen, TCOs) and prior consultation as specified in the aforementioned legal instruments. Despite the fact that plurinational Indigenous autonomy is supported in the new constitution, some government officials resisted it, claiming it would break regional limits and national unity—interestingly, a nationalistic argument similar to the administration's criticisms of regional autonomy demands made by Santa Cruz elite

(Gustafson 2009). Although peasant organization Sole Confederation of Rural Workers of Bolivia (Confederación Sindical Única de Trabajadores Campesinos de Bolivia, CSUTCB) officially rejected the march and affirmed support for Morales, internal divisions emerged. The secretaries of natural resources of the organizations affiliated with CSUTCB stated that for a long time they had been on the war path against the extractivist and developmentalist policies of the "Indigenous" government. According to one source, the Morales administration wanted to restrict the right to consent because it could result in an "Indigenous veto" of the administrations' initiatives, which includes fossil fuel and mining development (*Bolpress* 2006).

Asymmetrical power relations among the state, oil corporations, and Indigenous peoples have already manifested through contradictions in implementation. In October 2008 the Morales administration announced that the state oil company, Yacimientos Petrolíferos Fiscales Bolivianos (YPFB), would join with its Venezuelan counterpart, forming Petroandina Sociedad Anonima Mixta (SAM)—with 60% of the shares owned by YPFB, and 40% owned by Venezuelan state oil company Petróleos de Venezuela, S.A., PDVSA)—to carry out oil exploration and extraction in the northern La Paz Department, including Madidi National Park. The park, which spans from the Andes to the Amazon Basin, is home to several Indigenous groups[2] and is one of the most biodiverse places on Earth. Featured on the cover of *National Geographic* magazine, Madidi is a tourist haven, a hotbed for "ecofriendly" development projects[3] touted for curbing logging and agricultural clearing. News of the project sparked a wave of protest on the part of environmental organizations and some affected Indigenous communities. The case has become a litmus test for how the government will balance hydrocarbons development with Indigenous rights and environmental protection. The administration's conduct thus far has been criticized for weighting the former over the latter, exemplified by controversy surrounding consultation with affected Indigenous peoples.

The broad contours of issues surrounding consultation in the Madidi case are strikingly similar to the Cuiabá case, except that with Madidi the state took the lead (and criticism), rather than transnational oil corporations. Throughout the conflict, the state downplayed criticisms regarding consultation, declaring that it had been carried out properly and had not generated division amongst Indigenous groups. It dismissed Indigenous representatives and NGOs that claimed otherwise. Carlos Espinoza, the social and environmental director of Bolivia's hydrocarbons ministry,

proclaimed that all Mosetene Indigenous communities had been consulted and agreed to support the project before it began: "We explained all
aspects of the project to them and all possible impacts. Division among the
Mosetene does not exist. It does not exist! Some foundations and NGOs
have commented a lot about potential environmental risks. There has been
a lot of speculation. We have been there, and have not observed risk to the
environment; there is no risk, none. We understand that subsistence agriculture that the Mosetene practice is totally compatible with oil activities"
(qtd. in Schipani 2009, translation by author).

Too often, states interpret "consultation" in a self-serving manner, as
merely an exchange of views that excludes decision making on the part of
Indigenous peoples concerned (Carmen 2010:124). Espinoza's statement
suggests he views consultation as a one-way flow of information from the
state and technical "experts" to affected Indigenous peoples, rather than as
a meaningful, dialectical exchange of knowledge in accordance with Indigenous customs and traditions, as required by UNDRIP. As his job title
suggests, he was supposed to serve as a liaison with communities, yet rather
than advocating for respectful dialogue, his statement suggests he viewed
Mosetene communities as children who needed to be taught about the
project's benevolence. His erroneous proclamation that there is no environmental risk and that subsistence agriculture is totally compatible with
oil activities reveals his overt bias toward oil development.

Project consultants did initially consult with the Central Organization
of Indigenous Peoples of La Paz (Central de Pueblos Indígenas de La Paz,
CPILAP), a regional organization representing eight Indigenous peoples
and their organizations. CPILAP clarified that it was not opposed to the
project but simply wanted to ensure that meaningful consultation and
oversight occurred (Costas 2010). It tried to use the project for leverage to
pressure the government to finish the land titling process for some pending TCOs, placing this as a condition to approval of the consultation process (Costas 2010). Ultimately, though, when the companies and Indigenous
organizations reached an impasse, the state bypassed CPILAP and the two
Indigenous organizations whose territories would be directly affected by
development, Organización del Pueblo Indígena Mosetén (OPIM) and
Organización del Pueblo Indígena Leco y Comunidades de Larecaja,
(PILCOL) (Costas 2010). The state repeated what Enron and Shell's consultants did in the Cuiabá case, bypassing a regional Indigenous organization and instead negotiating directly, community by community. In both
cases, a series of internal divisions emerged within and among communities, and some leaders lost credibility (Costas 2010). In the Madidi case,

Espinoza's declaration that division had not occurred was clearly false. Vilma Mendoza, a leader from Simay, a community opposed to the project, viewed infighting as the greatest negative consequence of the project: "Besides environmental effects, which will change our quality of life and the quality of our food, this above all is dividing our community. There have already been fights among Mosetene" (qtd. in Schipani 2009, translation by author).

The Simay community blocked company machines, which caused conflict with communities supportive of oil development. This point was made by Simay leader and Catholic priest Daniel Gigasi: "We had to stop protesting due to constant threats and intimidation from other fellow Mosetene who had been bought by the government and the oil companies. We did this to avoid bloodshed" (qtd. in Schipani 2009, translation by author).

On July 2, 2009, one day after the ministries of environment and hydrocarbons granted Petroandina an environmental license, several Indigenous organizations from the region presented a legal demand opposing the license on the grounds that consultation had not been carried out properly (Costas 2010). At a press conference they announced: "The problem we have is about the consultation and participation process. As leaders we have tried to ensure that steps in the consultation process have been complied with. However, the technical experts from the Ministry of Hydrocarbons, who carry out consultation, went over the heads of the leadership. They tried to make their rounds to the communities, but began to buy off leaders. That is why we have leaders that are not in line with what we want. Therefore, we asked that they comply with these steps and norms" (Costas 2010, translation by author).

Several Indigenous leaders leveled accusations that other leaders and communities had accepted bribes to support the project. A leader from one of the communities supporting development denied these claims, stating that his and other communities had consented to generate investment in potable water and improved living conditions. Yet, a representative from CPILAP alleged that this leader did not consult with the community but, rather, that the government had merely searched for a leader who would support the project (FM Bolivia 2009). Gigasi criticized the project for overlapping various Indigenous communal territories. He further claimed the government was running roughshod over Indigenous rights and not complying with ratified international laws (FOBOMADE 2010). Indigenous representatives also criticized the state for not providing sufficient information and for not giving leaders sufficient time to plan the consultation process in coordination with their communities as required by

FPICon (Costas 2010). Some alleged that the company gathered signatures from children and at community members' houses at night (FM Bolivia 2009). Despite these issues, in December 2009 the minister of hydrocarbons issued a resolution rejecting the Indigenous organizations' legal demand opposing the project license (Costas 2010). Exploration commenced. The state's interest in hydrocarbons had superseded Indigenous rights to consultation.

Within the course of a year, this setback was followed by yet another. In the beginning of 2010 the president of YPFB, the state oil and gas company of Bolivia, commented that consultation and participation with Indigenous peoples was an obstacle to investment and announced changes to the hydrocarbons law (Costas 2010). In October 2010, the Morales administration approved a presidential decree (Gaceta Oficial del Estado Plurinacional de Bolivia 2010) that opened up fifty-six new areas for oil development, many of which overlap Indigenous territories and protected areas, including Madidi (Stephanes 2010). The decree inaccurately asserts that companies will mitigate social, environmental, and cultural impacts within protected areas by merely employing adequate technology. On the one hand, the decree cites provisions in the 2009 constitution that establish the state's duty to protect Indigenous cultures (Article 98), carry out consultation (Article 30), and promote sustainable development of hydrocarbons (Article 360). Yet it invokes another article that establishes nonrenewable resources as state necessities and public utilities (Article 356) and argues that under the 2005 hydrocarbons law, hydrocarbons activities are permitted in protected areas when studies have determined their viability.

These contradictions show the state is privileging rights to hydrocarbons development over Indigenous rights and environmental protection. This trend must be understood in the context of Andean-Amazonian capitalism, a so-called Indigenous form of state capitalism espoused by influential figures in the MAS political party, particularly Vice President Álvaro García Linera (Webber 2011:64). Such individuals view an intermediary stage of industrial capitalism as necessary to build the material conditions required for a transition to socialism. Using a train metaphor, García Linera views this model as comprised of six carriages: (1) state synthesis of popular will, strategic planning, and steering the economic locomotive, (2) Bolivian private investment, (3) foreign investment, (4) small business, (5) peasant economy, and (6) Indigenous economy (Toussaint 2010).[4] As Jeffrey Webber (2011:99) has argued, Indigenous liberation for MAS has been separated from the struggle for socialist transformation. Indigenous interests are subordinated to the interests of capital since the administration is wedded to the macroeconomic foundations of neo-liberalism (Webber 2011:144). Given this strategic ordering of the economy, the state's right and collective societal interest trumps Indigenous rights, as evidenced by García Linera's view on the need for oil development in the northern La Paz Department. In response to the question "What if the communities said the state couldn't come in either?" he stated:

> This is the debate. What happened? When we consulted the Central Organization of Indigenous Peoples of La Paz (CPILAP), they asked us to go negotiate in Brussels with their legal firm and that we respect some environmentalist principles published by USAID. How is this possible? Who wants to prevent the State from exploring petroleum in the north of La Paz? Indigenous Tacana communities? An NGO? Or foreign countries? This is why we went to negotiate community by community, and there we found support from the Indigenous communities to continue to explore for and exploit petroleum. The Indigenous-popular government consolidated the long struggle of the peoples for land and territory. In the case of the minority Indigenous peoples of the lowlands, the State consolidated millions of hectares as a historic territoriality for many peoples of low demographic density; but together with a people's right to land is the State's right, (the State led by the Indigenous-popular and peasant movement), to prioritize the higher collective interest of all the peoples. And this is how we proceeded afterwards. (qtd. in Svampa et al. 2009b)

García Linera's statement yields additional evidence that the state bypassed Indigenous organizations and went directly to negotiate with communities. His assertion that "together with a people's right to land is the State's right" does not appear to be real recognition of Indigenous territorial rights as outlined in UNDRIP. Rather, it implies that if energy resources on Indigenous lands can benefit the broader Bolivian population, then the state's right to the lands takes precedence over Indigenous peoples' sovereignty; ancestral rights are irrelevant. Such a "discourse of dominance" (Gedicks 2001:21) involves belittling Indigenous subsistence economies (the sixth carriage) under the pretext of introducing modern economic development to the "primitive" natives (Johnston 1994:10). This process is common in resource battles with Indigenous peoples. In northern Wisconsin, an Exxon Minerals biologist classified the Sokaogon Chippewa's wild rice–based subsistence economy as "a bunch of lake weeds" (Gedicks 2001:61).

García Linera's commentary reflects the administration's broader concerns over US intervention in domestic affairs, particularly in relation to meddling with economic sovereignty over oil and gas resources. The US Agency for International Development (USAID) had been involved in conservation initiatives in Madidi, supporting Indigenous territorial planning, community-based ecotourism, park management, and environmental education (USAID 2012). It had funded and partnered with Conservation International, Wildlife Conservation Society, and the Nature Conservancy on various projects. In April 2011, Congressman Antonio Molina (MAS) stated that the Morales administration was gathering evidence to expel USAID's environment program, on grounds that the United States wanted to damage Bolivian/Venezuelan relations and gain control over hydrocarbons in the region (*La Razón* 2011). Although such actions garnered attention in the Bolivian press for being outlandishly conspiratorial, information released by Wikileaks in 2011 lent credibility to the administration's concerns. A cable sent from the US embassy in Lima, Peru, titled " 'Evo Morales Is Our President': The Anti-System Project," revealed the US government's fear that "the anti-system movement" in leftist South American countries, including Venezuela, Bolivia, and Ecuador, would undercut "the pro-growth model," which supports transnational corporate control of Indigenous lands and natural resources (Toensing 2011).

García Linera's remarks also reveal his belief that the state has already gone beyond the call of duty to title lands for lowland Indigenous groups with small populations; by extension, any adverse impacts that arise as a result of hydrocarbons activities are simply a necessary evil that lowland Indigenous peoples must bear for the sake of the greater good. Yet, discursively, García Linera, like Espinoza, claims that preservation of Indigenous peoples' environment is compatible with hydrocarbons development: oil development in the Amazon is fine as long as it is carried out by the state and not foreign oil corporations: "In the case of the gas and oil exploration north of La Paz, we are trying to produce hydrocarbons to balance geographically the society's sources of collective wealth, to generate a State surplus and simultaneously preserve the spatial environment in coordination with the Indigenous communities. Today we are not opening a passage in the northern Amazon to allow the entry of Repsol or Petrobras. We are opening a passage in the Amazon to allow the entry of the State" (qtd. in Svampa et al. 2009a).

In response to the Morales administration's push for oil development in and around Madidi National Park, Bolivian NGO FOBOMADE launched a campaign called Amazon Without Oil, inspired by Ecuador's Yasuní Ishpingo, Tambococha, and Tiputini oil fields initiative (Ortiz 2011). The latter had been proposed by Ecuadorian environmental and Indigenous groups' social movements opposed to drilling and formalized by the Correa administration in order to establish a trust fund to compensate for not extracting oil from Yasuní National Park (FOBOMADE 2010; Ortiz 2010). The Ecuadorian constitution states that even if Indigenous peoples do not consent, the state can invoke the principle of national interest and call for a referendum. The administration raised this option as funding shortages began to threaten the initiative (*Hoy* 2010). Countering state rumblings to push ahead with oil development, in March 2011 Ecuador's main Indigenous organization, Confederación de Nacionalidades Indígenas del Ecuador (CONAIE) filed a suit against Correa and other officials over "genocide" of two uncontacted tribes (*China Post* 2011). In contrast to the Ecuadorian case, the Morales administration never considered leaving oil in the ground in the Amazon. Morales denounced the campaign as part of a strategy to interfere with his government and proclaimed that oil revenues from the Amazon were vital for the Bolivian people: "Some NGOs call for an 'Amazon without oil,' which means that there will not be gas or oil for Bolivians. So then what will Bolivia live on if some organizations say Amazon without oil? They are saying, in other words, that the Bolivian people should not have money, that there would be no IDH [direct hydrocarbons tax], that there would be no royalties" (*Jornada* 2009, translation by author).

Speaking more broadly about Indigenous opposition to development, Morales criticized fellow Indigenous brothers and sisters of being manipulated by NGOs and extorting the government and companies: "When we want to build roads there's no lack of Indigenous brothers and sisters, influenced by some NGOs, that don't want them. When we want to explore for oil, they don't want it. When we want to build dams they also oppose. . . . It is a necessity to have more oil, more gas, more roads, industry. . . . Consultation is constitutionalized, but consultation does not exist so that Indigenous brothers and sisters extort the government and [private] companies. Consultation serves to avoid environmental problems" (Evo Morales, July 15, 2011, qtd. in Plataforma Energética 2011a, translation by author).

Morales's view presumes that Indigenous peoples are being manipulated by "supporting" NGOs to oppose development projects, overlooking evidence where the former have done so freely, on their own accord. His analysis neglects that while some communities have requested compensation, such appeals are supported by Bolivian and international law. More broadly, his statement reflects a common pattern in resource conflicts in which governments and companies use the presence of NGOs and other actors to discredit protests under the argument that they are politically motivated rather than genuinely justified (Bebbington et al. in press). Commenting on a controversial highway, which was planned to cut through the Isiboro-Sécure Indigenous Territory and National Park (TIPNIS), Morales went even further to suggest that consultation, although supported by the new constitution, is neither binding nor obligatory: "We are going to do the consultations, but I want you to know that they are not binding. [The road] won't be stopped just because they [the Indigenous peoples] say no. Consultation is constitutionalized, but is not binding, and therefore, the great desire we have for 2014 is to see the Villa Tunari-San Ignacio de Moxos road paved; we have the money and the company (OAS) is contracted" (Evo Morales, July 31, 2011, qtd. in Chipana 2011, translation by author).

The Madidi, TIPNIS, and Yasuní cases cast doubt on the argument that left-leaning, populist administrations, bolstered by progressive new constitutions and legislation, will depart significantly from conventional forms of extractive development. Elsewhere, in Latin America, governments across the political spectrum continue to support megaprojects that violate Indigenous rights. In May 2011, the Andean Coordinating Committee of Indigenous Organizations (Coordinadora Andina de Organizaciones Indigenas), which represents Indigenous groups from Bolivia, Ecuador, Peru, Chile, Colombia, and Venezuela, blasted the Brazilian government for calling itself "progressive" and "leftist" yet advancing regional hegemony by financing megaprojects sponsored by the Initiative for the Integration of Regional Infrastructure in South America, such as the Belo Monte dam, in violation of Brazilian, Peruvian, and Bolivian Indigenous peoples' rights to self-determination, consultation, and free, prior, and informed consent (Quispe 2011).

The Madidi case reveals the triumph of a Western view of modernization and industrialization over Indigenous cosmologies of respect for Mother Earth and living well (*Vivir Bien*) that are ironically enshrined in the new constitution. Propelled by state interest in oil revenues, this developmentalist vision contravenes Article 390 of the constitution, which considers the Amazon a strategic space that should be protected due to its heightened environmental sensitivity, biodiversity, water resources, and ecoregions.

In addition to revealing disjunctures between policy and practice, the Madidi case highlights how the extractive model of development pursued under Morales builds on oil exploration carried out in the region by transnational oil corporations during the neoliberal period. Although Total (France) and Petrobrás (Brazil) conducted seismic explorations and then withdrew, their activities raised oil interest in the area (Chávez 2010). Reportedly, the two companies, along with Repsol-Yacimientos Petrolíferos Fiscales (YPF) (Spain) might carry out oil development in Madidi in the future (Stephanes 2010). Although exploration in Madidi during the Morales presidency had been conducted by a joint venture of the state oil companies from Bolivia and Venezuela, the Houston-based company Geokinetics was the subcontracted operator (Cingolani 2010).

Ultimately, whether Bolivian Indigenous peoples' right to FPIC will be recognized may be determined in the courts. In 2010 Bolivia's Constitutional Tribunal issued a historic sentence upholding Bolivian Indigenous peoples' right to consultation, noting their right to veto megaprojects (Observatorio Petrolero Sur 2011). The case had been brought by the departmental road service of the Department of Tarija against the Guaraní. The Guaraní alleged that the road service had reached a private agreement with oil company Petrosur to use the Guaraní TCO of Itika Guasu without consulting with them. The sentence made reference to the landmark 2007 case *Saramaka People v. Suriname*, noting the Inter-American Court of Human Rights' consideration: "Regarding large-scale development or investment projects that would have a major impact within Saramaka territory, the state has a duty, not only to consult with the Saramakas, but also to obtain their free, prior, and informed consent, according to their customs and traditions" (Observatorio Petrolero Sur 2011; qtd. in Inter-American Court of Human Rights 2007:40). The court also cited the UN Committee on the Elimination of Racial Discrimination, which observed that merely consulting Indigenous communities before exploiting subsoil resources did not meet the requirements of the committee's general recommendation on the rights of Indigenous peoples and recommended that prior informed consent be sought. That Bolivia's Constitutional Tribunal made reference to the *Saramaka* case illustrates the significant impact of the international Indigenous movement, of which Bolivian Indigenous peoples are a part.

Similar to Ecuador's 2008 constitution, the Bolivian Constitution creates a popular action through which individuals, groups, the Public Ministry, and the Public Defender may defend rights and interests "related to patrimony, space, security, public health, the environment" and other subjects that are similar in nature (Article 135). By establishing a public civil action that does not preclude individual initiation (Oquendo 2009), the provisions open up new avenues through which Indigenous peoples can safeguard their livelihoods and the environment. As the next section argues, regardless of what happens in the legal arena, Chiquitanos are well aware that they must exercise their rights and selectively consent to development projects:

> We demand our rights because we were born here, raised here, and will die here. Therefore, for us territory is our mother, our life, our big house and thus cannot be violated, cannot be impacted, because this is the guarantee for our children's lives. So we demand attention to education, attention to health, organizational strengthening, and respect for the uses and customs of each people. Therefore, we demand that the mining companies, oil companies, logging companies, cattle ranchers, and transnationals first consult with Indigenous peoples and later initiate their activities if we give our consent. We will agree to megaprojects if they are compatible with the interests of the people living where they are undertaken. (Chiquitano leader, interview by author)

Advancing the Emerging Indigenous Rights Regime

UNDRIP, now law in Bolivia, is an emerging Indigenous rights regime that represents the minimum international standard on Indigenous rights (Lightfoot 2010:84). By recognizing and protecting Indigenous peoples as both individual citizens and collectives ("peoples") with rights to land and self-determination, it has fundamentally challenged key tenets of Western law and human rights. Creation of UNDRIP arose through more than two decades of negotiations and lobbying by Indigenous peoples and supporters (Carmen 2010:126). Events that led to UNDRIP occurred in the 1970s, and the Working Group on the Draft Declaration labored on the document from 1995 to 2006 (Deer 2010:18, 21). As the Cuiabá case exemplifies, with national adoption of UNDRIP, Bolivian Indigenous peoples deepened their engagement in a long-term dialectical struggle over implementation by exercising newly afforded rights. They continue to simultaneously exchange lessons learned with other Indigenous peoples at international forums, actively constituting Indigenous identity and the struggle for rights with the international Indigenous movement (Lightfoot 2010:95). They not only influence international law but also invoke the international Indigenous rights discourse in their domestic struggles.

Given all the issues noted with the Madidi, Cuiabá, and Yasuní cases, one might ask what the point is of having laws on paper that are so poorly applied. All three cases illustrate the pragmatic manner in which Indigenous groups appropriate Western law, while at the same time working outside of it. Though these struggles are rife with internal conflict and contradictions, they show how the process by which Indigenous peoples and supporters shape international and domestic law is dialectical and dynamic, reflecting evolving cultures and shifting social and environmental realities. In the Cuiabá case, since the election of Morales, Chiquitano leaders are increasingly studying the language of the 2005 hydrocarbons law, UNDRIP, and 2009 constitution and using these legal instruments to demand that the state enforce their new rights and that other sectors of society respect them. They are keenly aware that for this to happen they must exercise their rights to the fullest extent. Chapter 1 describes how one leader, enthusiastic about the fact that UNDRIP had been adopted as law, was eagerly memorizing the entire declaration so that he could master it and disseminate it across Chiquitano communities. This individual expressed that Chiquitano communities are concerned that UNDRIP must now be applied and that the broader Bolivian society must be educated about Indigenous peoples' new rights; advances in the new constitution and various laws are not up for negotiation. He further argued that Bolivian society must comply with such legislation because Chiquitanos are demanding a dignified life and want sustainable use of the environment in order to safeguard the future. Speaking about the need to reshape the Indigenous Development Plan, he invoked UNDRIP, highlighting its significance in advancing Indigenous rights, particularly with respect to consultation:

We need to retake and restructure the agreement with the participation of all the affected communities in order to make companies comply, because that is what the regulations and laws of the state establish. A company can't just easily enter Indigenous territory or Indigenous communities without prior consultation, first with the government and later with the communities, to see if the communities are or are not in agreement. As happened with the construction of the pipeline, the communities were not consulted in time and therefore felt surprised by the project and that the companies didn't take them into account. The communities were affected, or, more precisely, our rights were violated. . . . This current government administration, led by comrade Evo Morales, has generated another opportunity to support our rights more through the United Nations [UNDRIP]. After discussing rights and recognition for twenty years, the Indigenous peoples of the world achieved an agreement that was approved by the United Nations. This is a great step forward for recognition of Indigenous peoples of the world. This law, which was approved by the United Nations, is for us a great advance because it supports Indigenous organizations and Indigenous peoples significantly with respect to our rights. . . . The national government of Evo Morales made this international law [UNDRIP] a Bolivian law for Indigenous peoples on November 7, 2007. It is law number 3760, which represents yet another comprehensive argument we can use because this law has forty-six articles, and in these forty-six articles it specifies Indigenous peoples' rights section by section. So this is the argument we have through which we can demand compliance. This is not only a problem for Bolivians, but for the world, for many countries that are protected by these laws established by the United Nations and the International Labor Organization. (Chiquitano leader, interview by author)

The Chiquitanos view UNDRIP as an important tool to claim control over lands and natural resources, precisely the worry of Phillip Goldberg, the former US ambassador Morales expelled in September 2008 for conspiring against his government (Kohl 2010). In a cable released by Wikileaks in 2011, Goldberg stated, "If the draft constitution passes, it would take precedence over other Bolivian laws and could therefore carry more weight in judicial interpretation when it contradicts existing land laws. Although most indigenous leaders seem to view the UN Declaration as a 'feel good' document that will give them more inclusion in the public sector, some leaders are citing the Declaration in support of concrete aims like self-governance and control over land and resources." Goldberg added that the embassy would "watch for further developments, particularly with regards to property rights and potential sovereignty or self-rule issues" (Toensing 2011).

García Linera (qtd. in Gómez Balboa 2004b, cited in Lucero 2008:108) poignantly elaborated on the sophistication of the lowland Indigenous movements in embracing Western law as a tool to consolidate rights, in contrast to those in the highlands: "In the *oriente* [eastern lowland] we are talking about Indigenous movements that make up a minority of the population. This influences their methods of struggle, making it difficult for them to directly confront the state. For this reason they opt to negotiate. They are more sophisticated in their understanding of the law, of statutes, because it is there they have found the best way to obtain rights. However, highland Indigenous populations have the numbers to force the state to back down. Moreover, the direct enemies of lowland Indigenous people have been business interests, and only more recently the state. In the Western highlands, the main adversary has been the state, as the political force of the national elite."

Ironically, however, even under Morales both the state and its "transnational partners" were adversaries in the Madidi case, directly challenging lowland Indigenous movements that questioned the administration's modernist development agenda. Moreover, by 2011, a seminal march spurred by lowland Indigenous groups in defense of TIPNIS would cast doubt on García Linera's assertion about the former's ability to confront the state while simultaneously working within Western law.

Bolivian Indigenous groups and other popular sectors belonging to the Unity Pact, whose platform was made public in 2006 in advance of the Constituent Assembly, called for the coexistence of Indigenous and Western legal systems. As a result, in a shift toward legal pluralism, Bolivia's 2009 constitution granted Indigenous peoples their own jurisdiction, with the caveat that Indigenous rights must respect all rights and guarantees established in the constitution (Article 190).[5] In December 2010, the Bolivian legislative assembly passed the jurisdictional law (Law 73), which recognized Indigenous judicial authorities and set forth the jurisdiction of these tribunals in relation to the central court. This upheld national and international human rights laws and accords such as UNDRIP and ILO Convention 169. However, the law does not define Indigenous territory and identity and does not clearly specify how Indigenous and peasant authorities must coordinate with each other and with the regular court system (Banks 2011). Furthermore, it excludes mining law and hydrocarbons law from Indigenous jurisdiction (Article 10).

In this chapter, I argued that although Bolivia's 2009 constitution makes many advances in the areas of Indigenous rights and environmental protection, internal inconsistencies and various conflicts over extractive development illustrate significant issues regarding application and enforcement. I claimed that at its core, Andean-Amazonian capitalism prioritizes a Western, modern vision of development over Indigenous beliefs that espouse harmonious coexistence and respect for the earth. Finally, I demonstrated how Indigenous peoples have forcefully employed the emerging Indigenous rights regime to prevent their rights from being violated by the state and other actors. The key rights that the Chiquitanos and Ayoreos fought

for since 1999 in the Cuiabá case—genuine consultation, consent, compensation, self-determination, and territory—have resurfaced again in the
Madidi and TIPNIS conflicts, underscoring the relevance of the Cuiabá
conflict. Chapter 9 returns to the Cuiabá case, looking at key changes and
continuities under Morales.

CHAPTER NINE

Cuiabá under Morales

Although mobilization related to the Cuiabá pipeline subsequent to the election of Evo Morales was marked by sporadic moments of direct action, overall there was a general decline in such activities during the first years of his presidency. Intermittent acts of rebellion emerged primarily in defense of livelihood, most notably in 2006 when the Chiquitanos took over a pipeline valve to push GasOriente Boliviano[1] to extend the Cuiabá pipeline Indigenous development plan (IDP). In part, decreased mobilization mirrored a broader dampening of radical social movements throughout Bolivia as they channeled their energies toward electoral politics, and as the ideology of the Movement Toward Socialism (Movimiento al Socialismo, MAS) party became more reformist (Webber 2011:23). Like during the neoliberal period, Chiquitano engagement with other actors reflected flexible pragmatism. Sometimes they directed their grievances through electoral channels, working with a Chiquitano senator, Carlos Cuasace, and with other lowland representatives. One Chiquitano leader referred to such avenues when he offered his view that the Morales administration and the state oil company, Yacimientos Petrolíferos Fiscales Bolivianos (YPFB), were easier to deal with than transnational oil corporations:

I think that we have more facility to present our complaints to YPFB or the government because we have people in positions in this very same government that help us to have easier access. On the other hand, private companies are different. They don't know us. But, for example, through the government, Carlos Cuasace, who is one of ours, is always helping us. We tell him to present various demands to the government, and he does it. Through him we execute things. Also, the minister of rural development is a person we know, as is Congresswoman Chacoyo. There are other representatives, too, through whom we can execute things. These are people from communities, Indigenous peoples, and through them we can execute things. (interview by author)

In other instances, they bypassed the state altogether, carrying out direct actions or dealing directly with international financial institutions, the companies, and conservation organizations. Such decisions paralleled how the MAS tacked back and forth between mass activism and electoral politicking (Postero 2010:31). They typified broader processes of repositioning that occurred across Indigenous movements in Bolivia since the 1990s (Lucero 2008:78).

During the initial years of the Morales presidency, the Chiquitanos judiciously directed their demands to the state, taking care to not rock the boat and destabilize the country's first Indigenous regime. This was particularly important as Chiquitano leaders had been elected to Congress under the MAS banner. While incorporation of Chiquitano leaders into government did not neutralize a movement that had participated in bringing down the neoliberal governments of presidents Gonzalo Sánchez de Lozada or Carlos Mesa (Kohl 2010), it did dilute more radical forms of resistance.

The Chiquitanos pragmatically forged coalitions to attain their aims, mirroring in some ways how MAS grew out of a coalition of social movements rather than a traditional political party, eventually evolving into a broader, more inclusive party. Such "coalitional strategies of Indigenous political and cultural engagement" (Albro 2006:408) congealed disparate identities under a wider umbrella (Lucero 2008:140), forming new alliances through a "politics of articulation" (Hall 1986).

For the Chiquitanos, alliances with nongovernmental organizations (NGOs) across multiple scales continued to be key, though to a lesser degree as support from allied organizations dwindled. At the international level, pressure from NGOs that had previously supported the Chiquitanos waned significantly after 2002. Friends of the Earth's pressure on Enron and the Overseas Private Investment Corporation essentially ended after 2001, and Amazon Watch's formal support ended in 2002 when I stopped working with the organization and their Bolivia program ended (see chapter 3). However, I continued to collaborate independently with the Chiquitanos thereafter. Domestic support waned as well; Santa Cruz–based NGO

Collective for Applied Studies and Social Development (Colectivo de Estudios Aplicados y Desarrollo Social) only sporadically assisted communities affected by the pipeline. The organization closed its Santa Cruz office in 2008 and began initiatives in Cochabamba and the highlands.

With the passage of time and changing leadership among Chiquitano organizations, waning institutional memory also took a toll on mobilization efforts related to the pipeline. In addition, when the Chiquitanos learned that the pipeline had stopped exporting gas in 2007, they questioned whether mobilization would lead to company concessions if its coffers were depleted—an argument the company did not hesitate to use. Nonetheless, although mobilization dampened under Morales, the Chiquitanos continued occasional protests and ongoing negotiations with companies, the government, and conservation organizations over the compensation program, conservation program, and impacts. Pragmatic decisions about whether to carry out more radical actions or direct negotiations continued to be contingent on changing conditions. Such choices were analogous to other cases in which Indigenous communities affected by extractive industries considered options carefully, deciding on resistance in some cases and concessions in others (Ali and Grewal 2006). As time wore on, the adoption of the UN Declaration on the Rights of Indigenous Peoples (UNDRIP) in 2007 and the Bolivian Constitution in 2009 breathed new life into the Chiquitanos' struggle. Moreover, overall sentiment across communities changed from not wanting to rock the boat, with Morales in power, to a growing impatience, one that paralleled rising resistance by other Indigenous groups throughout Bolivia. The battles over Madidi National Park and Isiboro-Sécure Indigenous Territory and National Park (Territorio Indígena y Parque Nacional Isiboro-Sécure, TIPNIS) were but two prime examples among many.

Chapters 7 and 8 examined key changes related to extractive development, Indigenous rights, and the environment during the Morales presidency. This chapter returns to the case of the Cuiabá pipeline, focusing on the central topics previously analyzed in chapters 3–6, updating them with new developments under Morales: the struggles to democratize the Chiquitano Forest Conservation Program, achieve a just compensation program, secure land tenure, and address environmental impacts of the pipeline. I close by considering hidden, synergistic impacts that emerged at a regional scale because the pipeline fueled two gas-fired power plants and the Don Mario gold mine and was linked to the El Mutún iron ore mine.

Cracks in the Fortress

The FCBC [Fundación para la Conservación del Bosque Chiquitano]
wanted to negotiate with the Indigenous organizations but didn't want us
to be part of the program board, only to support the initiative, and they
continue to operate just as they did before. We didn't accept this because it
is not beneficial for us to be a puppet. They carry out activities on their
own, and we don't know about them. So we didn't accept their proposal
because they didn't accept our proposal to allow Indigenous representa-
tives to become part of the program board with at least 51% control. That's
where the negotiations stopped, and they didn't bother us anymore. We
haven't received any of the funds from the program. We don't know what
they are using the funds for.

—CHIQUITANO LEADER (INTERVIEW BY AUTHOR)

Under Morales, conflict over the Chiquitano Forest Conservation Program, administered by the FCBC, continued but in a much more nuanced form than during earlier years of unified opposition. Across the region, after years of seemingly futile resistance, the Chiquitanos ceased mobilizing to gain control of the program board, their initial demand from 1999. Despite numerous acts of defiance, the governance structure remained unchanged, with the conservation NGOs and companies maintaining control. Despite an era of reputedly progressive "community-based" conservation, fortress conservation had prevailed. The Cuiabá case corroborated other research showing that top-down, exclusionary conservation programs are still commonplace throughout the world (Robbins et al. 2009; Brockington 2002; Malleson 2002) and fraught with inevitable and ubiquitous conflict (Brockington 2002; Neumann 1998; Peterson et al. 2005). Indeed, under Morales, fractured relations persisted among the conservation organizations, the companies, the state, the Chiquitanos, and allied NGOs. Divisions emerged across the Chiquitanos as well. A few communities reluctantly agreed to work with the program, whereas most remained opposed. The latter instead redirected their energies toward pressuring the companies to comply with land titling and to extend compensation agreements, once again demonstrating prowess in pragmatism. Widespread resentment persisted that the program was still not transparent with respect to its motivations, interests, and aims. Across those communities opposed to the program, some Chiquitanos had forgotten about the issue entirely or were not even aware that the program was still operating. Yet those leaders and community members who had been most active in struggling to democratize the program during the 1999–2005 period maintained their belief that it should be governed by Chiquitanos, not "illegitimate" conservation NGOs and oil corporations that they argued had no right to conserve the forest: "The FCBC asked the transnational companies for 90 million dollars for the conservation of the Chiquitano dry forest, for compensation for the [impacts of the] pipeline. But who was it that negotiated the program? Just the NGOs who have nothing to do with the Chiquitano forest, not us, the natives who live in the area. We have been living in and conserving the forest for many years. These funds should go to the communities" (Chiquitano leader, interview by author).

The Chiquitanos continued to insist that they should administer the funds themselves because they were rightful stewards of the forest, which they depended on for livelihood. As one Chiquitano leader put it, the forest was "life for the future." As during the pre-Morales period, such arguments invoked place-based claims to ancestral rights over resources. Chiquitanos opposed to the program fortified their demands with the discourse of Traditional Ecological Knowledge (Berkes 1999; Kimmerer 2002), underscoring the intimate knowledge of the forest they had acquired over time. In an act of identity construction and cultural revival, they played up their dependence on the forest while recognizing that most communities were now largely dependent on small-scale farming, supplemented by off-farm employment (sometimes in ranching, logging, and mining). Such larger material political economies framed their strategic selection of an identity that would be most viable in their contemporary geographical and historical context (Escobar 2008; Humphreys Bebbington and Bebbington 2010). Reinventing themselves as harmonious forest dwellers and conservation champions served to bolster their material claims to manage the conservation program (Sundberg 2003). Like the struggle for land titling, at its core, Indigenous mobilization to democratize the Chiquitano Forest Conservation Program was not as much about "conservation" of the forest from the perspective of Western environmentalism as it was about safeguarding control over territory and natural resources essential for livelihood. The latter are historic struggles that challenge the very structure of society as a whole and strike at the heart of the dominant order (Clark 2002:414). For the Chiquitanos, these were long-standing struggles over social and economic power reframed as fights over the environmental (Robbins 2004). This had been evident ever since the program's inception, when the Chiquitanos first demanded that the program aid community development projects that would simultaneously meet material needs and sustain the forest. Their demand persisted under Morales, even in those communities that decided to work with the program.

Those communities that chose to participate made a pragmatic decision to extract as much benefit as possible from the program given the recalcitrant position of the companies and conservation organizations. Once
again, this act reflected a kind of *dynamic pragmatism*, in which some
communities made a calculated political move based on their historical
assessment of the situation. This choice was exemplified by a Chiquitano
leader who had been adamantly opposed to the program but reluctantly
changed his mind: "Our Indigenous organizations saw that the companies
only wanted us to be part of the consultative body of the conservation program, but not in the program board, where we could ensure that the program favors Indigenous peoples. We met with them and said we want to
be part of the board and assume shared responsibility but they haven't
wanted to do so" (Chiquitano leader, interview by author). Invoking language from the UNDRIP, he insisted that even if the program could not
be governed by the Chiquitanos, the board should at least grant them
more autonomy over administering funds "according to our uses and customs." While this did not occur, the communities that acquiesced to working with the program did manage to persuade the board to support land
titling for Turubó Este, a large-scale native communal land (tierras comunitarias de origen, TCO) they had applied for in 1997. Consequently, the
board provided technical assistance, delimited boundaries, and aided in
land use planning and management. It also provided institutional support,
dug some wells, and undertook community-supported forest, water, and
wildlife management. Communities belonging to the TCO viewed this
support as a partial victory, given that they had managed to convince the
conservation organizations to support territorial consolidation and community development after all, not merely "Western wilderness preservation."
Nonetheless, they still felt that the conservation organizations could go even
further toward supporting projects more closely aligned with community
interests and collaborate more closely. They also pointed out the irony that
despite the efforts of the $20 million initiative, development activities con-
tinued to encroach upon the forest, jeopardizing their livelihood—the
conservationists were not doing enough conservation: "What is happening
now? Deforestation. Are there any personnel from the FCBC here? No,
there aren't any personnel. Therefore, all of their work is just office work. We
are demanding that personnel from the FCBC come here and work with
the Indigenous peoples because that should be the policy. It's not just about
saying 'I work for you and you are going to do the work that I should be
doing.' . . . There's no technical support" (Chiquitano community member,
interview by author).

A painful rift surfaced between Chiquitano communities working with the conservation program and those who remained opposed. The latter, particularly those leaders and community members who were most active in the democratization struggle, resented the former for "caving." Some of the Chiquitanos most opposed to the program alleged that fairer-skinned elites, whom they viewed as less "authentic" Chiquitanos, had pressured other community members into working with the program because of their interests in profiting from community logging organizations (Local Social Associations [Asociaciónes Sociales del Lugar, ASLs]). One community member complained that the conservation program was complicit in supporting an inequitable ASL in his community: "With regards to management of our TCO, the FCBC has been involved with community forestry management. This has focused on critical locations where outsiders can access the forest and where community members can benefit. Currently, however, only the ASL is benefiting, which is a group of fifteen to twenty people, but in reality there are only three people who benefit, not the rest of the community members" (interview by author).

The conservation program had revealed and reinforced class division within communities now working with the FCBC and had highlighted a racial divide based on skin color. This new conflict was really a political battle over identity, about inclusion and belonging, over who was and was not an "authentic" Chiquitano. This was a significant departure from the pre-Morales period, when Chiquitano communities affected by the pipeline had unified and petitioned to become legally recognized as "Indigenous" in order to gain land titles. During the prior era, the Chiquitanos had shown significant flexibility in their acceptance of who was "Chiquitano," in a manner that was very similar to the way that the MAS party and the coca growers exhibited a "broad notion of Indianness" (Lucero 2008:187).

If the Chiquitanos choose to reengage in the struggle to democratize the conservation program, they may find themselves aided or thwarted by an article in the new constitution that grants the state exclusive authority over use and conservation of natural resources and states that sovereignty over natural resources may not be compromised (Article 346). The political charter clearly indicates that property rights over natural resources are administered by the state in the name of the Bolivian people (Articles 309, 311). While Chiquitanos could use these provisions to pressure the companies and conservation organizations to step down from the program board, the state could also claim the exclusive right to administer the program, excluding Indigenous representatives. The Chiquitanos would have to insist upon application of Article 388, which expressly indicates that Indigenous "communities situated within forest areas will hold the exclusive right to its use and management, according to the law." And this will be further clarified as legislation is made to implement the new constitution.

Struggling for the Future

Here is the valve for the Cuiabá pipeline, which goes from Bolivia to Brazil. In September 2006 CIRPAS and the other organizations that were impacted by the pipeline carried out a protest in which all the affected communities participated as well as leaders from OICH, Turubó, and CPESC. We made demands about the benefits that they [the company] must provide. That's why we were here for twelve days. We brought members from all the communities here, who, thank God, all supported us, because if we hadn't carried out the protest demanding that which we have the right to and deserve according to the law, GasOriente Boliviano would not have continued supporting us by providing compensation for all of the pipeline's environmental impacts.

—CHIQUITANO LEADER

The brothers and sisters from San Matías and all the Chiquitano organizations from the region took over the pipeline valve so that the company would extend the IDP and also comply with it according to the agreement. This is one of the most drastic measures that the Chiquitano people take when the company doesn't comply. And we will also continue to take action by informing the government when the companies don't comply.

—CHIQUITANO LEADER

After two years of failed negotiations, in early September 2006 the Chiquitanos and Ayoreos peacefully took over GasOriente Boliviano's offices, demanding the company extend the IDP, which had been established in 1999 to compensate for impacts of the Cuiabá pipeline on communities, the Chiquitano forest, and Pantanal wetlands (*El Deber* 2006). Seeing little progress, later that month community members and leaders reached their limit and threatened to close one of the pipeline valves. They reasoned that if they did not take such drastic action, the company would not extend compensation as supported by law, despite persistent pipeline impacts. Chiquitano and Ayoreo organizations deliberated in an assembly, pragmatically evaluating their various options. They ultimately issued a joint statement criticizing the company for its intransigence, for adversely affecting communities, and for inciting internal division (CCICH-Turubó, CIRPAS, and OICH 2006). They amassed at the valve for twelve days but could not close it because the Morales administration sent troops to protect the pipeline in a display of divided loyalties to its new transnational partners and Indigenous supporters. Nonetheless, as a result of this pressure, on September 26, 2006, Indigenous leaders signed a three-year agreement with GasOriente Boliviano to extend the IDP from 2007 to 2010, for a total of $655,000. The company specified that it would sign a subsequent extension in 2010 if its evaluation of implementation was positive. The Chiquitanos' radical actions were insurgent acts of "postmulticultural citizenship" (Postero 2007) and were calculated moves in defense of livelihood (Friedmann and Rangan 1993). The takeovers were carefully planned assertions of identity, an exercise of new rights afforded since the neoliberal multicultural reforms of the 1990s.

Rather than pressuring the companies through a more supportive state, at times the Chiquitanos selectively and pragmatically chose to work outside it to uphold new forms of citizenship, identity, and governance based on Chiquitano epistemes and practices—an alternative "statecraft" from below (Hecht 2011). During deliberations, community members and leaders decided in assemblies how to reform the IDP. Most communities decided to redirect funds into more successful cattle projects over other community development projects (pig farming, chicken farming, crop farming, aquaculture, handicrafts), citing various classic development failures: shortage of funding, lack of markets, insufficient technical assistance, and poor oversight. Community members across the region pointed out that the IDP was destined for failure since the companies committed only to short-term funding. A community member from TCO Turubó Este complained that project performance worsened after the departure of a technician who was contracted for only two years. Various livestock projects lacked veterinary support and funding for feed. In a number of communities, the company brought animals that could not adapt to the local environment. Perhaps most marginalized was the one Ayoreo community affected by the pipeline, which received only negligible benefits from the IDP: "They promised cattle, but I haven't seen any cattle that they [the company] have brought. And there's a lot of land where cattle could be raised in this TCO. It goes on for 120 kilometers" (interview by author).

In addition to citing specific issues, overall many community members felt that the IDP would have been stronger had it been designed from the bottom up (by the communities) rather than from the top down (by company consultants):

We have cattle projects, which is the only program that has resulted in the area. There were other programs, such as pig farming and beekeeping, but they brought the pigs and bees at the wrong time of year. The project didn't emerge from the community. . . . They brought the pigs at a time of year when there wasn't anything for them to eat. They didn't provide information about potential problems related to the project or how to manage the animals. So they brought the animals, but they began to die and get sick. Technical assistance was lacking too. There wasn't any. (Chiquitano community member, interview by author)

A minority of communities opted to continue projects other than small-scale cattle ranching, particularly where success rates had been higher. In addition, the Chiquitanos decided to fund organizational development, school supplies, university scholarships, technical assistance, and leadership training. They further convinced the company to include additional communities in the IDP that were less directly affected by the pipeline.

The Chiquitanos' pragmatic restructuring of the program showed resistance to its initial top-down design in defense of autonomous ways of life. By asserting their rights to self-determination over development, the Chiquitanos highlighted their political agency and brought forward "legitimate development alternatives" to more environmentally destructive forms of conventional development (Hecht 2011:209). Yet these efforts were not simply resistance to Western development but rather an assertion of lifeways, or "life projects" (Blaser 2004), that had been impeded by a modernist agenda. Such acts were not uncommon among the Chiquitanos and had occurred in other cases. The Chiquitanos' experience of IDP community development projects in the Cuiabá case was analogous in some ways to how Chiquitanos associated with the Indigenous Center for Native Communities of Lomerío (Central Indígena de Comunidades Originarias de Lomerío, CICOL) tried to redirect money that international donors had earmarked for forestry into agriculture (McDaniel 2002). As had occurred in the past, the Chiquitanos' response to the IDP's market-based development projects were "attempts to articulate historical identity, values, social organization, and economies with the opportunities and challenges presented by outsiders" (McDaniel 2003:344). More broadly, their adaptation of community development projects imposed by the companies reflected how subsistence-oriented economies have persisted through a mixture of resistance, acquiescence, and adaptation, key ingredients of James C. Scott's (1976) "moral economy."

The Chiquitanos' pursuit of alternative forms of development is better understood as an attempt to improve their living conditions in accordance with Chiquitano visions of "Living Well" (*Vivir Bien*) than as striving to

achieve conventional development ends, with their value-laden notions of
wealth accumulation, technological progress, and control of nature (Blaser
2004). Their pragmatism in adapting the IDP to their needs was also apparent in their syncretization of the IDP for the pipeline with a subsequent
IDP for the Don Mario gold mine. Preceding chapters describe how the
Chiquitanos, in collaboration with supporting NGOs, strategically leveraged the Cuiabá pipeline's undisclosed provision of gas to the mine and
subsequent audit by the World Bank to pressure Orvana Minerals Corporation to create a separate IDP in 2006, a full three years after the mine
had begun to operate. Negotiations began at $3.6 million, an amount rec-
ommended by an independent consultant, but eventually ended with an
agreement totaling $620,000. Chiquitanos balked, viewing this as "crumbs"
compared with the mine's profits and as excluding communities outside
the immediate vicinity of the mine (Hindery in press). Nevertheless, the
Chiquitanos landed yet another compensation agreement, building on
lessons learned from mobilizing around the pipeline's IDP. Communities
affected by both the pipeline and the mine (those living in TCO Turubó
Este) strategically pooled resources from the two IDPs. One community
member explained how he did this for his community's cattle ranch: "I have
cattle from the IDP for the pipeline and I asked for cattle from the mine
IDP since they saw I did well with the cattle." Learning from the outcome
of the pipeline IDP, these communities insisted on greater autonomy and
decided on a diverse array of projects, including land titling, educational
support, sanitation, purchasing of community goods and services, organizational strengthening, environmental monitoring, crop farming, cattle
ranching, pig farming, fish farming, beekeeping, and carpentry. Although
problems with the mine IDP emerged, communities were more content
with it than with the pipeline IDP: it was born more out of community
needs, and community members generally felt that it had better planning
and technical assistance.

In addition to the pipeline IDP, separate agreements with GasOriente
Boliviano were pragmatically negotiated by Chiquitano communities, including schools, handheld radios, road improvements, and wells. The
company had a checkered record in complying with such accords. Rewarded most were those communities that were more politically savvy or
undertook direct action. A Chiquitano from a community near the Brazilian border described how the company fulfilled promised commitments
only when parent organizations and other communities organized and carried out a regionwide protest: "For example, with regards to obtaining water
we achieved success here, but only because of a protest that we carried out

for fourteen days. We had support from CIRPAS and the other communities because the companies didn't want to give us anything. We achieved getting a well, motorized pump, an office, and a bathroom" (interview by author).

Looking back at the pipeline IDP, most Chiquitanos viewed the program as having brought modest benefits. A leader representing the Chiquitanos of the San Matías region remarked that most communities were better off thanks to the cattle ranching project but that, overall, very few improvements had been realized. Others regretted not engaging in more radical actions with the company and being too accommodating. Representatives from parent organizations criticized the IDP for lacking independent assessment, a demand that had been made from the beginning. In response to pressure from Chiquitano leaders and Chiquitano senator Cuasace, GasOriente Boliviano did produce an evaluation report in 2009, but it was based on a one-month field study and evaluated only the first year of the IDP's extension (GasOriente Boliviano 2009a, 2009b). Looking forward, foremost on the Chiquitanos' minds is the need to continue pressure to ensure extension of the IDP and to restructure it into an autonomous, independent, long-term trust fund. Refashioning the IDP projects further will depend on funding, ongoing evaluation, and shifting needs. A female community leader stressed the need for ongoing funding and suggested refocusing the program around health, conservation, and education, alluding to gendered differences in development priorities:

> The pipeline won't only be here for 40 years but rather for eternity. We want more funding for community development. Personally, I would like them to create a health post within our community because you must realize that sometimes diseases come in the middle of the night, and sometimes we don't have transportation. So in order to arrive more quickly we want a health post, and it would be even better if the company did it. It is an obligation because the pipeline passes by our community, and these crumbs that they have given us are not sufficient. We want our forests to be conserved within our territory, and we are open to other organizations that are willing to assist us. Always thinking of our children's future, education, and health are the most important priorities in our territory, because the children will be tomorrow's future. . . . The women here would like more support for materials, and we would also like more funding for our children to pursue higher education at locations outside of the community, because the economic situation at the community level is often quite bad. (interview by author)

Compensate? Over Enron's Dead Body

Under Morales, anxiety among the Chiquitanos grew when it became evident that the pipeline was not exporting gas to Cuiabá, Brazil. Leaders remembered that GasOriente Boliviano had cited financial woes in the past when it failed to disburse funds for the IDP. They feared the company would do so again when exports dropped. In a March 2010 filing with the US Securities and Exchange Commission, GasOriente Boliviano's parent company, Ashmore Energy International, reported that the Cuiabá pipeline and power plant had generally not operated since August 2007 due to lack of gas supply (AEI Services LLC 2009). The company reported a loss of $37 million in 2008 and $132 million in 2009, with a net debt of $73 million in December 31, 2009. Lamenting losses, in January 2009 an Ashmore representative told me that for Indigenous groups to demand further compensation would be like extracting money from a corpse, a fitting metaphor given Ashmore had acquired a deceased Enron's shares in the pipeline.

Nonetheless, the Chiquitanos demanded that the companies compensate them regardless of whether or not the pipeline exported gas since impacts to communities, the Chiquitano forest, and Pantanal wetlands continued and multiplied. Aware that GasOriente Boliviano's forty-year concession did not end until 2039, they renewed their initial demand for a long-term, autonomous trust fund (Ashmore Energy International 2010). Despite the Chiquitanos' posturing, the company maintained its recalcitrant decision that it would sign only three-year agreements that could be renewed upon favorable evaluation. Aiding the Chiquitanos' claim for continued compensation, in 2011 Brazilian state company Petrobras revived the pipeline when it took over operations at the Cuiabá power plant and began pressuring the Bolivian government to resume gas export from the Cuiabá pipeline (Hidrocarburos Bolivia 2011). The dormant plant, the state of Mato Grosso's largest private investment, had become a source of political embarrassment and had fostered local mobilization in Brazil to get it online once again. Ultimately, in September 2011, Bolivia's state oil company, YPFB, signed a contract with Brazil's Petrobras to supply 2.2 million cubic meters of natural gas per day to the Cuiabá plant (Reuters 2011). If export volumes increase to a profitable level, analysts predict that the Morales administration might nationalize the pipeline. Should this happen, it would generate a new series of issues related to liability and transference of compensation agreements.

Compensation: Deepening Dependency and Reducing Resistance

Now that Bolivian Indigenous groups have achieved adoption of International Labor Organization Convention 169 (1991), the new hydrocarbons law (2005), and UNDRIP (2007), rights to compensation for development projects that affect them have been solidified. Recent legal developments in the international arena have further bolstered these gains. The 2007 decision by the Inter-American Court of Human Rights in the *Saramaka* case and the observations by the UN Committee on the Elimination of Racial Discrimination (CERD) that the court cited (see chapter 8) recognize the right of communities to share equitably in the benefits of major exploration activities on their traditionally owned lands (Inter-American Court of Human Rights 2007). Paradoxically, however, such advances in some cases have had the effect of dampening resistance to these projects, particularly when prospects for paralyzing them are slim. To the contrary, they have provided incentives for Indigenous peoples to consent to those development activities that have historically damaged their lands and livelihoods (Engle 2010:206) and deepened dependence on extraction. As noted in chapter 7, as a result of intense lobbying by Bolivian Indigenous groups and supporting organizations, the 2005 hydrocarbons law directly channeled hydrocarbons revenues into an Indigenous fund, enshrining dependence on degrading development activities.

In the Cuiabá case, compensation agreements in the form of the IDP and land titling support stifled more radical opposition to the pipeline and its potential long-term impacts. Yet the Chiquitanos made a pragmatic decision that the benefits outweighed potential adverse impacts and used threats of "opposition" to leverage greater funding from the companies. Their strategy stemmed from lessons learned from the case of the Bolivia-Brazil pipeline in 1997. The Chiquitanos knew that it had been built despite resistance and that the Guaranís had been granted an IDP as a result of mobilization. By accepting compensation agreements, the Chiquitanos knowingly became dependent on revenues from the companies. And the same was true for Chiquitano communities that ultimately agreed to work with the Chiquitano Forest Conservation Program. Yet this was by no means the first time they had been faced with dilemmas of dependence since the neoliberal period began. Historically, they had been weary of engaging with development and conservation organizations for fear of becoming dependent on outside organizations for knowledge and resources (McDaniel 2003:343). They had strategically sought funds, technical support, and political leverage associated with such relationships (McDaniel 2002:393). In the Cuiabá case, the Chiquitanos' unanswered demand for a long-term, autonomous trust fund stood as a reminder that they sought to sever ties with the companies and foster endogenous forms of sustainable "development":

> I think that we have to improve policies regarding relations and resource use, based on a sustainable development plan that includes a revolving fund so that funds can be used for a longer period of time. Instead of diminishing, the funds will grow to benefit even more communities, because we can't only talk about communities directly affected by the pipeline in the area of influence. There are other communities that are not benefiting, and somehow they must become part of this revolving fund so that the benefits reach them, too, because the idea is to improve the quality of life for everyone and for all of the communities that belong to the affected Indigenous organizations. (Chiquitano leader, interview by author)

Dependencies and contradictions stemming from both the conservation program and IDP help to explain the complexities of Morales's political project. In some respects, Chiquitano pragmatism paralleled decisions the government made at a national level. The administration continued hydrocarbons development with transnational "partners" in order to generate surplus for the greater good, despite adverse impacts and resistance from affected Indigenous peoples. Such pragmatic choices resonate with those made by Indigenous groups around the world (e.g., tar sands exploitation in Canada, oil extraction in Alaska). In the long term, it remains to be seen whether the Morales administration will have the ability or political will to avert adverse environmental impacts or equitably distribute the benefits derived from such "deals with the devil," particularly in light of structural dependence on extractive industries.

Divisions caused by the Cuiabá pipeline also mirrored those caused by other megaprojects, such as the Madidi and TIPNIS cases. In the case of Madidi National Park, from the beginning Indigenous organizations stated that they were not against drilling but rather sought to improve the conditions under which it occurred and obtain benefits to which they were legally entitled (e.g., land titling) (Costas 2010). Similar to the Cuiabá case, some community members who initially consented to oil exploration and compensation were later outraged about community impacts, environmental degradation, and issues with community compensation projects (Cingolani 2010). One individual felt torn in weighing the potential benefits of oil exploitation against possible cultural and environmental impacts: "We have the right to consultation. We want to know what impact it is going to have on our streams, our animals, and infrastructure. It brings diseases and cultural change. We want the government to give us a guarantee so we can see whether or not we want it, whether or not it is prudent. We know about the environmental impact, but on the other hand, we want the project. However, we know that the money will not be sufficient if it destroys our habitat. Many say development, but for us there is also going to be destruction" (qtd. in Costas 2010, translation by author).

Land Reform under Evo: A Checkered Record

Morales's 2006 agrarian reform raised expectations on the part of Bolivian Indigenous groups and supporters that lands would be redistributed from the landed elite, thereby ameliorating asymmetrical power relations. Its passage resulted from years of mobilization, punctuated by the 2006 National March for Land and Territory, in which Indigenous groups from across the country marched on La Paz to propel passage of the law (CEJIS 2010). Yet five years into its implementation, various left and popular movements—including the Bolivian Workers' Center (Central Obrera Boliviana), Bolivia's national trade union federation; the Movement of People Without Land (Movimiento Sin Tierra); and the National Council of Ayllus and Markas of Qullasuyu (Consejo Nacional de Ayllus y Markas del Qullasuyu), the main highland Indigenous organization—denounced the Morales administration for claiming to have carried out radical land reform while simply continuing to favor the landed elite and transnational corporations. In fact, neither the 2006 land reform nor the 2009 constitution significantly shifted lands from large-scale landholders to small holders: existing large-scale properties were merely grandfathered in (Redo, Millington, and Hindery 2011); only future landed estates were capped at 5,000 hectares.

The 2009 constitution does contain progressive provisions related to land tenure, including an article that specifies the state will grant lands to Indigenous, peasant, Afro-Bolivian, and intercultural communities that do not possess lands, or possess insufficient lands, in compliance with the state's sustainable development policies (Article 393). Other advances are present as well, including a provision for women to be granted lands regardless of marital status (Article 393) and that communal lands such as large-scale TCOs are irreversible and not subject to taxation and are to be recognized, protected, and guaranteed (Article 392). Indigenous peoples have the right to land, collective titling, and use and exclusive management of renewable natural resources located in their territories (Articles 30, 403), but as noted above, the state could limit this right (Article 346). Moreover, the state owns and is responsible for all mineral resources found in the soil and sub-soil, which includes hydrocarbons.

Despite legislative progress around collective titling, the Morales administration had a mixed record with respect to supporting TCOs. TCO titling advanced more under the first four years of the Morales presidency than during previous neoliberal regimes (Chumacero Ruiz 2010:18–19). Between 1996 (the year TCOs were enacted) and 2005, only sixty-eight TCOs were titled, covering 5.7 million hectares. In contrast, between 2006 and 2009, the Morales administration titled eighty-one TCOs, covering 9.8 million hectares, accounting for both the greatest number of TCOs and the largest TCOs. On the institutional front, Morales created a Vice Ministry of Lands (Viceministerio de Tierras) and appointed Guarayo Indigenous representative Bienvenido Sacu as director of native communal lands (tierras comunitarias de origen, or TCOs) within the institution. As described previously, Sacu had advocated forcefully for the Chiquitanos and Ayoreos in the Cuiabá case. Passage of the 1996 agrarian reform law had led to a disproportionate granting of TCOs to lowland Indigenous groups compared with highland groups during the neoliberal period (Lucero 2008:137). However, under Morales the balance shifted, and lowland organizations, including the Chiquitanos, expressed resentment over their perception that highland groups were being granted TCOs more swiftly than lowland groups.

Mobilizations challenging Morales, such as the July 2010 march for Indigenous autonomy and the August 2011 march protesting a road that would cut through TIPNIS, exposed serious contradictions in how the administration was defending Indigenous territories. A study by Fundación Tierra (2011) concluded that despite advances in communal titling and greater political will, the Morales administration was more defiant than previous administrations in enforcing Indigenous peoples' constitutional rights, including the right to consultation, self-government, and autonomy. It called on the government to respect consultation for megaprojects and exploitation of nonrenewable resources.

By 2011, after more than a decade of pressure in the form of letter writing, press outreach, lobbying, and direct actions (e.g., blockades, strikes, takeover of company camps), nearly all Chiquitano communities that had requested "simple" small-scale land titles had received them. Extensive mobilization had been necessary to persuade GasOriente Boliviano to comply with its contractual and legal obligations. As in cases in the adjacent

Amazon and elsewhere, Chiquitanos undertook acts of "insurgent citizenship" (Holston and Appadurai 1996), asserting their cultural identity to claim territorial rights. One Chiquitano leader insisted that the companies had provided legal, technical, and financial support only because of community resistance and oversight: "They complied [with simple land titling] but only when the community members and their leaders pushed the process along. To the contrary, when they didn't do this the process was delayed, or lands were not titled" (interview by author).

Although most small-scale simple titles were granted, under Morales the company continued to drag its feet regarding titling of the two large-scale TCOs related to the pipeline, despite the fact that this was required by the IDP and environmental law. Recognizing that they needed additional funding, Chiquitanos from TCO Turubó Este, located by San José de Chiquitos, pragmatically negotiated additional funding from the IDPs for the Don Mario mine and the Chiquitano Forest Conservation Program. Their efforts were rewarded: their TCO was completely titled with an area of 101,279 hectares. In contrast, Chiquitano communities from TCO Pantanal, who refused to work with the conservation program and did not obtain funding from the Don Mario gold mine (because they were not located near it), struggled to cobble together support. They had been stymied by a controversial addendum they signed with GasOriente Boliviano in December 2000 in which the company included a clause limiting funding for the TCO to $40,000, an amount that was insufficient (GasOriente Boliviano et al. 2000). Leaders contemplated asking for funds from the government's Indigenous fund (a product of the direct hydrocarbons tax; see chapter 7) but insisted that in principal the companies should pay for titling. As of 2010, only 494,627 hectares had been titled out of a requested total of 1,085,764 hectares.

Under Morales, Chiquitanos for the most part felt that state institutions responsible for land reform tilted in their favor, as evidenced by improved titling and support against third parties (*terceros*) that had competing land claims. In 2006, the Morales administration issued Administrative Resolution 0219 in favor of Indigenous communities living in TCO Pantanal over the logging corporation Compañía Industrial Maderera Ltda. (CIMAL) and two peasant communities that overlapped the TCO. The decree overturned Administrative Resolutions 018/98 and 2840/04 that previous neoliberal administrations had issued in favor of the company. CIMAL went so far as to present a claim against the head of the National Institute of Agrarian Reform, which was rejected in 2007 (Tribunal Agrario Nacional 2007).

The long-term integrity of Chiquitano lands titled through the Cuiabá pipeline IDP will depend in part on how new constitutional provisions related to territorial management and development are implemented, enforced, and supported. Chiquitanos living within TCO Turubó Este and TCO Pantanal emphasized the need for more funding to manage their territories and keep out unwanted development, including logging, mining, commercial farming, and cattle ranching. As the Cuiabá and CIMAL conflicts illustrate, Chiquitanos will continue to face David-and-Goliath battles against powerful economic interests, and much work remains to organize and develop management plans that effectively manage natural resources within their territories. As one community member put it:

> There is still a lack of awareness among community members about what a PC [*propiedad comunal* (communal property)] or TCO is and how they are related to development and defense, because they [the community members] were independent [prior to PCs and TCOs]. Outsiders are entering our territory, and we don't have [the capacity to deal with them]. We are very docile and accommodating. We are seeing that outsiders are pushing community members into individual partnerships and enter the territory to log. There isn't a regulation that specifies how natural resources within the territory are to be managed. This is what we are lacking. (interview by author)

Indigenous groups living in the lowlands, including Chiquitanos and Ayoreos, are only a small fraction of the total lowland population, and representatives of the landed elite have used force to protect their property, which they feel is jeopardized by both the 2009 constitution and 2006 agrarian reform. Paradoxically, the latter had the unintended consequence of encouraging agroindustrial farmers to clear more forest in order to prove "productive" use (Redo, Millington, and Hindery 2011).

Still Struggling for the Forest

Indigenous peoples are not accustomed to seeing this. They are not accustomed to facing all of these problems because it is not part of our customary life. We live from subsistence, from our own labor in accordance with the uses and customs of our communities.
—CHIQUITANO LEADER (INTERVIEW BY AUTHOR)

Like during the neoliberal period, under Morales the Cuiabá pipeline continued to cause impacts in Chiquitano communities and despoil the Chiquitano forest. Because of a lack of reforestation and ineffective barriers, secondary impacts along the pipeline route and access roads continued, including hunting, logging, farming, and mining (see figures 9.1 and 9.2). Gas supply fueled the rise of new synergistic impacts associated with the Don Mario gold mine (figure 9.3) and two gas-fired power plants, neither of which were disclosed in the pipeline's environmental impact statement.

Although Chiquitano communities and organizations continued to monitor impacts and pressure GasOriente Boliviano and the state to miti-gate adverse impacts, their actions were more muted than during the first couple years after pipeline construction. Nonetheless, they continued to exert their influence, insisting it was necessary to ensure company compli-ance. They used both older language from International Labor Organiza-tion Convention 169 as well as new legal provisions from UNDRIP and the 2009 constitution to augment their claims. Such actions were neces-sary, particularly because the Chiquitanos lost key allies that had been active in the early 2000s, as described previously. Because of decreased pressure, GasOriente Boliviano and the government's environmental min-istry scaled back their efforts to address the pipeline's aftereffects. The company did keep producing biannual reports for the ministry, which in turn carried out superficial inspections on occasion, yet Chiquitano lead-ers complained that GasOriente Boliviano did not inspect the pipeline

Figure 9.1 Burned vegetation along a section of the Cuiabá pipeline route that was not reforested. Author's photo

Figure 9.2 GasOriente Boliviano vehicle driving along a section of the Cuiabá pipeline that was not reforested. Author's photo

with them despite repeated requests. Interviews conducted with officials at the environmental ministry in 2008 and 2010 reveal that they were seriously understaffed and lacked resources. Despite these deficiencies, reports and resolutions generated by the agency suggest it went through the motions of attempting to address adverse impacts. However, field visits conducted by the author and the Chiquitanos show that such actions did not significantly reduce impacts on the ground. This revelation is at odds with strong provisions on "socioenvironmental monitoring" of hydrocarbons projects in Indigenous territories found in the 2009 constitution and various laws[2] that had emerged out of intense pressure from the Indigenous movement.

Like many other facets of the Cuiabá case, the Chiquitanos' handling of pipeline impacts intersected heavily with identity politics. Indeed, throughout Bolivia, Indigenous identities have been cultivated around claims relating to adverse effects of resource extraction (Humphreys Bebbington and Bebbington 2010:142). The Chiquitanos asserted their identity as forest dwellers, emphasizing their dependence on the forest for livelihood and cultural reproduction. First and foremost, they were concerned with pressuring the company to continue compensating them through IDP community development projects that had become part of their subsistence. Nevertheless, they were also concerned with attending to those impacts that directly affected their livelihood. After all, doing so was not merely a matter of maintaining "environmental quality" in the Western sense but rather a critical fight for cultural survival (Clark 2002): "The Cuiabá pipeline crosses the Chiquitano Forest and has directly affected this fragile, unique forest that is the resource and hope that guarantees the lives and future of the Chiquitanos. It has been socially and environmentally affected by the oil companies. And consequently, we have asked for compensation for these direct impacts so that the communities that are directly affected by the project are compensated" (Chiquitano leader, interview by author).

As the conflicts over the conservation program and IDP illustrate, the Chiquitanos' efforts to address adverse impacts were simultaneously power struggles for social justice and nature, with "nature" in the Western sense taking a back seat to those impacts more immediately affecting livelihood (see Perreault 2008; Hecht 2011). Like many other cases involving Indigenous peoples, the Chiquitanos had been historically marginalized and subjected to development activities pushed by powerful interests that threatened their survival (see Clark 2002). Their plight adds weight to existing evidence that Indigenous peoples worldwide bear a disproportionate share of the human costs of resource-extractive industries (Stavenhagen 2004).

Particularly harmful to the Chiquitanos were those impacts that affected their water and food supply. One community near San Matías alleged that a leak from the pipeline killed fish in their pond. Other communities in the region complained for years that pipeline construction had damaged water sources. A community leader voiced the urgency of the matter: "When the company was building the pipeline it degraded a pond, which hurt us a lot. They should compensate us for this. And our community is desperately in need of water. We don't have enough water to raise our horses or cattle. Now, when the dry season comes the pond dries up, but it didn't used to" (interview by author). Access roads, poor control, ineffective barriers, and insufficient reforestation of the pipeline route all triggered encroaching development that also threatened the Chiquitanos' livelihood. A Chiquitano leader vehemently expressed his concern about the potential for an explosion, explaining how it was rooted in the company's lack of oversight:

"Unauthorized persons prohibited from entering" [reading GasOriente Boliviano sign]. And the other sign says "The forests are sources of life.

Protect them!" But, also if we are talking about the environmental impacts caused by the construction of this pipeline, if you look [pointing to
a burned area on the pipeline right-of-way], this is one of the dangers for
us because the pipeline is below the ground, but there is no control of
forest fires started by hunters or people who enter or cross the right-of-way.
There is no control or oversight to protect and care for this right-of-way.
So we see the forest is burned, and this is a danger for us. . . . If there were
a gas leak it would be extremely dangerous because what we see is that
what has grown back are young bushes that dry out, which is dangerous
because they are susceptible to fires . . . the company is not complying
with what was agreed upon and is not complying with what the environmental law says . . . and we demand compliance. (interview by author)

A leader from the one Ayoreo community affected by the pipeline echoed
the same sentiment, poetically pointing out how company rhetoric did not
match reality, arguing for community-based monitoring, a demand the
company had rejected from the outset:

We are here across from the community. We are looking at the pipeline
right-of-way. We are seeing that there is no control. We have seen that
the vegetation is burned, even though they put a fence there so nobody
can enter. But they ought to control it well. There ought to be people, a
community member, to control it, because here the sign says to conserve
[the forest] but the sign doesn't "sing" [i.e., is false] because here we see
the fire has entered the right-of-way. There are many fires in the area
[for agriculture] and along the right-of-way behind the fence, so there
should be more protection because this barrier doesn't do anything
because the people jump over it, and the fire burns on the other side
too. Animals die because of the fire. (interview by author)

Lack of reforestation had led to growth of grasses and other combustible
vegetation along the pipeline route, enabling fires to enter. It was well
known that fires were common in the area and set regularly by farmers and
ranchers whose properties encompassed the pipeline right-of-way. Soil
degradation occurred because of inadequate reforestation, vehicular traffic,
and livestock walking on the route.

The pipeline's environmental license required GasOriente Boliviano to
restore and reforest affected areas to their original conditions to the best
extent possible. Areas considered fit for natural reforestation were not to be
disturbed by assisted reforestation. However, the company was required to

reforest and restore soils at places where pipeline construction caused soil erosion. GasOriente Boliviano carried out assisted reforestation along only a third of the length of the pipeline and left the rest for "natural" regrowth (GasOriente Boliviano 2009a). In small sections along the pipeline, Gas-Oriente Boliviano cut vines and weeded to increase natural reforestation. The company hired the Noel Kempff Mercado Museum of Natural History, implicated in the conservation program controversy, to help develop a native plant nursery for the effort. Most Chiquitanos felt the company's reforestation effort was miniscule, as described by one leader from the San Matías region: "That's how it is. There's been reforestation at some little sections along the pipeline. One passes by and it appears that everything is nicely reforested, but if we go past, deeper [into the forest] that's not the case" (interview by author). Even in areas where forest has regrown, an eight-meter-wide maintenance road remains along much of the pipeline route. Given ineffective barriers and poor oversight, the road practically guarantees that encroachment will continue in the future.

The aftereffects of the pipeline's access roads and right-of-way were anything but benevolent. Chiquitanos were particularly alarmed by land speculators and traffickers of timber, cattle, contraband, drugs, and wildlife: "Some people have taken advantage of using the pipeline access roads to get to cattle ranches. For them this was a benefit. But others have used them to traffic wood, cattle, and wildlife" (interview by author).

In self-critique, a number of community members admitted that their efforts to control logging and hunting were not very effective because of resource constraints and internal corruption. The lure of additional income in a setting of limited opportunities and powerful economic actors was difficult to resist. Logging was an important source of employment for some community members belonging to TCO Turubó Este. During field-work I observed new Brazilian timber mills supplied by unauthorized loggers, which had accelerated as a result of access roads created or improved for the Cuiabá pipeline and Don Mario gold mine, secondary impacts not anticipated in the projects' environmental impact statements. One unauthorized Bolivian logger told me that Brazilians were increasingly entering Bolivia due to stricter environmental laws in Brazil and lax enforcement in Bolivia. Electricity provided by a new gas-fired power plant in Ipias, at the southwestern end of the pipeline, had provided the energy that fueled such enterprises and their new cumulative and synergistic impacts.

Synergistic Side Effects

Extractive industry projects such as the Cuiabá pipeline are part of a broader reorganization of Latin America's geopolitical economy and economic geography (Bebbington and Bury in press). The extractive boom across Latin America is characterized by what Bebbington and Bury (in press) call an "extractive complex" of interconnected activities that comprise a network of infrastructure and built environments that aims to extract minerals, hydrocarbons, energy, and water. Social and environmental impacts arising from such projects aggregate and generate cumulative synergies that are often not predictable and can be multiplicative and more serious than singular projects alone (Dourojeanni et al. 2009:129; Hindery in press). In this section I argue the Cuiabá pipeline triggered a wave of secondary development activities and associated impacts in the Chiquitano forest and Pantanal wetlands by supplying gas to the Don Mario gold mine and gas-fired plants in the towns of Ipias and San Matías. Enron and Shell placed gas outtake valves at these and other locations along the pipeline, yet neither the outtakes nor provision of gas to the mine and power plants was disclosed in the pipeline's environmental impact studies. This pattern is significant to note because it highlights both the deceptive tactics used by the industry and the importance of assessing the impacts of related projects in their totality.

Under Morales, the Don Mario gold mine (see figure 9.3) continued to extract gas from the Cuiabá pipeline, generating significant cumulative and synergistic impacts also not mentioned in the studies. According to company documents, it will continue to operate through 2019 (Orvana Minerals Corp. 2009, 2010). Curiously, since 2003 various Bolivian governments, including those of Sánchez de Lozada and Morales, supplied gas to the mine even at times when no gas was exported to Cuiabá, Brazil (Hindery in press). Most recently, under the Morales administration, the mine company Empresa Minera Paititi signed another natural gas contract that will not expire until 2016 (Orvana Minerals Corp. 2010), further evidence of Morales's prioritization of economic development based on extractive industries. In 2011, Orvana began production in the Upper Mineralized Zone, located inside the Don Mario hill (known as Cerro Pelado, or Bald Hill). Previously, it had only exploited the Lower Mineralized Zone through underground and open pit methods.

Road improvements for the mine continued to increase forest clearing for cattle ranching, as well as unauthorized logging and hunting at the mine itself, along the mine road, and along the pipeline right-of-way (Hindery in

Figure 9.3 Don Mario gold mine. Author's photo

press). Chiquitano community members were especially concerned with those impacts that threatened their livelihood: "We are observing unauthorized loggers, wood thieves, and narcotraffickers using the mine's road and CIMAL's road, which are in very good condition. They use them to get to San Matías. And this was one of the reasons we established a guard post, to be able to control outsiders passing through the area" (interview by author). One community leader reprimanded the company for people speeding through the community and insisted they respect specific speed limits, particularly since company vehicles sometimes carried toxic chemicals. He called upon the company to comply with requirements to provide information periodically, use a bypass road, and prepare a contingency plan:

Recently, two months ago, I spoke with a representative from the mine and suggested to him that they were forgetting to inform us, that they are obliged to come every three months and provide information about the project's progress, the mine's condition, because recently we were stunned to see mining trucks carrying chemicals passing through our communities. Therefore, we asked them to create a bypass road 300 meters away from the community because a child came and found a hollow barrel with a substance leaking out of it. The ground was steaming, so it was acid, but when a representative from the mine came he said that it was hydrogen peroxide. We said it wasn't hydrogen peroxide because it wouldn't have steamed. Because of this we sent a serious letter stating that the next time this happened we would send a commission to Santa Cruz. Due to this they built the road around the community. But just suppose that a barrel were to spill on the bypass road. . . . On one occasion when the mining trucks passed by the community we asked them what their plan was if by chance a spill happened inside the community. They said they had a contingency plan. But imagine, it takes two hours to get from the mine to our community. I asked them if they think they are prepared with a contingency plan if an accident were to happen. This is serious. They didn't respond. Unfortunately, they are located at the mine and don't have an office here. (interview by author)

Some community members living in the vicinity of the mine alleged that the mine's tailing pond had overflowed. Mining staff denied this, instead claiming the fresh water reservoir had overflowed. A community leader who inspected the mine on a number of occasions reasoned this could not have been the case and urged for an independent commission to investigate potential contamination:

Nobody tells us the truth. They themselves don't want to notify us. They say it was something else and that it wasn't the tailing pond that overflowed, but rather the fresh water reservoir, but I don't think this is true because the fresh water reservoir is located higher and the tailing pond is lower. I don't think the overflow would have gone another way. So I think it would really be worth it to assemble a more serious commission, go to the site and take samples for analysis, including soil samples a meter deep, perhaps deeper or shallower, as well as plant and water samples, and possibly hunt a nearby animal to analyze its tissue for contamination from the chemicals used to extract and clean the minerals. (interview by author)

The company monitored only groundwater contamination, generating periodic reports of contaminant levels. Independent monitoring was absent, and insufficient numbers of wells were placed around the tailing pond and other facilities.

Synergistic impacts associated with the mine, which was fueled by gas from the Cuiabá pipeline, were also related to rural electrification schemes powered by the pipeline's gas. Under Morales, rural power lines and two power plants fueled by the Cuiabá pipeline were erected in the Chiquitanía, none of which was disclosed in the pipeline's environmental impact studies but all of which led to synergistic impacts. In December 2007, the gas-fired power plant located in Ipias began producing electricity for the town of Roboré, the Don Mario gold mine, and Chiquitano communities belonging to TCO Turubó Este. Mine officials had lobbied long and hard for electrification. Chiquitano community members were generally pleased to receive electricity as a result of the plant but were concerned that it would increase production in local timber mills, which in turn would lead to more logging on their lands. During the Morales presidency the Ministry of Hydrocarbons and Energy initiated planning for rural electrification of the Chiquitano and Pantanal regions using gas from the Cuiabá and Bolivia-Brazil pipelines. Five hundred forty-five kilometers of transmission lines were planned between the towns of El Carmen and Puerto Suárez (80 km), El Carmen and Ipias (185 km), and El Carmen and San Matías (280 km) (see figure 1.2). In July 2011, Morales proudly inaugurated a state-funded power plant fueled by the Cuiabá pipeline in San Matías (where the Cuiabá pipeline crosses into Brazil), providing electricity for more than eighteen hundred families that had been importing energy from Brazil (Observatorio Boliviano de los Recursos Naturales 2011). The government also planned a five-megawatt gas-fired plant in Puerto Suárez, a town bordering Brazil, to supply electricity to the world-class El Mutún iron ore mine. In 2007 the Morales administration resurrected the decades-old Mutún project and signed a joint-venture contract with Indian corporation Jindal Steel and Power Ltd. to develop the mine (Agencia Boliviana de Información 2002; Guzman et al. 2006; Press Trust of India 2010). The $2.1 billion project included construction of a 1.7 million tons per annum (MTPA) steel plant, a 6-MTPA sponge iron plant, a 10-MTPA iron ore pellet plant, and a 40-year contract to mine approximately half of the deposit (Economic Times 2011). Jindal proudly proclaimed that the sponge iron plant would produce more than any other facility in the world. Given the El Mutún mine's national significance, the government repeatedly pressured Jindal to begin production, but by August 2012 the project was suspended after a heated dispute between the company and the government (Siddiqui 2012). El Mutún is expected to either tap into the main Bolivia-Brazil pipeline through a new lateral pipeline (Heredia García 2011) or be fueled by an entirely new pipeline that would be built to the mine from the Río Grande gas field in Santa Cruz (*Cambio* 2012). None of the aforementioned projects—the Don Mario and El Mutún mines; the gas-fired power plants in Ipias, San Matías, and Puerto Suárez; or rural electrification—were disclosed in the environmental impact studies of the Cuiabá and Bolivia-Brazil pipelines, despite the fact that the pipeline companies built gas outtakes precisely where the plants and mines were located. This suggests that the companies were aware the pipelines would be tapped. All of these projects are likely to generate new synergistic impacts in conjunction with industrial waterways, roads, and railways already online or forthcoming from the Initiative for the Integration of Regional Infrastructure in South America (Hindery in press).

In the future, prospects for dealing with such impacts may be improved by provisions in new legislation and the 2009 constitution. The latter requires that all energy development preserve the environment (Article 378) and includes provisions that could result in better prevention and mitigation of adverse impacts: "Article 347. I. The State and society will promote mitigation of harmful effects on the environment and of environmental liabilities that affect the country. II. Those who conduct activities that impact the environment must, at all stages of production, avoid, minimize, mitigate, remediate, repair and compensate for damages caused to the environment and the health of persons, and shall establish security measures necessary to neutralize the possible effects of environmental liabilities."

Although the document introduces new provisions for environmental protection that were previously absent, its conception of territorial integrity is merely reduced to state border security and does not adequately address secondary development. Nor does it consider diverse Indigenous perceptions of territorial integrity, which are intimately tied to identity, culture, and place. Perhaps more important, it remains to be seen to what extent the government will legislate and enforce these provisions. Evidence thus far from the Madidi, TIPNIS, and Cuiabá cases does not bode well, as pipelines and roads have fragmented Indigenous territory, eroding control over natural resources. As I have shown above, the combined effects of these related development projects, that is, what I have termed synergistic impacts, were obscured by companies touting the projects as singular entities rather than as part of an overarching regional plan to integrate extractive industries into the global economy.

Cuiabá in Closing

In chapters 7, 8, and 9 I have examined the Cuiabá case as it has changed under Morales. In chapter 7, I examined liability for social and environmental impacts caused by Enron, Shell, and OPIC, particularly in the context of Enron's bankruptcy and nationalization. In chapter 8, I elaborated on the Cuiabá case in relation to Indigenous peoples' struggle for just compensation, consultation, and consent, underscoring how the Chiquitanos used new legal instruments such as UNDRIP and the 2009 constitution to demand that the state enforce Indigenous peoples' rights. In chapter 9, I argued that, as during the neoliberal period, the Chiquitanos and Ayoreos employed *dynamic pragmatism* in dealing with the companies, conservationists, and governments. Similar in some ways to the tactics deployed by the MAS political party, they alternated between electoral politics, transnational advocacy, and direct actions. While most Chiquitano communities continued to reject working with the Chiquitano Forest Conservation Program, others pragmatically opted to take part in it, viewing it as a means by which to secure land tenure and improve living conditions. I further argued that the program's continued existence highlights the persistence of fortress-style initiatives despite the reputed rise of community-based conservation. Regarding the Indigenous compensation program, I contended that the Chiquitanos and Ayoreos pragmatically adapted it in new ways according to their cultural priorities, yet outcomes varied, and new issues and dependencies arose. With ongoing and new social and environmental impacts, communities continued to engage in intermittent acts of resistance and protagonism, still focusing on those impacts that impinged on livelihood. Finally, this chapter describes how the Cuiabá pipeline gave rise to several related development projects (mines, power plants, transmission lines) that generated synergistic effects on Indigenous communities and environments at a regional scale. This pattern must be situated within broader geopolitical and economic plans to integrate the region into the global economy.

Looking forward, despite the fact that the Morales administration continues to aggressively promote extractive-oriented development on Indigenous lands, overall Chiquitano and Ayoreo community members are cautiously optimistic that the government will be more responsive than previous regimes in pressuring GasOriente Boliviano to address adverse impacts and extend compensation programs. In the face of weak application and enforcement, the Chiquitanos and Ayoreos continue to exercise rights recognized in the 2009 constitution, UNDRIP, International Labor

Organization Convention 169, and other laws to ensure this happens. Although recent marches and other unrest illustrate frustration with the Morales administration's violation of Indigenous rights, the Chiquitanos and Ayoreos are cognizant of gains recognized under his tenure (e.g., land titling and revenue redistribution) and perceive that increasing numbers of Indigenous representatives in Congress are helping them defend their rights, especially since some representatives are from the region. Yet they also realize that unrelenting insurgent citizenship will still be crucial, a conclusion Indigenous groups also reached during the renowned TIPNIS mobilization, described in chapter 10.

CHAPTER TEN

Evo's Double Game on
the Environment?

In this chapter I argue that while the Evo Morales administration has
made some advances with respect to the environment, such as the modest
pursuit of renewable energy initiatives, its green discourse has been coupled
with practices on the ground that degrade the environment and threaten
Indigenous peoples' livelihood, such as support for genetically modified
organisms (GMOs) and for the road through the Isiboro-Sécure Indigenous
Territory and National Park (TIPNIS). I show how the still unfolding TIPNIS
case, perhaps one of the most testing conflicts the Morales administration
has faced, resurrects struggles over many of the same rights that the Chiquitanos and Ayoreos defended in the Cuiabá conflict: the rights to free,
prior, and informed consultation, compensation, self-determination, and
territory.

Internationally, Morales has been hailed for his poignant criticism of
capitalism and northern countries' dismal progress on climate change at the
2009 UN Climate Change Conference in Copenhagen and at the World
People's Conference on Climate Change and the Rights of Mother Earth,
hosted in Cochabamba in 2010. Speaking at the UN climate conference in
Cancun on December 9, 2010, Morales said:

> It causes me a lot of pain as President to listen to my brothers and sisters
> talking about permanent droughts. . . . Without water, there is no produc-
> tion, and without production we lack food. It may be easy for us here in
> an air-conditioned room to continue with the policies of destruction of
> Mother Earth. We need instead to put ourselves in the shoes of families

in Bolivia and worldwide that lack water and food and suffer misery and hunger. I feel that many delegates here have no idea what it is like to be a victim of climate change. (qtd. in World People's Conference on Climate Change 2010)

Domestically, the administration took credit for enacting what has been viewed as the most radical environmental law in the world, the Mother Earth law. According to Raul Prada, an adviser to the Unity Pact (Pacto de Unidad), a coalition including Bolivia's main Indigenous organizations, the initial full bill (Anteproyecto de Ley de la Madre Tierra) was crafted by Bolivia's largest social movements in reaction to their perceived exclusion by the Movement Toward Socialism (Movimiento al Socialismo, MAS) (Buxton 2011). It would have dealt a harsh blow to extractive industries, as it mandated a fundamental ecological restructuring of Bolivia's economy and society and required all laws to be modified around it. It went well beyond the weak language of the 2009 constitution, which merely requires the state to "develop and promote research, as well as the use of new forms of production of alternative energy, compatible with the conservation of the environment" (Article 379). The bill would have required the government to transition from nonrenewable energy to renewable energy and to develop policies of renewable energy sovereignty. It also granted nature the intrinsic right "to not be affected by mega infrastructure and development projects that affect ecosystem balance and local communities" (Agencia Boliviana de Información 2011b), which, if interpreted strictly, could have blocked extractive projects.

This longer and more controversial bill did not pass, in part because it challenged the modernist development agenda of the Morales administration. Instead, a shorter, truncated version of the law (Ley de Derechos de la Madre Tierra) was passed by Bolivia's Plurinational Legislative Assembly in December 2010. In October 2012, following more than a year of intense conflict over the government-backed road through TIPNIS, a fuller, yet watered-down version of the Unity Pact's bill was enacted, the "Framework Law of Mother Earth and Integral Development for Living Well" (Ley Marco de la Madre Tierra y Desarrollo Integral para Vivir Bien). The 2012 law clearly reflects both the more environmentally progressive ideals pushed by the Unity Pact and the extractivist agenda of the Morales administration. Rooted in Indigenous cosmologies, both the 2010 and 2012 laws state that Mother Earth (*Pachamama*) is "a dynamic living system formed by the indivisible community of all life systems and living beings whom are interrelated, interdependent, and complementary, sharing a common destiny"

218 · *From Enron to Evo*

(qtd. in Domínguez 2012 and Buxton 2011, with translation errors corrected by author). Similar to the 2009 Bolivian Constitution, it calls for public policy to be guided by the principle of "Living Well" (*Vivir Bien*), but goes further in that it grants nature legal rights. According to Vice President Álvaro García Linera, the 2010 law "establishes a new relation between humans and nature, harmony that should be preserved as a guarantee of its regeneration" (qtd. in Agencia Boliviana de Información 2011b). Yet, the 2012 law clearly reveals that the Morales administration considers extractive development based on mining and hydrocarbons development to be compatible with the principle of "Living Well" (*Vivir Bien*). The day that Morales promulgated the law, García Linera suggested equilibrium could be reached between development and environmental protection: "If there must be production, there must be production. If minerals must be extracted this must be done, but finding equilibrium between satisfying needs and taking care of Mother Earth" (Página Siete 2012a). The law assumes technology, coupled with adequate regulation, will be able to address any adverse environmental effects resulting from such activities: "Activities associated with exploration, exploitation, refining, treatment, industrialization, transport and marketing of mining and hydrocarbons resources will be undertaken in a progressive manner, using the most adequate and clean technologies, with the objective of maximizing reduction of environmental and social damages" (Article 26—Mining and hydrocarbons). The law only alludes to free, prior, and informed consultation (Art. 16) but does not grant Indigenous peoples the right to free, prior, and informed consent as required by UNDRIP (Art. 32). Indigenous peoples affected by mining and hydrocarbons development are merely granted the right to participate in auditing the impacts of these activities in order to ensure they comply with the law. Given such shortcomings, Bolivia's main highland and lowland Indigenous federations, CONAMAQ and CIDOB, disassociated themselves from the law because they considered it to contravene the principles of *Vivir Bien* and the original Mother Earth bill that they had helped devise as part of the Unity Pact (Achtenberg 2012c).

These sorts of contradictions illustrate how the nationalist development agenda pursued by the Morales administration parallels the policies of other left-leaning governments in Latin America that have increased state revenues from extractive industries (Gudynas 2009). Yet, such forms of ostensibly progressive "neo-extractivism" (Gudynas 2009:1) typically generate adverse social and environmental impacts much like other less-progressive forms of development. And paradoxically, as the various cases examined in this book reveal, increased social spending has at times had the effect of placating the demands of populations adversely affected by extraction.

Thus far, under Morales, modest developments in the area of renewable energy have occurred, with support from both neoliberal institutions and the governments of Cuba and Venezuela. The World Bank–funded Decentralized Infrastructure for Rural Transformation project, which is integrated with the government's Electricity to Live with Dignity program, claims to have provided 9,200 solar home systems to marginalized rural populations, benefiting an estimated 45,000 people; an additional 87 systems were installed in schools and clinics, benefiting another 30,000 individuals (World Bank 2010). As part of a national literacy program, the Cuban and Venezuelan governments installed 8,350 solar panels to provide electricity to rural communities (Baspineiro 2008).

Despite these domestic advances, other projects that are purportedly "green" have been taken to task for precipitating environmental degradation. International pressure to mine lithium, a key component of electric vehicle batteries, has generated controversy over potential impacts to local communities and the environment. A study carried out by the Democracy Center (Hollender and Shultz 2010) points out that mining of lithium reserves in Bolivia—home to half the world's supply of the mineral—in the renowned salt flats of the Salar de Uyuni region could provoke a major water crisis, affecting quinoa farmers and llama herders, as well as tourism and drinking water sources. There is also potential for significant contamination of soil, water, and air from chemicals used to process the estimated 30,000–40,000 tons of lithium that are predicted to be mined. Such pollution has marred Chile's Salar de Atacama.

In the Cuiabá case, some Chiquitano community members are open to decentralized, renewable forms of energy instead of electricity produced by gas. This could include small-scale solar, wind, and hydroelectric systems: "In thinking a lot about how we, as Indigenous peoples, talk about ecology and conservation, I think that one of the possibilities we should pursue is modern energy technology, like solar panels, so we wouldn't be dependent on oil and would not contaminate the air. These are mechanisms that we have to look for if we are talking about sustainability and conservation within the Chiquitano territory" (Chiquitano community member, interview by author). A small number of solar panels already exist in some communities. However, now that transmission lines are being built from the Ipias gas-fired plant (see chapter 9), incentive to pursue renewable options has been reduced. Practical issues also daunt community members interested in using renewable energy. One Ayoreo community complained of a broken solar panel that was damaged by lightning.

Despite the existence of renewable energy initiatives and the new Mother Earth laws, if Ecuador's enactment of similar legislation is any guide to the future, extractive development will continue to be prioritized over environmental protection. This is particularly significant given that research within the field of political ecology has shown that as reputedly progressive governments rush toward extraction, the political spaces for struggle have been reduced, and heightened dependence on extraction limits prospects for progressive political, economic, and ecological agendas (Moore and Velásquez in press; Bebbington and Bury in press-a).

A long-term look back at Bolivia's history suggests that it will be difficult for the country to break its historic, structural dependence on extractive industries (Gray Molina 2007; see Galeano 1971). Throughout the country's history, liberal, statist, and neoliberal regimes alike have been tied to an extractive model. That said, as Benjamin Kohl (2010:108) notes, evaluation of the Morales administration's (in)ability to extricate itself from this path must be understood in relation to a number of interrelated issues: (1) pressures from national oligarchies, (2) inadequate state capacity, (3) deeply embedded corruption, (4) the constant of popular resistance to marginalization and exploitation, and (5) the influence of transnational actors. Nonetheless, it still seems reasonable to ask why, with Morales's reelection in December 2009, with 64% of the popular vote and MAS control of Congress, there was not a greater shift away from extraction. To some degree, the administration's contradictions in policy and practice reflect savvy politicking and political compromise and perhaps reveal a broader fiscal and legitimation crisis of the state (O'Connor 1973). But while it is unfair to expect the MAS to correct the legacy of almost five hundred years of colonial and republican rule, followed by twenty years of neoliberal doctrine (Kohl 2010:107), it would seem reasonable to hold the party accountable to its core principles, including those related to Indigenous rights and the environment.

As the cases examined in this book have shown, the Morales agenda is rife with contradictions, and Morales has been accused by some Indigenous leaders of "double-talk" and of playing a "double game" on Bolivia's environment: "We thought that he represented hope. We identified with him. He won. We gave him all the power. But the 'process' [a reference to the government's 'process of change'] has given us nothing. It has been all discourse, no application. He speaks of Mother Earth, yet he is the foremost violator of Mother Earth" (Rafael Quispe, qtd. in Weinberg 2010). Conflicts over GMOs and road development in the TIPNIS Indigenous territory and protected area further illustrate this point. Regarding GMOs, sharp disagreement arose over an agrarian law (Ley de Revolución Productiva, Comunitaria y Agropecuaria) that reputedly fused Indigenous knowledge with modern science to revolutionize agricultural production. The law was crafted by farmers and intellectuals working toward food sovereignty but received harsh criticism from environmental and Indigenous organizations over a provision that allows use of GMOs (Chávez 2011b). The highland Indigenous organization National Council of Ayllus and Markas of Qullasuyu (Consejo Nacional de Ayllus y Markas del Qullasuyu, CONAMAQ) and the environmental organizations Bolivian Forum on Environment and Development (Foro Boliviano sobre Medio Ambiente y Desarrollo) and League for the Defense of the Environment (Liga de Defensa del Medio Ambiente) called for all-out rejection of GMOs because of their adverse effects on health and the environment and because they would deepen dependencies on transnational corporations. CONAMAQ issued a statement criticizing Morales for caving to the interests of agribusiness, calling him out for double-talk and for being "'two-faced' because 'in his discourse he emphatically defends Mother Earth, yet in practice, with the [agrarian] law in hand, gives a death sentence to Mother Earth [*Pachamama*]" (Servicios en Comunicación Intercultural Servindi 2011, translation by author). The law contravenes the 2010 and 2012 Mother Earth laws, which grant nature itself eleven basic rights, including the right to not be altered genetically. In October 2012, when the 2012 Mother Earth law was enacted, Santa Cruz agroindustrial producers protested, and pressured the government into negotiations over conflictive articles related to GMOs (*El Deber* 2012). In November 2012, Morales announced that he was open to modifying these provisions and asked the Association of Oilseed and Wheat Producers (Asociación de Productores de Oleaginosas y Trigo, ANAPO), which largely represents the agroindustrial elite of Santa Cruz, to relay his decision to the agricultural sector because he considered guaranteeing food production and expanding the agricultural frontier to be a high priority.

At the surface, Morales's stance appears contradictory given his past active involvement in global farmer organizations Via Campesina and the International Federation of Organic Agriculture Movements, which advocate for food sovereignty and agrobiodiversity in Bolivia (Zimmerer 2009:169). Adoption of the GMO-friendly law lends support to Pablo Regalsky's (2010) argument that in reality the Morales administration aims to build a centralized nation-state that merely balances Indigenous claims with those of agroindustrial elites and oil corporations, rather than radically transforming the state. Regalsky was a member of the advisory team for the Unity Pact during the Constituent Assembly of 2006–2007.

In June 2011, the conflict over road development in TIPNIS garnered increasing attention when Morales declared, "Whether they like it or not, we will build that road," referring to the Villa Tunari–San Ignacio de Moxos interdepartmental highway. The government made clear its desire to route the road directly across TIPNIS, despite opposition from some Mojeño, Yuracaré, and Chimane Indigenous peoples (Cabitza 2011a).[1] Morales's infamous remark raised concern that his administration would dismiss constitutional guarantees regarding free, prior, and informed consultation. Three months earlier, Denis Racicot, the representative in Bolivia of the UN High Commissioner for Human Rights, had remarked that consultation with affected Indigenous groups about the project had been insufficient and recommended that the government expand legislation guaranteeing Indigenous peoples' right to it (*Periódico Boliviano–Cambio* 2011). Carlos Romero, the minister of presidency, said, "The Constitution doesn't recognize consultation as binding" (qtd. in Cabezas 2011). Yet representatives of the Mojeños, Yuracarés, and Chimanes admonished the government for pushing ahead with the project without consulting with its rightful owners. Pedro Nuni, a MAS congressman and Mojeño representative from TIPNIS, lambasted the administration for advancing a destructive modernist project aimed at "civilizing" the Indigenous peoples living within the territory:

> The government suffers because of its haughtiness, because of its abuse, because of its arrogance. The government suffers when the march departs and is in route. I think that is our strength, and obviously we Indigenous peoples are going to continue ahead, despite all the questioning, despite all the insults, despite all the discrimination to which we have been subjected. They have even said we are savages, and therefore they (the government) want to build the highway through TIPNIS, so that we stop being savages as a result of the highway. This is an attack against our dignity as the Indigenous peoples whom we are. We live in communities. We live in the forest. But that does not mean we are savages. But if our president of the Plurinational State of Bolivia sees us this way and is constructing a "process of change" like that, I think they are very mistaken. (qtd. in Comisión de Comunicación de la Marcha 2011, translation by author)

Like the case of Madidi National Park (see chapter 8), the TIPNIS case was another high-profile battle that drew substantial scrutiny both domestically and abroad. The conflict can be traced back to 1990, just a few years into the neoliberal period, when the first major march initiated by lowland Indigenous groups was triggered by the government's repeated refusal to grant lands in the heart of the Chimanes forest, where logging was most lucrative (Roper 2003:141; see Lehm 1993). Recognition of TIPNIS as an Indigenous territory grew out of this mobilization. Yet, ironically, in 2011, once again, the Chimanes, along with the Mojeños and Yuracarés, renewed their struggle for livelihood against road development pushed by Bolivia's first Indigenous, "anti-neoliberal" president. While TIPNIS leader Adolfo Moye expressed support for the road being built to San Ignacio, he clarified that opposition was not to the project itself but rather to a route that would cut through TIPNIS (ERBOL and Fundación Tierra 2011). Guarayo congressman Bienvenido Sacu, who was active in the Cuiabá conflict in the early 2000s and later served as Morales's director of native communal lands (tierras comunitarias de origen, TCOs) in the Vice Ministry of Lands (Viceministerio de Tierras), used the Cuiabá case to highlight the possible adverse consequences the road might bring (CIDOB 2011). His statement (see chapter 1) was another indication of the importance of historic memories about Indigenous mobilization surrounding resource conflicts.

TIPNIS Indigenous leaders denounced coca farmers entering the park and expressed concern that the highway would lead to further colonization. This was a sensitive issue, given Morales's own roots as a leader of the coca-grower (*cocalero*) movement in the Chapare. Morales aligned himself with the coca growers, whose leadership supported expanding farming into TIPNIS and desired the road to facilitate transport of coca. A 2011 survey released by the UN Office on Drugs and Crime (UNODC) reported that while coca cultivation remained stable between 2009 and 2010 and was less than during the 1990s, it increased by 9% in TIPNIS and by 6% in Carrasco National Park (UNODC 2011). In September 2009, the vice minister of land, Alejandro Almaraz, voiced his suspicion that new settlements were associated with drug trafficking (Chávez 2011a). He subsequently resigned in February 2010 and joined the mobilization against the road through TIPNIS. As described in chapter 1, Morales went so far as to suggest that men from the Chapare region should woo Yuracaré females into accepting the road.

Pabla Pamuri, president of a Mojeño women's organization, lamented that the Morales administration had bypassed her people like previous administrations and feared invasion by coca farmers: "I marched together with my daughter for our lands and the government agreed to respect them, but now it wants to bypass us. . . . The colonists, the coca growers are going to enter, and over time will subdivide our lands. They are going to charge us to enter our own lands" (qtd. in Apaza Mamani 2011, translation by author). Her statement was emblematic of sentiment that if coca growers entered TIPNIS, it would infringe upon the integrity of the territory and would set a precedent that encroaching development could penetrate other TCOs.

Writing for *Pukara*, a Bolivian journal on Indigenous rights based in La Paz, Iván Zavaleta Delgado (2011) referred to the TIPNIS colonists as a new bourgeoisie class of *cocaleros*, Morales's "infantry," operating in the interests of narcotraffickers, transnational oil corporations, and a new bureaucratic class within the "Bolivian Kremlin." He further called Morales's attempts to blame the opposition on the United States "distractionism," covering up the above interests as well as the geopolitical ambitions of Chile and Brazil in expanding into Bolivia, such as financing of the road by Brazil's national development bank (Banco Nacional de Desenvolvimento Econômico e Social). The leftist newsletter *La Protesta*, affiliated with the Revolutionary Bloc of Neighborhood Committees (Bloque de Juntas Vecinales Revolucionarias) from El Alto, elaborated on such links and criticized the administration for its ties to Brazilian and Spanish oil and logging corporations:

> This highway, which the government says is for Bolivia's "progress," is, in reality, meant to facilitate oil exploitation by Repsol and Petrobras, logging (benefiting large Brazilian companies) and capitalist narcotrafficking mafias. The government agreed to the construction of this highway with Lula [former Brazilian President Luiz Inacio Lula da Silva] in 2008, overpaying by approximately $US 200 million above its total price, $US 415 million. The highway was subcontracted to a company called OAS, which is very linked to Lula, precisely at the moment when Lula intervened so that the right-wing opposition (the so-called "Media Luna") would sign an agreement with Evo Morales. Furthermore, the highway is part of the IIRSA [Initiative for the Integration of Regional Infrastructure in South America] plan, an agreement made between Bolivia's ex-dictator and former president, Banzer, and Brazil's Cardoso, both of whom were neoliberal. (*La Protesta* 2011a, translation by author)

A growing body of evidence suggests the project was spurred by the administration's aim to link the Amazon to global trade (part of the Initiative for the Integration of Regional Infrastructure in South America) and to facilitate extractive industries in TIPNIS. A study conducted by the Center for Studies of Labor and Agrarian Development (Centro de Estudios Para el Desarrollo Laboral y Agrario, CEDLA), a well-respected nongovernmental organization (NGO) research center based in La Paz, found that in the center of TIPNIS, 17.7% of the TCO (230,528 hectares) had been concessioned to YPFB Petroandina SAM, a joint venture between the Bolivian state oil company, Yacimientos Petrolíferos Fiscales Bolivianos (YPFB), and the Venezuelan state oil company PDVSA (CEDLA 2011). Further, the proposed route would cut directly across this concession. Another 9.8% (127,923 hectares) had been destined to exploration by Brazil's Petrobras and France's Total. In addition, approximately 1 million of the park's 1.3 million hectares (78%) had been classified as areas of permanent forest production, and private logging concessions amounted to 25,000 hectares. Another 1,000 hectares were open to private mining. Only 39,686 hectares were classified as inhabited by Indigenous peoples. Like the synergistic impacts that emerged in the Cuiabá case, this evidence similarly suggested that the TIPNIS project was but one component within a larger geopolitical and economic scheme and could not be viewed in isolation.

The TIPNIS case is useful for considering a question posed by Alexandre Surrallés and Pedro García Hierro (2005:9): "Is it possible for the State to adopt an alternative perspective to that of the prevailing official vision whereby the territorial resources to which Indigenous peoples are entitled eventually become market commodities?" Different perspectives within the administration emerged, revealing a fractured state, with a multiplicity of "official visions." Senator Julio Salazar (MAS), a representative of the coca growers, labeled Indigenous peoples opposed to the project as "enemies of the Bolivian people" (*Eju!* 2011). Reminiscent of government discourse surrounding the Madidi case, Wálter Delgadillo, minister of public works and housing services, viewed the project as an opportunity to incorporate Indigenous peoples living in the region into the government's national development agenda, insisting environmental protection and development were compatible and that the project was consistent with the doctrine of "Living Well" (*Vivir Bien*) (Lazcano 2011a). Yet, Adrián Nogales Morales, a Yuracaré from TIPNIS, who, coincidentally, was the head of the government's National Service for Protected Areas, recommended the road not be built because it would degrade the biodiverse area and adversely affect climate change (*Bolpress* 2011d). Vice Minister of the Environment Juan Pablo Ramos resigned rather than approving an environmental license for the project.

In a move toward reconciliation, proclaiming the need to comply with the new constitution and cogovern with fellow Indigenous peoples, in July 2011 MAS senator Julio Salazar, president of the party's commission on territory and environment, announced the creation of a commission composed of Indigenous leaders from the region, government authorities, and experts in order to choose the least damaging route (*Los Tiempos* 2011). Yet some Indigenous leaders from the region alleged that the government would not agree to another route because there were oil deposits in the area (Apaza Mamani 2011). In August 2011 the conflict culminated in yet another historic Indigenous march from the lowlands to La Paz, the Eighth Indigenous March, with various social groups participating or expressing solidarity, including leaders of the Cochabamba water war, as well as both lowland and highland Indigenous federations (CIDOB and CONAMAQ).

A young Chiquitano leader who had been active in the Cuiabá case died in a plane accident when traveling to support the march. He became a symbol and increased the resolve of those who participated in the TIPNIS mobilization (Comisión de Comunicación de la Marcha 2011). I had accompanied him to observe impacts of the Cuiabá pipeline on communities living in the vicinity of San Matías. Some Guaraní erected road blockades in the Chaco region, simultaneously expressing support, while leveraging their own demand that the government stop oil exploration in Aguragüe National Park (ERBOL 2011). Indigenous organizations from elsewhere in Latin America quickly rose to the occasion to enforce the emerging international Indigenous rights regime. Indigenous groups from Mexico, Central America, and South America showed support, calling upon the government to respect rights to territorial integrity, consultation, and consent outlined in the UN Declaration on the Rights of Indigenous Peoples (UNDRIP) and International Labor Organization Convention 169 (Enlace Indígena 2011). The Coordinator of Indigenous Organizations of the Amazon River Basin (Coordinadora de las Organizaciones Indígenas de la Cuenca Amazónica, COICA), to which Federation of Indigenous Peoples of Bolivia (Confederación de Pueblos Indígenas de Bolivia, CIDOB) belongs, sent representatives to negotiate with the Morales administration and issued a strong statement of support for the march, calling on the government to practice what it preached: "COICA firmly supports the demands of our Indigenous brothers and sisters of the Bolivian lowlands, and we demand enforcement of our rights as Indigenous Peoples. We support a sincere dialogue and urge the Bolivian Government to demonstrate what its discourse says at an international level, to be an Indigenous government that respects real participatory democracy with tolerance toward its peoples" (COICA 2011). As he had done in the past, Rafael Quispe, leader of CONAMAQ, similarly called out Morales for double-talk regarding the environment: "Morales isn't a defender of Mother Earth. His rhetoric is empty" (qtd. in Cabezas 2011).

During the march, a faction of colonists and coca growers confronted the marchers in a countermarch, breaking windshields of support vehicles and blocking supplies and the march itself (Achtenberg 2011a). A colonist leader from Caranavi, located in the adjacent Yungas region, dismissed countermarchers as a miniscule group that had betrayed its base, driven by MAS senator Fidel Surco (*Bolpress* 2011b). Various acts of violent police repression occurred during the march, along the main route and at other locations where acts of solidarity were carried out. Defense Minister Cecilia Chacon resigned in protest to the government's decision to deploy police to intervene in the march when alternatives existed (BBC News 2011). Migration chief Maria Rene Quiroga also stepped down because of the "unforgivable" crackdown. After significant pressure and criticism for defending the police assault, Interior Minister Sacha Llorenti followed suit (AFP 2011).

Morales blamed the United States for inciting opposition to the project and for conspiring with orchestrators (Arias 2011). Demonstrating phone records and photos, he accused Pedro Nuni (a MAS congressman and Mojeño representative from TIPNIS), Roxana Marupa (wife of CIDOB's president, Adolfo Chávez), and Rafael Quispe of conspiring with Eliseo Abelo, the head of Indigenous affairs at the US embassy. Morales argued to the press that the United States supported the march to destabilize the Bolivian government: "It's a strategy of U.S. imperialism to prevent the national integration (of Bolivia), and to provoke a confrontation between peoples of the east and west" (qtd. in Achtenberg 2011a). The embassy denied these allegations, instead accusing the Morales administration of illegally spying on the United States. Morales, who insisted the road would be built regardless of the march, lamented that popular movements in Cochabamba and Beni that had previously supported him did not rally to persuade Indigenous peoples living in the park to accept the project:

> Imagine the benefit. Who could be opposed? I lament greatly and believe that the social movements of the departments of Cochabamba and Beni, especially the transportation workers, [ought to] persuade the Indigenous brothers and sisters who are being confused by NGOs to flatly reject the NGOs, who are enemies of integration, enemies of the national economy, enemies of the Indigenous peoples who don't have electricity, because it is not only the matter of the road, but also about oil and gas as well as dams. (qtd. in Rojas 2011, translation by author)

Morales was clearly disturbed that his modernist project was at risk. His alarmist rhetoric mirrored discourse used by Ecuadorian president Rafael Correa, who over the course of his administration similarly veered toward criminalizing environmental organizations and Indigenous groups opposed to extractive "development." Morales's remark raises the specter that Bolivia may join the ranks of other countries in Latin America—including Chile, Ecuador, Peru, and Mexico—where in recent years Indigenous leaders and community members challenging development have faced criminal prosecution in charges that are disproportionate and politically motivated (Amnesty International 2011).

As described in chapter 1, in January 2012 coca-dependent communities supportive of the highway through TIPNIS marched to La Paz, provoking a rift between those government officials who supported the controversial route and those who did not. Partly due to this pressure, the government designed a controversial consultation plan that was rejected by communities opposed to the highway's proposed route. In late April 2012, these communities embarked on a sixty-two-day march, the Ninth Indigenous March, in which they renewed their demand that the road not be routed through TIPNIS and protested the consultation scheme (Achtenberg 2012a). The marchers objected to the government's consultation proposal on grounds that it was untimely, lacked good faith, and bypassed legitimate Indigenous authorities in order to convince communities to back the project (Amnesty International 2012).

The government engaged in various actions to debilitate the march, such as providing community compensation packages to marchers who agreed to end their protest (Achtenberg 2012a). The mobilization was further weakened when, on July 10, the leadership of lowland Indigenous organization CIDOB was replaced by new leaders who supported the government's consultation process. In mid-July 2012, the marchers returned home after the government refused to speak directly with the march leadership, even going as far as to spray the marchers with tear gas and water cannons. Some then rejected the consultation process altogether, while others chose to participate, albeit under intense pressure.

During and after the march, the government doled out gifts to some TIPNIS communities and managed to sign agreements with forty-five of sixty-three authorities to back its consultation plan (Achtenberg 2012a; Página Siete 2012b). This provoked debate over the legitimacy and Indigeneity of the authorities who signed these pacts. In late July 2012, Morales personally visited the TIPNIS community of Oromomo to deliver radio equipment, solar panels, and school supplies, ironically claiming that he had not come to gain support for the road: "I do not come to campaign, but rather to defend consultation, because it is a right for Indigenous peoples. The people should decide the terms of the consultation, but to reject it for political motives is a grave error" (Página Siete 2012b, translation by author).

Throughout the consultation process, tensions rose as allegations continued to surface that the government was dividing communities, offering more "gifts," and detaining leaders who were coordinating opposition to government-sponsored consultation. Fernando Vargas, an Indigenous leader from TIPNIS, railed against what he called the "power and arrogance" of Morales against the Indigenous peoples of TIPNIS who defended the area: "If they want to put me in prison, then put me there, but they should imprison all of the Indigenous peoples of TIPNIS and all the Bolivians who oppose the destruction of this patrimony" (qtd. in Correo del Sur 2012). Similar to previous periods of the conflict, some factions of the government, including the ombudsman and Constitutional Tribunal, called upon those officials who were committing such acts to comply with international and domestic laws regarding consultation. The ombudsman recommended that consultation be carried out with mutual respect for involved parties, excluding penalties and without issuing arrest warrants that violate consultation requirements established in International Labor Organization Convention 169 and the 2009 constitution.

In August 2012, Amnesty International circulated a document titled "Governments must stop imposing development projects on Indigenous peoples' territories," which criticized the governments of Argentina, Bolivia, Brazil, Canada, Colombia, Ecuador, Guatemala, Mexico, Paraguay, and Peru for not complying with internationally recognized requirements regarding the right to consultation and free, prior, and informed consent (Amnesty International 2012). It blasted the Bolivian government for making key decisions regarding the TIPNIS highway—including a call for bids and selection of a company to build the project (OAS)—before consulting affected populations. As various cases examined in this book show, consultations conducted after projects have been approved often foster bad faith, distrust, polarization, and conflict.

TIPNIS is perhaps the strongest case in recent years in which diverse social movements within Bolivia have coalesced around the notion that culture or environment should not be subordinated to economy (Escobar 2006). This and other cases explored in this book suggest that "insurgent citizenship" will need to continue in order to guarantee the rights of "invisible" cultures (Holston and Appadurai 1996). Bolivian sociologist Silvia Rivera Cusicanqui has argued that since the 1980s, the beginning of the neoliberal period, due to its exclusionary nature, "Bolivian democracy, as it currently exists, is incapable of processing Indigenous and popular demands unless forced to do so by insurgent action" (qtd. in Postero 2007:217). Nancy Grey Postero (2007) explains that such unrest resulted in part because the neoliberal multicultural reforms of the 1990s, particularly the Law of Popular Participation, offered only limited forms of inclusion for Indigenous peoples; with decentralization, municipalities exhibited increased patronage, clientelism, and corruption through political parties and NGOs. While legal advances in Indigenous and environmental rights are undeniable under Morales, it is clear that Indigenous groups will need to push hard for implementation. Challenging "progress" and reshaping the institutions of conventional infrastructure and regional planning will be an uphill battle (Hecht 2011); lack of region-scale governance and resource organization has been a long-standing deficiency in Bolivian environmental management (Zimmerer 2009:168, 173).

Although structural dependencies on fossil fuels, improper consultation, and exclusion of the right to consent dampen prospects for outright rejection of extractive industries, existing examples in Bolivia and beyond show this is not out of the question, even in neoliberal contexts. Rejection of mining in Tambogrande, Peru, by more than 90% of the town's voters (of the 70% who voted) illustrates that even in states that have not ratified UNDRIP, along with its consent requirement, local populations can still use popular referendums to veto unwanted extractive projects (Schertow 2008). In 2011 approximately 41,000 Indigenous peoples living in two Guatemalan municipalities rejected mining in such plebiscites. In 2011, Bolivian Aymara communities living in the highland region of Puno, bordering Peru, blocked roads and called for a "mining-free zone," using the slogan "agriculture yes, mines, no" (*La Protesta* 2011b), a page borrowed from the Tambogrande case in Peru. The unrest was fueled by fears that a mine operated by Canadian company Bear Creek would contaminate Lake Titicaca, jeopardizing fishing and farming in the area (Guerrero 2011). Several weeks of intense strikes, protests, and blockades on the Peruvian side pressured outgoing neoliberal president Alan García Pérez to cancel the company's contract and place a three-year moratorium on future mining in the region (Dangl 2011).

Whether under neoliberalism, Andean-Amazonian capitalism, or communitarian socialism, development that safeguards both Indigenous rights and the environment will need to heed the principles enshrined by the notion of *Vivir Bien*. Raul Prada, one of the advisers to the Unity Pact, notes that a transition to an economy based on such tenets will be difficult, but vital:

> It is going to be difficult to transition from an extractive economy. We clearly can't close mines straight away, but we can develop a model where

this economy has less and less weight. It will need policies developed in participation with movements, particularly in areas such as food sovereignty. It will need redirection of investment and policies toward different ecological models of development. It will need the cooperation of the international community to develop regional economies that complement each other. . . . Our ecological and social crisis is not just a problem for Bolivia or Ecuador; it is a problem for all of us. We need to pull together peoples, researchers, and communities to develop real concrete alternatives so that the dominant systems of exploitation don't just continue by default. This is not an easy task, but I believe with international solidarity, we can and must succeed. (qtd. in Buxton 2011)

CHAPTER ELEVEN

Conclusion: Reconsidering Development, Indigenous Rights, and the Environment

The manifesto of the Fourth Global Minga in Defense of Mother Earth,[1] circulated October 12, 2011, reads as follows:

> Five hundred nineteen years ago, the European invasion of our continent, Abya Yala (today known as America), abruptly interrupted the life of our civilizations, which knew how to coexist in dialogue and harmony with the Mother Earth. The plunder, depredation, and physical and cultural extermination began. Five centuries later, the neoliberal project was imposed on the world as the new colonization, and the war of extermination against Indigenous peoples gathered new strength.
>
> Now this neoliberal model is in crisis: economically, financially, politically, and climatically. The paradigms of the free market and the mono-national State are collapsing. The climate catastrophes (droughts, hurricanes, floods, freezing colds) multiply, battering the poorest. And those who are responsible, with their extreme consumerism and dependence on fossil fuels, those who emit the greatest volumes of greenhouse gases, only respond by commodifying nature through false solutions (REDD,[2] green economies, carbon markets, clean development mechanisms, etc.). . . .
>
> For this reason States impose a neoliberal economic model in constitutions and laws that obliterate human and collective rights and grant all sorts of incentives for extractive investment. For this reason they agree to megaprojects within the framework of the Initiative for the Integration of Regional Infrastructure in South America, such as the Inambari

dam in Peru, the Belo Monte dam in Brazil, and the highway through TIPNIS [Territorio Indígena y Parque Nacional Isiboro-Sécure] in Bolivia, multiplying social conflicts.

Mining occurs in the headwaters of the basin, contaminating our waters, our lands, our air. It destroys our subsistence activities, such as agriculture and cattle raising. Our Amazon is allotted to gas and oil companies. . . .

But we Indigenous peoples are no longer invisible. We have moved from resistance to proposal and action. We have organized and made ourselves visible. We depend on our knowledge and ancestral practices that permit us to conserve and enrich the biodiversity with which we have been blessed. We depend on the rights recognized by international treaties: the right to territory and self-determination, rights from which the right to free, prior, and informed consultation and consent; the right to decide our ways of living; and the right to our natural assets are derived. We have proposals to confront the crisis of Western civilization and the climate crisis: *Living Well* in dialogue and harmony among peoples and the Mother Earth, which we offer to the world to save all forms of life. . . .

For all of the above reasons, today, October 12, at the fourth Global Minga for Mother Earth, in every corner of Abya Yala and other parts of the world, we raise our voices and unite our hands in defense of life, for the rights of Mother Earth, for the full exercise of the rights of Indigenous peoples, against the imposition of extractive activities. For the collective construction of the Good Life (*"Buen Vivir,"* or, in Bolivia, *"Vivir Bien"*).

In defense of life. . . . No to mining, no to false solutions for climate change. . . . Yes to self-determination of Indigenous peoples. Coordinadora Andina de Organizaciones Indígenas (CAOI), Coordinadora de Organizaciones Indígenas de la Cuenca Amazónica (COICA), Consejo Indígena de Centro América (CICA), Consejo Indígena de Meso América (CIMA), CONACAMI, CONAMAQ, ECUARUNARI, ONIC, FOCO, FUNDAMAYA, COMKADES, No a la Mina, CRIC, CONAFROIC, CRIDEC, CONAVIGUA, Minga Informativa de los Movimientos Sociales, TONATIERRA, Peruanos en Acción, Movimiento Indígena Nacional (México), Grito de los Excluidos, Plataforma 12 de Octubre: ¡Nada qué celebrar!, GTEPIC-15M, SICSAL, ECOPORTAL, Centro de Derechos de la Mujer de Chiapas, otras organizaciones indígenas del Abya Yala. (Coordinadora Andina de Organizaciones Indígenas et al. 2011, translation by author)

This powerful statement illustrates that although contexts differ, conflicts involving Indigenous peoples and extractive development in Latin America share a number of core features. In many situations, neoliberal policies (e.g., deregulation, privatization) have eased the entrance of transnational corporations and deepened structural dependence on extractive industries. In turn, transnationals, states, and international financial institutions have implemented extractive initiatives in violation of Indigenous peoples' right to free, prior, and informed consultation and consent. As many of the cases examined in this book show, projects are often predetermined by preexisting contracts and financing agreements.[3] Indigenous peoples generally find benefits are minimal and short-term and do not adequately compensate for problems caused by extraction (Anaya 2011:13). Upon implementation, extractive projects and policies often usurp or degrade natural resources on which Indigenous peoples depend and cause significant social, cultural, and health effects. While affected Indigenous peoples have a long history of resistance and protagonism, the advance of extractive activities often sparks new waves of insurgent mobilization in defense of livelihood. Frequently, and even under left-leaning governments that claim to safeguard Indigenous rights and the environment (e.g., Bolivia, Ecuador), mobilization is met with state repression and government attempts to criminalize or discredit instigators.

The central case for this book, Enron and Shell's Cuiabá pipeline, a project that spanned the time from the height of the neoliberal era through the adoption of Andean-Amazonian capitalism under Evo Morales, offers important insights on these matters. The project's aftermath—a conflictive conservation program, a problematic compensation program, rising secondary impacts—is still unfolding, yet the neoliberal players that set these effects in motion—including the World Bank, the US government–based Overseas Private Investment Corporation, Enron, and an exiled Bolivian president, Gonzalo Sánchez de Lozada—have, for the most part, washed their hands of responsibility. At least in nearby Ecuador, an audacious Chevron-Texaco is still caught in the midst of the world's largest environmental lawsuit, though it is boisterously defying its liability. In 2009, then-corporate spokesperson Donald Campbell described the company's legal strategy succinctly: "We're going to fight this until hell freezes over. And then we'll fight it out on the ice" (qtd. in Klasfeld 2011a). As I argued in chapter 7, the Morales administration, although it has taken some steps to hold transnationals liable for their impacts prior to nationalization, will have a challenging time compiling evidence distinguishing the culpability of transnationals versus the state, since it did not conduct comprehensive audits prior to nationalization.

The conservation nongovernmental organizations (NGOs) complicit in convincing the US government to fund the Cuiabá pipeline through the heart of the Chiquitano forest also are largely unscathed and continue to manage the conflictive conservation program to the exclusion of the Chiquitanos and Ayoreos, in violation of International Labor Organization Convention 169—a contemporary illustration of the persistence of fortress-style conservation. Some of the Chiquitano communities dispossessed by the program have pragmatically diverted some of the funds the companies and conservationists accumulated toward land titling, but this has created other dependencies that may dilute more transformative mobilization.

Chapter 1 outlined the specific ways in which the arguments made throughout this book advance emerging research on extractive development within political ecology. It also explained how other claims I make are related to other areas of inquiry within the field. While I do not repeat all of the arguments summarized at the end of each chapter, here I elaborate on some of my principal claims. I have argued that the continued advance of the extractive frontier under Morales is an outgrowth of new dependencies set in motion during the neoliberal era, which itself builds on five hundred years of exploitative extraction. I have identified neoliberal trajectories that took hold in the 1980s and 1990s, explaining how the continuities that persisted under Morales are crucial for understanding Andean-Amazonian capitalism. I have claimed that mobilization by Indigenous peoples and supporters affected by extractive development reflect their agency in negotiating, challenging, and shaping the structural confines delimited by these development models. The structural conditions created by neoliberal players in the 1990s (partial privatization of the oil and gas sector, deregulation) still persist to a significant extent under Morales, as do mushrooming synergistic impacts on Indigenous communities and the environment. Singular projects such as the Cuiabá pipeline and TIPNIS road must be seen not in isolation but as part of larger geopolitically and economically integrated projects that have synergistic outcomes. In some ways the duplicitous arguments used to justify the neoliberal projects of the 1990s (poverty alleviation, sustainable development, the Chiquitano Forest Conservation Program) parallel the Morales administration's use of discourse about environmental protection and Indigenous rights to greenwash and justify oil development in the northern La Paz Department and road development in TIPNIS, advanced under the guise of the collective good and the state's rights. In the TIPNIS case, Indigenous groups and NGOs challenging the road's route lambasted the government for bowing to a neoliberal development agenda since the project was linked to the Initiative for the Integration of Regional

Infrastructure in South America regional development agreement and because it would grant transnationals access to their preexisting oil concessions in the territory. Brazilian interests were particularly significant because Brazil financed the road (through the Brazilian Development Bank) and had concessions in the territory (through the state oil company, Petrobras); moreover, Brazilian company OAS was contracted to execute the project.

Under Morales, the state has continued to facilitate the conditions for the accumulation of capital, and many of the same transnationals present during the neoliberal era remain in Bolivia (Webber 2011:228). Although there has been increasing foreign investment from beyond the United States and Europe (e.g., Venezuela, Brazil), ironically, the persistent onslaught of extractive development under Morales is arguably neocolonial, despite the administration's pursuit of "decolonization." Investment reached $1 billion in 2011, more than four times what it was in 2005, prior to the so-called nationalization (Shahriari 2011). Bolivia's extractive boom, under Morales's nationalist and production-oriented model of resource use, has challenged fundamental rights won during recent decades (Gustafson 2009:1005).

Conflicts related to extractive industries under Morales show how Indigenous peoples, while mindful of gains realized during his tenure, are increasingly dissatisfied with the administration's development model, particularly when it infringes upon their rights to self-determination. These cases further demonstrate how Indigenous groups affected by extractive development continue to exercise their rights and carry out direct actions in dynamic and pragmatic ways—what I term *dynamic pragmatism*—when the state violates them. This is, ironically, consistent with a statement Morales made at the UN climate talks in Cancun in 2010, several months before the TIPNIS conflict exploded: "If governments don't act, it will be the people who will force their governments to act" (qtd. in *Climate and Capitalism* 2010).

Deconstructing Development

I have argued that to grasp the contradictions of development under Morales, it is necessary to recognize how Andean-Amazonian capitalism privileges a modern vision of development over Indigenous cosmologies that promote harmonious coexistence and respect for Earth. And it is useful to recall the multiplicity of views that are present in a fractured government— that is, as Vice President Álvaro García Linera describes, a government of social movements that drive the Movement Toward Socialism (Movimiento al Socialismo, MAS) party's "process of change" (qtd. in Natanson 2007). As Benjamin Kohl (2010:112) explains, the administration has called upon these movements to take to the streets when pressure is needed to advance policies. Yet as the TIPNIS case illustrates, splintering has occurred, where some of the Indigenous groups that previously supported Morales use direct actions to oppose the administration's moves (e.g., the marches against the road's route), while other core groups use them to back the government's policies (e.g., the January 2012 countermarch led by coca-dependent communities). Such contentious actions have a long history in Bolivia and reflect how popular movements have understood and exercised democracy as a direct participatory process (Kohl 2010; Tapia 2007:62; Regalsky 2010). Although the government has supposedly established various mechanisms to guarantee social movement control (Natanson 2007), in practice, when Indigenous groups have contested megadevelopment projects, the administration has often dismissed or discredited them as linked to right-wing conspiracies and US imperialism. Unrelenting insurgent action has been essential in challenging such accusations and shifting the government's position—witness Chief of Staff Carlos Romero's affirmation in October 2011 that the TIPNIS march was part of the MAS party's "process of change" (Achtenberg 2011b) after previously discounting TIPNIS leaders for opposing the road to protect illicit transnational timber and agribusiness interests (Achtenberg 2011a).

In this context, it is important to recognize that MAS representatives hold varying degrees of sympathy for modernist ideologies versus Indigenous cosmologies (e.g., "Living Well" or *Vivir Bien*)—as exemplified by those Indigenous leaders who either resigned their posts in the government or distanced themselves from the party during the TIPNIS conflict (e.g., the Indigenous caucus that formed in January 2012). The new constitution itself reflects the manifold views held by the document's architects; this can be seen in progressive provisions advancing Indigenous rights and environment protection that are contravened by those that advance a modernist development agenda. This helps explain how, in practice, the Morales administration has often prioritized the latter over the former. Similarly, in Ecuador, where the left-leaning administration of Rafael Correa also continues to advance extractive development, Indigenous groups have criticized the government's modernist agenda for being at odds with Indigenous ideals. A resolution signed in February 2012 by affected Indigenous groups and Ecuador's main Indigenous organization, Confederation of Indigenous Nationalities of Ecuador (Confederación de Nacionalidades Indígenas del

Ecuador), demanded a permanent moratorium on drilling in a region of the Amazon bordering Peru "out of respect for our world view, our collective rights and the rights of nature" (qtd. in Fraser 2012)—rights established in the country's 2008 constitution as a result of mobilization. Such statements are not isolated; they are consistent with a broader push by Indigenous coalitions in Latin America for alternative ways of living that depart from the prevailing modern, extractive, neoliberal model—the declaration at the beginning of this chapter is but one example. In April 2012, the fourth Indigenous Leaders Summit of the Americas proposed the Indigenous model of the "good life" (*el buen vivir*), based on harmonizing human–environment relations, in place of modern forms of development rooted in resource exploitation and environmental destruction.

While such mobilization challenges administrations entrenched in extractive forms of development to consider Indigenous models, broader shifts in markets may have a similar effect. In January 2012, recent massive hydrocarbon discoveries in Argentina and Brazil prompted Morales to express concern about losing Bolivia's two largest markets for gas: "If they no longer want our gas, who do we sell our gas to? . . . Some will say that we're going to industrialize. Of course, we're already beginning with two natural gas liquid separation plants . . . but even so, the Bolivian market is small. Who are we going to sell these products to?" (qtd. in *Latin American Herald Tribune* 2012). This statement underscores that Bolivia remains vulnerable to shifts in the global market and is still highly dependent on exporting primary resources, despite Morales's move toward industrialization. And although the government is pursuing a more nationalist agenda, its development model, Andean-Amazonian capitalism, continues to rely heavily on the capitalist market as the main means of advancing development (Webber 2011:232).

For many countries in Latin America, natural resource extraction contributes a substantial proportion of domestic revenue and is often carried out on Indigenous peoples' territories. In contrast to previous neoliberal regimes, the Morales administration has increased the state's share of the economic surplus generated from extractive industries and redirected it toward industrialization and social spending, exacerbating dependence on resource extraction. Bolivian Indigenous peoples are now, paradoxically, even more directly beholden to extractive industries, given an Indigenous development fund derived from hydrocarbons taxes—itself the result of persistent Indigenous mobilization. Many Chiquitanos are eager to access these funds and excited at the prospect of spending them on various priorities, including health, education, sanitation, housing, institutional development, and the environment. And as the Cuiabá case illustrates, Indigenous peoples receiving compensation (e.g., in the form of land titling, institutional strengthening, or basic infrastructure) experience even deeper dependencies, particularly in situations where states do not provide adequate support—often a product of neoliberal austerity measures. In this context, communities affected by extractive development are encouraged to consent to activities that have historically dispossessed them of natural resources upon which they depend.

Opposition Versus Acquiescence

Extractive industries infringe upon a number of rights outlined in the UN Declaration on the Rights of Indigenous Peoples (UNDRIP), including the right to self-determination; the right to free, prior, and informed consent; the right to be secure in subsistence and development; the right to traditional lands, territories, and resources; and the right to conservation and protection of the environment and the productive capacity of lands. That the UN Special Rapporteur on the rights of Indigenous peoples, James Anaya, prioritized developing guidelines on operationalizing the rights of Indigenous peoples in the context of extractive industries by 2013 speaks to the urgency of the matter. His 2011 report on the topic found the "ever-expanding operations of extractive industries[4] to be a pressing issue for indigenous peoples on a global scale" and noted that natural resource extraction and other development projects have "become one of the foremost concerns of indigenous peoples worldwide, and possibly also the most pervasive source of the challenges to the full exercise of their rights" (Anaya 2011:9, 14).

Indigenous peoples deciding whether to allow resource extraction and development on their lands are forced to weigh a number of challenging considerations while under intense pressure from development proponents. The fact that potential long-term impacts are difficult to predict further complicates the decision-making process, especially as project sponsors frequently do not provide complete, adequate, and timely information. Although in some cases Indigenous groups oppose extractive projects or policies altogether (e.g., the U'wa in Colombia), frequently they choose to accept forms of extraction that they think will respect their cultures, livelihoods, and territories (Arellano-Yanguas 2012). Demands typically include genuine consultation and consent, secure land tenure, control over natural resources, equitable benefit sharing, and reparation for environmental damages (Anaya 2011). Similar to the Cuiabá case, in the TIPNIS case opposition emerged over the proposed route of the Villa Tunari–San Ignacio de Moxos interdepartmental highway, not over the highway itself. This demonstrates the importance of opening broader national debates on where extraction should and should not occur as well as the forms and terms of extraction (Bebbington 2012).

The kinds of decisions Indigenous peoples made in each of these cases reflect what I term *dynamic pragmatism* that the Chiquitanos and Ayoreos employed in the Cuiabá conflict—strategically using their Indigeneity, judiciously interacting with allies, carefully choosing multiscaled mobilization tactics, and thoughtfully deliberating whether to consent to "development." In the Cuiabá case, the Chiquitanos and Ayoreos, though initially opposed to Enron and Shell's pipeline, ultimately acquiesced in exchange for a compensation program they hoped would guarantee land tenure and improve living conditions. At the time, they viewed this as a pragmatic act of self-determination, albeit a decision made with limited information given the companies' deficient environmental impact studies. However, more than a decade after construction, while mobilization had brought some of the anticipated benefits (fairer compensation, land titles, lessons in organizing), dependency relations had deepened, inequities had surfaced, and territorial integrity had been compromised by multiplying secondary impacts—for example, logging, hunting, and trafficking along the pipeline route and access roads, new power plants, and the Don Mario gold mine. Nonetheless, I argue that, confronted with these quagmires, the Chiquitanos and Ayoreos once again employed *dynamic pragmatism*, adapting the compensation program in novel ways according to their cultural priorities and prioritizing those impacts that threatened livelihood. These and other actions illustrate how, on one level, the Cuiabá conflict can be seen as a struggle for environmental justice.

Strengthening the Indigenous Rights Regime on the Ground

Despite the persistent progression of an extractivist model under Morales, Indigenous groups continue to master the rights gained since the mobilizations of the 1990s and, with the aid of supporters, are becoming increasingly savvy at using new legal tools, such as UNDRIP and the 2009 Bolivian Constitution, in combination with direct action to more forcefully compel states, corporations, and international financial institutions to comply with their rights. As the Cuiabá, Madidi, and TIPNIS cases demonstrate, Bolivian Indigenous groups have pressed for their rights to be respected by mobilizing through electoral and legal channels while simultaneously dealing directly with transnationals and international financial institutions and engaging in direct acts of "insurgent citizenship" (Holston and Appadurai 1996), such as marches, blockades, strikes, and takeovers of facilities. The Cuiabá conflict highlights unique insights about the inner workings of transnational "boomerang" advocacy (Keck and Sikkink 1998) and emphasizes the value of community-based monitoring in increasing awareness about rights and amassing evidence to pressure states, companies, and international financial institutions to address adverse impacts and provide adequate benefits.

This sort of mobilization is part and parcel of broader efforts by Indigenous groups and supporters worldwide, which has led to significant international and domestic legal policy reforms and favorable court decisions[5]—albeit with serious challenges in the area of understanding, implementation, and enforcement; in the last few years several international and regional financial institutions have developed policies and guidelines regarding projects affecting Indigenous peoples (Anaya 2011).[6] In January 2012, the World Bank's International Finance Corporation implemented a new Performance Standard that requires Indigenous peoples' free, prior, and informed consent.[7]

The Chiquitanos' and Ayoreos' dynamic and pragmatic use of UNDRIP and other legal instruments as a means to guarantee their rights illustrates the importance of these tools, imperfect as they are. And it underscores, as Anaya (2009:63) has argued, that while there should not have to be a declaration on the rights of Indigenous peoples, it is needed because Indigenous peoples' rights to equality, self-determination, and related human rights have been denied, with disregard for their character as peoples. As Erica-Irene Daes, former chair of the UN Working Group on Indigenous Populations, has stated, Indigenous peoples, in their pursuit of self-determination, desire not merely to be assimilated as citizens of the state but to be recognized and incorporated as distinct peoples according to mutually agreed upon and just terms (Anaya 2009:61). The actions carried out by the Chiquitanos and Ayoreos are part of a broader global Indigenous politics that is "pushing the international community toward a new vision of self-determination, territoriality, and sovereignty which is postcolonial" (Lightfoot 2010:86). They are part of a movement for intercultural citizenship, demanding greater social inclusion, equality, and cultural diversity while rejecting cultural homogeneity and concentration of political power (Molina Barrios and Albó 2006:18), a far cry from the lip service paid by neoliberal multiculturalism, in which technocratic proponents acquiesced to minimal reforms related to Indigenous rights to preserve the integrity of their broader hegemonic project.[8]

Although the saga surrounding TIPNIS and other conflicts continues to unfold with formidable challenges, one remarkable outcome has been the emergence of a national dialogue—what Amitai Etzioni and David Carney (1997) call a "megalogue"—on the viability of the current development model in the context of Indigenous rights and the environment. This is a lesson that should be noteworthy to other countries trying to chart a path for a more sustainable future. Various cases worldwide, from TIPNIS in Bolivia to the Keystone pipeline in North America, continue to underscore the importance of insurgent action in realizing this trajectory. As the preceding chapters suggest, excising Bolivia from a development model that is so structurally dependent on extractive industries and transnational capital will be a daunting task, but with the stakes so high, Indigenous peoples, NGOs, and others are nonetheless pushing ahead. As Bolivia's former ambassador to the United Nations under Morales stated in the midst of the TIPNIS conflict at the World Peoples' Conference on Climate Change and the Rights of Mother Earth, a more comprehensive and genuine debate will be crucial in achieving this end:

> Since 2006, Bolivia has shown leadership to the world on how to tackle the most profound challenges of our time. We have achieved the approval of the Human Right to Water and Sanitation in the United Nations and promoted a vision for society based on *Vivir Bien* (*Living Well*) rather than consuming more. . . .
>
> As the country that initiated the International Day of Mother Earth, we have a profound responsibility to be an example on the global stage. We cannot repeat the same recipes of failed "developmentalism" that has already brought the relationship between humanity and Mother Earth to a breaking point. . . .
>
> In order to stop the manipulation of the Right, who wish to use this protest to return to the past, we must be even more consistent in defending human rights, indigenous peoples' rights and the rights of Mother Earth.
>
> It's not too late to resolve this crisis if we suspend permanently the construction of the road through the TIPNIS, bring to justice those responsible for the repression to the indigenous march, and open up a

broad and participatory national and regional debate to define a new
agenda of actions in the framework of *Living Well*. (Solón, 2011)

It was indeed an ironic twist of fate that Morales's former ambassador needed
to remind Morales to comply with the charge he had given the world at the
opening of this book: to obey the Indigenous principle of "Living Well"
(*Vivir Bien*), not the capitalist, modernist concept of "Living Better" (*Vivir
Mejor*).

Notes

Chapter 1

1. In contrast to Indigenous communities living elsewhere in TIPNIS that are more dependent on hunting, fishing, and subsistence farming, these coca-dependent communities work as wage laborers for coca harvests, have small plots, or are affiliated with Morales's coca growers' union (Achtenberg 2012b).

2. In a 2001 Census, 112,271 individuals self-identified as Chiquitano. Ramiro Molina Barrios and Xavier Albó (2006:179–180) estimate a total population of 195,624 (2.4% of the Bolivian population), inferring the addition of Chiquitanos younger than 15. In the 2001 census, approximately 66.4% of Bolivia's population was registered as Indigenous, totaling 5,033,814 people (UNECLAC 2005:42, 46). Aside from the Chiquitanos, Bolivia's largest Indigenous groups are Quechua (2,530,985, or 30.6%), Aymara (2,001,947, or 24.2%), Guaraní (126,159, or 1.5%), and Mojeño (68,771, or .8%) (UNECLAC 2005:47). The Ayoreos, the other major Indigenous group affected by the Cuiabá pipeline, number approximately 1,236 (Molina Barrios and Albó 2006: 179). For a map of Bolivia's Indigenous peoples, see en.wikipedia.org/wiki/File:Pueblos _originarios_de_Bolivia.png.

3. This included a call to limit temperature increases during the next century to 1°C as well as a proposal for an international court for climate crimes (Kohl and Bresnahan 2010a).

4. I explain this model more fully in chapters 7 and 8.

5. Dan Brockington (2002) describes "fortress conservation" as an approach that preserves wildlife and habitat by enclosing ancestral lands used and occupied by local people, excluding them from the very environment they have historically depended on for their livelihood.

6. David Harvey's term "accumulation by dispossession" (2003) builds on Karl Marx's concept of primitive accumulation, extending it to such dimensions as privatization, environmental degradation, and exploitation.

7. For seminal early work in political ecology, see Blaikie 1985, Blaikie et al. 1987, and Watts 1983. For a history of the field, see also Neumann 2005, Robbins 2004, and Zimmerer and Bassett 2003.

8. Stephen Cote, e-mail message to author, June 2, 2012.

9. That is to say, Gulf Oil was financially compensated approximately $US 78 million.

Chapter 2

1. UMA was consolidated in 2000 by the World Bank's Hydrocarbon Sector Reform and Capitalization Credit (credit no. 2762 BO). The Hydrocarbon Sector Social and Environmental Management Capacity Building Project (credit no. 33780), informally known in Bolivia as the LIL project, was also implemented in the same year.

2. The Pacific LNG consortium comprised British Petroleum, British Gas, the major Spanish oil company Repsol YPF, and Pan American (Energy British Petroleum and the Argentinean oil company Bridas).

Chapter 3

1. This text is cited from a website of Enron and Shell that is no longer available. It promoted the significance of the Cuiabá project.

2. The Guaraní pressured the companies building the pipeline (including Enron, Shell, and Petrobras) to reroute the pipeline away from their territories because they feared that encroaching development (e.g., ranching, farming, and logging) would follow along the path of the pipeline, as described in chapter 2.

Chapter 5

1. This included small-scale cattle production (for meat and milk), poultry production (for eggs and meat), and crops (corn, rice, beans, cassava, and plantains). Production was for subsistence, with excess sold in the market.

2. These impacts included degradation of community roads, illegal logging and hunting along the pipeline route, and construction of an unauthorized five-kilometer pipeline to tap gas from the Cuiabá pipeline to supply Bolivian president Gonzalo Sánchez de Lozada's Don Mario gold mine.

3. Technically, the pipeline was illegal until the government granted a retroactive environmental license after the pipeline had already been built.

4. The Amazon Alliance is a coalition of Indigenous groups from the Amazon Basin and a variety of northern and southern NGOs.

5. State institutions responsible for land titling include the National Institute of Agrarian Reform (Instituto Nacional de Reforma Agraria) and the Vice Ministry of Indigenous and Native Peoples' Affairs (Viceministerio de Asuntos Indígenas y Pueblos Originarios).

6. The authoritarian regime of García Meza inequitably granted vast quantities of Indigenous lands to political cronies and powerful economic actors.

7. Retitling was the mechanism of the 1996 agrarian reform (Urioste 2010:2).

Chapter 6

1. Erick Reyes Villa is the brother of Manfred Reyes Villa (New Republican Force party), who was mayor of Cochabamba four times and presidential candidate against Sánchez de Lozada in 2002 and Evo Morales in 2009. Erick Reyes Villa subsequently fled to the United States to avoid being prosecuted on corruption charges.

2. The leaders were from Santa Cruz parent organization CPESC, the main Chiquitano organization (OICH), and the two key regional Chiquitano organizations affected by the pipeline (CCICH-Turubó and CIRPAS).

3. In 2011, Avalos, then a senator from the Movement Toward Socialism party, would support construction of a controversial highway through the Isiboro-Sécure Indigenous Territory and National Park (Territorio Indígena y Parque Nacional Isiboro-Sécure) protected area, in opposition to some of the Indigenous peoples living in the area and the country's main Indigenous organizations.

Chapter 7

1. According to the 2001 census (UNECLAC 2005:42, 46).

2. Prior to nationalization, Article 5 of the hydrocarbons law (Law 3058, May 2005) had declared that property of hydrocarbons had been recuperated at the well head (i.e., on site, where hydrocarbons are extracted) for the state.

3. One fertilizer plant, to be located in Carrasco, Cochabamba, would produce 600,000 metric tons of ammonia and 720,000 metric tons of urea per year. The second plant would be sited based on Brazilian demand.

4. YPFB expects the polyethylene and diesel production plants to be located in the Chaco region, where the country's major gas fields are located.

5. A 2010 report produced by the NGO Centro para el Desarrollo Laboral y Agrario states that only a third of the capital necessary for YPFB's proposed industrial projects exists (*La Patria* 2010).

Chapter 8

1. For all activities that exploit natural resources, albeit, with respect for their norms and procedures (2009 Bolivian Constitution, Article 352, Article 30; see also Article 403).

2. The Indigenous groups in or near Madidi National Park include the Mosetén, Leco-Larecaja, Tsimane, Quechua-Tacana, Tacana, Ese Ejja, Toromona, and Leco-Apolo.

3. Such "ecofriendly" projects include small-scale shade-grown coffee and cocoa production.

4. García Linera's view of Indigenous economy parallels what Stefano Varese (1996:126) describes as "a moral economy, founded mainly on the logic of reciprocity and on the right to subsistence, and secondarily on the necessity of exchange in the capitalist market." Although this claim is essentialist, it reflects a predominant perception.

5. Indigenous jurisdiction is granted the same legal hierarchy as ordinary jurisdiction.

Chapter 9

1. GasOriente Boliviano is Enron and Shell's subsidiary that owned and operated the Cuiabá pipeline. After Enron's bankruptcy, Ashmore Energy International purchased the company.

2. Examples include the 2005 hydrocarbons law (Law 3058) and 2007 Presidential Decree 29103 on regulation of socioenvironmental monitoring of hydrocarbons activities in Indigenous territories.

Chapter 10

1. For a translation of a resolution by some Indigenous peoples of TIPNIS rejecting the highway on May 18, 2010, see Carwil Without Borders (2011).

Chapter 11

1. *Minga* is a collective, traditional form of work performed in the public interest. In this context, the term signifies a collective meeting aimed at improving society.

2. Reducing Emissions from Deforestation and Forest Degradation (REDD) is a controversial market-based approach claiming to reduce deforestation and alleviate poverty.

3. For instance, in the TIPNIS case, Law 3477 (September 22, 2006) declared the road through the territory a national and departmental priority. Law 005 (April 7, 2010) approved an agreement between Brazil and Bolivia regarding financing of the project. In August 2008, Brazilian company OAS was contracted to execute the project.

4. These extractive industries particularly include mining, forestry, oil and natural gas extraction, and hydroelectric projects.

5. Examples of legal policy reforms include internationally, UNDRIP (2007), and domestically, laws regarding consultation and sectorial laws in the areas of mining, forestry, and water resources (Anaya 2011:11–12). Favorable court decisions include Colombia's Constitutional Court striking down a Mining Code reform (Law 1382) in May 2011 that had been passed by the Colombian Congress, finding that it was unconstitutional because of a lack of prior consultation with Indigenous and Afro-Colombian peoples (see Armeni 2011).

6. For instance, the European Bank for Reconstruction and Development's 2008 environmental and social policy recognizes the 2007 UNDRIP and requires free,

prior, and informed consent (albeit with a limited definition of "consent"). In 2011, the Organization for Economic Cooperation and Development updated its guidelines on corporate standards regarding human rights (including Indigenous peoples).

7. The new standard is Performance Standard 7. The previous 2006 performance standards required only free, prior, and informed consultation.

8. On interculturality versus multiculturalism, see Johnson (2010:141–142) and Rivera Cusicanqui (2006).

References

Aboriginal Affairs and Northern Development Canada. 2008. "Update paper: United Nations Declaration on the Rights of Indigenous Peoples." Communications Branch, Aboriginal Affairs and Northern Development Canada, Government of Canada; www.aadnc-aandc.gc.ca/eng/1100100014161.

Achtenberg, Emily. 2011a. "Bolivia: TIPNIS marchers face accusations and negotiations." North American Congress on Latin America, August 26; nacla.org/blog /2011/8/26/bolivia-tipnis-marchers-face-accusations-and-negotiations (accessed April 12, 2012).

Achtenberg, Emily. 2011b. "Bolivia's TIPNIS conflict moves to La Paz." North American Congress on Latin America, October 14; nacla.org/blog/2011/10/14/bolivias-tipnis -conflict-moves-la-paz (accessed April 12, 2012).

Achtenberg, Emily. 2012a. "Bolivia: TIPNIS marchers return home, pledge to resist government consulta." North American Congress on Latin America, July 13; nacla .org/blog/2012/7/13/bolivia-tipnis-marchers-return-home-pledge-resist-government -consulta (accessed August 22, 2012).

Achtenberg, Emily. 2012b. "Bolivia's TIPNIS highway redux." North American Congress on Latin America, January 21; nacla.org/blog/2012/1/20/bolivia%E2%80%99s -tipnis-highway-redux (accessed April 10, 2012).

Achtenberg, Emily. 2012c. "Earth First? Bolivia's Mother Earth Law Meets the Neo-Extractivist Economy." North American Congress on Latin America, November 16. nacla.org/blog/2012/11/16/earth-first-bolivia%E2%80%99s-mother-earth-law -meets-neo-extractivist-economy.

Adams, W.M., and D. Hulme. 2001. "Conservation and communities: Changing narratives, policies and practices in African conservation." Pp. 9–23 in *African wildlife and livelihoods: The promise and performance of community conservation*, edited by David Hulme and Marshall W. Murphree. Cape Town; Portsmouth, NH: D. Philip; Heinemann.

AEI Services LLC. 2009. "AEI Form 20-F, commission file number: 000-53606—filed with the United States Securities and Exchange Commission." www.sec.gov/Ar chives/edgar/data/1387685/000095012310030967/c98338e20vf.htm (accessed April 11, 2012).

AFP. 2011. "Bolivia leader asks for pardon after massive strike." September 28; www .google.com/hostednews/afp/article/ALeqM5ibPWns-XP0gPvsUlLcG884VgHhFw ?docId=CNG.d2b3a8ccf23254b4d5ac2261f83673f7.6c1 (accessed April 12, 2012).

Agarwal, Bina. 1992. "The gender and environment debate: Lessons from India." *Feminist Studies* 18(1):119–158; www.jstor.org/stable/3178217.

Agencia Boliviana de Información. 2002. "Existen tres interesados en explotar El Mutún." *El Diario, Economía*, June 12; www.eldiario.net/noticias/2002/2002_06 /nt020614/3_02ecn.html.

Agencia Boliviana de Información. 2011a. "BM dice que es socio de Bolivia en el proceso de cambio y lucha contra la pobreza." *Agencia Boliviana de Información*, June 13; www.derechoshumanosbolivia.org/noticia.php?cod_noticia=NO20110613085721 (accessed April 8, 2012).

Agencia Boliviana de Información. 2011b. "Nueva legislación boliviana otorga 11 derechos básicos a la naturaleza." *Los Tiempos*, May 4; www.lostiempos.com/dia rio/actualidad/nacional/20110504/nueva-legislacion-boliviana-otorga-11-derechos -basicos-a-la_124217_249268.html.

Agencia de Noticias Fides. 2011. "Hasta 2015, gas natural cubrirá el 48% de la matriz energética." *La Patria*, March 29; www.lapatriaenlinea.com/?nota=63560.

Albó, Xavier. 1991. "El retorno del indio." *Revista Andina* 9(2):299–366.

Albro, Robert. 2005. "The Indigenous in the plural in Bolivian oppositional politics." *Bulletin of Latin American Research* 24(4):433–453.

Albro, Robert. 2006. "Actualidades Bolivia's 'Evo phenomenon': From identity to what?" *Journal of Latin American Anthropology* 11(2):408–428.

Ali, Saleem H., and Andrew Singh Grewal. 2006. "The ecology and economy of Indigenous resistance: Divergent perspectives on mining in New Caledonia." *Contemporary Pacific* 18(2):361–392.

Amazon Watch. 1999. Atossa Soltani and Derrick Hindery, "The case of the Bolivia-Cuiabá pipeline: A report on the failures of Enron international to comply with Bolivian environmental laws and OPIC loan conditions in the construction of the lateral gas pipeline." December 8.

Amazon Watch. 2002. Derrick Hindery, Jon Son, and Nadia Martinez, "Field audit of Enron and Shell's Cuiabá and Bolivia-Brazil pipeline impacts." December 10.

Amnesty International. 2011. "Americas: Sacrificing rights in the name of development: Indigenous peoples under threat in the Americas." www.amnesty.org/en/library/info /AMR01/001/2011/en (accessed April 10, 2012).

Amnesty International. 2012. "Governments must stop imposing development projects on Indigenous peoples' territories." www.amnesty.org/en/library/asset/AMR01/005 /2012/en/d6fc82a0-661c-4509-8fbf-d4a6ac7631dc/amr010052012en.pdf (accessed August 21, 2012).

Anaya, S. James. 2009. "Why there should not have to be a declaration on the rights of Indigenous peoples (speech delivered at the 52d Congress of Americanists, Seville, July 2006)." *International human rights and indigenous peoples*, edited by S. James Anaya. New York: Aspen.

Anaya, James. 2011. "Report of the Special Rapporteur on the rights of Indigenous peoples, James Anaya: Extractive industries operating within or near indigenous territories." United Nations; www.ohchr.org/Documents/Issues/IPeoples/SR/A-HRC -18-35_en.pdf (accessed April 3, 2012).

Andersen, Lykke E., and Mauricio Meza. 2001. *The natural gas sector in Bolivia: An overview.* La Paz: Instituto de Investigaciones Socio-Economicas, Universidad Católica Boliviana.

Andersson, Vibeke. 2002. "Indigenous authority and state policy: Popular participation in two villages in rural Bolivia." Working Paper no. 106, Development Research Series. Aalborg: Research Center on Development and International Relations and Institute for History, International and Social Studies, Aalborg University.

Apaza Mamani, Ana. 2011. "Indígenas del TIPNIS advierten a Evo: 'Esa carretera no va a pasar por aquí.'" *ERBOL Agencia de Noticias Indígena,* June 22; plataforma energetica.org/content/2890.

Aramayo Montes, Jorge. 2002. "Opinión: Por fin se aclara el ingreso irregular de Enron a Bolivia." *El Diario,* February 3.

Arellano-Yanguas, Javier. 2012. "Mining and conflict in Peru: Sowing the minerals, reaping a hail of stones." Pp. 89–111 in *Social conflict, economic development and the extractive industry: Evidence from South America,* edited by Anthony Bebbington. New York: Routledge.

Arias, Sandra. 2011. "Evo: Se declaró 'parque' al Tipnis para evitar peleas." *Los Tiempos,* August 22; www.lostiempos.com/diario/actualidad/economia/20110822/evo-se -declaro-%E2%80%9Cparque%E2%80%9D-al-tipnis-para-evitar_138698_284005 .html.

Armeni, Andrea. 2011. "Mining: The risks for Afro-Colombians and the Indigenous." *Americas Quarterly,* Fall; www.americasquarterly.org/node/3040 (accessed April 12, 2012).

Ashmore Energy International. 2010. "AEI–Cuiabá–GOM, GOB, TBS." www.aeien ergy.com/?id=225 (accessed April 11, 2012).

Baeza, Gonzalo. 2002. "Enron deals under scrutiny in Bolivia." UPI; www.upi.com /Business_News/2002/04/04/Enron-deals-under-scrutiny-in-Bolivia/UPI-9215101 7948266/ (accessed April 5, 2012).

Bailey, Jennifer L., and Torbjorn L. Knutsen. 1987. "Surgery without anaesthesia: Bolivia's response to economic chaos." *World Today* 433:47–51.

Banks, Emma. 2011. "Bolivian jurisdictional law: A step in the right direction, but requires further clarification." AIN–Andean Information Network, March 28; ain -bolivia.org/2011/03/bolivian-jurisdictional-law-a-step-in-the-right-direction-but -requires-further-clarification/ (accessed April 11, 2012).

Bascopé Sanjinés, Iván. 2010. *Lecciones aprendidas sobre consulta previa.* La Paz: Centro de Estudios Jurídicos e Investigación Social; servindi.org/pdf/Lecciones_Apren didas_sobre_consulta_previa%20FINAL%20pdf.pdf.

Baspineiro, Alex Contreras. 2008. "Bolivia: Territorio libre de analfabetismo. ALAI, América Latina en Movimiento 'Proceso de cambio, no de contrabando.'" América Latina Unida, December 21; americalatinaunida.wordpress.com/2009/01/04 /bolivia-territorio-libre-de-analfabetismo/ (accessed April 11, 2012).

BBC. 2007. "Bolivian president delivers state of the nation address." BBC Monitoring International Reports, January 23.

BBC News. 2011. "Bolivia minister quits in growing row over road protest." BBC News, September 26; www.bbc.co.uk/news/world-latin-america-15065442 (accessed April 12, 2012).

Bebbington, Anthony. 1993. "Modernization from below: An alternative Indigenous development?" *Economic Geography* 69(3):274–292.

Bebbington, Anthony. 2009. "The new extraction: Rewriting political ecology in the Andes?" *NACLA Report on the Americas* 42(5):12–20.

Bebbington, Anthony. 2012. *Social conflict, economic development and the extractive industry: Evidence from South America.* New York: Routledge.

Bebbington, Anthony, and Jeff Bury, eds. In press-a. *Subterranean struggles: New dynamics of mining, oil, and gas in Latin America.* Austin: University of Texas Press.

Bebbington, Anthony, Jeff Bury, and Emily Gallagher. In press-b. "Conclusions." In *Subterranean struggles: New dynamics of mining, oil, and gas in Latin America,* edited by Anthony Bebbington and Jeff Bury. Austin: University of Texas Press.

Bebbington, Anthony, and Denise Humphreys Bebbington. 2011. "An Andean avatar: Post-neoliberal and neoliberal strategies for securing the unobtainable." *New Political Economy* 16(1):131–145.

Bebbington, Anthony, Denise Humphreys Bebbington, Jeff Bury, Leonith Hinojosa, and Maria-Luisa Burneo. In press. "Anatomies of conflict: Social mobilization and new political ecologies of the Andes." In *Subterranean struggles: New dynamics of mining, oil, and gas in Latin America,* edited by Anthony Bebbington and Jeff Bury. Austin: University of Texas Press.

Berkes, Fikret. 1999. *Sacred ecology: Traditional ecological knowledge and resource management.* Philadelphia: Taylor and Francis.

Berkes, Fikret. 2008. *Sacred ecology: Traditional ecological knowledge and resource management.* New York: Routledge.

Bicker, Alan, Paul Sillitoe, and Johan Pottier. 2003. *Negotiating local knowledge: Power and identity in development.* London: Pluto Press.

Birk, Gudrun. 2000. *Dueños del bosque: Manejo de los recursos naturales por indígenas Chiquitanos de Bolivia.* Santa Cruz de la Sierra, Bolivia: Apoyo para el Campesino-Indígena del Oriente Boliviano.

Blaikie, Piers M. 1985. *The political economy of soil erosion in developing countries.* London: Longman.

Blaikie, Piers M. 1994. *Political ecology in the 1990s: An evolving view of nature and society.* East Lansing: Center for Advanced Study of International Development, Michigan State University.

Blaikie, Piers M., Harold C. Brookfield, and Bryant Allen. 1987. *Land degradation and society.* London: Methuen.

Blaser, Mario. 2004. "Life projects: Indigenous people's agency and development." Pp. 26–44 in *In the way of development: Indigenous peoples, life projects, and globalization,* edited by M. Blaser, H. Feit, and G. McRae. London: Zed Books.

Boelens, Rutgerd, and Bernita Doornbos. 2001. "The battlefield of water rights: Rule making amidst conflicting normative frameworks in the Ecuadorian highlands." *Human Organization: Journal of the Society for Applied Anthropology* 60(4):343.

Bolanos, Omaira. 2011. "Redefining identities, redefining landscapes: Indigenous identity and land rights struggles in the Brazilian Amazon." *Journal of Cultural Geography* 28(1):45–72.

Bolivian Government. 1985. *El decreto 21060 y Santa Cruz: Ponencias del Primer Seminario sobre la Política Económica del MNR.* Edited by Seminario sobre la Política Económica del MNR and Unión de Instituciones de Santa Cruz. Santa Cruz: Unión de Instituciones de Santa Cruz.

Bolpress. 2006. "¿Por qué son legales y constitucionales todas las demandas indígenas?" June 29; www.bolpress.com/art.php?Cod=2010062904 (accessed April 11, 2012).

Bolpress. 2011a. "Bolivia: La VIII Marcha Indígena en construcción de una casa nueva." October 6; www.bolpress.com/art.php?Cod=2011100519 (accessed April 6, 2012).

Bolpress. 2011b. "Colonizadores de Caranavi apoyan a la marcha indígena." September 21, Retrieved April 12, 2012

Bolpress. 2011c. "Justicia libera a dos ex ministros de Goni." July 9; www.bolpress.com /art.php?Cod=2011090711 (accessed April 6, 2012).

Bolpress. 2011d. "Pronunciamiento publico de la Campana en Defensa del TIPNIS." May 20; http://www.bolpress.com/art.php?Cod=2011052009 (accessed April 12, 2012).

Bonifaz, Carlos Romero. 1999. "Tierra y territorio: Avances, dificultades y conflictos." Pp. 138–141 in *Miradas, voces y sonidos: Conflictos ambientales en Bolivia,* edited by J. Gruenberger. La Paz; Santiago, Chile: FOBOMADE; Observatorio Latinoamericano de Conflictos Ambientales.

Borda, Alberto, and A. Jerzy de la Barra. 2007. *Plan nacional de desarrollo: "Bolivia digna, soberana, productiva y democrática para vivir bien": Lineamientos estratégicos, 2006–2011.* La Paz: Ministerio de Planificación del Desarrollo.

Bosque, Hugo. 1999. "Superposición de concesión forestal con reserva de la biosfera y territorio indígena Pilon Lajas." Pp. 144–146 in *Miradas, voces y sonidos: Conflictos ambientales en Bolivia,* edited by J. Gruenberger. La Paz; Santiago, Chile: FOBOMADE; Observatorio Latinoamericano de Conflictos Ambientales.

Bosshard, Peter, and Roger Moody. 1997. "Brave new World Bank?" *Higher Values* 11:7–11.

Brass, Tom. 2002. "Latin American peasants—new paradigms for old?" *Journal of Peasant Studies* 29(3/4):1–40.

Brass, T. 2005. "Neoliberalism and the rise of (peasant) nations within the nation: Chiapas in comparative and theoretical perspective." *Journal of Peasant Studies* 32(3/4):651–691.

Brenner, N., J. Peck, and N. Theodore. 2010. "Variegated neoliberalization: Geographies, modalities, pathways." *Global Networks* 10(2):182–222.

Bridge, Gavin. 2011. "Past peak oil: political economy of energy crises." In *Global political ecology,* edited by Richard Peet, Paul Robbins, and Michael Watts. New York: Routledge.

British Gas Group. 2001. "Brazil." www.bg-group.com/international/int-brazil.htm (page no longer available; accessed November 21, 2011).

Brockington, Dan. 2002. *Fortress conservation: The preservation of the Mkomazi Game Reserve, Tanzania.* Oxford; Bloomington: International African Institute in association with James Currey; Indiana University Press.

Bryant, Raymond L. 1992. "Political ecology: An emerging research agenda in third-world studies." *Political Geography* 11:11–36.

Brysk, Alison. 2000. *From tribal village to global village: Indian rights and international relations in Latin America.* Stanford, CA: Stanford University Press.

Buechler, Hans Christian. 2009. "The Cristo del Gran Poder and the T"inku: Neoliberalism and the roots of Indigenous movements in Bolivia." Pp. 83–99 in *Beyond neoliberalism in Latin America? Societies and politics at the crossroads*, edited by J. Burdick, P. Oxhorn, and K.M. Roberts. New York: Palgrave Macmillan.

Bury, Jeffrey. 2005. "Transnational corporations and livelihood transformations in the Peruvian Andes: An actor-oriented political ecology." *Human Organization* 67(3):307–321.

Bury, Jeffrey, and Timothy Norris. In press. "Rocks, rangers, and resistance: Mining and conservation frontiers in the Cordillera Huayhuash, Peru." In *Subterranean Struggles: New Dynamics of Mining, Oil, and Gas in Latin America*, edited by Anthony Bebbington and Jeff Bury. Austin: University of Texas Press.

Business News Americas. 2007. "Morales Nationalizes Vinto Smelter." February 9; www.bnamericas.com/news/metals/Morales_nationalizes_Vinto_smelter.

Buxton, Nick. 2011. "The law of Mother Earth: Behind Bolivia's historic bill." *Yes! Magazine*, April 21; www.yesmagazine.org/planet/the-law-of-mother-earth-behind -bolivias-historic-bill.

Byrne, John, Leigh Glover, and Cecilia Martinez. 2002. "A brief on environmental justice." Pp. 3–17 in *Environmental justice: Discourses in international political economy*, edited by John Byrne, Leigh Glover, and Cecilia Martinez. New Brunswick, NJ: Transaction.

Cabezas, Stanislaw Czaplicki. 2011. "Indigenous activists gain momentum in Bolivia." *Al Jazeera–English*, August 29; www.aljazeera.com/indepth/opinion/2011/08/2011 82810278552745.html.

Cabitza, Mattia. 2011a. "Evo Morales plays a double game on Bolivia's environment." *Guardian*, July 4; www.guardian.co.uk/global-development/poverty-matters/2011 /jul/04/bolivia-evo-morales-hypocrisy-environment.

Cabitza, Mattia. 2011b. "Peru leads the way for Latin America's indigenous communities." *Guardian*, September 12; www.guardian.co.uk/global-development/poverty -matters/2011/sep/12/peru-land-rights-indigenous-communities.

Cáceres, Eduardo. 2008a. "Interview with Carlos Cuasace." Translated by Oxfam.

Cáceres, Eduardo. 2008b. "Territorios y ciudadanía: La revolución de los Chiquitanos." P. 12 in *De la pobreza al poder: Cómo pueden cambiar el mundo ciudadanos activos y estados eficaces*, edited by D. Green. Barcelona: Intermón Oxfam; www .oxfam.org.uk/resources/downloads/FP2P/FP2P_Bolivia_Territories_citizenship _CS_SPANISH.pdf.

Cadena, Marisol de la, and Orin Starn. 2007. *Indigenous experience today*. Oxford: Berg.

Calle Quiñonez, J. Osvaldo. 2001. "'Bolivia la Nueva': El despertar de un acto de ilusión." In *Temas Sociales 22 Foro YPFB versus capitalización*. La Paz: Universidad Mayor de San Andrés, Facultad de Ciencias Sociales.

Calvo Mirabal, Tristán. 1996. *Transnacionales petroleras en Bolivia La Paz: Impresiones La Amistad*. La Paz: Impresiones La Amistad.

Cambio. 2012. "Gasoducto al Mutún demandará $US 1.000 millones de inversión." March 22; www.cambio.bo/economia/20120322/gasoducto_al_mutun_demandara _$us_1.000_millones_de_inversion_67191.htm.

Carlos Rocha, Juan. 1996. "Mine spill has president in awkward position." *IPS Inter Press Service*, October 23; ipsnews.net/news.asp?idnews=61532.

Carmen, Andrea. 2010. "The right to free, prior, and informed consent: A framework for harmonious relations and new processes for redress." In *Realizing the UN Declaration on the Rights of Indigenous Peoples: Triumph, hope, and action*, ed. P. Joffe, J. Hartley, and J. Preston, 120–134. Saskatoon: Purich Pub.

Carruthers, David V. 2007. "Environmental justice and the politics of energy on the US-Mexico border." *Environmental Politics* 16(3):394–413.

Carvajal, Roger E. 2001. "Análisis de los riesgos toxicológicos en la salud humana, Anexo de la auditoría ambiental." *ENSR International Corporation* 2:11.

Carwil Without Borders. 2011. "Resolution by indigenous communities of Isiboro-Sécure rejecting Cochabamba-Beni highway on May 18, 2010." *Carwil Without Borders*; woborders.wordpress.com/2011/07/15/resolution-by-Indigenous-communities-of-isiboro-secure-rejecting-cochabamba-beni-highway/ (accessed April 11, 2012).

CCICH-Turubó. 2008. "Demandas: Tierra y territorio. Esta información se ha obtenido gracias al seguimiento del directorio de la central a través de la secretaria de tierra y territorio el Señor Lorenzo Suárez y el Señor Víctor Padilla Robles ex-dirigente." www.ccich-turubo.org/d_tierraterritorio.html (accessed April 8, 2012).

CCICH-Turubó, CIRPAS, and OICH. 2006. "Voto resolutivo." plataformaenergetica .org/obie/system/files/voto.pdf (accessed April 10, 2012).

CEDIB. 2001. "Los grandes negocios de Enron en Bolivia: corrupción y transnacionales." *Petropress* 6. Cochabamba: Centro de Documentación e Información Bolivia.

CEDLA. 2011. *Compendio de espaciomapas de TCO en tierras bajas. Tenencia y aprovechamiento de recursos naturales en territorios indígenas*. La Paz: CEDLA.

CEJIS. 2010. *Información general de Bolivia*. La Paz: Inicio–Tierra y Recursos Naturales–Titulación de tierras Indígenas y Campesinas; www.cejis.org/node/75.

Centellas, Miguel. 2000. "Decentralization and democratization in Bolivia." Paper presented at the International Congress of the Latin American Studies Association; www.iisec.ucb.edu.bo/projects/Pieb/archivos/Centellas-DecentandDemocrat.pdf (accessed April 5, 2012).

Chávez, Franz. 2010. "Madidi National Park and the Curse of Petroleum in Bolivia." IPS Inter Press Service, December 13; www.galdu.org/web/index.php?odas=5001 &giella1=eng (accessed April 11, 2012).

Chávez, Franz. 2011a. "Bolivia: Rainforest road will have environmental and cultural impacts." IPS Inter Press Service, September 6; ipsnews.net/news.asp?idnews=105002 (accessed April 12, 2012).

Chávez, Franz. 2011b. "New food policy to boost small-scale farms." IPS Inter Press Service, July 19; ipsnews.net/news.asp?idnews=56544 (accessed April 11, 2012).

Chávez, Walter, and Álvaro García Linera. 2005. "Rebelión Camba: Del dieselazo a la lucha por la autonomía." *El Juguete Rabioso* 65. January 23, La Paz.

China Post. 2011. "Ecuador indigenous group files suit over 'genocide' at government's hands." March 31; www.chinapost.com.tw/international/americas/2011/03 /31/296767/Ecuador-Indigenous.htm.

Chipana, Willy. 2011. "La consulta por el TIPNIS no será vinculante." *La Razón*, August 1; www2.la-razon.com/version.php?ArticleId=134806&EditionId=2608.

Chiquitano Indigenous Organization. 2000. "Resolution of the Chiquitano Indigenous organizations related to the conservation of the Chiquitano forest." Santa Cruz, Bolivia.

Chumacero Ruiz, Juan Pablo. 2010. *Reconfigurando territorios reforma agraria, control territorial y gobiernos indígenas en Bolivia: Informe 2009.* La Paz: Fundación Tierra.

CIDOB. 1999. "Letter from CIDOB to George Munoz, President of OPIC." June 23, Santa Cruz, Bolivia.

CIDOB. 2000. "Letter from CIDOB to US State Department, US Embassy in La Paz, and United States Agency for International Development in La Paz." February 8, Santa Cruz, Bolivia.

CIDOB. 2011. "Diputados indígenas advierten sobre impactos que traería la carretera para el TIPNIS." August 13; www.cidob-bo.org/index.php?option=com_content&view=article&id=569:diputados-indigenas-advierten-sobre-impactos-que-traeria-la-carretera-para-el-tipnis&catid=82:noticias&Itemid=2 (accessed April 6, 2012).

Cingolani, Pablo. 2010. "Geokinetics se va, el dolor y el descontento se quedan con los Mosetenes." *Bolpress*, January 6; www.bolpress.com/art.php?Cod=2010010608.

Clara Galvis, María. 2011. *The right of Indigenous peoples to prior consultation: The situation in Bolivia, Colombia, Ecuador, and Peru.* Due Process of Law Foundation/ Oxfam; www.oxfamamerica.org/publications/the-right-of-indigenous-peoples-to -prior-consultation-the-situation-in-bolivia-colombia-ecuador-and-peru (accessed April 3, 2012).

Clark, B. 2002. "The Indigenous environmental movement in the United States: Transcending borders in struggles against mining, manufacturing, and the capitalist state." *Organization and Environment* 15(4):410–442.

COICA. 2011. "La COICA respalda la gran marcha de los hermanos Indígenas de las tierras bajas de Bolivia, en ejercicio de sus legitimo derechos como pueblos Indígenas." Diplomacia Indígena, August 14; www.diplomaciaindigena.org/wp-content /uploads/2011/08/pronunciamiento-de-la-coica-sobre-la-marcha-indigena-por-el -TIPNIS-de-Bolivia.pdf (accessed April 12, 2012).

Comisión de Comunicación de la Marcha. 2011. "VIII Marcha Indígena: 'El gobierno sufre cuando estamos en el camino.'" *Bolpress*, September 11; www.bolpress .com/art.php?Cod=2011091108.

Conaghan, Catherine M., James Michael Malloy, and Luis A. Abugattas. 1990. "Business and the 'boys': The politics of neoliberalism in the Central Andes." *Latin American research review* 25(2): 3–30.

Conduru, Guilherme Frazão. 2001. "The Roboré agreements (1958): A case study of foreign policy decision-making in the Kubitschek administration." Working Paper CBS-24-01. Centre for Brazilian Studies, University of Oxford; www.brazil.ox.ac .uk/__data/assets/pdf_file/0004/9409/Conduru24.pdf.

Conklin, Beth A., and Laura R. Graham. 1995. "The shifting middle ground: Amazonian indians and eco-politics." *American Anthropologist* 97(4):695–710.

Coordinadora Andina de Organizaciones Indígenas et al. 2011. "Manifesto of the 4th Global Minga for Mother Earth." www.movimientos.org/madretierra/show_text .php3?key=19898 (accessed October 12, 2011).

CORE International. 1994. "Report 1, Executive Summary." In *Definitional mission report: Privatization and capitalization of state enterprises in Bolivia: Final report*, edited by A. Cook, W. Fenton, and V. Shrivastava. Washington, DC: Core International.

Correo del Sur. 2012. "Los Indígenas celebran su día divididos por el lío del Tipnis." August 10. www.correodelsur.com/2012/08/10/19.php.

Cortés, Jorge. 2003. "The influence peddlers: Enron in Bolivia." iacconference.org /documents/11th_iacc_workshop_The_Influence_Peddlers_ENRON_in_Bolivia .pdf (accessed April 10, 2012).

Costas, Patricia. 2010. "Entre el requisito y el derecho: La consulta y participación de los pueblos indígenas." Fundación Tierra, February 10; www.ftierra.org/ft/index .php?option=com_content&view=article&id=2509:rair&catid=130:ft& Itemid=188 (accessed April 11, 2012).

CPESC. 2003. "Letter to compliance advisor/ombudsman, World Bank regarding non-compliance with World Bank's operational guidelines in the Don Mario mining project in Bolivia." June 27, Santa Cruz, Bolivia.

CPESC and CEADES. 2003. "Dossier informativo FCBC: Delitos, ilegalidades, contravenciones con los recursos naturales del Estado." November, Santa Cruz, Bolivia.

CPESC, OICH, and CEADES. 2003. *Inspección "in situ" del Gasoducto Río San Miguel–San Matías–Cuiabá, Tramo Boliviano, del 14 al 28 de Abril del 2003.* Santa Cruz, Bolivia: CPESC, OICH, and CEADES.

Cray, Charlie. 2000. "Export credit agencies out of control." *Multinational Monitor* 21(3):22; www.multinationalmonitor.org/mm2000/032000/.

Crespo Flores, Carlos. 2000. "Superintendencias: Nuevos super poderes (democracia y regulación en Bolivia)." Unpublished manuscript. Cochabamba, Bolivia: Centro de Estudios Superiores Universitarios–Universidad Mayor San Simón.

Dangl, Benjamin. 2011. "Showdown in Peru: Indigenous communities kick out Canadian Mining Company." Upside Down World, September 21; upsidedown world.org/main/peru-archives-76/3229-showdown-in-peru-indigenous -communities-kick-out-canadian-mining-company- (accessed April 12, 2012).

Deer, Kenneth. 2010. "Reflections on the development, adoption, and implementation of the UN Declaration on the Rights of Indigenous Peoples." Pp. 18–28 in *Realizing the UN Declaration on the Rights of Indigenous Peoples: Triumph, hope, and action,* edited by P. Joffe, J. Hartley, and J. Preston. Saskatoon: Purich.

de Franco, Nelson. 2001. *Project report: Gas SCTR dev project.* L/C/TF no. SCL-4265. Washington, DC: World Bank.

de Franco, Nelson, and Peter L. Law. 1998. *International gas trade—the Bolivia-Brazil gas pipeline.* Washington, DC: World Bank Group; documents.worldbank.org/cu rated/en/1998/05/441757/international-gas-trade-bolivia-brazil-gas-pipeline.

Delgado, Iván F. Zavaleta. 2011. "La infantería cocalera, cuerpo a cuerpo: Nueva clase dominante, petroleras y burocracia estatal." *Pukara,* September; www.periodicopu kara.com/archivos/pukara-61.pdf.

Democracy Center. 2009. "The trial of Gonzalo Sanchez de Lozada." Blog from Bolivia; www.democracyctr.org/blog/2009/05/trial-of-gonzalo-sanchez-de-lozada.html (accessed accessed April 8, 2012).

Denevan, William M. 1992. "The pristine myth: The landscape of the Americas in 1492." *Annals of the Association of American Geographers* 82(3):369–385.

Denvir, Daniel, and Thea Riofrancos. 2008. "Ecuador: CONAIE Indigenous movement condemns President Correa." Upside Down World, May 16; upsidedown world.org/main/ecuador-archives-49/1288-ecuador-conaie-Indigenous-movement -condemns-president-correa (accessed April 12, 2012).

De Souza Martins, José. 2002. "Representing the peasantry? Struggles for/about land in Brazil." *Journal of Peasant Studies* 29(3/4):300–335.

Díez Astete, Álvaro. 1993. "Las etnias en Bolivia." Pp. 109–147 in *Enciclopedia Bolivia mágica*, edited by H. Boero Rojo. La Paz: Editorial Vertiente.

Dinerstein, Eric, et al. 1995. *A conservation assessment of the terrestrial ecoregions of Latin America and the Caribbean*. Washington, DC: World Bank.

Domínguez, Luis. 2012. "Mother Earth will have its own ombudsman in Bolivia." *PV Pulse*. www.pvpulse.com/en/news/world-news/mother-earth-will-have-its-own-ombudsman-in-bolivia.

Dourojeanni, Marc J., Alberto Barandiarán Gómez, and A. Diego Dourojeanni. 2009. *Explotación de recursos naturales e infraestructuras*. Lima: G y G Impresores Sociedad Anonima Cerrada.

Dussan, Manuel. 2004. "Bolivia: Enormous reserves, political restrictions." Pp. 37–70 in *Gas market integration in the Southern Cone*, edited by P. Beato and J. Benavides. Washington, DC: Inter-American Development Bank.

Economic Times. 2011. "JSPL to export iron ore from Bolivia in 2–3 months." *Economic Times*, March 15; articles.economictimes.indiatimes.com/2011-03-15/news/28691468_1_iron-ore-bolivia-s-el-mutun-jspl-vice-chairman.

Economist. 2007. "Tin soldiers: The political vendetta behind another nationalization." February 15; www.economist.com/node/8706.

Economist Intelligence Unit. 2002. *Country profile 2002: Bolivia*. London: Economist Intelligence Unit.

Edwards, Rob. 1996. "Toxic sludge flows through the Andes." *New Scientist*, November 23; www.newscientist.com/article/mg15220570.200-toxic-sludge-flows-through-the-andes.html.

EFE. 2011. "Indians occupy US company's gas plant in Argentina." November 24; latino.foxnews.com/latino/news/2011/11/24/indians-occupy-us-companys-gas-plant-in-argentina/ (accessed April 4, 2012).

Eju! 2011. "Evo analiza cambiar trazo de carretera por TIPNIS; Brasil condiciona financiamiento a acuerdos con indígenas." April 8; eju.tv/2011/08/evo-analiza-cambiar-trazo-de-carretera-por-tipnis-brasil-condiciona-financiamiento-a-acuerdos-con-indigenas/.

El Deber. 1999. "Gasoducto: Un equipo multidisciplinario marcara variación del trazado." August 17.

El Deber. 2000. "La empresa transportadora puede ser sancionada: Transredes: No entrega forraje tal como instruyó el Gobierno." August 11.

El Deber. 2002. "Ex ministro Reyes Villa avaló tendido del ducto a Cuiabá." May 10.

El Deber. 2004. "Congreso investiga daños en bosque seco Chiquitano: Comisión. Averiguan anormalidades en obras de ducto." April 4.

El Deber. 2006. "Indígenas y GOB sin acuerdo Hidrocarburos. Ayoreos y Chiquitanos ahora definirán la toma del gasoducto." September 7.

El Deber. 2011. "Bolivia será accionista del BID con aporte de $US 14.7 millones." July 6; www.eldeber.com.bo/bolivia-sera-accionista-del-bid-con-aporte-de-us-147-millones-/110706132810.

El Deber. 2012. "Evo Da Un Paso Atrás Contra Transgénicos." November 11; www.eldeber.com.bo/evo-da-un-paso-atras-contra-transgenicos/121110224549.

El Diario. 1997. "Organismos multilaterales, presionan al gobierno: Ganaran SUS 600 millones de deuda si privatizan SEMAPA de Cochabamba." July 1.

El Diario. 1999. "La enajenación de nuestra riqueza petrolera. Evaluación CDAEN." March 14.

Elliott, Stuart. 2011. "Bolivia to start increased gas exports to Argentina June 30: YPFB–Natural Gas." *Platts*, June 21; www.platts.com/RSSFeedDetailedNews/RSSFeed/NaturalGas/8027038.

Embassy La Paz. 2006a. "Transredes and Goni on trial." WikiLeaks cable 06LA PAZ1842; wikileaks.vicepresidencia.gob.bo/TRANSREDES-AND-GONI-ON-TRIAL (accessed April 4, 2012).

Embassy La Paz. 2006b. "Transredes sale decreases U.S. investment in Bolivian hydrocarbons." WikiLeaks cable 06LAPAZ1491; wikileaks.vicepresidencia.gob.bo/TRANSREDES-SALE-DECREASES-U-S (accessed April 4, 2012).

Energy Information Administration. 2011. "EIA country analysis briefs Bolivia." www.eia.gov/cabs/Bolivia/Full.html (accessed April 4, 2012).

Energy Sector Management Assistance Programme. 2003. *Cross-border oil and gas pipelines: Problems and prospects*. Joint UN Development Programme/World Bank Energy Sector Management Assistance Programme; www.esmap.org/esmap/node/383 (accessed April 5, 2012).

Engle, Karen. 2010. *The elusive promise of indigenous development: Rights, culture, strategy*. Durham, NC: Duke University Press.

Enlace Indígena. 2011. "Declaración del Foro Indígena del Abya Yala. Llamado al diálogo para solucionar el caso del TIPNIS." August 25; movimientos.org/enlacei/show_text.php3?key=19718 (accessed April 12, 2012).

Enron and Shell. 1999. "GasOriente Boliviano response to Amazon Watch allegations." cuiabaenergy.com (accessed August 15, 2001).

ENSR International Corp. 2001. *Auditoría ambiental del derrame de hidrocarburos en el Río Desaguadero*, Vol. 2. Westford, MA: ENSR International Corporation.

Entrix-Bolivia. 1999. *Gasoducto Río San Miguel–San Matías/plan de desarrollo Indígena*. Santa Cruz, Bolivia: Entrix–Bolivia.

Environmental Defense Fund. 1999. *A race to the bottom: Creating risk, generating debt and guaranteeing environmental destruction: A compilation of export credit and investment insurance agency case studies*. Washington, DC: Environmental Defense Fund.

Equipo Nizkor and Derechos Human Rights. 2004. "Marcha para impedir la consolidación del latifundio improductivo y la entrega de los bosques indígenas a las madereras." May 12; www.derechos.org/nizkor/bolivia/doc/gmarcha1.html (accessed April 8, 2012).

ERBOL. 2011. "Guaraníes deciden continuar en la marcha y radicalizar bloqueos." *ERBOL Comunicaciones*, September 21; erbol.com.bo/indigena/noticia.php?identificador=2147483949862 (accessed April 12, 2012).

ERBOL and Fundación Tierra. 2011. "Indígenas: 'No nos oponemos a la carretera.'" August 24; www.indigena.erbol.com.bo/noticia.php?identificador=2147483948693 (accessed August 11, 2012).

Ergueta S., Patricia, and Cecile B. de Morales. 1996. *Libro rojo de los vertebrados de Bolivia*. La Paz: Centro de Datos para la Conservación.

Escobar, Arturo. 2006. "Difference and conflict in the struggle over natural resources: A political ecology framework." *Development* 49(3):6–13.

Escobar, Arturo. 2008. *Territories of difference: Place, movements, life, redes*. Durham, NC: Duke University Press.

Etzioni, Amitai, and David Carney. 1997. *Repentance a comparative perspective*. Lanham, MD: Rowman and Littlefield.

Ewing, Andrew, and Susan Goldmark. 1994. *Privatization by capitalization: The case of Bolivia: A popular participation recipe for cash-starved SOEs.* Washington, DC: World Bank, Finance and Private Sector Development; www-wds.worldbank.org /external/default/WDSContentServer/WDSP/IB/1994/11/01/000009265 _3980420172933/Rendered/PDF/multi0page.pdf.

Fabricant, N. 2010. "Between the romance of collectivism and the reality of individualism: Ayllu rhetoric in Bolivia's landless peasant movement." *Latin American Perspectives* 37(4):88–107.

FAN, Missouri Botanical Garden, Museo de Historia Natural Noel Kempff Mercado, Wildlife Conservation Society, and World Wildlife Fund. 1999. *The San Miguel– Cuiabá pipeline project. An independent supplemental environmental assessment (ISEA).* Santa Cruz, Bolivia: Enron International.

Farthing, Linda C. 2009. "Bolivia's dilemma: Development confronts the legacy of extraction." *NACLA Report on the Americas* 42(5):25–29.

Fernández Terán, Roberto. 2009. *Gas, petróleo e imperialismo en Bolivia.* La Paz: Centro de Estudios Superiores Universitarios (CESU) University Mayor San Simón (UMSS); International Budget Partnership (IBP): Plural Editores.

Finer, Matt, Clinton N. Jenkins, Stuart L. Pimm, Brian Keane, and Carl Ross. 2008. "Oil and gas projects in the western Amazon: Threats to wilderness, biodiversity, and Indigenous peoples." *PLoS ONE* 3(8):e2932; dx.doi.org/10.1371/journal.pone .0002932.

Finer, Matt, and Martí Orta-Martínez. 2010. "A second hydrocarbon boom threatens the Peruvian Amazon: Trends, projections, and policy implications." *Environmental Research Letters* 5(1):014012; iopscience.iop.org/1748-9326/5/1/014012.

Flores, Paolo. 2006. "Bolivia seeks prosecution of ex-president." *USA Today,* June 24; www.usatoday.com/news/world/2006-06-24-bolivia-enron_x.htm.

FM Bolivia. 2009. "Indígenas anuncian retención de motorizados de Petroandina: Noticias de Bolivia de último momento." July 30; www.fmbolivia.com.bo/noticia 14394-indigenas-anuncian-retencion-de-motorizados-de-petroandina.html (accessed April 11, 2012).

FOBOMADE. 2000. *Comments on the consultation process and new project documents for the Learning and Innovation Project (LIL): Strengthening environmental management capacity in the hydrocarbons sector.* La Paz: FOBOMADE.

FOBOMADE. 2001a. "Brutalidad y violencia contra indígenas y sus asesores en Bolivia" (e-mail bulletin). La Paz: FOBOMADE.

FOBOMADE. 2001b. *The environmental audit of the oil spill in Rio Desaguadero.* La Paz: FOBOMADE.

FOBOMADE. 2010. "La exploración petrolera en la Amazonía presenta nuevos desafíos al proceso de cambio." *Rebelión,* January 15; www.rebelion.org/noticia.php ?id=98701.

Fraser, Barbara. 2012. "Indigenous leaders call for Ecuador government to stop oil leasing plans." *Indian Country Today Media Network.com,* February 10; indian countrytodaymedianetwork.com/2012/02/10/indigenous-leaders-call-for-ecuador -government-to-stop-oil-leasing-plans-97010.

Friedmann, John, and Haripriya Rangan. 1993. "Introduction: In defense of livelihood." Pp. 1–21 in *In defense of livelihood: Comparative studies on environmental action,* edited by John Friedmann and Haripriya Rangan. West Hartford, CT: Kumarian Press.

Friends of the Earth International. 2004. "Global day of action on World Bank's 60th birthday: Actions were held in various places including Indonesia, United Kingdom and Bolivia." www.foei.org/en/what-we-do/mining/global/extractive-indus tries-review/j22.html#bolivia (accessed April 8, 2012).

Fundación Tierra. 2011. *Territorio Indígena originario campesinos en Bolivia; entre la Loma Santa y la Pachamama*. La Paz: Fundación Tierra.

Gaceta Oficial del Estado Plurinacional de Bolivia. 2010. "Decreto Supremo 676: Fecha de emisión: 20-10-2010 Edicion: 183NEC–Publicado el: 2010-10-2. Modifica el Artículo 2 del Decreto Supremo n° 29130, de 13 de mayo de 2007, modificado por Decreto Supremo n° 29226, de 9 de agosto de 2007." www.gacetaoficialdebolivia .gob.bo/normas/buscar/676 (accessed April 11, 2012).

Galeano, Eduardo H. 1971. *Las venas abiertas de América Latina*. México: Siglo XXI.

Garcia-Guinea, Javier, and Matthew Harffy. 1998. "Bolivian mining pollution: Past, present and future." *Ambio* 27(3):251–253.

García Linera, Álvaro. 2004a. "Los impactos de la capitalización: Evaluación a medio término." In *Diez años de la capitalización: Luces y sombras*. La Paz: Delegación Presidencial para la Revisión y Mejora de la Capitalización.

Garzón, Biviany Rojas. 2010. "Forest resources in Indigenous territories and REDD projects in the Amazon basin." Pp. 21–74 in *Avoided deforestation (REDD) and indigenous peoples: Experiences, challenges and opportunities in the Amazon context*. São Paulo: Instituto Socioambiental and Forest Trends; www.gcftaskforce.org /documents/REDD_indigenous_peoples.pdf.

GasOriente Boliviano et al. 1999. *Convenio para la ejecución del Plan de Desarrollo Indígena*. Santa Cruz, Bolivia: GasOriente Boliviano Ltda., CIDOB, CPESC, OICH, CANOB, CCICH-Turubó, and CIRPAS.

GasOriente Boliviano et al. 2000. *Addendum al convenio para la ejecución del Plan de Desarrollo Indígena (PDI)*. Santa Cruz, Bolivia: GasOriente Boliviano Ltda., CIDOB, CPESC, OICH, CANOB, CCICH-Turubó, and CIRPAS; www.gasori enteboliviano.com/docs/631b_pdi_adendum_convenio.pdf (accessed April 6, 2012).

GasOriente Boliviano 2009a. "15avo Informe Socioambiental fase de operaciones." GasOriente Boliviano Ltda. Santa Cruz, Bolivia.

GasOriente Boliviano. 2009b. "Evaluación técnica y financiera. Plan de desarrollo indígena." GasOriente Boliviano Ltda. Santa Cruz, Bolivia.

Gavaldá, Marc. 1999. *Las manchas del petróleo boliviano: Tras los pasos de REPSOL en el territorio indígena Parque Nacional Isiboro Sécure*. La Paz; Tarija, Bolivia; Santiago, Chile: FOBOMADE; Red Alerta Petrolera; Observatorio Latinoamericano de Conflictos Ambientales.

Gedicks, A. 2001. *Resource rebels: Native challenges to mining and oil corporations*. Cambridge, MA: South End Press.

Gentry, Alwyn H. 1995. "Diversity and floristic composition of neotropical dry forests." Pp. 146–194 in *Seasonally dry tropical forests*, edited by S. Bullock, H. Mooney, and E. Medina. New York: Cambridge University Press.

Gerlach, Allen. 2003. *Indians, oil, and politics: A recent history of Ecuador*. Wilmington, DE: Scholarly Resources.

Getter, Charles, Elliott Taylor, and Gavin Macgregor-Skinner. 2000. "Managing agricultural resources during oil spills: Case of the OSSA II pipeline spill in Bolivia." US Environmental Protection Agency; www.epa.gov/oem/docs/oil/fss/fss02/getter paper.pdf (accessed April 5, 2012).

Gill, Lesley. 2000. *Teetering on the rim: Global restructuring, daily life, and the armed retreat of the Bolivian state.* New York: Columbia University Press.

Goldman, Michael. 2005. *Imperial nature: The World Bank and struggles for social justice in the age of globalization.* New Haven, Conn.; London: Yale University Press.

Gómez, Luis A. 2004. *El Alto de pie: Una insurrección Aymara en Bolivia.* La Paz: HdP; Comuna: Indymedia.

Gómez Balboa, Miguel E. 2004b. "La sociología de los movimientos sociales. Interview with Álvaro García Linera." *La Prensa,* December 12, 17–18.

Gomez Wichtendahl, Carla. 2009. "Annex II: Bolivia country report (February 2009)." Pp. 127–185 in *Payments for ecosystem services: Legal and institutional frameworks,* edited by T. Greiber. IUCN Environmental Policy and Law Paper No. 78. Gland, Switzerland: International Union for Conservation of Nature.

Gordon, Gretchen. 2005. "Interview with Carlos Villegas Quiroga."

Gordon, Gretchen, and Aaron Luoma. 2008. "Oil and gas: The elusive wealth beneath their feet." Pp. 77–216 in *Dignity and defiance: Stories from Bolivia's challenge to globalization,* edited by J. Shultz and M. Draper. Berkeley: University of California Press.

Gray Molina, George. 2007. "El reto posneoliberal de Bolivia." *Nueva sociedad* 209:118–129.

Griffiths, Thomas. 2000. "World Bank projects and Indigenous peoples in Ecuador and Bolivia. Paper for the Workshop on Indigenous Peoples, Forests and the World Bank: Policies and Practice." Washington, DC: Forest Peoples Programme and Bank Information Center; www.forestpeoples.org/region/bolivia/publication/2010 /world-bank-projects-and-indigenous-peoples-ecuador-and-bolivia.

Griffiths, Thomas. 2007. *Exigiendo responsabilidad al BID y la CFI en Camisea II: Una revisión de estándares internacionales aplicables, y diligencia y conformidad debidas.* San Francisco, CA: Amazon Watch; www.forestpeoples.org/sites/fpp/files /publication/2010/08/perucamiseaiiidbifcsept07sp.pdf.

Grimaldi, James. 2002. "Enron pipeline leaves scar on South America: Lobbying, U.S. loans put project on damaging path." *Washington Post,* May 6; www.washing tonpost.com/ac2/wp-dyn/A37365-2002May5?language=printer.

Guardia, Henry M. 1999. "Gasoducto San Miguel–San Matías–Cuiabá." Pp. 88–89 in *Miradas, voces y sonidos: Conflictos ambientales en Bolivia,* edited by J. Gruenberger. La Paz; Santiago, Chile: FOBOMADE; Observatorio Latinoamericano de Conflictos Ambientales.

Gudynas, Eduardo. 2009. *Diez tesis urgentes sobre el extractivismo bajo el progresismo Sudamericano actual.* Quito: CAAP-CLAES. www.redge.org.pe/sites/default/files /GUDYNAS__El_nuevo_extractivismo_del_siglo_21.pdf.

Gudynas, Eduardo. 2010. "La ecología política de la crisis global y los límites del capitalismo benévolo." *Íconos: Revista de Ciencias Sociales* 2010(36):53–67.

Gudynas, Eduardo, and Alberto Acosta. 2011a. "El buen vivir mas allá del desarrollo." *Quehacer* 181:70–81.

Gudynas, E., and A. Acosta. 2011b. "La renovación de la crítica al desarrollo y el buen vivir como alternativa." *Utopía y Praxis Latinoamericana* 16(53):71–83.

Guerrero, Carlos. 2011. "Mine opponents paralyze city in Peruvian highlands." May 27; abcnews.go.com/Business/wireStory?id=13703305#.T4ZkvdlMiSo (accessed April 12, 2012).

Gustafson, Bret. 2002. "The paradoxes of liberal indigenism: State processes and intercultural reforms in Bolivia." Pp. 267–306 in *The politics of ethnicity: Indigenous peoples in Latin American states*, edited by David Maybury-Lewis. Cambridge, MA: Harvard University, David Rockefeller Center for Latin American Studies.

Gustafson, Bret. 2009. "Manipulating cartographies: Plurinationalism, autonomy, and Indigenous resurgence in Bolivia." *Anthropological Quarterly* 82(4):985–1016.

Guzman, Edwin, Helen Popper, and Carlos Villegas Quiroga. 2006. "Bolivia awards El Mutún mine deal to India's Jindal." World News Network, June 2; archive.wn.com/2006/06/02/1400/p/7e/ef23985453d4b9.html (accessed April 11, 2012).

Guzmán-Ríos, Senén. 2007. "The struggle for natural resources and for the rights of Indigenous peoples: From exclusion and plunder to return of the land." *Indigenous Affairs* 1–2(7):24–35.

Haglund, Christina. 2008. "A river turns black: Enron and Shell spread destruction across Bolivia's highlands." Pp. 45–76 in *Dignity and defiance: Stories from Bolivia's challenge to globalization*, edited by Jim Shultz and Melissa Draper. Berkeley: University of California Press.

Hale, Charles R. 2002. "Does multiculturalism menace? Governance, cultural rights and the politics of identity in Guatemala." *Journal of Latin American Studies* 34(3):485–524.

Hall, Stuart. 1986. "Gramsci's relevance for the study of race and ethnicity." *Journal of Communication Inquiry* 10(2):5–27.

Hamerschlag, Kari. 1999. *The Bolivia-Brazil pipeline: A "model" project.* Bank Information Center; www.bicusa.org/en/Article.454.aspx (accessed April 5, 2012).

Haraway, Donna. 1988. "Situated knowledges: The science question in feminism and the privilege of partial perspective." *Feminist Studies* 14(3):575–599.

Harris, Mark, and Stephen Nugent. 2004. *Some other Amazonians: Perspectives on modern Amazonia.* London: Institute for the Study of the Americas.

Harvey, David. 2003. *The new imperialism.* Oxford: Oxford University Press.

Harvey, David. 2005. *A brief history of neoliberalism.* Oxford: Oxford University Press.

Healey, Susan. 2009. "Ethno-ecological identity and the restructuring of political power in Bolivia." *Latin American Perspectives* 36(4):83–100.

Healy, Kevin. 2001. *Llamas, weavings, and organic chocolate: Multicultural grassroots development in the Andes and Amazon of Bolivia.* Notre Dame, IN: University of Notre Dame Press.

Hecht, Susanna B. 1993. "Of fates, forests, and futures: Myths, epistemes, and policy in tropical conservation." Albright lecture. Berkeley: Department of Environmental Science, Policy and Management, University of California; nature.berkeley.edu/site/lectures/albright/1993.php (accessed March 19, 2012).

Hecht, Susanna B. 2005. "Soybeans, development and conservation on the Amazon frontier." *Development and Change* 36(2):375–404.

Hecht, Susanna B. 2010. "The new rurality: Globalization, peasants and the paradoxes of landscapes." *Land Use Policy* 27(2):161–169.

Hecht, Susanna B. 2011. "The new Amazon geographies: Insurgent citizenship, 'Amazon Nation' and the politics of environmentalisms." *Journal of Cultural Geography* 28(1):203–223; www.tandfonline.com/doi/abs/10.1080/08873631.2011.548500.

Hecht, Susanna B., and Alexander Cockburn. 1990. *The fate of the forest: Developers, destroyers, and defenders of the Amazon*. Great Britain: Penguin Group.

Hendricks, Janet. 1991. "Symbolic counterhegemony among the Ecuadorian Shuar." Pp. 179–196 in *Nation-states and Indians in Latin America*, edited by G. Urban and J. Sherzer. Austin: University of Texas Press.

Heredia García, Hilton. 2011. "Katya Diederich K. Presidenta de Gas Transboliviano (GTB): 'No hay un requerimiento oficial para Mutún.'" *El Deber*, August 14; m.elde ber.com.bo/inota.php?id=110813181223.

Hidrocarburos Bolivia. 2011. "Solución confirmada: Petrobras se hace cargo de todas las operaciones en la Termoeléctrica de Cuiabá y revive el gasoducto Bolivia-Cuiabá." March 30; www.hidrocarburosbolivia.com/nuestro-contenido/noticias /41325-solucion-confirmada-petrobras-se-hace-cargo-de-todas-las-operaciones-en -la-termoelectrica-de-cuiaba-y-revive-el-gasoducto-bolivia-cuiaba.html (accessed April 11, 2012).

Hindery, Derrick L. 1997. "The effects of structural adjustment on deforestation in the Bolivian Amazon." MA dissertation. Los Angeles: Department of Geography, University of California.

Hindery, Derrick L. 2003a. "Multinational oil corporations in a neoliberal era: Enron, Shell, and the political ecology of conflict over the Cuiabá pipeline in Bolivia's Chiquitanía." PhD dissertation. Los Angeles: Department of Geography, University of California.

Hindery, Derrick. 2003b. "Government of Bolivia initiates inspection phase in environmental audit of Cuiabá gas pipeline." *Cultural Survival*, April 14; www.cultural survival.org/news/bolivia/government-bolivia-initiates-inspection-phase-environ mental-audit-cuiaba-gas-pipeline.

Hindery, Derrick. 2004. "Social and environmental impact of World Bank/IMF-funded economic restructuring in Bolivia: An analysis of Enron and Shell's hydrocarbon projects." *Singapore Journal of Tropical Geography* 25(3):281–303; onlinelibrary.wiley.com/doi/10.1111/j.0129-7619.2004.00187.x/abstract.

Hindery, Derrick. In press. "Synergistic impacts of gas and mining development in Bolivia's Chiquitanía: The significance of analytical scale." In *Subterranean Struggles: New Dynamics of Mining, Oil, and Gas in Latin America*, edited by Anthony Bebbington and Jeff Bury. Austin: University of Texas Press.

Hodges, Tina. 2007. "Bolivia's gas nationalization: Opportunities and challenges." *Petroleum World*, November 25; www.petroleumworld.com/SF07112501.htm (accessed October 5, 2012).

Hollender, Rebecca, and Jim Shultz. 2010. *Bolivia and its lithium: Can the "gold of the 21st century" lift a nation out of poverty?* Democracy Center, May 10; democracy ctr.org/blogfrombolivia/bolivia-and-its-lithium-can-the-gold-of-the-21st-century -lift-a-nation-out-of-poverty/ (accessed April 11, 2012).

Holston, James. 1996. "Spaces of insurgent citizenship." *Architectural Design* 66(11/12):54–59.

Holston, James, and Arjun Appadurai. 1996. "Cities and citizenship." *Public Culture* 8(2):187–204.

Howard, Rosaleen. 2010. "Language, signs, and the performance of power: The discursive struggle over decolonization in the Bolivia of Evo Morales." *Latin American Perspectives* 37(3):176–194.

Hoy. 2010. "ITT: Consulta exige autorización de Asamblea y no es vinculante." January 19; www.hoy.com.ec/noticias-ecuador/itt-consulta-exige-autorizacion-de-asamblea-y -no-es-vinculante-388233.html.

Human Rights Watch. 2012. "Bolivia country summary." www.hrw.org/sites/default /files/related_material/bolivia_2012.pdf (accessed April 6, 2012).

Humphreys Bebbington, Denise, and Anthony Bebbington. 2010. "Anatomy of a regional conflict tarija and resource grievances in Morales's Bolivia." *Latin American Perspectives* 37(4):140–160; lap.sagepub.com/content/37/4/140.

Hutton, Jon, William M. Adams, and James C. Murombedzi. 2005. "Back to the barriers? Changing narratives in biodiversity conservation." *Forum for Development Studies* (2):341–370.

Hylton, Forrest, Sinclair Thomson, and Adolfo Gilly. 2007. *Revolutionary horizons: Past and present in Bolivian politics.* New York: Verso.

ILO. 1991. "Convention concerning Indigenous and tribal peoples in independent countries (ILO No. 169), 72 ILO Official Bull. 59, entered into force Sept. 5, 1991." www1.umn.edu/humanrts/instree/r1citp.htm (accessed April 11, 2012).

Inter-American Court of Human Rights. 2007. "Inter-American Court of Human Rights case of the *Saramaka People v. Suriname,* Judgement of November 28, 2007 (preliminary objections, merits, reparations, and costs)." www.corteidh.or.cr/docs /casos/articulos/seriec_172_ing.pdf (accessed April 10, 2012).

International Energy Agency. 2003. *South American gas.* Paris: Organization of Economic Cooperation and Development/International Energy Agency.

International Finance Corporation. 2002. "Project Summary Sheet: IFC's Extractive Industries Projects FY1993–FY2001." Washington, DC: International Finance Corporation; irispublic.worldbank.org/85257559006C22E9/All+Documents/85257 559006C22E985256FDD0066C418/$File/Comsur.pdf (accessed June 30, 2012).

International Finance Corporation. 2003. "Assessment report: Complaint regarding COMSUR/Don Mario Mine Bolivia." Washington, DC: Office of the Compliance Advisor/Ombudsman of the International Finance Corporation; www.cao-ombuds man.org/cases/document-links/documents/AssessmentReportFinalSent12-05-03 .pdf (accessed June 30, 2012).

International Finance Corporation. 2004. "Final report, review of the capacity of COMSUR to manage environmental and social responsibility issues." Washington, DC: Office of the Compliance Advisor/Ombudsman of the International Finance Corporation; www.cao-ombudsman.org/cases/document-links/documents /COMSURcapacityreview-English-CAOweb.pdf (accessed June 30, 2012).

IPS. 2002. "The World Bank and fossil fuels: A clear and present danger." IPS Inter Press Service; www.ips-dc.org/reports/the_world_bank_and_fossil_fuels_a_clear _and_present_danger (accessed April 5, 2012).

Jackson, Jean E. 1995. "Culture, genuine and spurious: The politics of indianness in the Vaupés, Colombia." *American Ethnologist* 22(1):3–27.

Jessop, Bob. 2002. "Liberalism, neoliberalism, and urban governance: A state-theoretical perspective." *Antipode* 34(3):452–472.

Johnson, Brian B. 2010. "Decolonization and its paradoxes." *Latin American Perspectives* 37(3):139–159.

Johnston, Barbara Rose, ed. 1994. *Who pays the price? The sociocultural context of environmental crisis.* Washington, DC: Island Press.

Jones, James C. 1995. "Environmental destruction, ethnic discrimination, and international aid in Bolivia." Pp. 169–216 in *The social causes of environmental destruction in Latin America*, edited by M. Painter and W. Durham. Ann Arbor: University of Michigan Press.

Jornada. 2009. "Morales denuncia estrategias para evitar exploración de hidrocarburos en Bolivia." July 11; www.jornadanet.com/n.php?a=34302-1.

Kaimowitz, David, Graham Thiele, and Pablo Pacheco. 1999. "The effects of structural adjustment on deforestation and forest degradation in lowland Bolivia." *World Development* 27(3) (March): 505–520. doi:10.1016/S0305-750X(98)00146-6.

Kaup, Brent Z. 2008. "Negotiating through nature: The resistant materiality and materiality of resistance in Bolivia's natural gas sector." *Geoforum* 39(5):1734–1742; www.sciencedirect.com/science/article/pii/S0016718508000808.

Kaup, Brent Z. 2010. "A neoliberal nationalization? The constraints on natural-gas-led development in Bolivia." *Latin American Perspectives* 37(3):123–138.

Keck, Margaret E., and Kathryn Sikkink. 1998. *Activists beyond borders: Advocacy networks in international politics*. Ithaca, NY: Cornell University Press.

Kim, Sook-Jin, and Joel Wainwright. 2010. "When seed fails: The contested nature of neoliberalism in South Korea." *Geoforum* 41(5):723–733.

Kimmerer, Robin Wall. 2002. "Weaving traditional ecological knowledge into biological education: A call to action." *BioScience* 52(5):432–438.

Kirsch, Stuart. 2006. *Reverse anthropology: Indigenous analysis of social and environmental relations in New Guinea*. Stanford, CA: Stanford University Press.

Klare, Michael T. 2010. "The relentless pursuit of extreme energy." *Third World Resurgence* 237:6–8.

Klasfeld, Adam. 2011a. "Chevron takes offensive again after appellate defeat." Courthouse News Service, December 2; www.courthousenews.com/2011/12/02/41916.htm (accessed April 12, 2012).

Klasfeld, Adam. 2011b. "Ecuadoreans may face sanction in Chevron case." Courthouse News Service, August 14; www.courthousenews.com/2011/08/04/38736.htm (accessed April 8, 2012).

Klein, Herbert S. 2011. *A concise history of Bolivia*. Leiden: Cambridge University Press. public.eblib.com/EBLPublic/PublicView.do?ptiID=667625.

Kohl, Benjamin. 2003. "Democratizing decentralization in Bolivia: The law of popular participation." *Journal of Planning Education and Research* 23(2):153–164.

Kohl, Benjamin. 2004. "Privatization Bolivian style: A cautionary tale." *International Journal of Urban and Regional Research* 28(4):893–908.

Kohl, Benjamin. 2010. "Bolivia under Morales: A work in progress." *Latin American Perspectives* 37(3):107–122.

Kohl, Benjamin H., and Rosalind Bresnahan. 2010a. "Bolivia under Morales: Consolidating power, initiating decolonization." *Latin American Perspectives* 37(3):5–17.

Kohl, Benjamin H., and Rosalind Bresnahan. 2010b. "Introduction Bolivia under Morales. National agenda, regional challenges, and the struggle for hegemony." *Latin America Perspectives* 37(4):5–20.

Kohl, Benjamin H., and Linda C. Farthing. 2006. *Impasse in Bolivia: Neoliberal hegemony and popular resistance*. London: Zed Books.

Kohl, B., and L. Farthing. 2009. "'Less than fully satisfactory development outcomes': International financial institutions and social unrest in Bolivia." *Latin American Perspectives* 36(3):59–78.

Langman, Jimmy. 2000. "Clinton regime ripped for supporting pipeline; environmentalists contend project in Bolivia, Brazil harms ecosystems." *Washington Times,* January 11.

Langman, Jimmy. 2002. "Enron's pipe scheme: Energy giant bulldozed over environmental, human rights concerns to build Bolivian pipeline—with U.S. government backing." CorpWatch, May 9; www.corpwatch.org/article.php?id=2528 (accessed April 5, 2012).

La Patria. 2010. "YPFB no halla financiamiento para industrializar el gas." January 25; lapatriaenlinea.com/index.php?nota=15917.

La Prensa. 2000. "Por daño ambiental, prefiere proseguir con el proceso administrativo: Gobierno no quiere iniciar juicio contra Transredes." August 10.

La Prensa. 2002. "Gobierno pedirá nuevo informe ambiental sobre ducto a Cuiabá." May 10.

La Protesta. 2011a. "Evo Capataz De Las Transnacionales." September 22; old.kaosen lared.net/noticia/bolivia-justa-cabrera-evo-capataz-transnacionales.

La Protesta. 2011b. "Se reanudan bloqueos Aymaras en Puno contra las mineras." June 17; sites.google.com/site/laprotestabolivia/ (accessed April 12, 2012).

La Razón. 2000a. "El 30 de Enero se Rompió el Oleoducto Sica Sica-Arica: El derrame y los daños ecológicos." August 9.

La Razón. 2000b. "Las empresas petroleras invirtieron 1.985 millones de dólares desde 1997: Las reservas de gas crecieron 600%." August 6.

La Razón. 2000c. "No realizó el mantenimiento del oleoducto en el tramo que atraviesa por el río desaguadero, derrame de petróleo: Transredes fue multada con 114 mil dólares." August 9.

La Razón. 2000d. "Para proyectos energéticos petroleras: El FNDR se queda con las multas." August 10.

La Razón. 2000e. "To the government: The World Bank asks for counsel to be institutionalized." July 29.

La Razón. 2000f. "Viceministra de medio ambiente sostiene que hubo negligencia." August 10.

La Razón. 2006. "La fiscalía de la paz cierra el caso de la quebrada empresa Enron." December 21.

La Razón. 2009. "Los indígenas exigen empleos a Yacimientos." September 22; www .derechoshumanosbolivia.org/noticia.php?cod_noticia=NO20090922093650.

La Razón. 2011. "Confirman la expulsión de un programa de USAID." April 19; www .contrainjerencia.com/?p=15789.

Larner, W. 2003. "Neoliberalism?" *Environment and Planning. D, Society and Space* 21:509–512.

Latin American Herald Tribune. 2012. "Bolivian president frets about Argentina, Brazil gas demand." February 16; www.laht.com/article.asp?ArticleId=462500&Cate goryId=14919.

Lauermann, Paul David. 2011. "Boundless: Conservation and development on the southern African frontier." MA dissertation. Eugene: Department of International Studies, University of Oregon.

Laurie, Nina, Robert Andolina, and Sarah Radcliffe. 2002. "The excluded 'indigenous'? The implications of multi-ethnic politics for water reform in Bolivia." Pp. 252–276 in *Multiculturalism in Latin America: Indigenous rights, diversity, and democracy,* edited by R. Sieder. New York: Palgrave Macmillan.

Lazcano, Miguel. 2011a. "Convocan a indígenas por el TIPNIS." *La Razón*, July 11; www2.la-razon.com/version.php?ArticleId=133547&EditionId=2587.

Lazcano, Miguel. 2011b. "Evo no reculará respecto a la vía por el TIPNIS: Advertencia. Anunció que se construirá 'quieran o no quieran.'" *La Razón*, June 30; www2.la-razon.com/version.php?ArticleId=132963&EditionId=2575.

Lehm, Zulema. 1993. *El Bosque de Chimanes: Un escenario de conflictos sociales.* Trinidad, Bolivia: Centro de Investigación y Documentación para el Desarrollo del Beni.

Ley del Servicio Nacional de Reforma Agraria (commonly known as Ley INRA), October 18, 1996.

Lightfoot, Sheryl R. 2010. "Emerging international indigenous rights norms and 'over-compliance' in New Zealand and Canada." *Political Science* 62(1):84–104.

Lohman, Maria. 1999. "Revista 30 días en las noticias." February. Cochabamba: Centro de Documentación e Información Bolivia.

Los Tiempos. 2002. "El 'Ahorro' de la Enron." May 13; amazonwatch.org/news/2002/0513-el-ahorro-de-la-enron.

Los Tiempos. 2011. "Otro grupo indígena objeta carretera a Beni." July 14; www.lostiempos.com/diario/actualidad/economia/20110714/otro-grupo-indigena-objeta-carretera-a-beni_133686_271733.html.

Lovell, Nadia. 1998. *Locality and belonging.* London: Routledge.

Lowman, Sonia. 2011. *Broken promises gender impacts of the World Bank–financed West African and Chad-Cameroon pipelines.* Washington, DC; Amsterdam: Gender Action; Friends of the Earth International; www.genderaction.org/publications/11/chad-cam-wagp-pipelines.html.

Lucero, José Antonio. 2006a. "Interview with Richard Chase Smith, Instituto del Bien Común."

Lucero, José Antonio. 2006b. "Representing 'real Indians': The challenges of indigenous authenticity and strategic constructivism in Ecuador and Bolivia." *Latin American Research Review* 41(2):31–56.

Lucero, José Antonio. 2008. *Struggles of voice: The politics of indigenous representation in the Andes.* Pittsburgh: University of Pittsburgh Press.

Lynch, Richard. 2002. *An energy overview of Bolivia.* Fossil Energy International and US Department of Energy; www.osti.gov/servlets/purl/821117-Wmyost/native/ (accessed April 5, 2012).

Macdonald, Laura. 1995. "A mixed blessing: The NGO boom in Latin America." *NACLA Report on the Americas* 28(5):30–35.

Malleson, R. 2002. "Changing perspectives on forests, people and 'development': Reflections on the case of the Korup Forest." *IDS Bulletin* 33:94–101.

Malloy, James M. 1970. *Bolivia: The uncompleted revolution.* Pittsburgh: University of Pittsburgh Press.

Mares, David. 2006. "Natural gas pipelines in the Southern Cone." Pp. 169–201 in *Natural gas and geopolitics: From 1970 to 2040*, edited by D. Victor, A. Jaffe, and M. Hayes. Cambridge: Cambridge University Press.

Mares, David R., Peter R. Hartley, and Kenneth B. Medlock III. 2008. *Energy security in a context of hyper-social mobilization: Insights from Bolivia.* The Global Energy Market: Comprehensive Strategies to Meet Geopolitical and Financial Risks. James A. Baker III Institute for Public Policy.

Markowitz, L. 2001. "Finding the field: Notes on the ethnography of NGOs." *Human Organization* 60:40–46.

Martinez-Alier, Juan. 2002. *The environmentalism of the poor: A study of ecological conflicts and valuation.* Northhampton, MA: Edward Elgar; public.eblib.com /EBLPublic/PublicView.do?ptiID=472042.

McDaniel, Josh. 2002. "Confronting the structure of international development: Political agency and the Chiquitanos of Bolivia." *Human Ecology* 30(3):369–396.

McDaniel, Josh M. 2003. "History and the duality of power in community-based forestry in southeast Bolivia." *Development and Change* 34(2):339–356.

McDaniel, Josh, Deborah Kennard, and Alicia Fuentes. 2005. "Smokey the tapir: Traditional fire knowledge and fire prevention campaigns in lowland Bolivia." *Society and Natural Resources* 18(10):921–931. dx.doi.org/10.1080/08941920500248921.

Medina, Javier. 2006. *Suma Qamaña: Por una convivialidad postindustrial.* La Paz: Garza Azul Editores.

Mekay, Emad. 2003. "IMF policies at root of riots, say activists." Inter Press Service, February 13; ipsnews.net/print.asp?idnews=15922 (accessed April 8, 2012).

Mendía, Gina. 2000a. "Transredes aún no decide si pagará multa. La empresa puede recurrir a la Superintendencia y a la Suprema, pero aquí es inapelable." *El Deber,* August 10.

Mendía, Gina. 2000b. "Transredes no teme sanción del Gobierno." *El Deber,* July 26.

Merry Frank, Gregory Amacher, and Eirivelthon Lima. 2008. "Land values in frontier settlements of the Brazilian Amazon." *World Development* 36(11):2390–2401.

Meyer, Carrie A. 1993. "Environmental NGOs in Ecuador: An economic analysis of institutional change." *Journal of Developing Areas* 272:191–210.

Minister of Finance of Bolivia. 1994. "Bolivia: Capitalization program adjustment credit, letter of development policy to Lewis Preston, President, World Bank, La Paz, Bolivia."

Ministerio de Medio Ambiente y Agua. 2008. "Carta abierta del Presidente Boliviano Evo Morales Ayma: Cambio climático: Salvemos al planeta del capitalismo." www .mmaya.gob.bo/web_anexo/titulares/cartanacionesunidas.htm (accessed August 11, 2012).

Minzenberg, E., and R. Wallace. 2011. "Amazonian agriculturalists bound by subsistence hunting." *Journal of Cultural Geography* 28(1):99–121.

Molina, Patricia. 1999a. "El proyecto Cuiabá: Cómo comprar conservacionistas." Pp. 199–208 in *Miradas, voces y sonidos: Conflictos ambientales en Bolivia,* edited by J. Gruenberger. La Paz; Santiago, Chile: FOBOMADE; Observatorio Latinoamericano de Conflictos Ambientales.

Molina, Patricia. 1999b. "Explotación de hidrocarburos y conflictos ambientales en Bolivia." Pp. 71–104 in *Miradas, voces y sonidos: Conflictos ambientales en Bolivia,* edited by Jenny Gruenberger. La Paz; Santiago, Chile: FOBOMADE; Observatorio Latinoamericano de Conflictos Ambientales.

Molina Barrios, Ramiro, and Xavier Albó. 2006. *Gama étnica y lingüística de la población boliviana.* La Paz: Sistema de Naciones Unidas en Bolivia.

Montaño Aragón, Mario. 1989. *Guia etnografica linguistica de Bolivia (Tribus de la Selva). Tomo II.* La Paz: Editorial Don bosco.

Moore, Jennifer, and Teresa Velásquez. In press. "Water for gold: Confronting state and corporate mining discourses in Azuay, Ecuador." In *Subterranean struggles:*

New Dynamics of Mining, Oil, and Gas in Latin America, edited by Anthony Bebbington and Jeff Bury. Austin: University of Texas Press.

Muriel, Verónica. 2011. "Proyecto Petrocasas no se materializa, recibe críticas y advertencias." Energy Press, April 11; www.hidrocarburosbolivia.com/bolivia-mainmenu-117/semanarios-mainmenu-126/41656-proyecto-petrocasas-no-se-materializa-recibe-criticas-y-advertencias.html (accessed April 11, 2012).

Natanson, José. 2007. "Las reformas pactadas: Entrevista de José Natanson. Interview with Álvaro García Linera." Nueva Sociedad 209 (May–June):160–172; www.nuso.org/upload/articulos/3436_1.pdf.

Nepstad, Daniel, S. Schwartzman, B. Bamberger, M. Santilli, D. Ray, P. Schlesinger, P. Lefebvre, et al. 2006. "Inhibition of Amazon deforestation and fire by parks and Indigenous lands." Conservation Biology 20(1):65–73.

Neumann, Roderick P. 1998. Imposing wilderness: Struggles over livelihood and nature preservation in Africa. Berkeley: University of California Press.

Neumann, Roderick P. 2005. Making political ecology. London: Hodder Arnold.

Newell, Peter. 2008. "Contesting trade politics in the Americas: The politics of environmental justice." Pp. 49–73 in Environmental justice in Latin America: Problems, promise, and practice, edited by David V. Carruthers. Cambridge, MA: MIT Press.

Nugent, Stephen. 1993. Amazonian caboclo society: An essay on invisibility and peasant economy. Providence, RI: Berg.

Nygren, Anja. 2000. "Development discourses and peasant-forest relations: Natural resource utilization as social process." Development and Change 31(1):11–34.

Observatorio Boliviano de los Recursos Naturales. 2011. "Termoeléctrica sentará soberanía en San Matías." July 21; recursosnaturales-ceadl.blogspot.com/2011/07/termoelectrica-sentara-soberania-en-san.html (accessed April 11, 2012).

Observatorio Petrolero Sur. 2011. "Bolivia: Tribunal Constitucional reconoce derecho a consulta y propiedad de la TCO Itika Guasu, Declaración de la APG IG ante la Sentencia Constitucional 2003/2010-R." May 19; opsur.wordpress.com/2011/05/19/bolivia-el-tribunal-constitucional-reconoce-el-derecho-a-consulta-y-a-la-propiedad-de-la-tco-en-un-caso-que-afecta-a-la-asamblea-del-pueblo-guarani-itika-guasu/ (accessed April 11, 2012).

O'Connor, James. 1973. The fiscal crisis of the state. New York: St. Martin's Press.

Offen, Karl H. 2003. "The territorial turn: Making black territories in Pacific Colombia." Journal of Latin American Geography 2(1):43–73.

OICH. 1999. Informe de vigilancia socio-ambiental de los pueblos indígenas al gasoducto Bolivia-Brasil lateral Cuiabá. Santa Cruz, Bolivia: OICH.

OICH. 2000. Chiquitano Indigenous Organization (OICH) information on the conflict between the multinational oil corporations and Indigenous peoples over the conservation of the Chiquitano dry forest. Santa Cruz, Bolivia: OICH.

OICH and CEADES. 2002. Cuiabá gas pipeline: Social and environmental impacts on the Chiquitano forest: Indigenous organizations' monitoring report. www.eca-watch.org/problems/americas/bolivia/Cuiaba_Indigenous_Report.pdf (accessed April 3, 2012).

OICH and CEADES. 2004. Guía metodológica para la vigilancia social de la industria extractiva en territorios indígenas: La experiencia del Pueblo Indígena Chiquitano en el Gasoducto Lateral Cuiabá. Santa Cruz, Bolivia: OICH, CEADES, Oxfam.

OPIC. 1999a. List of conditions to the approval by the OPIC board of directors of the Cuiabá project. Washington, DC: OPIC.

OPIC. 1999b. *OPIC board approves Cuiabá project with unprecedented environmental safeguards*. Washington, DC: OPIC.

OPIC. 1999c. *Summary of environmental conditions in the Cuiabá project loan agreement*. Washington, DC: OPIC.

Oquendo, Ángel R. 2009. "Upping the ante: Collective litigation in Latin America." *Columbia Journal of Transnational Law* 47(2):248–291.

Orgáz García, J. Mirko. 2002. *La guerra del gas: Nación versus Estado Transnacional en Bolivia*. La Paz

O'Rourke, Dara, and Sarah Connolly. 2003. "Just oil? The distribution of environmental and social impacts of oil production and consumption." *Annual Review of Environment and Resources* 28(1):587–617; www.annualreviews.org/doi/abs/10.1146/annurev.energy.28.050302.105617.

Ortiz, Gonzalo. 2010. "Ecuador: Environmental inspection in Yasuni Park." IPS Inter Press Service, April 10; ipsnews.net/news.asp?idnews=50986 (accessed April 11, 2012).

Ortiz, Gonzalo. 2011. "Ecuador: Fate of untapped oil hangs in the balance—of trust fund." IPS Inter Press Service, July 14; ipsnews.net/news.asp?idnews=56483 (accessed April 11, 2012).

Orvana Minerals Corp. 2009. "Annual information form, fiscal year ending September 30, 2009." December 21. Canada: Orvana Minerals Corp.

Orvana Minerals Corp. 2010. *NI 43-101 technical report on the Don Mario upper mineralized zone project, eastern Bolivia*. Canada: Orvana Minerals Corp.

Osterweil, Michal. 2005. "Place-based globalism: Locating women in the alternative globalization movement." Pp. 174–189 in *Women and the politics of place*, edited by W. Harcourt and A. Escobar. Bloomfield, CT: Kumarian Press.

Otero, Gerardo, and Heidi A. Jugenitz. 2003. "Challenging national borders from within: The political-class formation of Indigenous peasants in Latin America." *Canadian Review of Sociology and Anthropology* 40(5):503–524.

Pacheco, Pablo. 1998. *Estilos de desarrollo, deforestación y degradación de los bosques en las tierras bajas de Bolivia*. La Paz: Center for International Forestry Research, CEDLA, Taller de Iniciativas en Estudios Rurales y Reforma Agraria.

Pacheco, P., D. Barry, P. Cronkleton, A. Larson, and I. Monterroso. 2008. "From agrarian to forest tenure reforms in Latin America: Assessing their impacts for local people and forests." In *XXII Conferencia de la Asociación Internacional para el Estudio de la Propiedad Colectiva (IASCP)*, 14–18. Cheltenham, Reino Unido. iasc2008.glos.ac.uk/conference%20papers/papers/P/Pacheco_118301.pdf.

Página Siete. 2012a. "Presidente Morales promulgó la ley de la Madre Tierra." October 15; www.paginasiete.bo/2012-10-15/Sociedad/Destacados/Promulga-Ley-de-la-Madre-Tierra.aspx (accessed November 26, 2012).

Página Siete. 2012b. "Evo entrega más regalos en el TIPNIS a 10 días de la consulta." July 19; www.paginasiete.bo/2012-07-20/Nacional/Destacados/3Nac00120-02.aspx (accessed August 21, 2012).

Parellada, Alejandro, Ana Cecilia Betancur, Aragón, Miguel Angel, Zurita, Iván Égido, Roca, Carla, Coronado, Noel, Solorzano, Gabriel, Winding, Diana, IWGIA, and Danmark. Ambassaden (Bolivia). 2010. The Rights of Indigenous Peoples: The Cooperation between Denmark and Bolivia (2005–2009). Copenhagen; La Paz: International Work Group for Indigenous Affairs (IWGIA); Royal Danish Embassy.

Parker, Theodore A. 1993. *The lowland dry forests of Santa Cruz, Bolivia: A global conservation priority*. Washington, DC; Santa Cruz, Bolivia: Conservation International; Fundación Amigos de la Naturaleza.

Parks, S.A., and A.H. Harcourt. 2002. "Reserve size, local human density, and mammalian extinctions in U.S. protected areas." *Conservation Biology* 16(3): 800–808.

Pató, Zsuzanna. 2000. *Piping the forest: The Bolivia-Brasil gas pipeline case study.* Liben, Czech Republic: Central and Eastern European Bankwatch Network.

Paz, Walter. 1999. "Superposición de concesiones forestales con tierras comunitarias de origen." Pp. 154–156 in *Miradas, voces y sonidos: conflictos ambientales en Bolivia*, edited by J. Gruenberger. La Paz; Santiago, Chile: FOBOMADE; Observatorio Latinoamericano de Conflictos Ambientales.

Peck, Jamie. 2004. "Geography and public policy: Constructions of neoliberalism." *Progress in Human Geography* 28(3):392–405.

Peck, Jamie. 2010. *Constructions of neoliberal reason*. Oxford: Oxford University Press.

Peck, Jamie, and Adam Tickell. 2002. "Neoliberalizing space." *Antipode* 34(3): 380–404.

Pedlowski, Marcos Antonio, E.A.T. Matricardi, D. Skole, S.R. Cameron, W. Chomentowski, C. Fernandes, and A. Lisboa. 2005. "Conservation units: A new deforestation frontier in the Amazonian state of Rondônia, Brazil." *Environmental Conservation* 32 (2): 149–155.

Peet, Richard, Paul Robbins, and Michael Watts. 2011. *Global political ecology*. New York: Routledge; public.eblib.com/EBLPublic/PublicView.do?ptiID=668182.

Periódico Boliviano–Cambio. 2011. "ONU recomienda profundizar las consultas a los pueblos indígenas: El alto comisionado de las naciones unidas en Bolivia presentó informe sobre derechos humanos." March 25; www.cambio.bo/noticia.php?fecha=2011-03-25&idn=41525.

Perreault, Tom. 2008. "Popular protest and unpopular policies: State restructuring, resource conflict, and social justice in Bolivia." Pp. 239–262 in *Environmental justice in Latin America: Problems, promise, and practice*, edited by David Carruthers. Cambridge, MA: MIT Press.

Perreault, Thomas. 2009. "Assessing the limits of neoliberal environmental governance in Bolivia." Pp. 135–155 in *Beyond neoliberalism in Latin America? Societies and politics at the crossroads*, edited by John Burdick, Philip Oxhorn, and Kenneth M. Roberts. New York: Palgrave Macmillan.

Perreault, Thomas. 2012. "Extracting justice: Natural gas, Indigenous mobilization and the Bolivian State." Pp. 75–102 in *The politics of resource extraction: Indigenous peoples, multinational corporations, and the state*, edited by Suzana Sawyer and Edmund Terence Gomez. New York: Palgrave Macmillan.

Perreault, Thomas, and Patricia Martin. 2005. "Geographies of neoliberalism in Latin America." *Environment and Planning A* 37(2):191–201.

Peterson, M. Nils, Markus J. Peterson, and Tarla Rai Peterson. 2005. "Conservation and the myth of consensus." *Conservation Biology* 19(3):762–767.

Plataforma Energética. 2011a. "Evo: La consulta no es para que los indígenas chantajeen al Gobierno." July 15; plataformaenergetica.org/content/2928 (accessed August 11, 2012).

Plataforma Energética. 2011b. "Pueblo Guaraní anuncia toma de una planta de gas de YPFB–Repsol." May 27; plataformaenergetica.org/content/2845 (accessed April 11, 2012).

Porro, Noemi, Iran Veiga, and Dalva Mota. 2011. "Traditional communities in the Brazilian Amazon and the emergence of new political identities: The struggle of the quebradeiras de coco babaçu-babassu breaker women." *Journal of Cultural Geography* 28(1):123–146.

Portillo-Quintero, C.A., and G.A. Sanchez-Azofeifa. 2010. "Extent and conservation of tropical dry forests in the Americas." *Biological Conservation* 143(1):144–155.

Postero, Nancy Grey. 2007. *Now we are citizens: Indigenous politics in postmulticultural Bolivia.* Stanford, CA: Stanford University Press.

Postero, Nancy Grey. 2010. "Morales's MAS government: Building Indigenous popular hegemony in Bolivia." *Latin American Perspectives* 37(3):18–34.

Prada, Paulo. 2006. "Bolivian nationalizes the oil and gas sector." *New York Times*, May 2; www.nytimes.com/2006/05/02/world/americas/02bolivia.html.

Pratt, Scott L. 2002. *Native pragmatism: Rethinking the roots of American philosophy.* Bloomington: Indiana University Press.

Presencia. 2000. "Gobierno amonesto a Gas Transboliviano por incumplir normas de medio ambiente: En la construcción de gasoducto a Cuiabá." February 24.

President of Bolivia. 2007. "Presidential decree n° 29033: Consultation and participation regulation for hydrocarbon activities." Reglamento de consulta y participación para actividades hidrocarburíferas, February 16.

Press Trust of India. 2010. "Jindal Steel asked to pay for Bolivia pact violation." May 11; www.financialexpress.com/news/jindal-steel-asked-to-pay-for-bolivia-pact-vio lation/617036/ (accessed April 11, 2012).

Price, Marie. 1994. "Ecopolitics and environmental nongovernmental organizations in Latin America." *Geographical Review* 84(1):42–58.

PROBIOMA. 1999a. "Letter from PROBIOMA to Neisa Roca, vice-minister of sustainable development, entitled 'Denuncia de Incumplimiento al EEIA por Parte de GOB en el Gasoducto a Cuiabá.'" Santa Cruz: PROBIOMA.

PROBIOMA. 1999b. "Propuesta acerca del fondo para el Plan de Conservación." Santa Cruz: PROBIOMA.

PROBIOMA. 2000a. "Algunas aclaraciones sobre la situación de San Matías." Santa Cruz: PROBIOMA.

PROBIOMA. 2000b. "Informe Cuiabá: Febrero de 2000." Santa Cruz: PROBIOMA.

PROBIOMA. 2000c. "Informe Gasoducto San Miguel—Cuiabá." Santa Cruz: PROBIOMA.

PROBIOMA. 2000d. "Las contradicciones prácticas del conservacionismo mercantilizado." Santa Cruz: PROBIOMA.

PROBIOMA. 2001. "Unidades de Trabajo." www.oocities.org/espanol/probioma/pro bioma/unidades_de_trabajo.htm (accessed August 9, 2012).

PROBIOMA. 2009. "Se conformo el comité de fiscalización socioambiental de la Chiquitanía y el Pantanal Voces del Pantanal Boliviano." Boletín no. 25. Santa Cruz: PROBIOMA.

PROBIOMA, Organización Indígena Chiquitana, H. Alcaldes, Comités Cívicos, Comités de Fiscalización de las Provincias Ángel Sandoval, Chiquitos y German Busch, Foro Regional de Medio Ambiente y Desarrollo de la Provincia German

Busch, Foro Departamental de Medio Ambiente y Desarrollo de Santa Cruz, and Foro Boliviano de Medio Ambiente y Desarrollo. 1999. "Public Declaration: Bolivia: Gasoducto a Cuiabá: Descubren Escandaloso Negociado De 'Conservacionistas.'" Santa Cruz: PROBIOMA.

Quiroga, Carlos Villegas. 2004. *Privatización de la industria petrolera en Bolivia: Trayectoria y efectos tributarios*, 3d ed. La Paz: FOBOMADE, Postgrado en Ciencias del Desarrollo–Universidad mayor de San Andrés, Diakonia, CEDLA.

Quispe, Miguel Palacín. 2011. "Brasil: Vergüenza internacional; secretario general de la OEA cuestiona medida cautelar emitida por la CIDH en caso Belo Monte." Diplomacia Indígena, May 10; www.diplomaciaindigena.org/2011/05/verguenza -internacional-secretario-general-de-la-oea-cuestiona-medida-cautelar-emitida -por-la-cidh-en-caso-belo-monte/?home=1 (accessed April 11, 2012).

Rabe, Stephen G. 1988. *Eisenhower and Latin America: The foreign policy of anticommunism*. Chapel Hill: University of North Carolina Press.

Ramos, Alcida Rita. 1998. *Indigenism: Ethnic politics in Brazil*. Madison: University of Wisconsin Press.

Redo, Daniel, Andrew C. Millington, and Derrick Hindery. 2011. "Deforestation dynamics and policy changes in Bolivia's post-neoliberal era." *Land Use Policy* 28(1):227–241.

Reed, Jean-Pierre. 2003. "Indigenous land policies, culture and resistance in Latin America." *Journal of Peasant Studies* 31(1):137–156.

Regalsky, P. 2010. "Political processes and the reconfiguration of the State in Bolivia." *Latin American Perspectives* 37(3):35–50.

Republica de Bolivia. 2006. *Diagnostico área identidad y pueblos Indigenas. Para el ajuste del Plan Departamental de Desarrollo Económico y Social (PDDES) 2006–2020*. Santa Cruz, Bolivia: Republica de Bolivia.

Retallack, Simon. 2000. "ECAs exposed why export credit agencies are the world's largest public financiers of environmental destruction." *Ecologist London and Wadebridge Then Slinfold* 30:56–57.

Reuters. 2007. "Ashmore Energy buys Shell assets in Brazil, Bolivia." May 29; www .reuters.com/article/2007/05/29/ashmore-shell-idUSN2936107920070529 (accessed April 8, 2012).

Reuters. 2011. "Bolivia agrees to supply more natgas to Brazil." September 13; af.reuters .com/article/commoditiesNews/idAFS1E78C28Q20110914 (accessed April 11, 2012).

Rich, Bruce. 2009. *Foreclosing the future coal, climate and public international finance*. Environmental Defense Fund; www.edf.org/documents/9593_coal-plants -report.pdf (accessed August 9, 2012).

Rival, L. 2003. "Review: From peasant struggles to indian resistance: The Ecuadorian Andes in the late twentieth century by Amalia Pallares." *Journal of Peasant Studies* 30:217–219.

Rivera Cusicanqui, Silvia. 2006. "Chhixinakax utxiwa: Una reflexión sobre prácticas y discursos descolonizadores." Pp. 3–16 in *Modernidad y pensamiento descolonizador: Memoria del Seminario Internacional*, edited by M. Yapu. La Paz; Lima: Universidad para la Investigación Estratégica en Bolivia; Instituto Francés de Estudios Andinos.

Rivero Guzman, Susana. 2007. "Bolivia—the Struggle for Natural Resources—from Exclusion and Plunder to Return of the Land." *Indigenous Affairs* 1:24.

Robbins, Paul. 2004. *Political ecology: A critical introduction*. Malden, MA: Blackwell.

Robbins, Paul, Kendra McSweeney, Anil Chhangani, and Jennifer Rice. 2009. "Conservation as it is: Illicit resource use in a wildlife reserve in India." *Human Ecology* 37(5):559–575.

Robertson, Morgan. 2010. "Performing environmental governance." *Geoforum* 41(1):7–10.

Robertson, Nina, and Sven Wunder. 2005. *Fresh tracks in the forest: Assessing incipient payments for environmental services initiatives in Bolivia*. Bogor, Indonesia: Center for International Forestry Research.

Robinson, John G. 2011. "Ethical pluralism, pragmatism, and sustainability in conservation practice." *Biological Conservation* 144(3):958–965.

Rojas, Germán. 2011. "Las elecciones de autoridades judiciales están empantanadas." *Eju!*, July 13; eju.tv/2011/07/las-elecciones-de-autoridades-judiciales-estn-empantanadas/ (accessed April 12, 2012).

Roper, J. Montgomery. 2003. "Bolivian legal reforms and local Indigenous organizations: Opportunities and obstacles in a lowland municipality." *Latin American Perspectives* 30(1):139–161.

Royuela Comboni, Carlos. 1996. *Cién años de hidrocarburos en Bolivia (1896–1996)*. La Paz: Editorial "Los Amigos del Libro."

Sachs, Wolfgang. 1993. *Global ecology: A new arena of political conflict*. London; Atlantic Highlands, NJ: Zed Books; Fernwood.

Salles Abreu Passos, Maria de Fátima. 1998. "Bolivia-Brazil pipeline." *Economy and Energy* 2(10); ecen.com/eee10/gas.htm.

Sánchez-Moreno, Maria MacFarland, and Tracy Higgins. 2004. "No recourse: Transnational corporations and the protection of economic, social, and cultural rights in Bolivia." *Fordham International Law Journal* 27(5):1663–1805.

San Sebastián, Miguel, and Anna Karin Hurtig. 2004. "Oil exploitation in the Amazon basin of Ecuador: A public health emergency." *Revista Panamericana de Salud Pública* 15(3):205–211; www.scielosp.org/scielo.php?script=sci_arttext&pid=S1020-49892004000300014.

Sawyer, Suzana. 2004. *Crude chronicles: Indigenous politics, multinational oil, and neoliberalism in Ecuador*. Durham, NC: Duke University Press.

Sawyer, Suzana, and Edmund Terence Gomez, eds. 2012. "Transnational Governmentality in the Context of Resource Extraction." Pp. 1–8 in *The politics of resource extraction: Indigenous peoples, multinational corporations, and the state*, edited by Suzana Sawyer and Edmund Terence Gomez. New York: Palgrave Macmillan.

Scandizzo, Hernán. 2012. "Oil drilling threatens Mapuche: Indigenous communities demand end to hydrocarbon industry on their lands." *Latinamerica Press*, January 19; lapress.org/articles.asp?art=6540 (accessed April 3, 2012).

Schertow, John. 2008. "Peru: Tambogrande mine returns amidst two other conflicts." *Upside Down World*, June 18; upsidedownworld.org/main/peru-archives-76/1337-peru-tambogrande-mine-returns-amidst-two-other-conflicts (accessed April 12, 2012).

Schipani, Andrés. 2009. "El reclamo de los últimos Mosetene." *BBC Mundo–Cultura y Sociedad*, September 30; www.bbc.co.uk/mundo/cultura_sociedad/2009/09/090921_mosetene_bolivia_mj.shtml (accessed April 11, 2012).

Schmink, Marianne, and Charles H. Wood. 1992. *Contested frontiers in Amazonia*. New York: Columbia University Press.

Schroeder, Kathleen. 2007. "Economic globalization and Bolivia's regional divide." *Journal of Latin American Geography* 6(2):99–120.

Scott, James C. 1976. *The moral economy of the peasant: Rebellion and subsistence in Southeast Asia.* New Haven, CT: Yale University Press.

Selby, Jan. 2005. "Oil and water: The contrasting anatomies of resource conflicts." *Government and Opposition* 40(2):200–224.

Servicios en Comunicación Intercultural Servindi. 2011. "Bolivia: Conamaq denuncia 'doble cara' del gobierno de Evo Morales en tema de transgénicos." *Servindi,* June 16; servindi.org/actualidad/46703 (accessed April 11, 2012).

Shahriari, Sara. 2011. "Bolivia Hydrocarbons Industry Sees Record Investment, YPFB Says." *BusinessWeek,* December 1. www.businessweek.com/news/2011-12-01/bolivia-hydrocarbons-industry-sees-record-investment-ypfb-says.html.

Shiva, Vandana. 1993. "The greening of the global reach." Pp. 149–156 in *Global ecology: A new arena of political conflict,* edited by W. Sachs. London; Atlantic Highlands, NJ: Zed Books; Fernwood.

Shultz, Jim. 2003. "Bolivia: The water war widens." *NACLA Report on the Americas* 36(4):34–36; www2.fiu.edu/~hudsonv/Shultz.pdf.

Shultz, Jim, Carolyn Claridge, Marcela Olivera, and Nicholas Verbon. 2005. *Deadly consequences: The International Monetary Fund and Bolivia's "Black February."* Cochabamba, Bolivia: Democracy Center.

Shultz, Jim, and Tom Kruse. 2000. "The World Bank speaks—we respond." Democracy Center; www.1worldcommunication.org/bolivia.htm#The%20World%20Bank%20Spea (accessed April 5, 2012).

Siddiqui, Huma. 2012. "Bolivia, JSPL close to settling dispute." Financial Express, August 13; www.financialexpress.com/news/bolivia-jspl-close-to-settling-dispute/987415/0# (accessed August 13, 2012).

Slack, Keith. 2009. "Digging out from neoliberalism: Responses to environmental (mis)-governance of the mining sector in Latin America." Pp. 117–134 in *Beyond neoliberalism in Latin America? Societies and politics at the crossroads,* edited by John Burdick, Philip Oxhorn, and Kenneth M. Roberts. New York: Palgrave Macmillan.

Smith, Richard Chase. 1985. "A search for unity within diversity: Peasant unions, ethnic federations, and Indianist movements in the Andean republics." Pp. 5–38 in *Native peoples and economic development: Six case studies from Latin America,* edited by Theodore Harney Macdonald, Jr. Cambridge, MA: Cultural Survival.

Soliz Rada, Andrés. 2002. *La telaraña del poder en la venta del gas.* Voltaire Network, September 15; www.voltairenet.org/La-telarana-del-poder-en-la-venta (accessed April 4, 2012).

Solón, Pablo. 2011. "There must be coherence between what we do and what we say." *Monthly Review (MR) Zine,* September 28. mrzine.monthlyreview.org/2011/solon 290911.html.

Soltani, Atossa, Kari Hamerschlag, and Derrick Leonard Hindery. 1997. *Urgent action: Bolivia Brazil pipeline.* Malibu, CA; Washington, DC: Amazon Watch; Bank Information Center.

Soltani, Atossa, and Derrick Leonard Hindery. 1999. *A world class disaster: A report on the failures of Enron International to comply with Bolivian environmental laws and OPIC loan conditions in the construction of the Cuiabá pipeline.* Malibu, CA: Amazon Watch.

Soltani, Atossa, and Tracy Osborne. 1997. *Arteries for global trade, consequences for Amazonia*. Malibu, CA: Amazon Watch.

Spronk, Susan, and Jeffrey R. Webber. 2007. "Struggles against accumulation by dispossession in Bolivia: The political economy of natural resource contention." *Latin America Perspectives* 34(2):31–47; hdl.handle.net/10625/46846.

Stavenhagen, Rodolfo. 2004. *Human rights and indigenous issues: Report of the Special Rapporteur on the situation of human rights and fundamental freedoms of Indigenous people*. Geneva: UN Commission on Human Rights.

Stefanoni, Pablo. 2005. "The MAS is of the centre-left. Interview with Álvaro García Linera, newly elected Bolivian vice-president." International Viewpoint, December; www.internationalviewpoint.org/spip.php?article938 (accessed April 8, 2012).

Stephanes, Giovanny Vera. 2010. "Bolivia transforma parque en la Amazonía en zona petrolera." *El Ciudadano*, October; www.elciudadano.cl/2011/03/29/33935/bolivia-transforma-parque-en-la-amazonia-en-zona-petrolera/.

Stern, Steve J. 1982. *Peru's Indian peoples and the challenge of Spanish conquest: Huamanga to 1640*. Madison, WI: University of Wisconsin Press.

Stern, Steve J. 1987. *Resistance, rebellion, and consciousness in the Andean peasant world, 18th to 20th centuries*. Madison, WI: University of Wisconsin Press.

Sundberg, Juanita. 2003. "Strategies for authenticity and space in the Maya Biosphere Reserve, Petén, Guatemala." Pp. 50–72 in *Political ecology: An integrative approach to geography and environment-development studies*, edited by K. Zimmerer and T. Bassett. New York: Guilford Press.

Sundberg, Juanita. 2006. "Conservation encounters: Transculturation in the 'contact zones' of empire." *Cultural Geographies* 13(2):239–265.

Sundberg, Juanita. 2008. "Placing race in environmental justice research in Latin America." *Society and Natural Resources* 21(7):569–582.

Surrallés, Alexandre, and Pedro García Hierro. 2005. *The land within: Indigenous territory and the perception of the environment*. Copenhagen: International Work Group for Indigenous Affairs.

Svampa, Maristella, Pablo Stefanoni, and Ricardo Bajo. 2009a. "Bolivia's vice-president defends MAS government's record. Interview with Álvaro García Linera, vice-president of Bolivia." English translation and notes by Richard Fidler; links.org.au/node/1241 (accessed April 8, 2012).

Svampa, Maristella, Pablo Stefanoni, and Ricardo Bajo. 2009b. "'El punto de bifurcación es un momento en el que se miden ejércitos.' Interview with Álvaro García Linera." www.rcci.net/globalizacion/2009/fg912.htm (accessed April 11, 2012).

Tapia, Luis. 2007. "El triple descentramiento: Igualdad y cogobierno en Bolivia." Pp. 47–70 in *Reinventando la nación en Bolivia*, edited by Karin Monasterios, Pablo Stefanoni, and Hervé Do Alto. La Paz: Consejo Latinoamericano de Ciencias Sociales/Plural.

Taringa! 2011. "Coca en el TIPNIS." September 10; www.taringa.net/posts/ecologia/12783575.R/Coca-en-el-TIPNIS.html (accessed April 12, 2012).

Tegel, Simeon. 2011. "Peru may be turning a corner on its treatment of indigenous people." *Guardian*, August 31; www.guardian.co.uk/commentisfree/2011/aug/31/peru-indigenous-peoples.

Toensing, Gale Courey. 2011. "Wikileaks: UN Declaration raised US fears over Indigenous land rights, sovereignty, anti–free market movements." Indian Country Today

Media Network, September 13; indiancountrytodaymedianetwork.com/2011/09/13 /wikileaks-un-declaration-raised-us-fears-over-indigenous-land-rights-sovereignty -anti-%e2%80%98free-market%e2%80%99-movements-53608 (accessed April 11, 2012).

Toussaint, Eric. 2010. "Is Bolivia heading for Andean-Amazonian capitalism?" Upside Down World, Bolivia Rising, March 11; upsidedownworld.org/main/news-briefs -archives-68/2401-is-bolivia-heading-for-andean-amazonian-capitalism (accessed April 11, 2012).

Transredes, S.A. 2000. "Derrame OSSA-2 al Río Desaguadero; informe socioeconómico y acciones del equipo CLO's." Oruro, Bolivia: Transredes.

Tribunal Agrario Nacional. 2007. *Sentencia Agraria Nacional S1ª Nº 18/2007. Expediente: Nº 114/06.* Sucre, Bolivia; tan.poderjudicial.gob.bo/cuerpo.asp?TPagina=1& TContenido=8&Codigo=SAN-S1-0018-2007 (accessed April 8, 2012).

UNECLAC. 2005. *Los pueblos indígenas de Bolivia: Diagnóstico sociodemográfico a partir del censo del 2001 [Proyecto BID/CEPAL "Los pueblos indígenas y la población afrodescendiente en los censos"]; documentos de proyectos.* Santiago, Chile; www .eclac.org/publicaciones/xml/3/23263/bolivia.pdf (accessed August 6, 2012).

UNODC. 2011. *Estado plurinacional de Bolivia: Monitoreo de cultivos de coca 2010.* Bolivia: UN Office on Drugs and Crime; www.unodc.org/unodc/en/frontpage/2011 /September/bolivias-coca-crop-cultivation-remains-stable.html?ref=fs1 (accessed April 12, 2012).

Urenda Díaz, Juan Carlos. 2009. "El estado catoblepas las contradicciones destructivas del Estado Boliviano." Pp. 177–192 in *Estudios sobre la constitución aprobada en enero del 2009,* edited by J. Antonio Rivera S. Cochabamba, Bolivia: Grupo Editorial Kipus.

Urioste, Miguel. 2010. "Land governance in Bolivia, working paper." La Paz: Fundación Tierra.

USAID. 2012. *USAID Bolivia: Geographic Focus > USAID Support: La Paz.* bolivia .usaid.gov/focus_lapaz.php (accessed April 11, 2012).

US Department of Energy. 2002. "An energy overview of Bolivia." www.fe.doe.gov /international/bolvover.html (accessed March 12, 2002; site now discontinued).

Valdivia, Gabriela. 2007. "The 'Amazonian trial of the century': Indigenous identities, transnational networks, and petroleum in Ecuador." *Alternatives: Global, Local, Political* 32(1):41–72.

Valdivia, Gabriela. 2010. "Agrarian capitalism and struggles over hegemony in the Bolivian lowlands." *Latin American Perspectives* 37(4):67–87.

Vallette, Jim, and Daphne Wysham. 2002. *Enron's pawns: How public institutions bankrolled Enron's globalization game.* Institute for Policy Studies/Sustainable Energy and Economy Network; www.seen.org/PDFs/pawns.PDF (accessed April 5, 2012).

Valle V., Luis Francisco, trans. 2010. *Constitution of the Plurinational State of Bolivia: Enacted on February 7th, 2009 by President Evo Morales Ayma.* (Translation of Bolivian constitution.)

Varese, Stefano. 1996. "The new environmentalist movement of Latin American Indigenous people." Pp. 122–142 in *Valuing local knowledge: Indigenous people and intellectual property rights,* edited by Doreen Stabinsky and Stephen B. Brush. Washington, DC: Island Press.

Vargas Salgueiro, Augusto. 1996. *Y.P.F.B.: Entre nacionalistas y liberales.* La Paz: Editorial "Los Amigos del Libro."

Viceministerio de Energía e Hidrocarburos. 2002. Home page. www.energia.gov. bo /paginas/sh_capitalizaciOn_2001.html (accessed April 5, 2012).

Walker, Peter A. 2006. "Political ecology: Where is the policy?" *Progress in Human Geography* 30(3):382–395.

Walker, Peter A. 2007. "Political ecology: Where is the politics?" *Progress in Human Geography* 31(3):363–369.

Watts, M.J. 1983. "On the poverty of theory: Natural hazards research in context." Pp. 231–262 in *Interpretations of calamity from the viewpoint of human ecology*, edited by Kenneth Hewitt. Boston: Allen and Unwin.

Watts, Michael. 2003. "Development and governmentality." *Singapore Journal of Tropical Geography* 24(1):6–34.

Watts, Michael J. 2005. "Righteous oil? Human rights, the oil complex, and corporate social responsibility." *Annual Review of Environment and Resources* 30: 373–407.

Webber, J. R. 2005. "Left-Indigenous struggles in Bolivia: Searching for revolutionary democracy." *Monthly Review* 57(4):34–48.

Webber, Jeffrey R. 2006. "The first 100 days of Evo Morales: Image and reality in Bolivia." *Against the Current* 21(3):11–20.

Webber, Jeffrey R. 2011. *From rebellion to reform in Bolivia class struggle, Indigenous liberation, and the politics of Evo Morales*. Chicago: Haymarket Books.

Weil, Gotshal, and Manges LLP. 2004. "In re Enron Corporation et al." Case No. 01-16034, Bankruptcy Court. DOC 43889.0003/Chapter 11 of the US Bankruptcy Code; bankrupt.com/misc/15303FifthAmendedPlan&DisclosureStatement.pdf (accessed April 6, 2012).

Weinberg, Bill. 2010. "Beyond extraction: An interview with Rafael Quispe." *NACLA Report on the Americas*, September/October; nacla.org/files/A04305023_8.pdf.

Weisbrot, Mark, and Luis Sandoval. 2008. "The distribution of Bolivia's most important natural resources and the autonomy conflicts." *Monthly Review—MR Zine*, April 8; mrzine.monthlyreview.org/2008/ws040808.html.

Weiss, Wendy. 1997. "Debt and devaluation: The burden on Ecuador's popular class." *Latin American Perspectives* 24(4):9–33.

Westra, Laura. 2008. *Environmental justice and the rights of indigenous peoples: International and domestic legal perspectives*. London: Earthscan; public.eblib.com /EBLPublic/PublicView.do?ptiID=430213.

White, Richard. 1991. *The middle ground: Indians, empires, and republics in the Great Lakes region, 1650–1815*. Cambridge: Cambridge University Press.

Wolf, Eric. 1972. "Ownership and political ecology." *Anthropological Quarterly* 45(3):201–205.

Wolford, Wendy. 2008. "Environmental justice and agricultural development in the Brazilian cerrado." Pp. 213–239 in *Environmental justice in Latin America: Problems, promise, and practice*, edited by D. Carruthers. Cambridge, MA: MIT Press.

World Bank. 1993. *Natural resource management in Bolivia: 30 years of experience*. Washington, DC: World Bank.

World Bank. 1994a. "Bolivia: Capitalization program adjustment credit initiating memorandum." Washington, DC: World Bank.

World Bank. 1994b. "Capitalization program adjustment credit, project ID 6BOLPA064." Washington, DC: World Bank.

World Bank. 1997. "Implementation completion report: Bolivia. Mining sector rehabilitation project (Credit 2013-BO)." Report no. 17239. Washington, DC: World Bank.

World Bank. 1998. "Implementation completion report: Bolivia. Major cities water and sewerage rehabilitation project (Credit 2817-BO)." Report no. 18009. Washington, DC: World Bank.

World Bank. 2000a. "Bolivia country assistance evaluation." Washington, DC: World Bank, Operations Evaluation Department; lnweb90.worldbank.org/oed/oeddo clib.nsf/DocUNIDViewForJavaSearch/74ADCEC08FF269EF852567F5005D66 F0/$file/cae_bolivia.pdf.

World Bank. 2000b. "Bolivia-hydrocarbon sector social and environmental management capacity building project—learning and Innovation Loan (LIL), project ID BOPE65902." Washington, DC: World Bank.

World Bank. 2004. "Report and recommendation of the president of the international bank for reconstruction and development, international development association, international finance corporation and the multilateral investment guarantee agency to the executive directors on a country assistance strategy for the Republic of Bolivia." Washington, DC: World Bank; www-wds.worldbank.org/external/de fault/WDSContentServer/WDSP/IB/2004/01/21/000090341_20040121130421 /Rendered/PDF/268380BO.pdf.

World Bank. 2006. "Project performance assessment report: Bolivia. Private enterprise development project (credit 2134-BO); capitalization program adjustment credit (credit 2761-BO); financial markets and pension reform TA (credit 2789-BO); public financial management operation II (credit 2279-BO)." Washington, DC: World Bank, Country Evaluation and Regional Relations Independent Evaluation Group.

World Bank. 2010. "Bolivia: decentralized infrastructure for rural transformation project (IDTR)." Washington, DC: World Bank; web.worldbank.org/WBSITE/EXTER NAL/PROJECTS/0,,contentMDK:22707543~menuPK:64282137~pagePK:41367 ~piPK:279616~theSitePK:40941,00.html (accessed April 6, 2012).

World Bank. 2011. "Projects–BM/Bolivia: Transportation cost to fall more than 50 percent in northern Amazonian highway." Press Release No:2011/473/LAC; web.world bank.org/WBSITE/EXTERNAL/PROJECTS/0,,contentMDK:22907782~menuP K:64282138~pagePK:41367~piPK:279616~theSitePK:40941,00.html (accessed April 8, 2012).

World People's Conference on Climate Change. 2010. "President Morales speaking at COP16 in Cancun." Presented at the World People's Conference on Climate Change and the Rights of Mother Earth; pwccc.wordpress.com/2010/12/09 /president-morales-speaking-at-the-un/ (accessed April 20, 2012).

WWF. 2000. *The institutional role of WWF Bolivia in relation to the conservation of the Chiquitano forest*. Santa Cruz, Bolivia: WWF.

Wysham, Daphne. 2001. "Leaked World Bank memo says oil, gas, and mining investments pose 'clear and present danger.'" Institute for Policy Studies; www.1worldcom munication.org/leakedworldbankmemo.htm (accessed April 10, 2012).

YPFB. 2009. "Yacimientos Petrolíferos Fiscales Bolivianos: Plan de inversiones 2009–2015." La Paz: YPFB.

YPFB. 2011. "Los ingresos por hidrocarburos marcan un récord histórico $US 1.688 millones." January 19; www.hidrocarburosbolivia.com/bolivia-mainmenu-117/ypfb

-petroleras-mainmenu-118/39588-los-ingresos-por-hidrocarburos-marcan-un-re
cord-historico-us-1688-millones.html (accessed April 8, 2012).

Zimmerer, Karl S. 2006. "Cultural ecology: At the interface with political ecology—
the new geographies of environmental conservation and globalization." *Progress in
Human Geography* 30(1):63–78.

Zimmerer, Karl. 2009. "Nature under neoliberalism and beyond: Community-based
resource management, environmental conservation, and farmer-and-food movements in Bolivia, 1985–present." Pp. 157–174 in *Beyond neoliberalism in Latin America? Societies and politics at the crossroads*, edited by John Burdick, Philip Oxhorn,
and Kenneth M. Roberts. New York: Palgrave Macmillan.

Zimmerer, Karl S., and Thomas J. Bassett, eds. 2003. *Political ecology: An integrative
approach to geography and environment-development studies*. New York: Guilford
Press.

Index

conflicts of interest, 33–36, 38, 53, 54, 72, 88, 91
Consejo Nacional de Ayllus y Markas del Qullasuyu (National Council of Ayllus and Markas of Qullasuyu) (CONAMAQ), 218, 221
consent, 168–170, 171, 179, 234, 241. *See also* consultation; UN Declaration on the Rights of Indigenous Peoples
conservation
    community-based conservation, 48. *See also* Indigenous peoples: environmental management by
    fortress conservation, 18, 78–79, 84–88, 90–97, 188, 235, 245ch1n5. *See also* Chiquitano Forest Conservation Program
    Indigenous management practices and, 71, 88–90
conservation organizations. *See also* individual organizations
    Chiquitano Forest Conservation Program and, 18, 73–74, 84–86, 91–93, 235
    collaboration with USAID of, 176
    Cuiabá pipeline and, 12, 63–64, 69, 70, 72–74, 75–79, 84–86
    greenwashing and green-stamping by, 12, 63–64, 76–77, 85–86
constitution (2009)
    contradictions of, 4, 160, 162, 165, 167, 237
    economic and developmental priorities of, 152, 161, 170, 217
    environmental protection in, 156, 160, 162, 167, 213
    Indigenous cosmologies and, 167–168, 237
    Indigenous rights and, 6, 166–167, 168–170, 179–180, 183, 222. *See also* consent; consultation
    Indigenous use of, 14–15, 165, 179–180, 187, 191–192
    limitations and enforcement of, 213
    overview of origins, goals, and adoption of, 149, 164–168
    provisions regarding land in, 200–201
consultation, 6, 99–101, 168–180, 222. *See also* consent

Convention 169. *See* International Labor Organization (ILO) Convention 169
Cooperative for Assistance and Relief Everywhere (CARE), 57
Coordinadora Andina de Organizaciones Indigenas. *See* Andean Coordinating Committee of Indigenous Organizations
Coordinadora de las Organizaciones Indígenas de la Cuenca Amazónica (Coordinator of Indigenous Organizations of the Amazon River Basin) (COICA), 226
Coordinadora de Pueblos Étnicos de Santa Cruz (Council of Ethnic Peoples of Santa Cruz) (CPESC), 83, 93, 99, 132, 192
Coordinator of Indigenous Organizations of the Amazon River Basin. *See* Coordinadora de las Organizaciones Indígenas de la Cuenca Amazónica (COICA)
CORE International Inc., 32
Corporación Minera de Bolivia (Mining Corporation of Bolivia) (COMIBOL), 33
Correa, Rafael, 169, 227–228
corruption, 31, 66, 117, 128, 153, 208, 220. *See also* Enron
Council of Ethnic Peoples of Santa Cruz. *See* Coordinadora de Pueblos Étnicos de Santa Cruz (CPESC)
CPESC. *See* Coordinadora de Pueblos Étnicos de Santa Cruz (Council of Ethnic Peoples of Santa Cruz)
CPILAP. *See* Central de Pueblos Indígenas de La Paz (Center for Indigenous Peoples of La Paz)
crime, 130, 143, 144–145, 208, 223, 224
CSUTCB. *See* Confederación Sindical Única de Trabajadores Campesinos de Bolivia (Sole Confederation of Peasant Workers of Bolivia)
Cuasace, Carlos, 185–186
Cuiabá pipeline, 6
    audits of, 95–96, 247ch6n2
    conservation organizations and, 12, 63–64, 75–79
    construction of, 5, 74

290 · *Index*

About the Author

Derrick Hindery is an Assistant Professor in the departments of International Studies and Geography at the University of Oregon. He holds a BA, MA, and PhD in Geography from the University of California, Los Angeles. His research focuses on Indigenous political mobilization in response to neoliberal and statist models of extractive development in Latin America, primarily Bolivia. His work also examines environmental, social, and political dimensions of Liquefied Natural Gas (LNG) projects along the supply chain. Prior to working at the University of Oregon, Hindery volunteered and worked for the nongovernmental organization Amazon Watch, where he spearheaded its campaign to hold the US government, Enron, and Shell accountable for social and environmental impacts caused by the Cuiabá gas pipeline.